Building a Religious Empire

ENCOUNTERS WITH ASIA

Victor H. Mair, Series Editor

Encounters with Asia is an interdisciplinary series dedicated to
the exploration of all the major regions and cultures of this vast
continent. Its time frame extends from the prehistoric to the
contemporary; its geographic scope ranges from the Urals and
the Caucasus to the Pacific. A particular focus of the series is the
Silk Road in all of its ramifications: religion, art, music,
medicine, science, trade, and so forth. Among the disciplines
represented in this series are history, archaeology, anthropology,
ethnography, and linguistics. The series aims particularly to
clarify the complex interrelationships among various peoples
within Asia, and also with societies beyond Asia.

A complete list of books in the series
is available from the publisher.

# BUILDING
# A RELIGIOUS
# EMPIRE

Tibetan Buddhism, Bureaucracy,
and the Rise of the Gelukpa

Brenton Sullivan

**PENN**

UNIVERSITY OF PENNSYLVANIA PRESS

PHILADELPHIA

Published by
University of Pennsylvania Press
Philadelphia, Pennsylvania 19104–4112
www.upenn.edu/pennpress

Printed in the United States of America on acid-free paper
10 9 8 7 6 5 4 3 2 1

Library of Congress Cataloging-in-Publication Data

Names: Sullivan, Brenton, author.
Title: Building a religious empire: Tibetan Buddhism, bureaucracy, and the rise of the Gelukpa / Brenton Sullivan.
Other titles: Encounters with Asia.
Description: 1st edition. | Philadelphia: University of Pennsylvania Press, [2021] | Series: Encounters with Asia | Includes bibliographical references and index.
Identifiers: LCCN 2020015353 | ISBN 9780812252675 (hardcover)
Subjects: LCSH: Dge-lugs-pa (Sect)—China—Tibet Autonomous Region—History. | Dge-lugs-pa (Sect)—Tibet Region—History. | Buddhist monasteries—China—Tibet Autonomous Region—History. | Buddhist monasteries—Tibet Region—History. | Buddhist monasticism and religious orders—Government—History. | Buddhism—China—Tibet Autonomous Region—History. | Buddhism—Tibet Region—History.
Classification: LCC BQ7576 .S85 2021 | DDC 294.3/92309—dc23
LC record available at https://lccn.loc.gov/2020015353

# Contents

# A Note on Language and Romanization

This book examines the expansion of the Geluk school of Tibetan Buddhism from its early base in Central Tibet, near the southern edge of the Tibetan Plateau, across the Tibetan Plateau and into Mongolia and parts of East Asia (particularly through its engagement with the Qing Court in Beijing). As a result, names and terms from a variety of languages, especially Tibetan (T.), Mongolian (Mo.), Chinese (Ch.), and Manchu (Ma.), appear in the relevant primary sources.

Chinese names and terms are transcribed using Pinyin. Mongolian names and terms follow the forms given in Christopher Atwood's *Encyclopedia of Mongolia and the Mongol Empire* (2004). Manchu names and terms are transcribed according to Jerry Norman's *Comprehensive Manchu-English Dictionary* (2013). Tibetan names and terms have been phoneticized in the body of the text using the Tibetan and Himalayan Library (previously the Tibetan and Himalayan Digital Library) Simplified Phonetic Transcription of Standard Tibetan (2003), developed by David Germano and Nicolas Tournadre. This system makes Tibetan names and words more or less pronounceable by the English-reading audience and does so in a consistent fashion according to the general rules of pronunciation in Central Tibet. Tibetan names and terms in the notes of the text are rendered using the Wylie transliteration system as described by Turrell Wylie (1959).

# Introduction

*Building a Religious Empire* is focused on the story of the Geluk (T. Dge lugs) school of Tibetan Buddhism, the most widespread school of Tibetan Buddhism, best known through its symbolic head, the Dalai Lama. The vast majority of the monasteries in Tibet and Inner Mongolia—a landscape that makes up a third of the territory of today's China—as well as those in Mongolia are Geluk monasteries. Historically, these monasteries were some of the largest in the world, and even today some of the largest Geluk monasteries house thousands of monks both in Tibet and in exile in India. To understand how this came to pass, this book reveals the compulsive efforts by Geluk lamas in the early modern period to prescribe and control a proper way of living the life of a Buddhist monk and to define a proper way of administering the monastery. These lamas drew on the sort of administrative techniques usually associated with state-making—standardization, record-keeping, the conscription of young males, the concentration of manpower in central cores, and so on—thereby earning the moniker "lama official" or "Buddhist bureaucrat" (T. *bla dpon*). They also thereby succeeded in establishing a relatively uniform and resilient network of monasteries stretching from Ladakh to Lake Baikal, from Beijing to the Caspian Sea.

Previous explanations of this success of the Geluk school over other schools of Tibetan Buddhism have focused on the brilliance of its founder or on the role played in later centuries by the school's powerful Mongol patrons in eliminating, often violently, rivals. What has not been appreciated is the zeal and thoroughness with which Geluk lamas organized, systematized, and administered their monasteries, thereby giving rise to a uniform and hegemonic school of Tibetan Buddhism. It is the deployment of bureaucratic techniques usually associated with the state for the purpose of extending the Geluk "liberating umbrella" over more and more lands and peoples that best justifies describing the Geluk project as "spiritual colonialism."[1]

The cumulative effect of the organizing efforts of Geluk lamas was the belief that monastic life must follow codified patterns of study, worship, conduct, and administration for the sake of the monastery and for Buddhism as a whole. The Geluk project of incorporating all peoples under its religious rule was designed to be a predictable one, whereby every aspect and every moment of the monastic life was subjected to bureaucratic scrutiny and control. This privileging of the monastery and its rules lent the Geluk school a consistency and an integrity that was conducive to Geluk ambitions to spread Buddhism across wide stretches of Inner Asia, and it is also the reason we talk today about a single, unified Geluk school of Tibetan Buddhism.

*Building a Religious Empire* traces the unique and overriding preoccupation of Geluk lamas with administering their religious empire from the time of their assumption of power in Central Tibet in the seventeenth century through their expansion and consolidation of power along the frontier with China and in Mongolia in the eighteenth century (roughly 1642–1750). In contrast to leaders of other schools of Tibetan Buddhism, Geluk lamas devoted an extraordinary amount of time worrying about the institutional framework within which every other aspect of monastic life—be that philosophizing, meditating, conducting rituals, or anything else—would take place. I argue that this privileging of the monastic institution fostered a common religious identity that insulated it from factionalism along the lines of any specific religious leader, practice, or doctrine. The construction and maintenance of a bureaucratic system of Geluk monasticism further provided legitimacy to the Geluk project of conversion and spiritual conquest.

The Geluk school's recipe for success was not just prioritizing the organization of its fixed monastic institutions. Equally important was the mobility of monks and lamas, which both ensured a degree of uniformity among Geluk monasteries and was facilitated by that uniformity. *Building a Religious Empire* addresses the "mother-child" (T. *ma bu*) or "branch" monasteries (T. *dgon lag*), the "monk streams" (T. *grwa rgyun*) or study-abroad relationships between monasteries, the institutional links based on liturgical traditions, and so on, that developed over this period and tied together into a single corporate entity the thousands of Geluk monasteries across Tibet and Mongolia. The shared practice of ensuring that one's own administrative and monastic practices were modeled on those of another, more centrally located monastery contributed to the formation of a system of overlapping networks and loyalties that collectively made up the Geluk school. Thus, by the mid-eighteenth century there developed a remarkable consistency in the forms of administration, study, and ritual across Tibet and Mongolia, making it relatively easy for a new monk to travel from the small, local temple where he first renounced to his temple's mother monastery for ritual training, or for the enterprising, young, scholar-monk to make the difficult journey to Central Tibet to seek advanced training at one of the major Geluk monasteries there.

Nor was this mobility between and among monasteries limited to young monks or monks engaged in studies. Lamas—the high-ranking clerics of the Geluk church—also frequently moved between monasteries. They did this, as did lamas of other schools of Tibetan Buddhism, for the sake of study and teaching, alms begging and the distribution of alms, pilgrimage, and the construction or restoration of temples.[2] But Geluk lamas also did this as part of their regular administrative duties, serving as abbot of first one monastery and then another or even holding concurrently the abbotship of two or more monasteries. This peregrinating and rotating cohort of Geluk lamas ensured an administrative continuity between monasteries located as far apart as different sides of the Asian continent. The Geluk school was polycephalous, or "multi-headed"; meaning, it did not rely on a single lama or monastic seat for promoting and maintaining its teachings and organization but on a proliferation of such lamas and monastic centers. One can even say that the Geluk school was "hydra-headed" because, like the mythic Hydra beast, it could regenerate new heads to help lead and administer the Geluk church when one died, was killed, or was otherwise unable to fulfill his duties. This, together with a common concern for consistency in monastic practices and institutions, aided the Geluk school in outperforming its rivals and helped to prevent the school from splintering into sub-schools or new schools and revelations.

To be sure, the Geluk school was not a homogeneous religious group. Other scholars have documented the various lines on which heated and even violent divisions could be drawn, from power politics and conspiracies in Lhasa,[3] to differences of opinion over the best future course of the Geluk school,[4] to endless legal battles over the ownership of temples and fiefs.[5] Nonetheless, I argue that what allowed for this diversity within the Gelukpa was precisely the rhetoric and preoccupation with consistency in its monastic forms. So, while different monasteries might have used one or another of a small group of scholastic manuals (T. *yig cha*), for instance, they all followed the same basic format of debate.

What the Gelukpa did exceptionally well was to make the *monastery*—the place and the institution—the essence of Buddhism. Certain aspects of the Geluk school were never questioned, such as the inerrancy of the school's founder and, significantly, the importance of monastic discipline. "Discipline" here refers not just to individual comportment and norms such as celibacy but also to the specificity with which the organization of the ideal monastery was laid out and the strictness with which its administration was carried out. Above all else, what was agreed upon was the idea that there existed a proper and *orderly* way of living out the monastic life and that that way was and ought to be made explicit and available to all who wished to submit to it. What we are talking about is the *systematization* of the monastic life and thereby of Buddhist liberation itself. The fact that intra-Geluk disputes can usually be cast as disputes between monasteries rather than as doctrinal or sectarian disputes—there are no Geluk sub-schools—demonstrates the success of the Gelukpa in making monasteries and disciplined monastic life the essence of "proper Buddhism." The relatively homogeneous system of "disciplined" monks and monasteries appealed to political rulers and laity, and it facilitated the socialization and control of its growing number of monks and monasteries in early modern Tibet and Mongolia.

## Legislating Proper Buddhism

The Geluk school's bureaucratic proclivities are most visible in the hundreds of "monastic constitutions" that Geluk lamas composed for monasteries flung across Tibet and Mongolia. Like Christian monastic "customaries," these constitutions (T. *bca' yig*) express the need to institute "proper" administrative procedures, scholastic curricula, liturgical sequences, financial protocols, and so on. They also appeal to notions of "impartiality" and "the common good" to underscore the idea that theirs are monasteries of order and of reason. Having traveled to dozens of monasteries in Tibet and Mongolia between 2008 and 2016 (including one extended stay at a monastery in Tibet from 2011 through 2012), I collected rare manuscripts of monastic constitutions dating principally from the eighteenth century. I further collected every available monastic constitution composed for a monastery before the mid-eighteenth century as well as a representative sample of constitutions from after that period. I have contextualized these constitutions by consulting Chinese-language gazetteers and Qing Dynasty imperial compendia and Tibetan-language histories, chronicles, biographies, and other sources.

My close examination of all these monastic constitutions has allowed me to identify the moment that Geluk lamas seized this genre of administrative document as one of the school's many methods for expressing and acting upon its concern for systematizing monastic administration and practice. Beginning with the compositions of the Fifth Dalai Lama (1617–1682), these constitutions reveal a palpable preoccupation with what sociologist Max Weber called *rationalization*, that is, the propensity for increasing the predictability of social life and interactions through the standardization of procedures. These constitutions reflect and call for bureaucratic techniques normally associated with state-making, including the standardization of administrative terminology and procedures, record-keeping (e.g., rosters of resident monks), the demarcation of monastic territories, and so on, all of which facilitated the growth and management of large-scale monastic cores and the proliferation of Geluk monasteries across the Tibetan Plateau and Mongolia.

Historically, each Geluk monastery would safely guard its monastic constitution. The monastery's highest officers would periodically reveal the constitution, read it aloud, comment on it, and appeal to its written word and meaning in order to exhort the monastery's resident monks to best comport themselves. The hope was to make the monastery a beacon of "proper" Buddhism and thereby attract new disciples and lay patrons alike to the monastery. Chapter 1 traces the development of this genre from its origins in the eleventh or twelfth century through the point when the production of monastic constitutions became prolific in the mid-eighteenth century. I demonstrate how the preeminent Geluk lama of the seventeenth century—the Fifth Dalai Lama—and his successors in the eighteenth century both drew upon and departed from earlier precedents. Geluk lamas did not invent the genre of monastic constitutions, but they did perfect it and capitalize on it.

As engineers of a new, far-flung religious empire, Geluk lamas deployed novel financial instruments and institutional arrangements to support and control its burgeoning body of monks and to insulate such resources from the monastery's highest officials. These lamas also regularly appealed to notions of "impartiality" and a "common good" that was to be protected from personal avarice by legal-bureaucratic norms. Such "expropriation of the means of administration" is arguably the lynchpin for a fully functioning bureaucratic administration.[6] Chapter 2 examines the promotion of these ideals as well as the actual application of new administrative techniques, which together contributed to the legitimacy of the Geluk project and to the school's ability to manage its growing body of monks.

In Chapter 3, I argue that Geluk lamas took special care to institutionalize tantra, the most potent source of both spiritual liberation and destruction (i.e., destruction of an individual's hope of liberation and destruction of real-world enemies). The lineages of tantric transmission that epitomized the early history of the Geluk school (and other schools) came to be overshadowed by the more standardized, routinized, and semi-public form of transmission through tantric colleges. As Buddhists, the power associated with meditation and esoteric ritual practice could not be altogether repressed; instead, they were channeled into institutions that served the interest of Geluk monasteries and the Geluk school.

In Chapter 4, I demonstrate the Fifth Dalai Lama's early concern with creating separate monasteries, such as Drepung, that specialized in the study of Buddhist philosophy. The systems of scholasticism that the Fifth Dalai Lama helped to standardize—curricula, methods of debate, the awarding of scholastic degrees, degree exams—were then instituted at monasteries along the frontier with China and ultimately in Inner Mongolia. This standardization and dissemination of "right knowledge" and "right ways of knowing" contributed to the uniformity of the Geluk school and, in conjunction with Geluk liturgy, informed and socialized scores of monks and promoted "brand loyalty" on an unprecedented scale. This standardization and exportation of Geluk scholasticism also contributed to the formation of explicit scholastic ties between monasteries, with certain monasteries becoming "feeder schools" for the more centrally located and prestigious monasteries. Thus, the growth in the number of monks as well as the geographic expansion of the Geluk school were facilitated by such novel and carefully devised institutional arrangements.

Chapter 5 describes the pathway or mechanism for Weber's contention that bureaucracy cultivates esprit de corps, namely, liturgy. It charts the standardization of recitations and ritual from the time of the founder of the Geluk school, and especially the Fifth Dalai Lama, through the exportation of the Geluk liturgy to Inner Mongolia by Geluk lamas from the Tibet-China frontier in the mid- to late-eighteenth century. Much as early modern states discovered that forcing a battalion to march together in formation contributed to the group's cohesion and group identity,[7] Geluk lamas fashioned an extensive liturgy (almost entirely in the Tibetan language) that was practiced in common by hundreds of thousands of monks. This contributed to the integrity of the Geluk school even as it extended farther and farther across the Tibetan Plateau and Mongolia, where Tibetan language was the "church language," or the "language of the dharma."

I conclude by explaining why religious institutions are often overlooked by scholars of Tibetan Buddhist history. A focus on religious ideas (philosophy) and virtuosos (meditators, ascetics, and saints), has obscured the decisive role of more down-to-earth practices by religious elite. Understanding the expansion of religious groups and the grip they have on a population requires scholars to attend to the techniques of administration and control they employ, techniques that are often the same as those used by political rulers. In the early modern and premodern worlds, "popular mass politics was religion, and religion was political."[8] Such an approach also allows one to appreciate the similarities and differences with other religious empires, such as the Catholic Church. Both the Catholic Church and the Geluk school depended on bureaucratic techniques of standardization and control, but the "polycephalous" nature of the Geluk school distinguished it from the pope-centered Catholic Church and lent the Geluk school a degree of flexibility and autonomy that was advantageous in the shifting political landscape of early modern Inner Asia.

The rest of this Introduction presents the theoretical framework for understanding the Geluk preoccupation with bureaucracy and the school's success. Max Weber's insights into the ethics (the sets of values) of the world's major religions, his concept of "rationalization," and his typology of the forms of rule and legitimation are applied to the Geluk school to reveal what made it unique and successful. In presenting the Gelukpa as bureaucrats, I hope that the reader learns something about the most prevalent form of monastic life on the Tibetan Plateau. In addition, we may together peer into the functioning of some of the most successful Buddhist monasteries and thereby learn something more generally about what makes religious organizations successful.

## The Growth of the Geluk School: Power, Money, *and* Organizational Capabilities

The spiritual, or religious, dimension of Tibet is its most noted feature. These range from hoary, romantic descriptions of life in Tibet, especially premodern Tibet, as a heaven on earth,[9] to more matter-of-fact observations

that the vast majority of Tibetans identify as Buddhist and that Buddhist practices and Buddhist myths have been some of the most important contributors
to the formation of a common identity across the Tibetan Plateau.[10] Perhaps
the most noted feature of Tibet's religious landscape is its great number of
monks. The usual estimate given for the proportion of the male population
that lived the life of the celibate monk until the twentieth century is nearly
one-third, that is, one-sixth of the overall population.[11] The pre-modern
censuses on which this estimate is based are not entirely reliable, and one more
conservative estimate suggests only 10 to 12 percent of the male population in
the more densely populated, agricultural regions of Tibet were monastics.[12]
Even so, this number situates Tibet well above other Buddhist countries, such
as Burma and Thailand, in terms of their estimated monastic populations.[13]

Statistics for the pre-1950 population of Tibet, including Tibet's monastic population, are sparse and not entirely reliable. However, several scholars
have pointed back to two censuses carried out shortly after the Geluk school
of Tibetan Buddhism came to power in 1642 under the direction of the Fifth
Dalai Lama (1617–1682) and his principal patron, the Oirat (particularly the
Khoshud) Mongol Güüshi Khan (1582–1655). R. A. Stein refers to a 1663 census documenting 50,900 Geluk monks and approximately 100,000 monks
and nuns of all schools.[14] The twentieth-century Tibetan scholar Dungkar
Lozang Trinlé appears to have arrived at a similar figure, citing the 1698[15]
history of the Geluk school by the Fifth Dalai Lama's prime minister, suggesting there were 97,528 monks across Central, Eastern, and Western Tibet
at that time.[16] Then, in 1737, another census found more than 302,500 monks
under the Dalai Lama's dominion (principally, in the Central Tibetan province of Ü) and another 13,700-plus monks under the Panchen Lama's dominion (in the neighboring province of Tsang).[17] These figures point to a
dramatic (at least threefold) increase in the number of monks in less than a
century.

The Geluk monastery known as Gönlung Jampa Ling, which is situated along the cultural frontier between Tibet and Mongolia and which figures prominently in this book, similarly underwent a major demographic
shift during this period. When it was first founded in 1604 by a high-ranking
lama from Central Tibet, it is said that "more than a hundred monks" gathered there, each in his own small hut.[18] By 1698, when the Fifth Dalai Lama's prime minister was compiling his history of the Geluk school, Gönlung
Monastery had 1,500 monks.[19] This made Gönlung the largest monastery
outside the direct dominion of the Fifth Dalai Lama and the fourth largest

Figure 1. Gönlung Jampa Ling Monastery.
Photo by the author, October 2010.

monastery on the entire Tibetan Plateau. On the eve of the monastery's destruction by Qing imperial forces in 1724, the monastery may have had as many as 2,400 monks.[20]

The establishment and growth of monasteries such as Gönlung point to another kind of monastic growth: the geographic expansion of the Geluk school of Tibetan Buddhism. As Gray Tuttle has demonstrated, the geographic region where Gönlung is situated, known in Tibetan as Amdo,[21] has been characterized by a pattern of "almost complete Dge lugs pa [Gelukpa] dominance of massive monastic institutions."[22] Although Tuttle's periodization of Geluk expansion into Amdo includes earlier periods, it is clear that the most significant and sustained growth began once the Gelukpa and their Khoshud (also written "Qoshot," "Hoshuud," etc.) and Zünghar (also written "Dzungar," "Junghar," etc.) Mongol patrons came to power in the mid-seventeenth century.[23] The same can be said of Mongolia.[24]

There is yet another feature of monasticism in Tibet in the aftermath of the Gelukpa's assertion of religious and political authority: institutional size.

While the 1737 census referred to above gives the number of monasteries as 3,150 under the Dalai Lama's dominion and 327 under the Panchen Lama's dominion,[25] the number of Geluk monasteries said to be recorded for the year 1882 is 1,026 *even while the number of Geluk monks increased to 491,242*.[26] "In other words," write the scholars who first drew attention to this phenomenon, "the sect was concentrating its monks in fewer monasteries."[27] Although one cannot place too much confidence in these statistics,[28] it is safe to say that the growth in the number of monastics did not always correlate with an increasing number of monasteries. It did mean bigger monasteries, however. This has led the anthropologist of Tibet, Melvyn Goldstein, to describe the characteristic and dominant form of monasticism in Tibet as "mass monasticism," defined as having "an emphasis on recruiting and sustaining very large numbers of celibate monks for their entire lives."[29] The sheer number of monks rather than their "quality" became the measure of a successful monastery.[30]

The explanations typically given to describe this phase of monastic growth and expansion are power and money. That is, the Fifth Dalai Lama (1617–1682) consolidated political and religious power over Central Tibet through the help of his new patrons, the Oirat or "Western Mongols." According to the redoubtable scholar Giuseppe Tucci,

> [The Fifth Dalai Lama] established firm ties between these monasteries and the central government, he appointed *mk'an po* [religious teachers] and abbots he could trust; by this time nothing happens without the Dalai Lama's sanction and consent; he deposes at his pleasure the abbots who arouse his suspicious, as was the case with the abbot of Šel dkar. . . .

> Moreover he neglects no opportunity of keeping this great monastic population attached to himself; in 1655 he restored the usage of reciting sacred texts and with this pretext he caused the monks of the great monasteries to come to Lhasa by turns.[31]

This portrait of the newly empowered Fifth Dalai Lama presents him as being everywhere at all times. He appoints the officers of monasteries, monitors their conduct, and dismisses them when necessary. He prescribes the rituals the monasteries were to conduct.

In addition to political power, scholars have identified the immense amount of economic and human resources to which the Dalai Lama was suddenly the beneficiary, which he allocated to his favored school of Buddhism. The Tibetan scholar Dungkar has written, "The fifth Dalai Lama, using his political power, built thirteen monasteries for all religious sects except the Bka' brgyud [Kagyü] sect, converted a part of Bka' brgyud pa's monasteries to the Dge-lugs sect, stipulated the number of monks in various monasteries and the monk corvée system, gave the three main [Geluk] monasteries— Se-ra, 'Bras-spungs, and Dga'-ldan—the right to manage their own manors and the people on them, and stipulated the amount of crops and money the government provided for the monasteries."[32] Dungkar concludes his overview of the economic and political power responsible for the Geluk success by criticizing the fact that all sects, but particularly the Gelukpa, were enmeshed in such economic activity: "The broad masses of the people called them *bla-dpon* (meaning "monk official," "lama official") to show their respect to them, but this term itself had profound satiric implication."[33]

When the Oirat Mongols (particularly the Khoshud and some Zunghars) settled in Amdo, the Geluk monasteries there, many of which had been established through earlier missionary activity, were the recipients of these patrons' largesse.[34] This, together with the "Eastern Mongols" predilection for the Gelukpa—a phenomenon often attributed to the charisma of the Third Dalai Lama and his meeting with the Tümed Mongol Altan Khan in the sixteenth century—positioned the Geluk school to expand across the Tibetan Plateau and into Mongolia. Later, in the eighteenth century, when a segment of the Oirat (the Torghud/Kalmyks) migrated to the Caucasus, they took their support for the Geluk school with them. Thus, the religious empire of the Geluk school stretched from its center in Lhasa, to the northern reaches of Mongolia, and to the western reaches of Eurasia. This process also resulted in construction of some of the Geluk school's most iconic, large-scale monasteries, such as Kumbum and Labrang in Amdo. In short, the independent variable in this sort of analysis is the patron, that is, the Mongols, who installed the Dalai Lama, paid for the Geluk monasteries, and carried their zeal for the Geluk school wherever they went.

One recent, innovative article that approaches the growth and expansion of the Geluk school from a different angle is McCleary and van der Kuijp's "The Market Approach to the Rise of the Geluk School, 1419–1642." They apply an economics-of-religion approach to the rise and success of the Geluk school. They argue that the Geluk school exhibited club-like characteristics that gave the school an edge in the competitive religious arena of sixteenth- and seventeenth-century Tibet. Moreover, it was these club-like characteristics, and not state intervention, that made the Gelukpa "organizationally capable of generating the violence that led to a monopoly outcome."[35] I have drawn particular inspiration from their attempt to explain the Geluk success by considering *institutional* factors apart from purely political or economic ones. My argument differs from McCleary and van der Kuijp's in that I focus more on the period that began *after* the Fifth Dalai Lama came to power in 1642 with the assistance of his Oirat Mongol patrons. As such, I am less interested in the Gelukpa's use of violence than in their passion for and ability in organizing their monasteries. Without denying the importance of such violence, I ask what the Gelukpa did with their newfound power and how they directed the resources they received in order to build their own school (and not just destroy their opponents). I want to draw attention to the fact that Geluk hierarchs were prodigious organizers with a proclivity for rationalizing all aspects of their monasteries, from doctrinal orthodoxy to the scheduling of major rituals and systems for administering and financing its monasteries. This, I argue, was just as important for the Geluk school's monopoly position and longevity as was its willingness to participate in violence or exhibit other club-like characteristics.

I also depart from McCleary and van der Kuijp's adoption of anthropologist Melvyn Goldstein's definition of mass monasticism. Mass monasticism, according to Goldstein, is a system devised to recruit as many monks as possible regardless of any detriment caused to the discipline or ideal of the monastery. In fact, he argues that monasteries lowered their standards in order to help as many monks as possible find their niche and to retain as many monks as possible.[36] The primary problem with this line of reasoning is that it actually inverts what the historical record reveals about the discipline of the largest monasteries. As Georges Dreyfus has written, "We should not assume that all Tibetan monasteries were equally lax in their discipline. . . . Since important aspects of the discipline are regulated by the particular code of each individual monastery or monastic unit [i.e., monastic constitutions], the strictness of monastic discipline varies greatly (as one might expect). In general, the large central monasteries of the tradition tended to be much stricter than the local smaller monasteries."[37] Just as the Chinese pilgrim Yijing had observed of the largest monasteries in seventh-century India,[38] a review of the historical record suggests that Dreyfus is correct and that some of the largest Geluk monasteries in Tibet were the most strictly regulated. A second problem with the concept of "mass monasticism" is its singular focus on the number of monks (the "masses"). I prefer to speak instead of "mega monasticism"—borrowing from the label "mega churches" applied to the twentieth- and twenty-first-century phenomenon among Protestant churches—in order to draw equal attention to the "volume" of (i.e., the number of monks at) the monastery and the institutional complexity of these monasteries.[39]

These explanations—of power and wealth provided by Mongol patrons, on the one hand, and of unique organizational capabilities of the Geluk school, on the other—are not incompatible. On the contrary, they may even be complementary insofar as the conservative and rule- and procedure-oriented Geluk school may have appealed to the Mongol leaders who patronized the Geluk school in much the same way that the teachings of the founder of the Geluk school in the fourteenth century appealed to the most important political power in Central Tibet from that time.[40] Moreover, the military and economic might of the Oirat Mongols may have cleared the way for Geluk lamas to operationalize their religious ethic of organization and rationalization.[41] In short, Geluk growth and dominance were not just the result of the Fifth Dalai Lama's direct rule and management of monastic affairs—although that did happen—nor should they be attributed solely to economic might—although their Mongol patrons gave them that.

Gene Smith once remarked on the integrity or robustness of the Karma Kagyü school relative to the other Kagyü schools: "Two subsects have branched off of the Karma pa, but there have been far fewer divisions than one might have expected. A possible explanation for this may be the well-developed organization of monasteries coupled with the prestige of the great incarnations."[42] As we shall see in Chapter 1, the Karmapas were the primary opponents to the Gelukpa through the first half of the seventeenth century and, as this quote suggests, the strength of the two competing schools may have shared a common basis in their organizational capabilities.

## Buddhist Bureaucrats

The above communist-infused critique of Geluk hierarchs by Dungkar as being "lama officials," which we might also gloss as "Buddhist bureaucrats,"[43] is true in ways that even he did not realize. Dungkar's critique is meant to imply that the typical Gelukpa was a monster of a sort—half monk, half political official—and not a complete or pure anything. The implication is that the Gelukpa were "bureaucrats" in the popular, negative sense of the term—functionaries and managers of an organization that exists only to perpetuate itself at the expense of the people and of progress. While this may be how Marxist-Leninist regimes think of bureaucracy,[44] this is not the way in which the concept was formalized by the sociologist Max Weber in the early twentieth century. In fact, Weber's understanding of bureaucracy and the bureaucrats who work in it can illuminate a lot more about the Geluk school than can the popular notion of the terms.

For Weber, bureaucratic rule is the purest example of rule that is based on the rule of law.[45] It is "the most rationalized known means of exercising authority over human beings."[46] It is important to remember that this is Weber's analytical evaluation concerning bureaucracy, not a normative one. It is true that Weber considers bureaucracy and the rational, legal authority on which it is founded to be most fully developed only in the modern period, but this is not because they are "better." After all, Weber famously used the image of the "iron cage" to describe the world ultimately transformed by rationalization and modern bureaucracy—an inescapable world of calculation and acquisition, devoid of value.[47] Moreover, rationalism is by no means found solely in modern states.

So, what does Weber mean by "rationalization" and how is that useful to our analysis of the Gelukpa? For Weber, rationalization is the desire for coherence. It is a reaction to the suffering and uncertainty of the world in which we live, "a stand towards something in the actual world which is experienced as specifically 'senseless.'"[48] It consists of the human "tendencies toward order in human thought."[49] It is a quest for meaning, although meaning need not be understood as a logical or cognitive ordering of the world. Indeed, Weber argues that one of the most common ways in which people have responded to the senselessness of the world is by seeking refuge in "sacred values," promises of material well-being and especially spiritual states of ecstasy or wholeness.[50] These religious states are essentially emotional states, and it is these states that become the focus of later, more abstract theological and philosophical speculations.[51] These speculations are often the products of intellectuals who seek to "sublimate" the acquisition of the sacred value into a sacrament or doctrine; they add "metaphysical meaning" to this emotional value (i.e., to the emotional satisfaction of experiencing a sacred state).

Rationalism, then, is a feeling of closure, of completeness, of order, or of control over the world provided by particular emotional states and by the abstract systems that give form to those states. Rationalism is not simply whatever accords with our modern-day, scientifically informed understanding of how the world works. Indeed, both the notion of a savior and that of karma are primary examples of rationalization (of suffering).[52] Rather, rationalization is the increase in predictability, order, and efficiency that comes with the observation and production of laws governing the cosmos, nature, and human relations.[53] Or, more technically, the maximization of "the calculability of means through the standardization of action."[54] It is this penchant for calculability and predictability through standardizing action that typifies the later Geluk approach to religious life.[55]

Rationalization in the form of the Protestant ethic has been credited with providing the "spirit" of modern capitalism and, more recently, with providing the "toolbox" for the construction of modern bureaucracy.[56] The latter argument has been made by historical sociologist Philip Gorski. In particular, Gorski describes the indignation and criticism that arose due to such practices as venality (the appropriation and sale of office) within the late medieval and early modern Catholic Church. These critiques were later reiterated by reformers such as Martin Luther, which prevented the uninhibited spread of such patrimonial forms of administration in Northern Europe. Later, pietist reformers extended this critique to the corruption and "spoils systems" as practiced in the early modern states. The proposals these Protestant reformers advanced, such as the rational use of remuneration of administrators (salaries), required technical qualifications (exams), written rules, and so on, were precisely the features of what we now recognize as the hallmarks of bureaucracy. Moreover, Gorski underscores the importance of attending to the *ideal* interests—the creation of a more predictable world in the pursuit of salvation—that gave rise to what is now the most widespread form of administration.

For Weber, much of early, Indian Buddhism was very rational. It exemplified the "genteel intellectual" approach to the problem of suffering. Apart from adopting and elaborating on the doctrines and worldview consisting of samsara, karma, and liberation, these intellectuals sought a purely "cognitive" solution to the fundamental problem of the world. Liberation from the cycle of suffering was coterminous with gnosis, knowing or wisdom, and thus it was in contemplation that one sought resolution and escape.[57]

However, this wisdom and liberation were fundamentally tinged by "emotion," and thus the goal of this path of contemplation was one of the "irrational *loci*" to which these intellectuals-cum-contemplatives retreated. Thus, the rationalization process of early Buddhists faltered upon the "mystical" grounds of quietism, "silence," "passivity," and "rest." The Buddhist virtuoso, the monk, was at his best a world-fleeing mystic.

The Buddhist mendicant's Western counterpart, the Christian monk, is understood by Weber to be "ascetic" rather than "mystic." That is, he *applied* himself to *changing* the world around him rather than merely "accepting" the world as it is and seeking to adjust to it. Thus, Weber prefers to call Christian monasticism a "world-rejecting asceticism"—an ethic that stands in tension with the world and seeks to transform its cruder aspects. Weber writes, "The occidental church is a uniformly rational organization with a monarchial head and a centralized control of piety. That is, it is headed not only by a personal transcendental god, but also by a terrestrial ruler of enormous power, who actively controls the lives of his subjects. Such a figure is lacking in the religions of Eastern Asia, partly for historical reasons, partly because of the nature of the religions in question."[58] In distinguishing Buddhist monasticism from Christian monasticism, Weber even anticipates the argument of this book by downplaying the similarities between Christian monasticism and Tibetan monasticism: "Even Lamaism, which has a strong organization, does not have the rigidity of a bureaucracy. The Asiatic hierarchs in Taoism and the other hereditary patriarchs of Chinese and Hindu sects were always partly mystagogues, partly the objects of anthropolatric veneration, and partly—as in the cases of the Dalai and Taschi [i.e., the Panchen] Lama—the chiefs of a completely monastic religion of magical character."[59] In other words, Buddhism, especially in its later stages, succumbed to the primitive belief in the extraordinary power inherent in particular objects, actions, and people to influence the material world.

Weber's analysis of Buddhism was limited by the paucity of rich historical and ethnographic literature on Buddhism. Research at that time was primarily oriented toward the study of early Buddhism as understood through later Pali doctrinal sources. Later, Mahayana Buddhism was written off as a popular and magical aberration. As the anthropologist David Gellner has written, "By paying no attention to the Vinaya (monastic discipline) texts, Weber underestimated the all-important role of the Sangha (monastic community) in the life of the monk. He also underestimated the degree to which early Buddhism had already accommodated itself to lay religious interests and therefore included elements of prayer, deification of the Buddha, and so on."[60] As a result, Weber overemphasized the "magical" aspects of Tibetan Buddhism and overlooked other aspects of early Buddhism where rationalization had taken hold, such as in monastic life. Actually, if we take what Weber had to say about Western (Christian) monasticism and apply it to Buddhist monasticism, much is revealed. Weber wrote, "Only in the Occident, where the monks became the disciplined army of a rational bureaucracy of office, did asceticism directed toward the outer world become increasingly systematized into a methodology of active, rational conduct of life."[61] We now know that early Buddhist monasticism, rather than being characterized by a "minimum of organization" and by lone mendicants cut off from society, consisted of complex economic and legal arrangements.[62] And if that is true of early Buddhism, then it is doubly true of the monasteries devised by the Gelukpa. After all, the Gelukpa did not flee from society; they ruled it. And their monasteries were the largest in the history of the world.

The renowned Tibetologist R. A. Stein's contention that Tibet be understood as an "ecclesiastical state"[63] alerts us to the possibility of applying Weber's analyses of "hierocratic associations" and the "church" to the study of Tibetan history and religion. "Hierocratic associations" are a type of corporate authority holding "a monopoly in the bestowal or denial of sacred values." Similarly, a "church" is "a community organized by officials into an institution which bestows gifts of grace."[64] Officials in a church are said to "fight principally against all virtuoso-religion and against its autonomous development."[65] This helps to explain a rather widespread discomfort among Gelukpa with institutions and practices more dependent on charismatic authority or other sources of authority apart from the legal authority of the institution itself. For instance, Geluk hierarchs frequently express a certain level of skepticism toward the process of identifying reincarnate lamas. Oracles and their mediums, too, although not dispensed with, are subjected to tight controls to protect from any potential "prophetic assault."[66]

Hierocratic associations share much in common with modern bureaucratic states, most importantly their reliance on rule of law. They also have a hierarchy of officials that both ranks and delimits the area of jurisdiction of each official and a separation of the "official sphere" from the "private sphere."[67] As we shall see, these traits epitomize the Geluk approach to organizing its monasteries.

A bureaucracy in its "pure form" is said to be characterized by "a single hierarchy of offices, meritocratic selection of personnel, and a systematic application of clearly defined impersonal legal norms in the form of abstract general rules regulating all procedures, as well as the rights and duties of officials."[68] It is perhaps this last characteristic—"clearly defined impersonal legal norms"—that most epitomizes Weber's concept of bureaucracy and the legal authority on which it rests.[69] Beginning in Chapter 1, we shall be looking at just such rules as they were codified by the Gelukpa in documents known as *chayik* (T. *bca' yig*), translated variously as "constitutions," "guidelines," or "constitutions," among other names.

Bureaucracies, moreover, "tend to evolve toward centralized control, functional differentiation, technical specificity, as well as depersonalization and impersonality."[70] The benefits of bureaucracy are greater speed, precision, and uniformity and predictability of operation. Bureaucracy also minimizes the personal, irrational, and emotional elements in official business[71] and improves "corporate coherence, esprit de corps, and useable knowledge and skills."[72] Thus, the predictable program of monasticism stipulated by its hierarchs was an efficient way for training its growing number of monks, and the uniformity of that program strengthened a corporate identity. A more cynical view of bureaucracy argues that it is merely the *conceit* of a transparent, meritocratic system that gives bureaucracy its allure.[73] Assuming this perspective, one can argue that the promotion of the idea of a depersonalized Geluk monasticism appealed to aspiring monks and commanded their loyalty,[74] while its presentation as a predictable and conservative approach to monasticism appealed to laity and potential patrons.

The Geluk church was not a "pure bureaucracy." The system of reincarnating lamas (T. *sprul sku*) competed with the superior at the head of the hierarchy of officials at the monastery (the abbot), which in some places may have eroded the efficacy of the abbot's power. The Geluk church also was not a pure "hierocratic association." The Dalai Lama's Ganden Phodrang government historically exercised political power over much of Central and Eastern Tibet, and, as such, it exhibits characteristics of a different social stratum, that of temporal ruler (e.g., some large-scale, public rituals are held more out of official or civic obligations to the state's subjects). But this is to be expected. As Weber wrote, "The great majority of empirical cases represent a combination or a state of transition among several such pure types."[75] Nonetheless, addressing the bureaucratic and hierocratic features of the Geluk school can help to explain historical outcomes that have previously been explained only in terms of material interests or doctrine.

## Tsongkhapa

Identifying the origin of Geluk bureaucracy is beyond the scope of this book and likely beyond the abilities of the current field of Tibetan history. Even the origin of bureaucracy in modern Europe is much debated despite the details of that political history being much better understood.[76] Nonetheless, it is clear that the figure of the founder of the Geluk school, Tsongkhapa (1357–1419), and his writings had a lasting impact on the identity of that school. Moreover, his creation of a totalizing "path" of Buddhist practice grounded in the ideas of discipline and reason provided what Weber calls the "world images" or "ideas" that have, "like switchmen, determined the tracks along which action has been pushed by the dynamic of [material and ideal] interests."[77]

Tsongkhapa Lozang Drakpa was posthumously credited with being the founder of the Geluk school or the New Kadam school as it was initially known. The earliest biographies of Tsongkhapa depicted him as both an ardent advocate of orthodoxy and, interestingly, as an institution builder.[78] Tsongkhapa's mark or "stamp," as Weber would call it, upon Tibetan Buddhism was an emphasis on ethics and monastic vows, an emphasis on a systematic study of Buddhist philosophy so as to acquire a correct view of the nature of reality, and the compatibility and integration of esoteric (tantric) practice and vows with exoteric, monastic vows.[79] Moreover, Tsongkhapa sought to systematize an approach to Buddhist salvation in which monastic discipline was prioritized. On that foundation one would pursue the systematic study of (exoteric) Buddhist philosophy. Only then would one be prepared to engage in beneficial contemplative (esoteric) practice, which was further limited by the sanction that such practice not contravene the more foundational monastic vows (such as celibacy). The biography of Tsongkhapa and, specifically, his decision to not engage in tantric practice with a consort further underscores his commitment to this ordering of priorities.

Tsongkhapa built a complete worldview that charts the way from one's present predicament to liberation. That "path" is a graded one that largely foreclosed upon the possibility of a "shortcut" to liberation through contemplative practices alone. In other words, the acquisition of "sacred values" is postponed and "sublimated" by elaborating a nonnegotiable metaphysical and intellectual path one has to traverse. That path and Tsongkhapa's philosophical works more generally were produced by relying on scholastic and Buddhist hermeneutical practices that emphasized the importance of scriptural authority and the determination of the definitive or correct meaning of scriptures, among other things.[80]

In addition to constructing a single, unified system of path and goal, Tsongkhapa is also remembered as an institution-builder. His "four great acts" are recorded in early biographical literature as restoring a Maitreya statue, lecturing on monastic discipline to monks at Namtsedeng[81] temple, founding the new year's Great Prayer Festival in Lhasa, and founding the Ganden Monastery.[82] As Kurtis Schaeffer has written, "The four acts single out Tsongkhapa's efforts at forging a strong monastic network through art, monastic ethics, and public ritual, yet do not mention his philosophical work, suggesting that he was known as an institution-builder as much as an intellectual in the period immediately following his death."[83]

Thus, if we can speak of a "religious ethic" that Tsongkhapa and his early disciples granted the nascent Geluk school, it was one of building an all-encompassing intellectual and soteriological system and of institution-building. This is the legacy that later generations of Gelukpa would inherit.


## The Great Fifth


The social and political arena for the full implementation of the Geluk religious ethic was the mid-seventeenth century. The violent end to the conflict there at the hands of the Fifth Dalai Lama's supporters, the Oirat Mongols, eliminated the Geluk school's main competitors for religious and political power, and it cleared the way for major institutional reforms. This parallels Gorski's observation that revolution in early modern Europe often catalyzed bureaucratization "by demolishing distributional coalitions that can stand in the way of reform."[84] Gorski has also identified the importance of an "ascetic Protestant monarch of severe habit and mind" for the full implementation of a rationalized administration. The Tibetan counterpart to this "ascetic Protestant monarch" was the Fifth Dalai Lama.

The Fifth Dalai Lama Ngawang Lozang Gyatso, or "The Great Fifth," and his Ganden Phodrang government (based in Lhasa) have received increased scholarly attention in recent years. As a result, we know more about how the Dalai Lama and his ministers were astute political strategists. He and his school emerged victorious from the centuries-long conflict between political and religious powers located in Tsang (western Central Tibet) and Ü (eastern Central Tibet) due to the fortunate alliances they formed with, first, the Tümed Mongols and, later, the Oirats or "Western Mongols." Later, the Fifth Dalai Lama would also visit the court of the rising Manchu Qing Empire, and the Gelukpa would capitalize on the unique relationship between their school and the imperial court.[85]

Once the Dalai Lama seized power in 1642, he and his ministers set about creating an image of the Dalai Lama and of his school fit for a bodhisattva king. Myths of the deeds of the Bodhisattva of Compassion, Avalokiteśvara, which had been developing and circulating in Tibet for centuries, were made the backdrop of the Dalai Lama's rule, as the Dalai Lama himself helped to spread the idea of his and his predecessors being emanations of the bodhisattva.[86] This connection had the important implication of also identifying the Dalai Lama with an earlier emanation of Avalokiteśvara, the dharma king Songtsen Gampo (d. 649), who is credited with catalyzing Tibet's golden age of vast, imperial rule. Various other efforts were made in print, architecture, ritual, and so on, to further legitimize the Dalai Lama's rule.[87]

The Dalai Lama and his ministers also sought to create an environment that would reflect the universal rule of a bodhisattva. They did so, for instance, by welcoming and patronizing intellectuals from India and elsewhere in South Asia who helped foster the study of language and medicine.[88] More generally, the Dalai Lama presented the Geluk school as the inclusive, "nonpartisan" bearer of Buddhism that was destined to spread across the world. Of course, it is much easier to be "universally-minded" or "non-partisan" when one is in power, having secured that position through violence. But this new authority based in Central Tibet did not rest after its Mongol patron-allies carried it to power. Moreover, the Dalai Lama and the Geluk school did not maintain its dominance through recourse to violence, nor did it legitimize its authority solely through drawing on tradition. Instead, the continuing success of the Dalai Lama's school had to do with their rationalizing tendencies that undergirded their unrestrained ambitions to "spread Buddhism vastly" and to "enlighten like the sun the darkness" of the East.[89]

Those tendencies may have had particular importance for legitimizing the Geluk dominance in places outside Central Tibet, particularly Mongolia, where customs and traditions from Tibet's past competed with local, non-Tibetan traditions and customs. To be sure, the legacy of the "priest-patron" or "royal donor and reverend donee" relationship between the earlier Mongol ruler Altan Khan (1507–1582) and the Third Dalai Lama (1543–1588) was important for legitimizing the Geluk school in these far-off places, but equally important may have been the stories of the Third Dalai Lama's "ethical rationalization" of life in Mongolia. One of the earliest records of this encounter is found in the biography of Altan Khan and his immediate descendants: "The errors of the non-Buddhist spirit dolls and fetishes were burned. / The mad and stupid shamans were annihilated and the shamanesses humiliated. / The State of the Supreme Dharma became like a silk protection cord."[90] Animal and human sacrifices were banned, and, as a later biography describes it, the Dalai Lama commanded that "all the Chinese, Tibetans, Mongols, and so on who live in this land [i.e., Kökenuur][91] abide by the rules of the ten virtuous actions."[92] Such ethical injunctions later informed Altan Khan's code of law for the Mongols.[93]

These stories of the "ethical" and "pure" Gelukpa in Mongolia were part of the legacy that the Fifth Dalai Lama and later Gelukpa inherited, and it was one they felt compelled to uphold. Thus, when another Geluk incarnate lama from Kökenuur (also "Kokonor") was traveling in Mongolia in the 1770s, he likewise sermonized on the importance of refraining from alcohol and of "avoiding the ten unwholesome deeds" of killing, stealing, and so on.[94] But the Gelukpa were known for more than just moral discipline. Equally important was the legacy of Tsongkhapa's institution-building.[95] The Gelukpa devised monasteries that were disciplined in the widest sense of the term, ensuring that the hundreds and thousands of monks that inhabited any one monastery were kept busy learning and memorizing its liturgy, its calendar of worship and tantric practice, its hierarchy of offices and functionaries, its system for redistributing wealth, its scholastic curriculum and methods of debate, and so on. These monks were also taught and knew of the ties that their own monasteries had with hierarchs and institutions in more centrally located areas and with branch monasteries and monasteries farther afield. This facilitated travel and communication between Geluk monasteries and contributed to the coherency of the Geluk school.

## A Religious Empire

The *expansionist* program of the Geluk school is one of its features that justifies referring to the Geluk school as a "religious empire." Of course, "empire" is almost always used in scholarly writing to refer to a *political* entity. "Empire . . . is a system of interaction between two political entities, one of which, the dominant metropole, exerts political control over the internal and external policy—the effective sovereignty—of the other, the subordinate periphery," writes one scholar of empire.[96] Religion is sometimes "used by" empires to provide a common sense of identity among its diverse peoples (e.g., *umma* for the Umayyad, Abbasid, and other Islamic polities; Christianity for the Carolingian Empire),[97] but it is seldom presented as the main actor or driver of history.

A more recent attempt to define "empire" provides a more complex and, for our purposes, more illuminating definition, although it too focuses on polities: "Empires are large political units, expansionist or with a memory of power extended over space, polities that maintain distinction and hierarchy as they incorporate new people."[98] This definition is slightly more applicable to the case of the Geluk school insofar as Geluk lamas were explicitly and actually expansionist and maintained and identified with a memory of power extended over space (that of the Tibetan Empire of the seventh through the ninth centuries). The school has also exhibited a longevity and staying power, which is a characteristic of any conventional empire.[99] Most important, thinking of the Geluk school as an empire encourages us to place its mechanisms of rule alongside those of states. It helps, moreover, to reveal the extent of the Gelukpa's ambitions, their proximity to and engagement with power, and the contributions that religious ideas and practices have made to political and social change.

Of course, conventional empires are also typically recognized by their command of "army and cannon" or the means and will to export it to other polities as part of their expansionist programs.[100] This is something the Gelukpa lacked, even if the Dalai Lama could muster troops in times of war and major monasteries maintained a corps of "punk monks" who would police major assemblies and who could be directed to attack other nearby monasteries or local enemies. But even the "ecclesiastical empire" of the Western Christian Church lacked this and often depended on temporal powers to enforce its will.[101] By considering the Geluk expansion across Inner Asia and its consolidation and systemization of power in the late seventeenth and the eighteenth centuries as a process of building a *religious* empire, we can better appreciate the religious control effected by its common body of doctrinal and practical norms[102] and the resulting uniformity and resilience of the Geluk school as a whole.

The key to the Geluk school's expansion and staying power, in any case, is its proclivity for and excellence in bureaucracy, a feature of most empires whether conventional (political) or religious. The following analysis of the Geluk "religious law"—the silken cord—reveals how the Gelukpa, beginning with the Fifth Dalai Lama, built a hierocratic organization that drew on legal authority to spread across the expanse of the Tibetan Plateau and into Mongolia. By plotting the administration of their monasteries, Geluk hierarchs left us with a record of their rationalizing minds and their path to success. They were "organization men" in the sense that they prioritized the organization (the monastery) and planned for (organized) its success by, among other ways, encoding its rules and procedures in monastic constitutions.[103] The success of the Geluk school was as much or even more the result of its hierarchs' organizing vision and methods as it was any other factor, such as political patronage or philosophical prowess.

Chapter 1

# The Geluk School's Innovative Use of
# Monastic Constitutions

By 1642, the Fifth Dalai Lama had forged an unparalleled priest-patronage relationship with the supreme political and military presence in Tibet, Köken-uur (in today's Qinghai Province), and Züngharia (in today's Xinjiang)—the Oirats or "Western Mongols"; specifically, the Zünghar and Khoshud tribes. From this relationship the Geluk school of Buddhism became reified in an unprecedented way and came in the subsequent centuries to dominate the religious landscape of Tibet, Mongolia, and even the Qing imperial court. One could imagine that this relationship and profound support accorded the Dalai Lama might have led to different historical trajectories. For instance, the Dalai Lama might have chosen to utilize a mobile court like that of the "great encampment" (T. *sgar chen*) of the Karma school or of the (later) lama Chagan Nom-un Khan in Kökenuur.[1] His very mobility, so characteristic of lamas throughout the centuries,[2] would have underscored his charisma and the importance of his personal lineage as the center of his religious and political rule. Flocks of disciples and devotees might have followed him, inhabiting makeshift huts (T. *spyil pu*) along the way, in the hope of receiving teachings, blessings, and empowerments that he would transmit from centuries past. Meanwhile, he would establish separate "teaching centers" (T. *bshad grwa*) and "practice centers" (T. *sgrub sde*) for intimate and focused study and meditation. His influence and domain would thereby grow in a more or less piecemeal and organic manner based on the places he traveled to and the personal interactions he had.

So, why did the Dalai Lama choose not to grow his brand of Buddhism in this manner? One monastic constitution that reflects an early move toward institutionalization provides an explanation: "The happiness of society[3] depends upon the Teachings of the Buddha, and the Teachings [depend upon] centers of the sangha. Those, moreover, depend upon the firm establishment of order. Even if there is a large sangha, without order, it is of no benefit other than causing great destruction to the Teachings."[4] That is, bigger is not necessarily better. A bigger sangha that is not regimented is actually a detriment to upholding and promoting the Buddha's Teachings.

The Dalai Lama chose regimentation and order. He took up residence in the Potala Palace at the top of the legendary Red Hill in Lhasa,[5] and he was disassociated from any *particular* monastery.[6] The order, or school, that he helped to shape, the Geluk, was not (like the Sakya or Kagyü) associated with a particular *place* nor even with the Dalai Lama himself. The Geluk school did not depend on a single monastic seat. One might say that it had *three* seats (T. *gdan sa gsum*)—the renowned Ganden, Drepung, and Sera Monasteries—but it would be more accurate to understand the Geluk school as an ideology grounded in a *system of monasteries and an ideal of proper monasticism.*[7] The inter- or pan-regional Mongol patrons presented the Dalai Lama and other Geluk prelates with the opportunity to devise a resilient religious group not tied to either a particular place or a particular lineage. Instead, what tied the Gelukpa together was its consistent messaging on the importance of monastic discipline and on its position that scholasticism and scriptural authority takes precedence over claims to insight grounded in meditative practices alone.

A primary medium of this messaging was the monastic constitution, or *chayik (bca' yig)* in Tibetan.[8] Short for "*trimsu jawé yigé*" (T. *khrims su bca' ba'i yi ge*), "documents that institute as law," these documents were and continue to be important for providing monasteries with a blueprint for how the monastery should ideally operate.[9] In addition, they provided legitimacy to the administrative structure of the monastery. Usually an illustrious lama would be sought out and even beseeched by the elder monks and administrators of a monastery to compose a constitution for the institution, which would lend the monastery legitimacy. Occasionally, these documents would be put on display on a monastery wall, although more often they were written on scrolls similar to secular legal documents.[10] The monastery's abbot or senior disciplinarian would act as the custodian of this precious document, regularly revealing it and giving "disciplinary sermons"[11] based on it throughout the year. This further legitimized the monastery's administrative structure and

Figure 2. A monastic constitution written on the wall of Zaplung Monastery (T.
*Zab lung rdo dkar bkra shis 'khyil*) in eastern Amdo.
Photo by the author, July 2016.

practices by repeatedly appealing to a code of conduct and foundational document[12] that transcended the interests of any individual administrator.

As mentioned in this book's Introduction, neither the Dalai Lama nor
the Geluk school invented the monastic constitution. The earliest extant constitution dates from an itinerant religious community of the eleventh
century that was built around the influential figure known as Rongzom
(1042–1136).[13] In addition, non-Geluk schools of Buddhism, especially the Kagyü school, are responsible for at least twenty extant constitutions dating
from before the time of the Fifth Dalai Lama and the climatic growth in
monasteries discussed in the Introduction.[14] Nonetheless, both a synoptic
view of all of the available constitutions as well as a close reading of all of
the constitutions through the middle of the eighteenth century reveal that
the Geluk school seized the genre of monastic constitutions in ways that
other schools only belatedly learned to do.

A representative survey of 151 extant monastic constitutions dating from
prior to the twentieth century reveals that two-thirds ($n = 100$) were composed

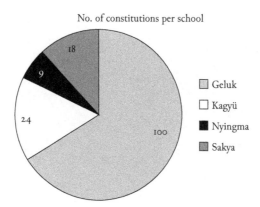

No. of constitutions per school

Geluk
Kagyü
Nyingma
Sakya

Figure 3. Representative sample of constitutions broken down by school.

by figures primarily associated with the Geluk school.[15] Geluk hierarchs dominated the production of monastic constitutions, particularly from the time the Fifth Dalai Lama assumed power through the first half of the eighteenth century, a period during which they composed almost 90 percent of the extant constitutions. After that, in the latter half of the eighteenth-century, non-Geluk authors doubled the rate at which they had been producing constitutions. Nonetheless, Geluk constitutions are still predominant, and Geluk authors, too, increased their rate of production.[16]

This growing interest in codifying the organization of monasteries in the mid-eighteenth century took place precisely at the moment that the influence of Central Tibetan hierarchs in Amdo began to wane.[17] This is also the period during which monasteries in Inner Mongolia were being founded at a historic rate.[18] In other words, the surge in the production of Geluk constitutions in the latter half of the eighteenth century reflects the institutionalization of the Geluk school beyond Central Tibet. After the death of the Fifth Dalai Lama, many of the constitutions that were composed were for monasteries on the frontier of Tibet, especially in Amdo (constitution nos. 58, 60–61, 65–67, and 69). Not only that, but they were also being composed increasingly by Geluk hierarchs *from* the frontier for monasteries in Amdo and beyond in Mongolia. Later still, we find Mongol authors of monastic constitutions, such as the Eighth Jibzundamba (1870–1924), who wrote at least three Tibetan-language constitutions.[19] The most prolific author of monastic constitutions prior to the twentieth century was the Second Jamyang Zhepa (1728–1791; nineteen constitutions), who

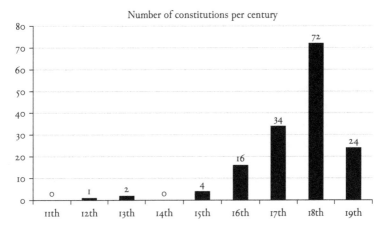

Figure 4. Representative sample of constitutions broken down by century of composition. This demonstrates the tremendous growth in production that coincided with the Geluk school's coming to power and spreading across the Tibetan Plateau and into Mongolia.

was the principle lama of Amdo's major Labrang Monastery. This shift in the locus of Geluk power from Central Tibet to Amdo—or, more precisely, the *decentralization* of power and its distribution into bureaucratic institutions—is connected to similar observations that have been made regarding a geographic shift in the production of collected works[20] and in the phenomenon of finding and recognizing the rebirth of an important religious master in a young child.[21]

In addition, this surge in the production of constitutions is an outgrowth of a standardization that was initially worked out by the Fifth Dalai Lama and other Geluk hierarchs in the decades immediately following his death. The Fifth Dalai Lama is the second most prolific author (after the Second Jamyang Zhepa) of constitutions prior to the twentieth century (eighteen constitutions), and, as I will show in later chapters, the influence of his constitutions on the language and content of the constitutions that followed is clear. Constitutions prior to the time of the Fifth Dalai Lama were mostly composed for "retreats" or "hermitages," and as such included (among other things) a preoccupation with maintaining the "boundaries" (T. *mtshams*; Sanskrit *sīma*) of the retreatants, with limiting their possessions, and with stressing the importance of meditation. The communities for which these constitutions were composed were relatively "guru-centric," being communities built around the charismatic personality of an individual or an individual lama lineage. The constitutions for these communities also exhibit a greater emphasis on the secret "commitments" (S. *samaya*) that bind together a "tantric family." And, significantly, they were composed by a lama for *his own* community.

In contrast, later constitutions—those composed by the Fifth Dalai Lama and by other Geluk hierarchs in the early decades of the eighteenth century—reveal concerted attempts to codify certain institutional arrangements: seating, debate topics and scholastic curricula, granting of degrees, ritual manuals to be consulted, requesting and granting of leaves, limiting and channeling the collection of "alms," the redistribution of "alms" (usually making it more equitable), the responsibilities of officers, and so on. We see a greater emphasis on the importance of impartiality among officers. These constitutions also sometimes make explicit reference to other, more centrally located monasteries (or to "mother monasteries") as models. And, finally, these constitutions were often composed for monasteries far away (often on the frontier with or in Mongol areas) that did not necessarily share any historical or institutional affiliation with the lama tasked with composing the constitution. The Gelukpa were doing something *qualitatively different* than earlier authors.

A review of the extant monastic constitutions reveals the opportunism of the Geluk school. As the Gelukpa consolidated their control in Central Tibet and expanded it into new areas, they used the power of the written word in a variety of ways to establish and legitimate their authority.[22] One such way was their prolific production of monastic constitutions. The expanding political and spiritual horizon afforded by the Geluk alliance with the Khoshud and Zünghar Mongols and, a little later, the Manchu Qing Empire, and a compulsion to fulfill the prophecy that "the Buddha's Pure Religion"—particularly that of the "Second Buddha," Tsongkhapa—"will spread in the East"[23] led to the creation of mega monasteries across the landscape of Inner Asia and to the success of the Geluk school.

## Retreats and Places of Practice

I have attempted to gather and read every available constitution through the 1740s, which amounts to nearly seventy constitutions,[24] and more than a dozen from after this period. The period between 1642 and the

1740s was the period during which the Geluk school consolidated its power in Central Tibet and, increasingly, in Amdo through the growth and institutionalization of its monasteries. Constitutions composed after this point are either inspired by or draw upon earlier constitutions, and they also represent a new historical phase in which the Geluk school's center of power gravitated toward Amdo and its new patrons in Mongolia and especially the Manchu Qing Court.[25] In addition, the dramatic increase in the production of constitutions after this period, including non-Geluk constitutions, makes the comprehensive study of later constitutions a task beyond the scope of this book.

The major takeaway from a review of the record of early constitutions is that until the time of the Fifth Dalai Lama in the mid-seventeenth century these constitutions are mostly concerned with small-scale centers often dedicated to meditation in retreat (T. *mtshams*). The earliest extant constitution, which is by Rongzom Chökyi Zangpo in the eleventh century (constitution no. 1), Tsongkhapa's 1405 constitution for his favorite hermitage of Lhazhöl (no. 5), the follower of Tsongkhapa Chenga Lodrö Gyeltsen's 1449 constitution (no. 6), a constitution by the Throne-holder of Drigung Monastery Rinchen Püntsok (1509–1557) for Reting Monastery north of Lhasa (no. 11), and even the constitutions composed by the Eighth Karmapa (1507–1554) for residents of his Great Encampment (T. *sgar chen*) (no. 8) and of his major monastery of Tsurpu (no. 9) all express concern for small-scale communities focused primarily on meditation.[26] The few exceptions to this pattern—nos. 3, 30, and 31—are exceptions that still fit the pattern described above: they are written by the heads of the non-Geluk schools for their own personal monasteries. Apart from these exceptions, the constitutions of the Ninth Karmapa (nos. 13–23) also stand out for exhibiting many of the same characteristics of Geluk constitutions, beginning with those of the Fifth Dalai Lama. Nonetheless, there is a striking and noteworthy difference between earlier constitutions and later ones in terms of the kinds of corporate bodies they envisioned and the mechanisms they specified for enacting and maintaining those bodies.

The earliest extant constitution is attributed to the important Nyingma, or "Ancient," schoolmaster from the eleventh century, Rongzom Chökyi Zangpo (1042–1136) (constitution no. 1), who composed it for his community of tantric "commitment-holders" (T. *dam tshig pa rnams*). Despite containing certain features that will come to be common to all constitutions,[27] Rongzom's constitution is set off from the later Geluk constitutions that will predominate in the seventeenth and eighteenth centuries by, in particular, the kind of ideal community it envisions and the considerations of such a community. Technically, Rongzom's constitution is not a "monastic constitution," since celibacy is not expected of the community's adherents. Dominic Sur has recently studied this constitution, and he explains how Rongzom's constitution and ideal community is a small, harmonious community maintained by faithful, interpersonal relationships. Rongzom's constitution "represents a resolutely tantric constitution that envisions the ethics of Rongzom's community in a way that is different from standard Mahāyāna ethics. The individual building block of Rongzom's social institution qua community is the *damtsikpa* (*dam tshig pa*): "committed disciples" or "those who are bound [to a teacher] by vows and pledges."[28] Considerable attention is paid by Rongzom to the proper relationship of the community's lama, or teacher, with his disciples. Disciples are to serve the teacher; the teacher is to teach clearly and equally to all disciples; and disciples are to avoid being boastful, critical, or divisive with respect to their vajra siblings.[29] The reason for this is that the community cannot survive without each member holding up his or her end of the bargain.

These relationships among members of Rongzom's community are defined by the very personal tantric commitments that members make to each other rather than by the individual commitments each makes to some abstract code of conduct, such as the Vinaya. So, although reference is made to the "five foundations of Mahāyāna precepts,"[30] which consist simply of five of the ten wholesome deeds (S. *kuśalakarmapatha*) found throughout Buddhist literature and societies, one may choose to take all five of these precepts or only "some."[31] Meanwhile, the primary organizing principle of Rongzom's constitution is that of the "eight vajra enclosures," which are characterized as "there being a harmony of views and commitments among the master and the vajra siblings, and thus an exercise of intimacy, good will, and friendship, without hatred."[32] Sur explains that "the constitution reflects the values and reality of the communities that emerge out of the dark age—small scale, non-institutional, highly focused on the growth and maintenance of healthy personal relationships between student and teacher, disciples of the same teacher, disciples of different teachers, and so on."[33]

To be sure, the later Geluk constitutions are equally concerned with the integrity of the sangha. After all, the canonical Vinaya itself warns against causing schism and disunion in the sangha, serious acts that invite probation.[34] Rongzom's constitution and later Geluk constitutions share other similarities, too, such as a desire to curtail sophistry in philosophical disputes and warnings against engaging in philosophical disputes without altruistic motivations.[35] Nonetheless, the context is clearly very different. The Geluk authors have in mind *institutions*—curricula, officers, disciplinary procedures, and so on—that will survive the foibles of an individual teacher; institutions that *contain* and *transcend* their communities and whose members are organized not by interpersonal commitments and loyalties to each other but by codes of conduct that preceded their existence and that will survive them until the end of the dharma itself. Even the community for which Rongzom composed his constitution is referred to simply as "the committed disciples" (T. *damtsikpa*) gathered together by Rongzom rather than, as is the case with later Geluk constitutions, having a unique eponymous name, that is, the monastery's proper name. In short, Rongzom's community is personal, lama- or guru-centric, and bound by intimate and sacred commitments (T. *dam tshig*; S. *samaya*).

Subsequent constitutions also envision communities far less institutionalized than later Geluk monasteries. For instance, a constitution composed by the seventeenth throne-holder of Drigung Monastery, Rinchen Püntsok (1509–1557) for the abbot of Reting Monastery (no. 11)—the monastery that the Fifth Dalai Lama would later compare to the palace of Avalokiteśvara and refer to as "the Headwaters of the Kadam [school]"[36]—has solely in mind retreatants embarked on "the path of practice, meditation, and insight."[37] There is a discussion of communal assembly and the proper comportment one must maintain while in assembly; however, it is sandwiched between ritual and meditation sessions that one is advised to conduct in one's own hut.[38] In fact, retreatants are advised to engage in the Great Perfection[39] contemplative practices of "Breakthrough" (T. *khregs chod*), "Direct Transcendance" (T. *thod rgal*), and "[Ego-]Severing" (T. *gcod*),[40] practices ordinarily associated with the Kagyü school or the Nyingma school. Apart from raising questions about the history of Reting, a monastery that comes to be closely associated with the Dalai Lama and the Geluk school, this constitution portrays a community concerned principally with practice (T. *sgrub*) and realization (T. *rtogs*).[41] As with all constitutions, this one insists on maintaining the integrity of the sangha, since it is the "foundation" (T. *gzhi rtsa*) of the Buddha's Teachings.[42] However, the consequence of this is not to look to the Vinaya for discipline, as do later Geluk constitutions, but rather to maintain strict spiritual practice. The closest the constitution comes to speaking of Vinaya-type morality is a brief insistence that practitioners should ideally maintain a vegetarian diet.[43]

## Early Inclinations Toward Organization: Tsongkhapa's Constitutions

Rinchen Püntsok's constitution for the abbot of Reting focuses explicitly on meditative *practice* in a way that even Rongzom's earlier constitution did not. Rinchen Püntsok's constitution actually presents a daily schedule of the community, albeit a rather basic one. In that schedule, one also learns of a clear separation between fully ordained (and presumably celibate) monks and novices and laity: the novices and laity are to take on various administrative and service roles in the community, while the monks are to remain in retreat and practice.[44] We also see references to certain officers in the community, the disciplinarian[45] and manager,[46] further suggesting a basic stage of institutionalization.

The precedent for these features of Rinchen Püntsok's constitution may be the two constitutions composed by Tsongkhapa (nos. 4 and 5), the founder of the Geluk school. In the constitution he composed for the Lhazhöl Hermitage (no. 5) that he had frequented in the 1390s, reference is made to a disciplinarian[47] and manager[48] and to lay workers that serve them.[49] The laity is required to stay below the retreat boundary (T. *mtshams mtho*) lest they face penalties,[50] and the retreatants are expected to stay inside the boundary, at least during the winter and summer meditation periods.[51] Women are prohibited from staying overnight at the hermitage and from even entering it unless they are seeking religious services. Moreover, it is clear from Tsongkhapa's other constitution (no. 4) that he has in mind a community of celibate renouncers, be they novices or fully ordained monks.[52]

That Tsongkhapa's constitutions show a concern for purely monastic discipline is not surprising for those familiar with Tsongkhapa's biography. One of Tsongkhapa's "Four Great Acts" is his discourse on Vinaya given at Namtsedeng Temple.[53] Near the opening to his "Constitution for the Sangha," which may have been composed around the same time,[54] Tsongkhapa stresses the importance of monastic discipline, which becomes a standard way of describing it in nearly all later constitutions, particularly Geluk ones:[55]

> As it is said in *The Entrance to the Way [of the Bodhisattva]*,
> The sole medicine for the suffering of wandering beings;

The source for all happiness;
May the Teachings abide long,
With support and honor.[56]

Here he begins by quoting from and commenting on Śāntideva's famous *Bodhicaryāvtāra*. Śāntideva's *Bodhicaryāvatāra* is a fitting scripture to invoke in a constitution that underscores the importance of monastic discipline because Śāntideva likely composed his text within the large Indian monastic complex of Nālandā in the eighth century.[57] Following his gloss on these verses, Tsongkhapa paraphrases a verse from Vasubandhu's *Abhidharmakoṣa*:[58]

> That, [the Teachings,] are twofold. As for all the Teachings of scripture, they are found with certainty in the Three Collections [i.e., the Tripiṭaka]. And, as for the Teachings of practice [T. *sgrub pa*], they are the three categories of precious Trainings. Moreover, as for the Training of Discipline, it is the support of the growth, stability, and flourishing of the other two Trainings. [The Buddha] spoke thus on more than one occasion. Therefore, here, most importantly, we begin from the Training of Discipline. So doing, one must speak about some of the rules that will serve to purify the behavior of those who reside in our monasteries.[59]

The idea that discipline is the foundation of the Buddha's dharma is not a new one. The Buddha himself is believed to have said that "when I enter Nirvana, this [the *Prātimokṣa Sūtra*[60]] will be your teacher."[61] However, Tsongkhapa and his followers in later centuries are the first ones in Tibet to take seriously and to effectively operationalize the idea. Tsongkhapa's "reform" of Tibetan Buddhism in Tibet was a prioritizing of monasteries and the monastic life.

This pairing of the line from the *Bodhicaryāvatāra* with the *Abhidharmakoṣa* and supporting commentary is found throughout later constitutions. For example, this section from Tsongkhapa's text is quoted nearly verbatim in the constitution for Gönlung Monastery, three centuries later.[62] The lines express a simple argument: the well-being and happiness of all beings depends on the Buddha's dharma. That dharma comprises two aspects: scriptures, or exegesis, and practice, or realization. Scriptures comprise the vast collection of texts that have been transmitted, translated, and studied over the centuries. Practice comprises proper comportment or discipline and the other two Trainings:

meditation and insight. Since neither meditation nor insight can be practiced or realized without a basis in discipline, discipline is most important.

This is precisely the argument, albeit in an abbreviated and modified form, that is presented in the quote at the beginning of this chapter: "The happiness of the public depends upon the Teachings of the Buddha, and the Teachings [depend upon] centers of the sangha. Those, moreover, depend upon the firm establishment of order. Even if there is a large sangha, without order, it is of no benefit other than causing great destruction to the Teachings." This quote happens to come from the constitution written by the Ninth Karmapa for members of his monastic estate, which was the only real contender for religious and political supremacy in Tibet in the sixteenth century. Other constitutions, beginning with that by Tsongkhapa's disciple (no. 6), also add logically that among scriptures the section that is most important is the one pertaining to discipline, namely the Vinaya.[63] Thus, an argument emerges that the ideal religious community is not only one that is grounded in order and discipline but also that that order and discipline are exemplified in the canonical Vinaya. As I will discuss below, the Fifth Dalai Lama especially exploits this idea.

If an emphasis on monastic discipline is the first distinguishing characteristic of Tsongkhapa's "Constitution for the Sangha," the second is how it attempts to comprehensively address every aspect of monastic life. His is the first constitution to codify punishments (confession before the assembly or expulsion) for infractions, to specify the responsibilities and powers of the disciplinarian (to grant leaves, to oversee conduct during assembly, etc.), to insist that one must be present at assembly in order to partake of food and offerings that are collected, to specify a liturgy to be recited at assembly, to specify that communal wealth be spent to care for a sick individual who cannot afford it, and to outline a general scholastic and practice calendar. All of these aspects became standard for many later constitutions.

The instructions regarding the sick speak to a process of institutionalization. Although the Rongzom constitution anticipates a sick member of the community, it does so by asking that each should individually vow to provide for the sick.[64] However, Tsongkhapa's constitution, which is copied nearly verbatim on this point in a constitution for the Gönlung Monastery in 1737,[65] adds a small layer of bureaucracy:

If a sick person appears, then the disciplinarian who oversees the region whence he came inspects, and, if there are provisions for an obstacle-clearing rite that is good.[66] If there are no provisions, then, if there are common resources [T. *spyi rdzas*], he [the disciplinarian] gives from those. If there are not, as it is said, then actions are to be undertaken beginning with prayers to the statues of the Buddha. If the sick person heals, then, if he has wealth, because he has enjoyed the wealth of the Precious Jewels, he should repay. Whether or not he is one who has [provisions or wealth], the sangha of that place must gather and apply themselves at reciting as many obstacle-clearing rites as are needed.[67]

Here we have an early reference to a common wealth, which is overseen by an officer.

Tsongkhapa's "Constitution for the Sangha" is the most important extant constitution in terms of its lasting impact on other constitutions. His constitution is quoted and is cited as the basis of later constitutions (such as the Fifth Dalai Lama's constitution for a certain Ganden Tupten Rabgyé Monastery, no. 42).[68] Tsongkhapa's constitution also addresses many features of a larger institution despite the fact that Tsongkhapa still has in mind more intimate monastic settings where meditation is given just as much attention as scholastic endeavors (winter and summer are for meditation, spring and fall are for scholastics[69]). This is not to say that Tsongkhapa himself created these ideas from whole cloth or that there were not earlier constitutions (yet to be uncovered) that contain some of these features. His own constitution refers to a profusion of "different kinds and numbers of rules for the sangha due to the exigencies of time and place," a profusion that resulted in uncertainty and necessitated the creation of his own constitution.[70] In addition, Tsongkhapa regularly directs the reader to the Vinaya itself as a source of information, and it is clear that the subject matter of the Vinaya—who can renounce and ordain, guidelines for proper attire and accoutrements for doing so, how to care for the sick,[71] and so on—also informs much of the general subject matter of his and other constitutions. Nonetheless, Tsongkhapa's "Constitution for the Sangha" and his constitution for the Lhazhöl Hermitage anticipate a need to *order* the administration of and life within monastic communities.

## The Karmapa's Great Encampment

Three and a half centuries of Geluk dominance might lead one to forget just how powerful the Karmapas and their school were and how close they were to monopolizing the political and religious landscape of Tibet. The domain of the Karma Kagyü school stretched from its center of power in Central Tibet to Kongpo in southeastern Tibet, Kham, and even the Jangsatam Kingdom in Yunnan. The power of the Karma Kagyü was centered on the figure of the Karmapa, or Gyelwang Karmapa,[72] the longest surviving incarnate lama lineage in Tibet. During this pivotal period of the fifteenth and sixteenth centuries, his power was manifest in his Great Encampment, *garchen* in Tibetan.[73] The *garchen*'s influence included even outposts in Ngari of far western Tibet,[74] and it maintained a significant presence at the major pilgrimage site of Tsari, or Crystal Mountain, along the border with Arunachal Pradesh.[75] By the end of the fifteenth century, the Karma Kagyü school had secured the patronage of the powerful Rinpung governor based at Zhigatsé, a role later appropriated by that governor's insubordinate counselor, the self-styled "king of Tsang." The successive "kings of Tsang" came to represent the nationalistic and conservative forces of Tibet,[76] which were defeated only in 1642 when the Geluk school called upon the Oirat, or "Western Mongols," to come to their aid in Tibet.

This period—the fifteenth and sixteenth centuries—was a cauldron of institution-building and internecine violence centering on the remnants of the Pakmodru Dynasty in Ü (eastern Central Tibet) and its insubordinate vassals, the Rinpung family in Tsang (western Central Tibet). In the first half of the fifteenth century, those clans still loyal to the Pakmodru Dynasty helped to establish a host of monasteries in the Lhasa region that were associated with the nascent Geluk school. In response, the Rinpungpa and the Karma Kagyü school, particularly that school's incarnate lama known as the Zhamarpa,[77] led a series of attacks on the Lhasa region, ultimately taking control of Lhasa in 1498.[78] Such fighting over control of this symbolically important area[79] continued into the next century and the first half of the seventeenth century.

The center of the Karma Kagyü power during this period was a mobile one, and its size and complexity both preceded and rivaled those of later Geluk monasteries. In fact, nearly every consideration that later Geluk authors would put into their constitutions can be found in one or another of the extant constitutions of the Eighth and Ninth Karmapas. The formation of the Karmapa's *garchen* effectively started in the aftermath of the Fourth Karmapa's visit to the Mongol Yuan court in 1356, when more and more lay and monastic followers began to congregate around him.[80] The size of the *garchen* is said to have grown under his successor, the Fifth Karmapa (1384–1415, who himself visited the Ming Dynasty's Yongle emperor), to the point that it was necessary for him to issue a constitution.[81] This is likely the "Great Legal Document" to which later Karmapa constitutions refer.[82]

The *garchen* is understood to have continually grown under the successive Karmapas until its destruction at the hands of the Gelukpa's new supporters, the Oirat, in 1642. The scholar Thupten Püntsok relates an old oral tradition that, during the time of the Sixth Karmapa (1416–1453), the size of the encampment was so great that every day, before breakfast, all 108 volumes of the *Kanjur* (the collection of scriptures attributed to the Buddha himself) would be recited by distributing a few pages to each of the residents of the encampment who would then recite his part.[83] The continuing growth and other transformations compelled the Seventh Karmapa (1454–1506) to issue another constitution or a supplement to the Great Legal Document.[84]

Although it is hard to reconstruct the contents and concerns of these early constitutions, which are either lost or unavailable, we are told that the Seventh Karmapa tamed the many "loud-speaking and unruly barbarian-sophists" that had increased in number and characterized a "decline" in the Kagyü teachings.[85] This is likely a polemical reference to the growing power of the Geluk school, which prioritized scholastic training over meditation in its institutions and which promoted debate as the best method for undertaking such scholastic training.[86] In his own supplemental constitution to the *garchen* (no. 9), the Eighth Karmapa warns against the prattle and vanity of his religious opponents:

> There is no time for the so-called "*Rapjam* debate circuits"[87] and titles and behaviors of the "Virtuous Friends" [T. *dge ba'i gshes gnyen*; i.e., *geshés*] [that take place during] the book retreats [i.e., when teachings and classes are not in session].[88] The conditions for [maintaining] that entail a depraved lifestyle. Embarking on such a thing, one acquires absolutely none of the positive qualities of listening, thinking, and meditation but rather, like a dog drinking blood, acquires desires. One attaches himself at the head of one monastic assembly and then another, and so doing brings no benefit and is an act of great danger. All of this should be put to rest! . . . One should speak and ask questions in the language of the dharma that expresses a wish for increasing wisdom and so forth; other than that, one must not engage in hurtful dharma

language that deprecates others such as condescension and the refutation of questions. Even if one is victorious in debate, one must not strike one's hands [together] or one's legs [on the ground] and point out the flaws of the other's lama, monastery, answer, and so on, nor should one in such an untimely manner boast about one's own lama, monastery, and so forth.[89]

This criticism of debate is clearly a reflection of the warfare and competition between the Tsang/Kagyü and Ü/Geluk factions at that time. We see the same sort of rhetoric reflected in the late-fifteenth-century retelling of the life of the Tibetan Saint Milarepa: whereas earlier stories blame a Bön (Tibet's "indigenous religion") priest for poisoning the saint, the later version by Kagyü "holy madman" Tsangnyön Heruka transforms the culprit into a scholar-monk *geshé*.[90] The Karma Kagyü constitutions reveal a sectarian identity that alerts us to the origin of Tibetan Buddhist sects, or schools, as we understand them today. The Seventh Karmapa is said to have specified in his constitution the proper and distinctive attire and hats of Kagyü monasteries,[91] something his successors as well as the Gelukpa will give considerable attention to. The Karma Kagyü sectarian identity is further underscored by numerous references to the founder of the school, the First Karmapa (1110–1193), who is placed within the *longue durée* of the history of Buddhism in Tibet.[92] The Ninth Karmapa even limits entrance at one of his monasteries to "those acquainted in general with the lineage of the Kagyüpas and with, in particular, the lineage of the Karmapas."[93]

Explicit promotion of a sectarian identity is just one of the features of the Karma Kagyü constitutions that anticipate the later Geluk ones. The Karmapa's *garchen* is clearly a complex institution necessitated by its great size and equally great ambitions. According to Tupten Püntsok, there were a thousand individuals at the *garchen* who received salaries during the time of the Eighth Karmapa (1507–1554)[94] and, on the eve of the *garchen*'s demise, there were two thousand monks prepared for battle.[95] What we know about the organization of the *garchen* comes from biographical sources[96] and the extant constitutions of the Eighth and Ninth Karmapas (nos. 8–10 and no. 17, respectively). What we see is a complex institution with many moving parts overseen by an extensive hierarchy of officers. Certain prelates of the encampment[97] were expected to alternate serving as "discipline master,"[98] overseeing some thirty "law officers."[99] The constitutions give great consideration to the ceremonial pageantry of the encampment as it is on the move,[100] monastic discipline, the liturgy to be followed, and the proper maintenance of relations with the patrons and laity that are encountered as this monolith moved about and descended upon populations.

Moreover, if one considers the other constitutions that the Ninth Karmapa composed for other Karma Kagyü monasteries (nos. 13–16 and 18–23), one even finds extensive discussion of the importance of scholasticism and debate (especially nos. 19 and 22), and, significantly, suggestions that the Karmapa was successfully developing a *network* of monasteries. The Ninth Karmapa composed eleven constitutions, which is more than any other figure prior to the Fifth Dalai Lama. It is difficult to identify the location of the monasteries for which he composed these constitutions, but it is clear that they were located across various regions of Tibet, from Ngari (no. 20) in the West to Dakpo (no. 23) and Tsari (no. 13) in the East and Southeast. In addition, although the Karmapa clearly saw himself as the most important figure for this growing network of monasteries, he nonetheless envisioned a system in which other monasteries and their representatives might cooperate for the sake of the Karma Kagyü Teachings. For instance, in his constitution for a monastery in Dakpo (no. 23), he describes the process for appointing the abbot: "As for the lama, the one who is able to bring benefit to the Teachings and wandering beings, without a doubt I myself scrutinize and make the appointment. However, if the encampment is far away, then the principal sites of responsibility for the Karma Teachings in Ü, Tsang, Dak[po], Kong[po], and so forth consult together and, in accordance with the inclination of all, make the appointment."[101] So, the Karmapa himself would make abbatial appointments at monasteries in far off places,[102] but he is also intent on building a monastic *system* that had some consistency and predictability to it.

The Karmapa's Great Encampment is deserving of a study of its own, and here I have only alluded to some of the institutional features of the encampment and the other monasteries related to it through the Karmapa. I will revisit certain aspects of the Karmapa's encampment and his constitutions in later chapters to compare his organizing efforts with those of later Geluk authors of constitutions. Here, however, I want to ask what prevented the Karmapa from succeeding like the Gelukpa eventually would given the Karmapa's early, earnest concern for institution-building.

An important part of the answer to this question is clearly patronage. That is, the Geluk school secured patronage from the most powerful Inner Asian power in the seventeenth century, the Oirats. Still, the Karmapas and their primary Tibetan patrons also had important Mongol supporters and, over the course of several centuries, had made significant inroads in those areas where the Gelukpa began to expand in the seventeenth century.[103] Other limiting factors may be able to help explain why the Karmapas did not succeed. The first limiting factor is reflected in the very word *Karmapa* and its ambiguity. It can refer both to the incarnate lama and to the followers of the Karma Kagyü teachings. No such ambiguity exists with the term "Gelukpa", a neologism that refers to the followers of "the tradition of virtue." The name of the school may seem incidental, but in fact it directs our attention to a major difference between the Karma Kagyü school and the Geluk school.[104]

The power of the Karmapa (i.e., the incarnate lama) is paramount in the monasteries aligned with him. In the Eighth Karmapa's constitutions for his encampment and other monasteries, he regularly reminds his audience that "unless permission has been given, servants, caretakers, the abbot, the master, and so on, in carrying out tasks however great or small, are not to transgress *my words*," and so on.[105] One rule in the constitution for the *garchen* expressly prohibits anyone from explicitly slandering the "father and sons,"[106] a reference to the Gyelwang Karmapa himself and to the other important Karma Kagyü incarnate lamas. Moreover, he reminds the audience of the constitutions that he wrote for other Karma Kagyü monasteries in which he states that there is a hierarchy at the pinnacle of which he sits: "In short, since my representative in body and speech is that master [T. *slob dpon*] of those residing at the monastic seat, then the cantor and disciplinarian or those together with the assembly of monks first and foremost must take as truth whatever the master says and must properly observe whatever he does."[107] These specifications regarding hierarchy and respect for authority are not that unusual. What is unusual are the Karmapa's numerous references to himself and his personal importance in the administration of these monasteries. To be sure, Geluk monasteries are often founded by a lama who then maintains a privileged position within the monastery, sometimes being referred to as the "lord" or "protector of the monastery" (T. *dgon bdag*). This was the case with the Gyelsé lama from Central Tibet who founded the Gönlung Monastery in Amdo, at least until the mid-eighteenth century when another, homegrown lama took on that status at Gönlung. But Geluk constitutions seldom make reference to such a founding figure. Geluk constitutions pay attention instead to the *administratives* position of abbot (T. *bla ma*; T. *khri pa*) and master (T. *slob dpon*).

The Karmapa himself clearly could not have involved himself in the daily administration of all the Karma Kagyü monasteries scattered across Tibet. However, the fact that he actually chooses the heads of these monasteries suggests a particular kind of relationship between this supreme lama and the monasteries belonging to his order. Moreover, the Karmapa's writing himself ("my commands") into his constitutions is something one seldom encounters in constitutions written by Geluk prelates, who receded into the background of an administrative structure. The Karmapa's system might better be called patrimonial rather than bureaucratic like later Geluk monasteries.

A second, related limiting factor to the Karmapa's monastic system is that its center was mobile. Being mobile no doubt conveyed certain advantages, especially in terms of acquiring and maintaining patrons. However, a mobile band of a thousand or two thousand practitioners must have been hard to handle, especially for the settled or nomadic populations that the encampment encountered along the way—which probably explains why so much of the Ninth Karmapa's constitution for his *garchen* (no. 17) is concerned with how alms are to be collected, how guests or patrons who visit the monastery are to be treated, and so on. More importantly, being mobile, his power followed him. His exercise of power is precisely the opposite of the idealized Chinese sage king, who merely faces south, whereupon the world revolves around him,[108] and, more relevant to Tibet, the Karmapa's exercise of power is more like that of the itinerant Second and Third Dalai Lamas than the Fifth Dalai Lama. The Fifth Dalai Lama, of course, would settle in the Potala Palace at the top of the Red Hill in Lhasa, and from there his power and the power of the Geluk school would course through the settled monasteries of Tibet.[109]

## The Fifth Dalai Lama's Constitutions

The intensive organizing efforts that began in the sixteenth century with the work of the Ninth Karmapa and his constitutions continued and grew in the subsequent century. There are approximately thirty-two extant constitutions dating from the seventeenth century, eighteen of which were composed by the Fifth Dalai Lama, making the Great Fifth the second most prolific author of constitutions prior to the twentieth century. (He is surpassed only by the Second Jamyang Zhepa in the following century, another institution-builder who helped to extend Geluk influence throughout Amdo and Mongolia.) These constitutions played an important role in the growth of the Geluk school—both in the scaling up of its institutions and in its geographic expansion into new areas, such as Kham and Amdo. They sometimes accompanied or followed the Dalai Lama's direct intervention in the affairs of monasteries in Central Tibet or Kham (such as appointing an abbot), although, importantly, they also provided extensive instructions on how the monasteries were to operate autonomously. In particular, the Dalai Lama's detailed instructions regarding liturgy and scholasticism set his constitutions apart from all earlier constitutions.

Nearly all of the Fifth Dalai Lama's constitutions show a level of concern with scholasticism—memorization, recitation, teaching, debate, and exams of scriptures and commentarial literature[110]—that is unprecedented in monastic constitutions. The frequency with which he discussed it and the detail of his curricula set an expectation that later constitutions, Geluk and non-Geluk alike, would follow. Furthermore, he presents scholasticism as essential to true Buddhism. Whereas Vinaya is "foundational" to Buddhism, the wisdom as conveyed through its scriptures is considered the "heart" of Buddhism,[111] and such wisdom begins with intensive memorization and extensive study of the Buddha's own words and the canonical commentaries on those scriptures.[112]

To be sure, earlier constitutions do sometimes discuss scholasticism. Usually it is in very general terms, such as when the Gelukpa Özer Gyatso describes the importance of teaching and studying the Tripiṭaka for the perpetuation of Buddhism: "Teachers must teach the five scriptures. Students must memorize, practice, debate, and so on."[113] The Ninth Karmapa, too, referred to these five scriptural areas as important and deserving study.[114]

There is one example of an earlier constitution that outlines an even more detailed curriculum, that by the Sakya[115] scholar-monk Shākya Chokden[116] (1428–1507) for his monastery of Serdokchen (constitution no. 7).[117] In it he insists that monks at his monastery not study the "baseless things transmitted to others and apart from the famed Sa[kya Paṇḍita][118] and Ngok [Lekshé Sherap]."[119] He specifies exactly which scriptures are to be studied: those attributed to Maitreya, those of the three masters credited with introducing Svatantrika Madhyamaka, Dharmakirti's *Pramāṇaviniścaya*,[120] and Tibetan commentaries and treatises on logic and epistemology by Sakya Paṇḍita and Ngok Lekpé Sherap, such as the former's *Treasury of Valid Cog-*

*nition.*[121] Apart from his clear and explicit parochial program, Shākya Chokden also insists on memorization and the practice of logical debate.

Shākya Chokden's constitution is perhaps the only example of a constitution prior to the time of the Fifth Dalai Lama that contains such a detailed curriculum. It is not incidental that the monastery in question, which was initially founded as a "scriptural seminary" by his teacher, is said to have housed several hundred monks.[122] We see that size and organization necessitate each other. In addition, Shākya Chokden saw the period in which he was writing, teaching, and building institutions as a time when "the later doctrines [of Tsongkhapa and his disciples] spread like fire among the fools and learned ones in the Land of Snows."[123] So, even this early example cannot be understood apart from the influence of the Gelukpa or the "New Kadampa."

As for the Dalai Lama's own constitutions, in addition to the steps he and his prime minister took to shore up his political and religious power, such as embedding himself in the cult of Tibet's patron saint, he also worked in his constitutions to associate himself with the paragons of scholasticism in Tibet. Four of his first seven constitutions show a proclivity for sites associated with the Indian scholar-monk Atiśa (nos. 33 and 36), Tsongkhapa (no. 37), and the past Tibetan ruler, Tai Situ Jangchup Gyeltsen (1302–1364; nos. 37 and 39) who is credited with initiating the practice of debate exams during the time of the new year celebrations. That one of his first constitutions was for Reting Monastery (no. 33) may be significant. This was the monastery that, according to a biography of Atiśa, "was a small satellite of [the major scholastic monastery in India,] Vikramaśīla. It was the Residence of the Lord [Atiśa], the spiritual construction of [his disciple] Géshé Tönpa, the chief ancestor protecting the precious Kadampa teaching, and the Lord's primary *caitya* [temple] in all the realm of snow, from West Tibet to the Center."[124] The Dalai Lama refers to Reting in his constitution as the "headwaters of the Teachings" and, more specifically, as the "headwaters of the Kadam [school]."[125]

Although he only makes passing reference to scholasticism in his Reting constitution, the Dalai Lama is concerned about what the declining conditions at the monastery might mean for the Geluk school. He gives most of his attention to the upkeep of the monastery's infrastructure and the purity and cleanliness of its grounds. The spiritual agents who reside at and protect the monastery are said to do so only as long as the Perennial Spring that flows from underneath the sacred image of the Buddha does not dry up. Their protection of the monastery is said to be intimately linked to the flow of this spring "like a shadow and one's body."[126] Tragically, "due to the [passage of] time and carelessness, there is no cleanliness, and thus, aside from the Perennial Spring, the other springs have dried up, and all the [symbolically important] junipers around the monastery have withered, too."[127] There is a real concern here that the next spring to go would be that linked to the very existence of the monastery's spiritual protectors, which would be quite inauspicious for the "Headwaters of the Kadam School" and its successor, the Geluk school. The constitution itself was meant to "clarify" profusion of earlier constitutions that were no longer heeded and to "renew" proper religious practices that had lapsed.[128]

In the first constitution that he wrote for the Great Prayer Festival—the major, annual ceremony founded by Tsongkhapa that was staged in Lhasa and coincided with the new year (no. 37)—the Dalai Lama argues that the scholastic debate competitions and awarding of scholastic titles (T. *rab 'byams grwa skor*) that were prevalent at that time actually began at Tsetang Monastery under the auspices of the Pakmodru ruler, Jangchup Gyeltsen.[129] He further describes how Tsongkhapa later established the custom of doing these debate competitions at the ceremonies for the New Year in Lhasa.[130] The Dalai Lama, as claimant to these traditions, wrote this "reminder text" to reassert discipline during the ceremony and to specify in great detail the procedures for the debates. Over several pages, he details exactly which sections of which texts are to be debated and for how many days they are to be debated. He even graciously makes accommodations for those of other schools who focus on other scriptures.

The final constitution that the Fifth Dalai Lama wrote for a monastery and his magnum opus is the constitution he wrote for Drepung (no. 51). It's one of the longest and most detailed constitutions ever written. His curriculum begins,

> First, having studied the Chain of Consequences [debate textbooks] of Madhyamaka and Perfection of Wisdom, it is permissible to apply one's mind to [these] classes as is fitting: the General Meaning [monastic manuals][131] and commentaries and sub-commentaries on the Perfection of Wisdom; the commentary on the *Mūlamadhyamakakārikā*; Vinaya and [*Abhidharma*]*koṣa*. However, because this monastery is of the class of Madhyamaka

and Perfection of Wisdom [monasteries], emphasize [Madhya-
maka and Perfection of Wisdom] together with the Special Topics
[classes on the same].[132]

Having specified these scripture-cum-classes (with the actual texts to be used
merely implied),[133] the Dalai Lama goes on to specify how debates are to be
carried out—who can participate, how degrees are to be awarded, and so on—
and rules regarding recitation lessons and attendance at such lessons.

The quote above that provides the curriculum at Drepung also alerts us
to the fact that the Dalai Lama was intent on constructing a monastery that
was *specialized*—that is, one where its residents are to be fully focused on
philosophy (T. *mtshad nyid*) and not ritual (T. *cho ga*; *bskang gso*; etc.).[134] This
is quite a departure from the ideal schedule devised by Tsongkhapa whereby
one would spend his fall and spring studying scriptures but his winter and
summer meditating. Meanwhile, other monasteries were specially assigned
to perform Accomplishment Offering rituals (T. *sgrub mchod*) for the principal Geluk patron deities. Good examples of this include Chökhorgyel (constitution no. 34 and, especially, no. 40), Zhalu[135] (constitution no. 45), and
Gaden Thupten Rapgyé Monastery,[136] the latter referred to as a "monastery
of *mantrins* following the tantras" (constitution no. 42).

The case of Chökhorgyel is interesting. This monastery was founded by
the Second Dalai Lama in 1509, and he identified the important deities Pelden
Lhamo ("Glorious Goddess") and Bektse ("Armored One") as the monastery's protectors. Chökhorgyel grew in importance as a place for the study
of tantra, including the Ritual Cake Offering (T. *gtor ma*) ritual for Lhamo;
for restoration rituals (T. *bskang gso*) for these protector deities; and for ritual dancing (T. *'chams*). The monastery's two principal protector deities were
also the personal protectors of the Dalai Lamas from as early as the time of
the Third Dalai Lama.[137]

The first constitution that the Fifth Dalai Lama wrote for Chökhorgyel
(no. 34) was completed in 1645. Near the end of that constitution he provides
a brief liturgy that residents at the monastery are expected to memorize:

Whether one is a "register monk" or a "faith monk,"[138] from the
moment one initially resides at the monastery to within six
months he is to be given an exam on the assembly recitations of
the breviary[139] from the Taking of Refuge onward. Then, based on

what is suitable [to his level], one is sequentially tested on the
mandala visualizations, the restoration rituals, and so forth for the
three: Guhyasamāja, Saṃvara, and Bhairava.

The assembly recitations are: Going for Refuge, Giving Rise to
the Mind of Enlightenment, the Confession of Downfalls,
Prostrations to the [Six]teen Arhats, and the two major scriptures.[140] Having gone to the first tea [in the morning], the
Glorious Three Realms,[141] the Two Paths,[142] Supplications to the
Lineage of Abbots, and so on. Also, apply oneself to the obstacle-
clearing rites,[143] the *Heart Sutra* and its apotropaic rite, *dhāraṇī* for
the [Buddha of Infinite] Life, and so forth for patrons.[144]

Then, just six years later, the Dalai Lama composed an update, a "correc-
tion," to his constitution (no. 40). This second Chökhorgyel constitution is
about twice as long as the first, and one of the sections that grew was that
pertaining to the monastery's liturgy. In fact, the updated liturgical section
is almost as long as the entire earlier constitution, running two and a half
pages in modern book print. It includes an extended list of protector deities
to be worshipped and whose rituals are to be memorized. It discusses in detail the separate ritual classes (T. *chog gra*), each made up of at least fifteen
monks, that are dedicated to the various deities. It discusses the revival of
an Accomplishment Offering ritual to the buddha Kālacakra based on the
manual by the renowned scholar-monk Butön (1290–1364), who was closely
associated with Zhalu Monastery in Tsang and whose tantric manuals come
to inform the ritual program of many Geluk monasteries.

The added attention given to Chökhorgyel's liturgy is no accident. In
1647, two years after finishing the first constitution for the monastery, the
Dalai Lama composed a ritual manual for invoking the protectors of the
monastery,[145] which he did on the occasion of consecrating several images of
deities that had been commissioned by the Third Dalai Lama. His second
Chökhorgyel constitution, then, was meant to direct the monks there to follow his ritual program:

"Maintain the detailed schedule of [ritual] texts to be memorized: the
ancient restoration ritual [manuals] from before for Three-Headed
Mahākāla,[146] Vaiśravaṇa, and the Makzorma Glorious Goddess,[147] together
with the newly compiled [manuals] for restoration rituals, ritual cake offerings, praises, and exhortations for Panjara Mahākāla and Four-Faced

Mahākāla and their two messengers, Putra[148] and Bektse."[149] He then proceeds to explain the various chapels and "groves" where each of these deities is to be worshipped and when that is to be done.

The saying that monastic life was "half worship, half study"[150] may be a result of the institution-building of the Dalai Lama. In his writing he was sure to give as much attention to the proper propitiation of the gods as he did to scholasticism. His "revival" of lapsed rituals and his new compositions on the same have been well documented by scholars such as Amy Heller and Chris Bell,[151] so it is not surprising that in his constitutions he directs monks and monastic administrators to adhere to these ritual protocols. What is innovative is his use of this medium—constitutions—to help design institutions to uphold and maintain these ritual traditions, ensuring that the ritual machinery runs without his immediate presence.

I am reminded of what a scholar-monk once told me when I asked him why much of the ritual program at a certain monastery in Inner Mongolia[152] was derived in part from Zhalu Monastery in Tsang, whereas his own monastery[153] in Amdo derived its program principally from Gyümé Monastery in Lhasa. He responded, "One monastery can't cover all the gods. So, our wise predecessors divided them up among the monasteries."[154] Of course, this is merely an anecdote, but the point is that Gelukpa today continue to look for *planning* and *organizing* in their monastic routines. Furthermore, this planning and organizing would extend across the Tibetan Plateau. For instance, the Dalai Lama issued edicts and constitutions to Nyingma and Sakya monasteries in Kham to ensure that they would "perform without impairment the special rites of the important protective rituals" of the Geluk school.[155] He instructed that the monastery in 'Ba', in particular, was to base its breviary for assembly on the main assembly hall of Drepung Monastery in Lhasa.[156]

The Dalai Lama's motivations for writing as many constitutions as he did and for instilling them with detailed programs of worship and study are clear. He possessed a strong faith in the protective (and destructive) powers of the gods,[157] which called for timely and proper worship. Beyond that, however, the Dalai Lama extolled and gave form to a religious ethic for his school, an ethic founded upon the Jewel or Refuge that is the sangha and an ethic that emphatically prioritizes philosophical orthodoxy before spiritual experiences. Commenting on the "two divisions" of Buddhism that Vasubandhu specified in his *Abhidharmakośa*—scripture and realization—the Dalai Lama writes, "First, having become established in properly listening to and thinking about the precious dharma of the scriptures, then, in reliance upon that, the accumulation of the qualities of realization emerges in one's mind-continuum."[158] For the Dalai Lama, scholasticism thus plays an essential and indispensable role in fostering enlightened beings.

There is an additional explanation of the Dalai Lama's motivations for composing all these constitutions: sectarianism. A conceit of pluralism runs through his constitutions. His constitution for the Great Prayer Festival makes accommodations for scholars from other schools, and his constitution for the medical college in Tsang (no. 46) presents medicine as "a type of non-sectarian or impartial knowledge" suitable for "healing the trauma of the recent Mongol-Tsang war."[159] He accuses the monasteries of *other* schools of being tainted by sectarianism,[160] while his monasteries are "impartial" and are otherwise "stainless" and "peerless."[161] The reality, however, is that his constitutions and the Geluk constitutions that follow are one of the primary vectors for the growth and dominance of an exclusively Geluk monasticism. His constitution for the Third Dalai Lama's outpost in Kham (no. 48) explains that it is written for a monastery that is once again flourishing thanks to the armies of the pro-Geluk leader of the Khoshud Mongols, Güüshi Khan, who "united and subjugated [the people] of all the Six Ranges of Dokam." In his constitution for Kumbum Monastery in Amdo (no. 41), a monastery he passed en route from Beijing to Lhasa, he harkens back to the Geluk founder Tsongkhapa by referencing the latter's general constitution for the sangha (no. 4). He also draws connections to the dharma kings of imperial Tibet whose influence is said to have reached the area around Kumbum. The Dalai Lama's forced conversion of the Nyingma Monastery of Ngesang Dorjé Ling[162] in Tsang is documented in his constitution for the monastery (no. 43): "The fabricated and corrupted false Treasures [of Nang, Sok, and Gong[163]] here are rejected; and so as to avoid opposing the Geluk Teachings and government, the Protector of the Earth, Treasurer Sönam Rapten,[164] commanded and Tratsangpa the Great Scholar-Adept Lodrö Chökyi Dorjé[165] was appointed abbot."[166] Such explicit sectarianism would become typical of later Geluk constitutions, in which Tsongkhapa is regularly referred to as the "Second Victor" (i.e., Buddha) and in which non-Geluk monks are barred from enrolling at Geluk monasteries.[167]

The Dalai Lama's approach to his school's success differed somewhat from that of the Karmapas: he removed himself from the process of administering the school's monasteries. To be sure, he did appoint abbots by decree to several monasteries throughout Central Tibet and Kham.[168] However, his intent was to devise a common monastic program of discipline, study, and worship that others would actually implement. Moreover, this monastic program and the ideology of the Geluk school did not depend on the Dalai Lama for their success. Other Geluk lamas could and would come along to do the same thing for monasteries across the Tibetan Plateau and Mongolia. Like franchisees, they would draw on the monastic constitutions of their forebears and their headquarters in more centrally located monasteries to draw up constitutions for places farther away.

## Geluk Expansion into Amdo and Beyond

Part of what makes bureaucracy so efficient and resilient is that it is not tied to any one individual. Alternatively, what makes bureaucracy so alluring is the *conceit* of fair, impersonal norms that guide it.[169] It is a *system* of rules and norms that is meant to avoid precisely the sort of unpredictability and transitory nature of strictly patrimonial forms of governance. In addition, being a system of rules and norms, which are encoded in writing, it is easily replicable. Through its intensive and innovative use of monastic constitutions, the Geluk school came to exercise dominion over Buddhist life in Amdo and Mongolia, far from its original center of power in Lhasa.

Shortly after the death of the Fifth Dalai Lama, we begin to see a proliferation of constitutions written by other Geluk hierarchs. Significantly, many of these were written for monasteries on the periphery and especially in Amdo. In the following chapters, we will be preoccupied with this geographic expansion of the Geluk system of monasteries. One monastery will be featured prominently, that of Gönlung Jampa Ling, "The Realm of Maitreya in the Valley of the Monastery."[170] Although Gönlung was founded outside of Central Tibet, in many ways it is an exemplary Geluk monastery the study of which can illustrate how the Geluk school was so successful. It was large and illustrious, and it spawned numerous "child monasteries," some of which grew to rival the reputation of their erstwhile "mother." Gönlung was intimately connected with both the most important Tibetan patrons of the Geluk school, the Kyishö family, and the primary Mongol patrons of the Geluk school, the Oirat.[171] And, significantly, it boasted a complex system of monastic organization, which attracted monks from elsewhere and, later, exported hierarchs from the monastery to monasteries elsewhere in Amdo and in Mongolia.

Gönlung was also similar to some of the other major Geluk monasteries founded in Amdo, such as Kumbum and Labrang, in being closely associated with Mongols. In fact, Gönlung was founded in the most northeastern corner of Amdo, a region known in Tibetan as Pari,[172] abutting the Mongol region of Alashaa. Much of Pari is today inhabited by a sedentary, Mongolic-speaking people known as "Monguor,"[173] a people thoroughly studied by the Belgian missionary-scholar Louis Schram in the early twentieth century. Gönlung has been overwhelmingly populated by local Monguors, a fact that sets Gönlung apart from most other Geluk monasteries on the Tibetan Plateau. Their geographic location, their native fluency in a Mongolic language, and their status as a minority people who, like other minority peoples on the Tibetan Plateau, were multilingual,[174] contributed to their positioning as representatives of the Geluk school in Inner Mongolia as well as at the Manchu Qing court.

Gönlung Monastery was founded in 1604 by an important Central Tibetan hierarch known as Ön Gyelsé Dönyö Chökyi Gyatso (d. ca. 1637) who was dispatched to Pari in Amdo to conduct the matter on behalf of the Fourth Dalai Lama. Ön Gyelsé's rebirth, Ön Gyelsé Lozang Tendzin (ca. 1638–1696) also visited the monastery in 1665, but it was Lozang Tendzin's rebirth, Ön Gyelsé Jikmé Yeshé Drakpa (1696–1743/1750),[175] who composed the constitution for Gönlung that came to be known as "the Great Constitution" of the monastery. This was one of three constitutions composed by Jikmé Yeshé Drakpa, all of which are contained in his *Collected Works*.[176] Aside from the Gönlung constitution, these were written for Narthang Monastery in Tsang (constitution no. 62) and Reting Monastery in Ü (constitution no. 64), both monasteries closely associated with the Kadam school from which the Geluk school claims descent. When he composed these, Ön Gyelsé was at the height of his power and influence. From 1728 to 1735, he served in the stead of the Seventh Dalai Lama, who was in exile, in presiding over the Great Prayer Festival in Lhasa.[177]

Jikmé Yeshé Drakpa's constitution for Gönlung, titled "The Constitution of the Mother Monastery, Gönlung, and Its Branches: The Sun That Brings Forth the Lotus Blooms of Benefit and Happiness," was composed in 1737 and stands at a turning point in the evolution of the Geluk school and its use of the monastic constitution. Gönlung Monastery had been destroyed by Qing imperial troops in 1724 for its involvement in the major revolt of Oirat Mongols living in Kökenuur, led by Lubsang-Danjin. For five years, it lay in ruins and its erstwhile population of over two thousand monks was scattered throughout the region. Then, with Qing imperial permission, the monastery was rebuilt in 1729 and a new "proper" name was bestowed on it by the Qing emperor: Youning si 佑寧寺, "the Monastery that Protects the Peace." Jikmé Yeshé Drakpa's constitution itself shows very little acknowledgment of this major sociopolitical shift in the governance of Amdo and Tibet. He continues referring to "Oirat" as well as to "Chinese" judges for capital crimes,[178] and, moreover, the constitution is similar to his other two constitutions for monasteries in Central Tibet in focusing on the codification of the optimal techniques for organizing monastic life. His Reting constitution was even more detailed than the earlier Reting constitution composed by the Dalai Lama, and both it and his Gönlung constitution advocated for ever greater bureaucratization.[179]

Jikmé Yeshé Drakpa's Great Constitution for Gönlung also sits at a historical turning point after which one sees less influence from the Ön Gyelsé lineage and other Central Tibetan hierarchs in the affairs of Amdo and more influence exerted by homegrown lamas such as Gönlung's Changkya Rinpoché and Labrang Monastery's Jamyang Zhepa.[180] Gönlung hosted numerous renowned and influential, local incarnate lamas. Among them, the best known are what I think of as the "three thirds," that is the Third Changkya, the Third Tuken, and the Third Sumba, who flourished in the latter half of the eighteenth century.[181] Changkya, Tuken, and Sumba are three of the so-called five great lamas at Gönlung.[182] The other two are Chuzang[183] and Wang.[184] The Second and Third Chuzang lamas[185] maintained a master-disciple relationship with the Seventh and Eighth Dalai Lamas.[186] The Wang lama is the least known of the bunch, although this lineage was quite influential both at Gönlung and beyond, promoting Geluk forms of monasticism in Inner Mongolia. In addition to these five "great lamas," there are "nine minor lamas" at Gönlung.[187] Incarnations within these lineages often served in leadership positions at Gönlung and elsewhere in Pari.[188]

Between Gönlung's lamas and the monastery itself there is an extensive network of forty-two to forty-nine "child" or "branch" monasteries.[189] Most of these are in Pari itself, which explains the later Chinese epithet for Gönlung, "mother of all the monasteries north of the Huang River."[190] However, Gönlung also had branches much farther away. As early as the eighteenth century, the monastery was being referred to as "the very origin of the flourishing of seminaries for the study of Geluk philosophy here in the land of Amdo"[191] and (in the early nineteenth century) as "the ancestress of all the commentarial schools in Domé [i.e., Amdo]."[192] Gönlung even established branches as far away as Xinjiang and Eastern Mongolia.

Thus, Gönlung is important for a couple of reasons. First, it is arguably the most important Geluk outpost in Amdo in the seventeenth and early eighteenth centuries.[193] A source from the 1640s already sees Gönlung as "the foremost among all the commentarial schools in Domé," although at that time Gönlung consisted of "two divisions," or "groups," a commentarial one and one for "practice."[194] Thus Gönlung did not have the level of integration and organization that the monastery would have by the end of that century. Gönlung's reputation was no doubt earned through the achievements of some of its most successful scholars[195] and also through its unique ties to the important Kyishö family from Central Tibet and to the rulers of the Oirat in Tibet and Kökenuur.

In addition, Gönlung is also important because its later (post-1724/1729) history also demonstrates a new phase in the growth of the Geluk school. This was a period during which Geluk systematic organization of its monasteries took off in the hands of new generations of Geluk hierarchs, many of them now from the area around the Tibet-China frontier. Gönlung, Kumbum, Labrang, Serkhok, and other Geluk monasteries were large-scale operations that instituted the complex systems of monastic administration and practice advocated earlier by the Fifth Dalai Lama. These monasteries thus began to act like monastic cores or centers on par or nearly on par with the centers of old in Central Tibet. For its part, Gönlung was no longer "merely" a monastery linked back to more centrally located figures and monasteries in Central Tibet. Now it was a "blueprint" or "ancestress"[196] for new institutions in Amdo and beyond. Gönlung was *both* the most successful early outgrowth of the Geluk school's systematic expansion *and* itself a "root" for continuous growth elsewhere in Amdo and Mongolia.

The Gelukpa's northern and eastern advance coincided with the period referred to as the "High Qing." Geluk lamas along the Tibet-China-Mongolia frontier adapted to the presence and intervention by Qing officials by utilizing the Qing's bureaucratic apparatus for their own or their monasteries' benefit. The future of Inner Asia was tied to the growing Qing Empire, and the Gelukpa adapted to this challenge by integrating themselves into the Qing. Moreover, the Geluk school became the Qing's Tibetan Buddhist school of choice, in part because of its reputation for discipline and order.[197]

That a monastery such as Gönlung could itself serve as a beacon of Geluk orthodoxy and orthopraxy is a result of the ideological underpinnings of the Geluk school. The Geluk school was not dependent on any one individual, including the Dalai Lama, but rather was dependent on adherence to a common project of rationalizing monastic life. Although much of this was the product of the Fifth Dalai Lama's rationalizing and state-building projects, later Geluk hierarchs played an equally valuable role. Nikolay Tsyrempilov has argued that, in fact, the Dalai Lama was motivated in general by nationalist (or proto-nationalist), state-building considerations. Later, Geluk hierarchs, coming from Amdo and not sharing these concerns of the Dalai Lama, were motivated more by sectarian or religious considerations.[198] They saw the future of the Geluk school in the Manchu Qing and the expansion into Mongolia. The Gelukpa could be "divided" in this way because membership required loyalty not to any single hierarch but to a system of monastic life and administration.

# Chapter 2

# Administering a Monastery
# for the "Common Good"

When someone is sick, the disciplinarian inspects [to see] whether the patient himself has the requisite provisions for [the performance of] an "obstacle-clearing ritual" [T. *rim gro*]. Or, if he does not, then [the disciplinarian] gives from the common possessions [T. *spyi rdzas*] of the monastic community. If there still are not [enough], then, do [ritual] actions beginning with those for the statues [lit. bodies] of the Buddha and so forth. After the patient's illness has improved, if he has wealth, since he has partaken of the riches of the [Three] Jewels, he should repay. No matter whether he has [wealth] or not, the monks belonging to that place are to congregate and exert themselves at reciting as many "obstacle-clearing rituals" as are needed.

In short, this precious vessel of freedoms and favors [i.e., the human body] is very valuable for monks—old, young, and middle-aged—who wish to do well. It is difficult to come by, and the time of death is uncertain. The sufferings of this frightening prison of samsara give rise to fierce depression. May [you] give rise to a wholesome mind of enlightenment for the benefit of others and thereby take whatever [one can] into his experience of mindfulness, conscientiousness, and shame as expressed by the precepts of the Three Vows [literature]. In particular, be conscientious of and protect one another, and through the gate of the nature of forbearing "quiescence" and "taming," strive at the three [knowl-

edges] of listening, thinking, and meditating. So doing, I pray you will make a foundation for benefiting the Teachings and all wandering beings. I offer this prayer with palms pressed together.[1]
—'Jigs med ye shes grags pa, constitution no. 66, *Dgon lung byams pa gling gi mtshon dgon ma lag dang bcas pa'i bca' khrims* [The Constitution of an Exemplary Mother Monastery, Gönlung Jampa Ling, and Its Branch Monasteries], 1737

Much of the language of the above epigraph may be familiar. The first half is copied nearly verbatim from Tsongkhapa's fifteenth-century instructions for treating a sick member of the sangha, which was translated in the last chapter. I included it there to show a difference between how Tsongkhapa addressed the issue of sickness and how it differed from the earlier constitution for mantrins by the Nyingma master Rongzom (no. 1), which simply instructed that "each of the brethren provide a great offering" to the sick individual.[2] Though subtle, the difference between the two is the centralization and institutionalization of communal resources (the "common wealth" of the monastery) in the Geluk constitutions. In later constitutions (after the 1720s), one finds this idea (and Tsongkhapa's language) repeated. Moreover, the fundamental idea that qualified and approved members of the monastery or the sangha more generally were entitled to certain resources and that those resources were provided by a stipulated "common" or "general" pool was an idea promoted most ambitiously by the Gelukpa.[3]

This chapter examines the manner in which the Gelukpa rationalized the system of collecting and distributing wealth so as to ensure a reliable livelihood for its growing body of monks. Some aspects of Tibetan monasticism are *less* centralized and collective than other forms of Buddhist monasticism found across Asia. For instance, unlike major Chinese or Japanese monasteries in which monks are assigned to divisions or offices and live in corresponding dormitories or halls,[4] Tibetan Buddhist monks live in private quarters (T. *grwa shag*) in which an older monk, often an uncle or other relative, looks after a younger monk(s) in exchange for his servitude. Meals, particularly dinner, are also often taken in these quarters apart from the rest of the congregation. Nonetheless, as Geluk monasteries grew in size and complexity over the course of the seventeenth and eighteenth centuries, they developed ideas and organizational arrangements to build institutions that were responsive to the needs of its monks and not susceptible to the whims of any one individual.

As a bureaucratic organization, the authority of a large-scale Geluk monastery rests especially on the rules and procedures that are codified in writing. Moreover, as Weber has explained, an organization exercising legal authority often includes offices with specified jurisdictions, a clear demarcation of private property from organizational property, and a strict system of discipline and control of the organization's officers, among other things.[5] In this chapter, we shall see precisely these characteristics being vociferously advocated by Geluk hierarchs for their monasteries. Their language emphasizes the importance of impartiality; it also places a unique emphasis on the idea of "the public" or "the common good" of the monastery (T. *spyi*) as opposed to "the private" or "the individual" (T. *sger*). Moreover, the Gelukpa specified an elaborate hierarchy of offices and officers within the monastery and their respective responsibilities. This also meant new policies and financial arrangements to exercise the vaunted impartiality that many monastic constitutions speak about.

Although there was variation between Geluk monasteries in the details of their organizational arrangements, there was a great deal of similarity, too. Besides a general passion for concocting elaborate schemes of organization and administration, this consisted of a desire to systematize the redistribution of wealth within the monastery, a desire to specify the parties responsible for funding the costly annual schedule of major ritual occasions and dharma sessions, an effort to separate the jurisdiction of the abbot or monastery head from that of the office responsible for the monastery's economic and other "worldly" affairs, an effort to utilize endowments and other financial instruments as a means to ensure a modicum of resources for the body of monks, and so on. Collectively, these efforts resisted the tendency to become completely beholden to the power of charismatic figures (incarnate lamas), and they fostered institutions capable of maintaining order (or of quickly restoring it when it was lost) despite the hundreds and thousands of monks who lived in them.

## Impartiality and Discipline: The Disciplinarian (T. *dge skos*)

Of all the officers in a Geluk mega monastery, the disciplinarian—T. "*dge skos*" (pronounced "*gegö*"), literally, "the one charged with [maintaining] virtue"—receives the most attention in Geluk constitutions. This reflects his importance in overseeing nearly every aspect of the operation of the monastery. A 1758 constitution composed for a small monastery in Amdo describes his position as follows:

> The disciplinarian,[6] having renounced karmic actions and
> their results, without flattery or partiality is to exhort young,
> middle-aged, and old—each according to his needs and place—
> in [worshipping] his tutelary deity, in practicing good conduct,
> in memorizing, reciting, and practicing in assembly and in the
> courtyard, and so forth. When there are infractions he is to
> [punish] in accordance with the severity of the infraction, includ-
> ing giving disciplinary sermons, beating, [fines] of butter and
> offering scarves, [collecting] fire-wood for assembly, [collecting]
> water for assembly, and prostrations as described herein.[7]

Notice the insistence that he transcend flattery and partiality and that he treat everyone equally according to his needs. This emphasis on impartiality in monastic officers is found first in those of the Fifth Dalai Lama. In his revised constitution for Chökhorgyel in southern Central Tibet (no. 40), the Dalai Lama writes, "Officers such as [those of the abbatial palace of] Lekshé Ling[8] and the disciplinarians must impose order, not following his own desires or falling into partiality."[9] In his constitution for Litang Monastery in Kham (no. 48), addressing what to do in the situation in which the monastery's abbot (T. *mkhan po*) or teachers (T. *slob dpon*) are absent, the Dalai Lama writes that "the disciplinarians, manager,[10] and assistants to the disciplinarian,[11] not forcing their own desires down the throats of others, are to consult together with the General Management Office and assemble, doing whatever is appropriate and most important for the monastery."[12] In her essay on the Great Fifth's constitution for Drepung Monastery, Berthe Jansen notes that the Dalai Lama specifically addresses the problem of disciplinarians accepting bribes in exchange for favors.[13] In fact, as early as his constitution composed to reform and regulate the Great Prayer Festival (no. 37), the Dalai Lama addressed the problem of disciplinarians bringing their personal interests into their administering of the ritual occasion.[14]

The Ninth Karmapa, too, had earlier insisted upon the impartiality of the monastery's top officers, which makes sense given what we know about the large size of his traveling encampment: "Since both the manager [T. *gnyer*] and disciplinarian officers [T. *chos khrims*] are public personnel [T. *spyi mi*], being neither of the monk class nor that of patrons, being partial neither to those inside nor those outside, near or far, and not focused on their own desires, they thus protect what is communal (T. *gzhung*)."[15] Here we see introduced the related concept of the "public" (T. *spyi*) or the "communal" (T. *gzhung*, a term that could also be translated as "the monastery government"), a subject to which we shall return. Notwithstanding the Karmapa's precedent, the Gelukpa, were the ones who devised the largest and richest monasteries, and it is they who therefore emphasized most the need for impartiality and fairness.

Jikmé Yeshé Drakpa's constitution for Gönlung (no. 66) insists that no one is above the law, including the disciplinarians: "If the lama, disciplinarians, managers, so forth later on cause bad arguments; and, other than removing themselves from [the process of karmic] actions and their consequences, if the major and minor officers of the law, in general, and the lama, disciplinarians, and general manager, in particular, are to engage in unallowable behavior such as partiality and bad arguments stemming from one's own past grievances, then the lama, [general] manager, disciplinarians, and so on are not to reside there long."[16] It is implied that the officers were held to an even higher standard, since they were models for everyone else and because they were the ones who enforced the governing order. As Sumba Kanpo, an Oirat Mongol-born monk from Amdo, wrote in one of his constitutions, "If one is partial and has favorites, then sin, suffering, and evil talk will arise at the same time and there will be the danger that the suffering of this life will become even greater in the next life. . . . The lords of discipline, by means of upright deeds and in accord with the dharma, impose the regular order. Strict and disciplined, everyone respects them. Internalize this discipline from your head to your toe!"[17]

The disciplinarian's status in the monastery was perhaps second only to that of the abbot.[18] His obligations are also some of the most onerous, since he would be expected to ensure all the proper comportment and routines laid out in the monastic constitution, from dharma classes to the nighttime rehearsal of the day's lessons that students were required to practice in their personal quarters. Monks would be regularly reminded of his authority by the two or three disciplinary sermons (T. *tshogs gtam*) he (or, otherwise, the abbot) would deliver at each of the dharma sessions throughout the year. These were "to be both broad and detailed like the monastic constitution, and, in particular, [the disciplinarian or abbot] is to give disciplinary sermons that look closely at the large and small infractions of the rules."[19]

These sermons that were "both broad and detailed" would invoke the specter of incrimination in each and every monk through the specificity of the announced misdemeanors and corresponding punishments of the monastery coupled with an equally *non*specific allusions to the wrongdoer.[20] Such systems of invoking the sensation of being surveilled are found, of course, in other hierarchical institutions. Talal Asad, drawing on the work of Michel Foucault, writes about the instruments of discipline in medieval Christian monasteries: "There was no single point of surveillance. Within the monastery there existed an entire network of functions through which watching, testing, learning, teaching, could take place. Mutual observation was urged on all, but the matter was too important to be left in the form of a general injunction. Because observation and imitation were defined as interlinked functions, the elevation of particular roles became necessary."[21] At Geluk monasteries, these elevated roles were filled by one's personal teacher in his quarters or residential house (T. *khangs tshan* or *khams tshan*; T. *mi tshan*) but especially by the disciplinarian. Monks were (and are) taught to run and hide from the disciplinarian should one encounter him in the streets of the monastery.

It is also interesting to consider the implications of the Geluk practices of discipline and surveillance for the success of the Geluk as a whole. The historical sociologist Philip Gorski has argued quite convincingly that the rise of the modern state is indebted to the disciplinary practices of observation that were the product of the Protestant Reformation:

> Like the industrial revolution, the disciplinary revolution was driven by a key technology: the technology of observation—self observation, mutual observation, hierarchical observation. For it was observation—surveillance—that made it possible to unleash the energies of the human soul—another well-known but little-used resource—and harness them for the purposes of political power and domination. . . .
>
> . . . By "infrastructure of governance," I mean a network of practices and institutions whose goal, to borrow Foucault's words, is "the conduct of conduct": the control of behavior and

the shaping of subjectivity. By "disciplinary revolution," I mean a revolutionary struggle, whether from below or above, which has, as one of its chief ends, the creation of a more disciplined polity. The state, from this perspective, may be defined as "pastoral" organization that claims clear priority (if not complete monopoly) over the legitimate means of socialization within a given territory.[22]

I do not intend here to attempt a description or analysis of the Tibetan Buddhist "subjectivity." Nor do I intend to enter fully into a discussion of the ways in which the Geluk school resembled a modern state, although I will note that one recent, novel definition of the modern state makes administration and bureaucracy—an area where the Gelukpa excelled—key components of that definition.[23] I do wish to reiterate that the entire Geluk project is grounded in the rhetoric of discipline. The Seventh Dalai Lama reminds us in one of his constitutions (no. 61), "To depart from this life and die is easy. If discipline degenerates and is destroyed, that is not so." That is, the pain that will ensue over innumerable lifetimes should one not maintain a disciplined life is worse than death itself. The Dalai Lama adds, "Therefore, the Buddha praised discipline to the utmost: 'Maintaining discipline, one encounters the arising of the awakening of enlightenment. Maintaining discipline is the most supreme of all adornments. Maintaining discipline is to be smeared with fragrances.'"[24] Disciplining or taming of the self is a virtue, as it is the ground on which Gelukpas built both their system of practice and their system of monastic expansion and control.

To return to the role of the disciplinarian and the theme of impartiality, Jikmé Yeshé Drakpa devotes several lines in his Gönlung constitution to underscoring the importance of maintaining the honor of the *position* of disciplinarian, a position that transcends any single individual who serves in that position for a year or two. (Usually, a monastery or a college (T. *grwa tshang*) within a mega monastery, has two disciplinarians, a junior one and a senior one. Often an individual serves a year in each position). If an infraction occurs during the tenure of a particular disciplinarian, but that disciplinarian is too busy and does not get around to administering the necessary punishment, he is to explain the situation to the next individual to serve in the position and that individual then carries out the punishment.[25] Similarly, an individual who commits an infraction cannot, because of condescension or malice toward the individual serving as disciplinarian, delay paying the fine or submitting himself to the punishment, waiting until a later individ-ual is appointed to the position. Such a delinquent is instead to be expelled from the monastery.[26] Even the disciplinarian may not, in an attempt to prove to the body of monks that he is a naturally "good guy," overturn a decision or sentence of his predecessor in the position.[27] The position of disciplinar-ian is inviolable. The disciplinarian, moreover, is supposed to stay above the fray, refraining from contributing to any complaining and negative talk that other monks may be engaged in.[28] As in most constitutions, Jikmé Yeshé Drakpa proscribes verbally or physically abusing the disciplinarian, and he warns of the consequences of harboring ill-content or disrespecting author-ity: "To make baseless accusations of the lords of discipline here, and for there to be reprisals, false accusations, and inappropriate words used among the lama, the disciplinarians, the general manager, and, moreover, among other officers and even [ordinary] monks, is like putting fire to straw."[29] The stok-ing of fear of social "conflagrations" and unrest that could occur when order breaks down is a common way of ensuring acceptance of a disciplin-ary regime.[30]

## The Lama

The "lama" of the monastery—here, the abbot—was the most powerful and respected position within a Geluk monastery unless there happened to be a resident incarnate lama at the monastery, such as the monastery's "lord" or "protector" (T. dgon bdag), who wielded even more influence (sometimes in tension with the position of abbot). The meaning and position of the lama within the monastery could change over time, but the idea of a *bureaucratic office* of the lama not tied to any one person or lineage persisted. "Lama" is a general religious title of respect in Tibetan, and it is used in at least four different ways. One is as a translation of the Sanskrit "*guru*" (lit. "weighty"). Scholars have suggested that the Tibetan translation of *guru*, "lama" (T. *bla ma*), may be interpreted literally as "without peer (i.e., peerless)" or as "mother of [one's] soul." Both of these interpretations are fitting for describing how a Buddhist is to think of his guru—that is, his spiritual (particularly tant-ric) teacher. A second use of "lama" is to refer to individuals who are be-lieved to exercise some level of control over the rebirth process so as to come back in a form conducive to saving more beings. These are *trülku*, the "ema-nation bodies" that I have referred to in this book as "incarnate lamas." The

Dalai Lama is the best-known example of this. A third way in which "lama" is used is as a title of respect for accomplished scholar-monks who have earned a degree, although often the scholastic title, such as "Geshé" ("spiritual friend") or "Khenpo" ("wise one"), is used instead. Finally, "lama" is used at times to refer to the abbot of the monastery and in this way may be interchanged with other titles, such as "Khenpo," "*lopön*" (T. *slob dpon*), or "*tripa*" (T. *khri pa*), depending on the context. These different uses of the term "lama" are not discrete and may overlap; for instance, Gönlung's abbot is often also an accomplished scholar and may also be a recognized rebirth in a spiritual lineage who also serves as the guru of many other monks.[31]

In the early days of Gönlung, the abbot would have, in principle, served in the stead and interest of Gyelsé Dönyö Chökyi Gyatso and his rebirths. Gyelsé, as Gönlung's founder, was understood to be the monastery's "lord" or "protector." Thus, when Gyelsé left Gönlung in 1609 to return to Central Tibet, he made the first of the Sumba incarnate lama lineage, Damchö Gyatso,[32] serve in his stead as the monastery's first abbot.[33] In theory, Gyelsé may have continued to exercise this power, appointing new abbots whenever the need arose. However, the historical record suggests that he only did this under rare, extenuating circumstances. For instance, it is said that in 1665 his successor Gyelsé Lozang Tendzin (ca. 1637–1697), chose the abbot[34] and also played a role in introducing a major institutional reform at the monastery (see below).

In general, a "lord" of a monastery, such as Gyelsé, would not need or even desire to play such an active role in choosing the abbots for a monastery located so far away. The next Gyelsé Lama, Jikmé Yeshé Drakpa, the author of the Gönlung constitution (no. 66), specified the procedure for choosing an abbot: "As for appointing the abbot, it is to be done based on the consultation of the old abbot, the cantor and disciplinarian,[35] the general manager,[36] the 'encampments' and hermitages,[37] and the senior monks."[38] The abbot was to be a rotating position chosen through deliberation by the monastery's highest officers and most senior monks.

Furthermore, like the disciplinarian, the abbot is to be an impartial, "public" figure. Jikmé Yeshé Drakpa continues, "Officers, with the lama as the lead, are not to indulge in favoritism, partisanship, or sycophancy and must not bring[39] private interests into a public [position]. This must be well enforced."[40] The abbot's position was a powerful one, endowed with great resources. In the constitutions, one finds a palpable fear of the abbot's needs or desires encroaching on the well-being of the monastery. For instance, the

First Jamyang Zhepa, in the constitution he wrote for his new monastery of Labrang in Amdo, says,

> Except for when there are numerous mass tea patrons [i.e., except for when there is no shortage], the manager [of the monastery] is to contribute to the number of mass teas of the lama palace [i.e., those provisions that the lama palace is responsible for producing].[41] Nowadays, the work and expenditures of the lama palace is tremendous, and so that custom is necessary. [Also,] for ancillary [private or more exclusive] mass teas, the patron provides as great a mass tea as s/he can with tea and butter. *Apart from this, the income of the sangha is never to be plundered.*[42]

"Plundered" here is clearly hyperbole; but what is being described is the use of the monastery's own, "common" funds to make up for the deficit of the abbot's office as well as the diversion of a patron's donations away from the common funds of the monastery and toward a more exclusive, private beneficiary. This was a "necessary custom," Jamyang Zhepa explains, due to the extenuating circumstances.

It is true that, as Jamyang Zhepa attests, the financial obligations of the abbot were tremendous. At Gönlung, for instance, he was responsible for providing the food and ritual provisions for those ritualists in charge of the major sacrificial cake offering to Yama during the Great Prayer Festival of the first month and to ritual dancers [T. *'chams*] who performed at that time.[43] Likewise, he was responsible for feeding the ritual dancers breakfast and lunch during their three-week-long annual practice retreat in the summer.[44] At the end of the year, the abbot was made responsible for provisioning the necessary supplies and food for the preparation of the sacrificial cake to Mahākāla and for providing food, tea, and fires for the entire gathered assembly.[45] He was also responsible for the foods and feasts associated with the Ritual Cake Offering of the First Day (the "Day *Torma*"), offered to Pelden Lhamo (the Glorious Goddess), an occasion to which all religious dignitaries (incarnate lamas, "encampments," and hermits associated with Gönlung) were invited and which all Gönlung monks were required to attend.[46]

The abbot and the disciplinarians, moreover, were responsible for ensuring that the "monastery teas" (T. *grwa ja*)—the food and tea not directly dependent upon a lay patron—did not run out, "lest the students grow weary

of attending the dharma sessions,"[47] and the abbot was responsible for check-
ing the quality of the offerings made by patrons.[48] Moreover, when there
were no communal funds available to pay for the monastery's expenses, as
was the case in the aftermath of the 1724 Lubsang-Danzin Rebellion, the
abbot would often be the one to pay.[49]

The early twentieth-century missionary and scholar, Louis Schram, describes the responsibilities of the figure who eventually took over many of
the responsibilities of the abbot (see below):

> The intendant of the monastery alone disposes of all the wealth of
> the monastery (not of the wealth of the community of the lamas
> or of the colleges), its revenues, investment of capital, loans, gifts,
> and alms received (but not of alms given to the community of
> lamas or to the colleges). He has to cope with all the expenses of
> the monastery, and to try to increase the collection of gifts and
> alms. He is in charge of the provisioning of the monastery, and
> must see that the procurator secures the colossal amounts of
> butter that a monastery requires. In the temples of Erh-ku-lung
> [i.e., Gönlung] eight butter lamps burn before the statues day and
> night. Each lamp consumes 180 pounds of butter every year,
> making 1,440 pounds for the eight lamps. The intendant told me
> that every year he had to provide a total of more than 3,000
> pounds of butter for lamps, kitchen, and tea, and had to send
> lamas to Kukunor and Mongolia in order to collect this enormous
> amount. The intendant, in short, is the biggest cog in the wheel
> of administration.[50]

Of course, the abbot also received more wealth than anyone else. According to the Gönlung constitution, the abbot, along with the cantor,
the disciplinarians, and the general manager,[51] would ordinarily receive an
extra share of cash disbursements and bread[52] donated at assemblies.[53] He
would also receive an extra pail of tea (as would the general manager and
the principal patron of the assembly) after the standard distribution of offerings (tea, noodles, and cash).[54] His allowance was increased greatly
during the Great Prayer Festival of the first month, when he alone received ten shares of cash tips, tea, or whatever was donated.[55] Offerings
would be given to the abbot on various other occasions, too, such as when
a monk asked to be considered to stand for the monastery's scholastic de-

gree or to purchase an "honorary degree" (in which case, the abbot received both a horse and another special "extensive offering" (T. *rnam gzhag rgyas pa*)).[56]

This largess notwithstanding, there appears to have been a push to place a cap on the amount to which the abbot was entitled. After all, receiving a single "extra share" alongside other major officers at an ordinary assembly at which there was a "mass tea offering" does not significantly set the abbot apart from the fray. Even the ten shares he was to receive during the Great Prayer Festival pales in comparison with what existed at certain other monasteries in the past (let alone the income gap that exists between modern CEOs and their lowest paid employees!). Meanwhile, at the *personal* monastery of the Amdo incarnate lama Tuken (T. Thu'u bkwan), the lama (i.e., Tuken himself) was to receive ten shares of cash tips and bread, a full pot of tea, plus a small pail of tea *under ordinary circumstances*.[57] Or take the case of Reting Monastery, for which Jikmé Yeshé Drakpa also composed a constitution (no. 64): "Previously, there was the custom of the abbot and the manager [T. *gnyer*] each taking forty shares. However, henceforth, the abbot is to get fifteen, the attendants [T. *dbon*] are to get seven [each], and the eight assistants [T. *g. yog*] one [each], totaling thirty, for example. When former abbots truly are residing at the monastery, their shares for allowance and cash offerings are to be five. Also, when the Tsenya[58] [Lama] is residing at the monastery, his share of allowance or cash offerings is three."[59] The earlier Reting constitution composed by the Dalai Lama was much briefer, and had left in the hands of the disciplinarian much of the decision-making power regarding distribution of offerings.[60] Apparently, this left things too vulnerable to abuse and was thus one of the "unsuitable" (T. *gnas min*) aspects of the earlier constitution that Jikmé Yeshé Drakpa intended to redress in his own constitution for Reting.[61]

Constitutions, beginning with the Fifth Dalai Lama's constitution for Drepung (no. 51) and extending to later texts written for new, important monasteries in Amdo (such as Labrang (no. 60) and Taktsang Lhamo),[62] began to show a concern for specifying and limiting the number of shares each member of the monastery was to receive. As Berthe Jansen has argued, this is in large part a reaction to the increased amount of wealth pouring into monasteries at the time of the Fifth Dalai Lama[63] and a desire on the part of Geluk hierarchs to formalize a system in which monks were directly dependent on the monastery. Therefore, they placed limits on the amount of direct interaction that monks had with the laity.[64]

This was part of the more general practice of the Gelukpa of *standardizing monastic routines so as to build and maintain a resilient system of norms and routines.*

## The Redistribution of Wealth

Jikmé Yeshé Drakpa's constitution for Gönlung gives us one of the most extensive and detailed overviews of the hierarchy of officers and functionaries within a Geluk mega monastery. We get a sense of one's status within the system by the number of shares of alms each individual is accorded during the Great Prayer Festival at the beginning of the year:

> As for shares, from whatever cash and bread appears [as donations from laity]: the master-throne-holder [T. *dpon slob khri pa*; i.e., the abbot] receives ten. Retired abbots and the Tantric College Lama receive five. The Sacrificial Cake Offering Lama,[65] the Lama-Cantor of the Tantric College,[66] the disciplinarian officers,[67] and the Great Cantor[68] receive three shares and a Great *Namshak.*[69]

> The chant-master,[70] disciplinarian, shrine caretaker,[71] and kitchen manager,[72] of the Tantric College,[73] the restoration ritual cantor,[74] the sacrificial cake offering cantor,[75] the Medicine Buddha Ritual cantor,[76] the contour-tone offering cantor,[77] the manager of the lama palace,[78] the managers of the hermitages,[79] the protector deity medium,[80] the three obstacle-clearing ritualists,[81] cooks,[82] assistants to the disciplinarians,[83] shrine caretakers, tea servers,[84] and water-carriers[85] get two shares.

> If those two cantors[86] are *Karam* scholars, then they [also] receive a great *Namshak.* If not, then they each receive a regular *Namshak.*[87]

> The contour-tone offering cantor,[88] and others, the two caretakers of the Maitreya receptacle [i.e., statue],[89] the leg-bone trumpet blowers,[90] the *gyaling* "oboe" players,[91] incense bearers,[92] umbrella bearers,[93] the two cushion caretakers,[94] the two sacrificial cake makers,[95] and Great Prayer Festival teachers[96] receive one share of cash tips and bread.[97]

After the abbot, the "second tier" of officers and dignitaries at the monastery comprises retired abbots and the lama or head of Gönlung's tantric college. The "third tier" consists of the ritual head of the Tantric College (the "Lama-Cantor"), the lama or head of the Offerings of Accomplishment to the monastery's principal deities, the head cantor of the monastery, and the disciplinarians of the monastery.

In addition to providing a clearly defined "single hierarchy of offices" within the monastery, which is one of the characteristics of a bureaucracy, the great range of roles points to the *specialization* of the work of running a monastery, another characteristic of a bureaucracy. The number of cantors, in particular, is outstanding. Gönlung today still maintains six cantors: the contour-tone offering cantor; the cantor of the Tantric College; that of the Gyelsé Hermitage up the valley, where traditionally the Medicine Buddha Ritual is carried out; the Restoration Ritual cantor; the Accomplishment Offering cantor; and, the cantor of the Great Assembly Hall.[98] The contour-tone offering cantor, for his part, sings numerous (more than twenty) liturgies between the third and sixteenth of the first month "in a drawn-out and complex manner which makes use of almost infinite varieties and combinations of the components of melody."[99] He, like other cantors, received *specialized training* to learn his job. Apart from learning to read the musical notation that serves as an aid for rehearsal, this training consists of imitating other monks during assembly and, in the case of large-scale monasteries with specified "voice sections" (such as Gönlung),[100] of one-on-one training from current or past cantors.[101]

The qualifications needed to serve in such a position are usually only generally described (e.g., for a cantor, that he have a "good voice"[102]). However, a great deal of attention is paid in monastic constitutions, particularly Geluk ones, to specifying the various positions within the monastery and their respective statuses and domains. Jansen has observed a trajectory toward uniformity in the administrative makeup of monasteries in the seventeenth century.[103] This uniformity is a result of the mobility of Geluk hierarchs (e.g., Jikmé Yeshé Drakpa was from Central Tibet and composed constitutions for monasteries there as well as for Gönlung in Amdo) and the Geluk penchant for standardizing and codifying the "proper" ways of running a monastery.

This same process of bureaucratization is reflected in the way monasteries began to handle "salaries" or "allowances" (T. *phogs*) at Geluk monasteries. Jikmé Yeshé Drakpa addresses the problem of freeriders at the Gönlung:

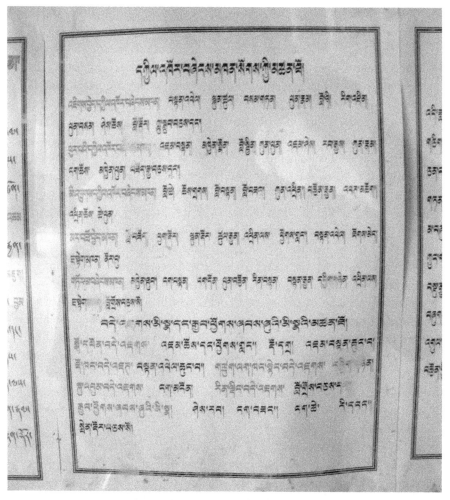

Figure 5. The Geluk passion for rationalization and documenting the relevant
offices and tasks for major ritual occasions continues today. This document,
posted alongside several others at the entrance to Pelkor Chödé (T. Dpal 'khor
chos sde) Monastery in Gyantsé (T. Rgyal rtse), assigns monks to the various
maṇḍala ritual groups for the upcoming *Saga* Month (fourth month).
Photo by the author, July 2009.

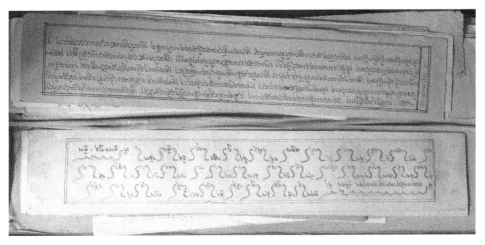

Figure 6. On top, an example of a melodic notation (T. *dbyangs yig*) from Gönlung Monastery. Cantors must learn to read this, although most of the specialized training is learned by ear while sitting at the feet of a senior, or more experienced, cantor. On bottom is a manuscript of the common Geluk hymn to Maitreya by Tsongkhapa, the "Vast and Deep [Knowledge]."
Photo by the author, March 2011.

"Drawing up the salary list once each year is a tremendous [task]. When the salary list has been completed, [people leave] to travel and to do what they wish. Except for during the twelfth month people do not congregate and there is limitless variation [in attendance]. Therefore, the salary list is drawn up [instead] at [each of] the four month-long dharma sessions, and salaries are distributed in accordance with this."[104] Historically, the use of salaries to support monks coincided with the Fifth Dalai Lama coming to power in the mid-seventeenth century.[105] This administrative practice of keeping salary lists as a way of monitoring the population of monks actually residing at the monastery would have followed this shift as a way of increasing the efficiency (and maintaining the solvency) of the monastery.

The standardization and codification of salaries also appear to be an effort to prevent jealousy and fighting among the monks. In the Gönlung constitution, new recruits are reminded to "exert themselves single-mindedly on the Teachings in general and on gathering [merit] and purifying [sin] and the welfare[106] of those beyond oneself."[107] To that end, the number of regular shares of offerings (usually bread and cash tips) and of the special *Nam-shak* are specified: the lama (abbot), disciplinarian, cantor, and general manager[108] each get an extra share.[109] Everyone else got a single share *if they were present* at assembly. Meanwhile, exceptions were made for retired abbots, incarnate lamas,[110] hermits, others of a "high class," functionaries[111] whose jobs kept them preoccupied, and those studying abroad in Central Tibet.[112] The idea is that by specifying and normalizing the redistribution of wealth, there would be greater acceptance and fewer complaints and instances of jealousy. Also, although additional, separate redistribution lists might be "privately compiled" (T. *sger sgrigs*) by the monastery's officers for the benefit of scholar monks (*Karam* scholars and those enrolled in the Philosophical College),[113] monks were explicitly advised never to exhibit jealousy or to interfere with such redistribution.[114]

A special group of redistributions known as *Namshak* (T. *rnam gzhag*) stand out as particularly important at Gönlung: there, knowing the typology and recipients of these are required for all new monks at the monastery.[115] Although it is not entirely clear from Jikmé Yeshé Drakpa's constitution *what* these *Namshak* consisted of, we do get some sense of the variation among them. The most opulent, the "extensive *Namshak*" (T. *rnam gzhag rgyas pa*) went only to the current and former abbots.[116] The "medium *Namshak*" was given to those who assisted in running assembly (T. *tshogs rim pa*) and other deserving functionaries. The "condensed" or "very condensed" *Namshak* (T. *rnam gzhag bsdus pa, rnam gzhag shin tu bsdus pa*) would go only to the two disciplinarians and the cantor.[117] While the above are defined principally by *who* receives the offering, the "great *Namshak*" and "normal *Namshak*" appear to be defined principally by what they are or their amounts. These could be given to various individuals, depending on the context. For instance, according to the schedule of cash and bread distributions, a certain set of cantors would receive a "great *Namshak*" in addition to their shares of bread and cash tips if they were *Karam* scholars. Otherwise, they received a "normal *Namshak*" in addition to their shares.[118]

Offerings from laity, too, were subjected to bureaucratic standardization. The "mass tea" offering (T. *mang ja*) was defined in the Gönlung constitution, for example, as follows: "The quantities of mass teas are to be at least [as follows]: considering that a single 'unit'[119] is twenty-four [bricks of] tea and serves three hundred monks, for six hundred monks [give] two units. Butter is to be three times that. Milk [is provided], too."[120] A similar example, though for 3,000 monks rather than 300, is found in the Seventh Dalai Lama's constitution for Sera Monastery.[121] Jansen has explained that this practice was intended to prevent the manipulation of the cost of rituals by monks and thereby avoid annoying lay donors and causing disputes.[122] Similarly, the amount needed to buy firewood to prepare the mass tea—something also to be provided by lay patrons—is specified as "normally ten ounces [T. *srang*] of tea or five ounces of tea and a piece of fabric."[123]

In short, the Gelukpa did not leave things to chance. They stipulated and codified the administrative arrangements of their monasteries, particularly those arrangements that had to do with wealth and money because those were and are often sites of contest and disagreement. All of these can be understood as measures taken to reach their sought after goal of impartiality and as attempts to enact a system of monastic administration that ran according to agreed upon norms of rightness and propriety. As we shall see in the next section, these attempts were never entirely successful and were challenged by the system of incarnate lamas among other things.

## Homegrown Lamas and Challenges to Rational Rule

Above, we examined the Gelukpas' emphasis on impartiality and the stipulations made in monastic constitutions to specify and demarcate the domain of its highest officers, particularly that of the abbot. These moves to bureaucratize the position of the monastery's leader were not immune to the influence of the proliferating phenomenon of identifying and reifying the rebirths of influential lamas. In Amdo, Gönlung had one of the earliest and most influential incarnate lama lineages: the Changkya (T. Lcang skya) lineage. By the eighteenth century, Changkya was the lama on the most intimate terms with the Qing emperors in Beijing. By the end of the eighteenth century, Changkya's power and reputation was so great, while that of the Gyelsé lineage had waned so much, that Changkya was referred to as the "lord" or "protector" (T. *dgon bdag*) of that monastery.[124]

As Gray Tuttle has shown, the number of new incarnate lamas in Amdo exploded in the eighteenth century,[125] and this was also true of Gönlung, where three other renowned lama lineages grew in importance—Tuken, Sumba (T. Sum pa), and Chuzang (T. Chu bzang)—and several other lesser known lineages surfaced. The prestige and wealth of these figures spelled the end of the ideal, bureaucratic office of abbot that Jikmé Yeshé Drakpa had implemented. As Gyelsé's power in Central Tibet waned, so did his interest in or ability to maintain any real relationship with his erstwhile branch

monastery of Gönlung Monastery. At the same time, the power of his puta-
tive representative at the monastery, the abbot, waned too.[126]

The later, 1885, constitution for Gönlung provides different instructions for how one of its key dharma sessions was to be financed, and it
obliquely signals the presence of a new kind of rule at the monastery: "The
mass tea at this time [i.e., during the First Spring Dharma Session] [is pro-
vided] by each of the four components of the 'lama-management council'
and so forth,[127] *by each of the major incarnation palaces,*[128] by each pair of
'alms-collectors,'[129] and, moreover, *by each grouping of three minor incarnation palaces in rotation.*[130] The community of the monks[131] must also make a
contribution."[132] The enhanced role of Gönlung's incarnate lamas expressed
in this passage is noteworthy because incarnate lamas are only mentioned
twice, in passing, in Jikmé Yeshé Drakpa's earlier constitution, and they
play no specified role in the administration of the monastery.[133] This
change in Gönlung's orientation—away from Gyelsé Rinpoché in Central
Tibet and toward Changkya and other lamas situated at Gönlung itself or
farther to the east in Beijing—and the concomitant change in its internal
hierarchy and administration helps explain the makeup of the monastery
as presented by Louis Schram. The Belgian missionary spent approximately
a decade (1911/12–1922) in Xining and surrounding areas studying the Monguor people.[134] His depiction of the typical monastery in the region de-
motes the abbot (Ch. *fatai*; T. *slob dpon, mkhan po*) of the monastery to the
position of a mere pawn in the hands of the monastery's lord or protector,
now a powerful, *local* incarnate lama who resides at the monastery.[135] The
abbot,[136] meanwhile, retains real financial obligations toward the body of
monks; however, his powers are "reduced to theoretical and honorary dimensions."[137] The real power-holder is the monastery's lord or protector
(the incarnate lama) and, in particular, his "intendant" (T. *phyag mdzod*).[138]
The intendant, Schram writes, is appointed by the monastery's lord or protector, which in Schram's day was said to be Tuken, Changkya, and Sumpa,
although Tuken was the de facto lord or protector, since the other two were
forced by circumstances to reside elsewhere.[139] The intendants were often
appointed for a lifetime and are said to have wielded immense power: "It is
not easy to handle intendants, and it is more difficult to dismiss them, according to the sayings of experienced old lamas."[140] In fact, the intendant
became so powerful that, in collusion with his second-in-command, the
"procurator,"[141] "they can easily dupe the supreme chief [i.e., the lord or
protector] for a long time."[142]

This account of the immense power accrued by local lamas at the monastery and the "intendants" that they personally appointed reflects numerous changes that took place in the decades and centuries after Gyelsé last intervened in Gönlung's affairs (i.e., after he composed Gönlung's constitution). These changes include the growing influence of the Qing Empire in Central Tibet and especially Amdo and, not least, the growth and maturation of monasteries on the periphery. As local lama lineages accumulated more wealth, they also took more of the power over the governance of monasteries. On the eve of the People's Liberation Army move into Amdo and Tibet, Gönlung and its incarnate lamas possessed some 37,000 *mu*[143] in what is now Huzhu County, the primary (but not the only) area of Gönlung's influence, of which only 10,000 *mu* was the common property of the monastery's monks.[144] The rest was owned by the monastery's incarnate lamas, especially Tuken, who alone reportedly controlled 14,000 *mu* of land. Also, the average tenure of a serving abbot had declined from about 4 years in the first 120 years of the monastery's existence to only 2 years in the nineteenth century. These facts suggest that the office of the abbot may not have endured to have any significant power independent of the growing influence of local lamas.

Nonetheless, the fact that the body of monks, what Schram called the "community of lamas," possessed as much land as it did attests to the enduring impact of the institutional changes implemented by earlier Geluk hierarchs to meet the demands of the growing, complex institutions and possibly even to slow the growing influence of incarnate lamas. It is to the institutionalization of this "common wealth" that we now turn.

## The General Management Office (T. *spyi sa/so/ba*)

The abbot's duties early on were quite onerous. Eventually, however, the financial and administrative needs of the monastic community exceeded the abilities of the abbot alone. The eighteenth-century chronicle of Gönlung, for instance, describes a major reform that took place in 1665 when the rebirth of the monastery's founder visited.[145] "The sixteenth abbot was the Expounder of Scripture and Reasoning, Pelden Gyatso. . . . [146] In the Wood-Snake year [1665], through the command of the Omniscient Gyelsé [who was visiting], he was installed as the abbot of Gönlung. Previously, abbots [T. *mkhan po rnams*] combined [the duties] of [religious]

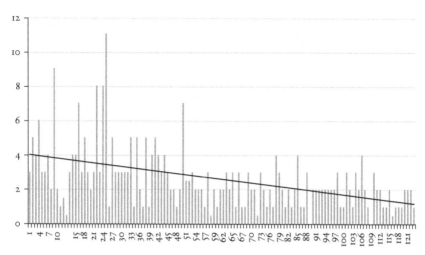

Figure 7. This chart shows the number of years (vertical axis) each of Gönlung's 123 abbots (horizontal axis; corresponding to the years 1604–1958) served in the position.

lama and [administrative] manager [T. *bla gnyer*]. This venerable separately established [the positions of] lama for religious affairs and manager for worldly affairs."[147] This reform is said to have been implemented on the heels of a time during which "the teachings had deteriorated."[148] This marks the establishment of a separate institution within the monastery that we might call the General Management Office (T. *spyi ba*), although it might be better understood as the "Office of the Common Good."[149] The Tibetan "*gzhung*" is sometimes used as a synonym referring to what is "common" rather than that which is "private" or "individual."[150] Three decades later, in the 1690s, Gönlung was recorded as the largest monastery in Amdo. By that time, one of its principal lamas, Changkya Rinpoché, had worked his way into serving as the Kangxi Emperor's court chaplain. It is difficult to assess the influence this reform might have had on the monastery's success; however, we do know that later leaders continued to recognize the importance of separating the domains of abbot and general management.

Despite Gyelsé's reform of 1665, by 1693, the monastery had slipped back into its old ways. The Second Changkya, who was staying at Gönlung at the time, recounts the situation he encountered and his reestablishment of the reform:

When Gyelsé Rinpoché [previously] went [to Gönlung in 1665],
he made separate the lama [T. *bla*; i.e. abbot] and general management office [T. *spyi*]. However, not long thereafter they were
merged into one [administration]. When lamas [T. *bla ma*; i.e.
abbots] are responsible for all worldly affairs such as resolving
disputes, it is difficult for them to do such things as teach [the
dharma]. Therefore, [in 1693,] all the lamas [T. *bla ma*] and
monks discussed this and came to an agreement that the managers of the general management office[151] will take responsibility for
all worldly affairs, and [these] managers will be separately appointed. A constitution was created clearly elaborating on all of
the tasks of the two traditions [of spiritual and temporal adminis-
tration].[152]

The abbot thereby became responsible for giving spiritual teachings and presiding over important rituals. The actual administration of the monastery
was handed over to the new general management office. This was not meant
merely to make the abbot's job easier. On the contrary, the primary benefi-
ciaries of this change were to be the monks themselves. Changkya's biographer clearly explains Changkya's motivation behind reestablishing such a
system at his other major monastery, Khökhe süme[153] in Dolonnuur: "Thinking of the benefit of the monastery, [Changkya] separately established the
general management office, and he appointed two general managers [T. *spyi
gnyer*]. From his own estate he gave to the public coffers[154] 120 stallions and
a family to care for the livestock. This he did as an endowment for the estate[155] of the temple and all [its] clergy."[156] In other words, the creation of a
general management office ensured that pedagogical, ritual, administrative,
and, most important, financial obligations were met for a growing number
of monks. Incidentally, such generous contributions by the estates of incarnate lamas to the public resources of monasteries may have been one of the
causes for the greater role of incarnate lamas in the life of these monasteries. After all, "help provided makes sympathy wax."[157]

This system of separating the abbot's position and duties from the direct
management of the financial assets of the monastery itself persisted in some
form into the twentieth century. In the 1940s and 1950s, an administrative
body comprising eleven or twelve individuals played a role in overseeing such
aspects of Gönlung and its common wealth. On it served the treasurer or
steward (T. *phyag mdzod* or *spyi phyag mdzod*) of the General Management

Office (who was perhaps the same as or had the same role as the "managers," *gnyer ba tsho*, referred to in the above quotations), two disciplinarians (i.e., those of the Philosophical College and Great Assembly), two senior elders (Ch. *laoye* 老爺) or "clerical supervisors" (Ch. *senggang* 僧岗), and six or seven other elders (Ch. *laozhe* 老者 or *laomin* 老民).[158] And, as colorfully recounted by Schram, this administrative group[159] possessed its own property and was responsible principally for the monks who populated the monastery, even going as far as to file suit against the "intendant" who was appointed by the principal local incarnate lama to oversee the entire monastery.[160]

When the Second Changkya reiterated in 1693 the need to separate the "spiritual" duties from the "worldly" ones and for a separate staff of people to manage the latter, he was not only referencing the earlier reform of 1665 by Gönlung's lord lama but also likely emulating his own guru, Ganden Sertri ("Golden Throne-holder of Ganden Monastery") Ngawang Lodrö Gyatso (1635–1688).[161] Before Ganden Sertri was the "Ganden Sertri" (i.e., the head of Ganden Monastery and the highest official position to which one can rise in the Geluk school), he served as abbot of the renowned Gomang College of Drepung Monastery.[162] His biographer, the Seventh Dalai Lama, describes his influential presence there as a teacher and the substantial changes he made to scholasticism at the college. In addition, Ganden Sertri also seems to have made a remarkable *administrative* change to the college:

> Formerly, the lama [T. *bla*; i.e. abbot] and general management office [T. *spyi*] did not exist separately [T. *so sor med pa*],[163] and thus there were no tea meals apart from those of the four major dharma sessions. For many—monks who had come from far away to study and so forth—this was very grueling. [Ganden Sertri] found this unbearable, and so consulted with the officers, teachers, and other decision-makers [of the college], whereupon they established additional "public goods" [T. *spyi pa'i dngos chas*] [and] established the custom of continuously providing two "monks' teas" [T. *gra ja*] in the mid-morning. Therefore, he is known as a most compassionate [contributor] to this college in terms of the two systems [i.e., spiritual and worldly].[164]

"Mass tea" (T. *mang ja*) is a common term that is still in use today. It refers to the distribution of tea (and often such food as bread or noodle stew) to *all of* the monastery's monks, including even certain high-status figures who are not present at assembly. Moreover, mass tea is generally donated by an individual, usually a lay patron. The meaning of "monastery tea" (T. *gra ja, grwa ja*), however, is less well understood. One informant suggests that it is given only to those monks actually present at the assembly.[165] It also appears to come from within the monastery itself rather than from an individual—a layperson, for example—outside the monastery. In other words, there is no immediate patron for the tea.[166] Instead, a monastery office, such as the General Management Office, would provide these meals from a fund it managed.[167]

Ganden Sertri's reform at Gomang College signifies a key turning point in the history of one of Tibet's foremost monastic institutions. Gomang College might have housed as many as 1,200 or 1,300 monks at the time Ganden Sertri implemented his reforms there.[168] To attract and sustain such a mass of monks, the availability of "monastery teas" and other sources of sustenance were essential. The Second Changkya, who ultimately followed Ganden Sertri to Beijing where he was introduced to the Kangxi Emperor, was no doubt influenced by Ganden Sertri's largess as well as by his administrative innovations, and this may have been the model for his reforms at Gönlung and elsewhere.

During Gönlung's ascendance, the administrative duties and powers of the General Management Office included helping to appoint the abbot, which, as we have seen, it did in consultation with the former abbots, the cantor and disciplinarians, the related "encampments" and hermitages, and the monastery's Elders.[169] It also regularly extended invitations to important lamas to visit Gönlung or to serve as its abbot. These responsibilities are significant insofar as they indicate that the General Management Office had certain executive powers in addition to its financial ones.[170] Nonetheless, the General Management Office's primary responsibilities were financial in nature.[171]

At Gönlung, the office was responsible for searching for patrons to cover the expenses of the Great Prayer Festival and all of the scholastic dharma sessions throughout the year. If the office failed to find such a patron, then fifty "ounces" (*srang*) of silver were to come from its coffers (the *spyi rdzas*, or "common wealth") to cover the year's expenses. Not having a dharma session was no excuse—if one were not held, then a suitable replacement was required of the office to ensure that the monks did not go without the provisions that such events usually entailed.[172] The General Management Office, moreover, was responsible for providing for or finding patrons for other major ritual occasions, such as the Twenty-fifth Offering commemorating the nirvana of Tsongkhapa (T. *lnga mchod*) and the commemoration ritual for the previous Gyelsé incarnations.[173] This requirement to track down patrons and goods for these occasions explains why the General Management Office was one of only two offices permitted to use pack animals (the other office was the abbot's palace).[174]

As was the case with the lama, the General Management Office was also entitled to vast amounts of income, which helped it to offset costs. The Gönlung constitution's section on the General Management Office begins, "With regard to the General Management Office, care must be taken that all donations given to those of the monk-class [T. *grwa rigs*] are given to the General Management Community." The constitution continues, "Whenever a great or minor lama is invited to this site, the monks of the General Management Office take turns receiving [his gifts] and offering as bountiful an offering as they can. . . . As for cash tips, bread, or whatever appears, [the General Management Office] gets three servings of each.[175] If there are helpers, they get one serving [each]."[176]

Such wealth came with great responsibility, however. At Gönlung, the General Management Office may have been responsible for overseeing all of the monastery's economic activity, including taxes and rents on land it owned, corvée labor, managing the products and reproduction of its herds, oil and grain mills, timber in the forests in controlled, bridge and ferry tolls, alms collections, moneylending, and taxes on merchants during fairs on monastery grounds.[177] At other Geluk monasteries, these responsibilities may have been divided among different "worldly" offices.[178]

As was the case at other Geluk monasteries,[179] the general managers (T. *spyi gnyer*) at Gönlung (there appear to have been two of them) were held to account for the monastery's wealth:

> Whoever is the manager responsible for the General Management Office's affairs must work for the benefit of the monastery on top of [properly] executing regular expenditures. Namely, he must give great attention to the building and refurbishing of [the monastery's] *sacra*, the shrine hall[180] and the General Management Building,[181] as well as the purchasing and repairs of ritual instruments and whatever is needed.

> When the lama and manager change, each must establish a visibly large endowment. As for the manager's living expenses, aside from

his food and drink, the common wealth should not be used. . . .
When changing the general manager, gifts are given to him based
on the greatness or smallness of his work.[182]

Thus it was that attempts were made to both centralize and systematize the
welfare of the hundreds and thousands of monks who congregated at expanding Geluk monasteries. This was to avoid the monastery's vast wealth
being squandered and to provide the financial support for the monastery's
ritual and scholastic programs.

This idea of a common wealth that is distinct from that of the monastery's lord or its abbot is one that the Gelukpa first promoted and, as such,
it became one of the vehicles for that school's success in Amdo and beyond.
Even a constitution for a Geluk hermitage for retreatants, one dating from
1727 in Amdo (no. 65), emphasizes the importance of safeguarding the common wealth: "The lama's wealth and the common wealth of the sangha must
be steadfastly valued and protected. The common wealth, however, except
for ordinary use, must not be used purposelessly by a few individuals. . . .
Should the common wealth and so forth be used by a few individuals through
force, and should some appear who engage in inappropriate acts such as fighting, then the lama and officers are to exact punishment."[183] Jamyang Zhepa
makes a similar point in his constitution for Labrang (no. 60): "Today," Jamyang Zhepa writes, "there is nothing apart from the general monastery fund
[T. *spyi ba*]. "[184] Transgressors must be "cut off at the roots."[185] In the same
way that there is a relative absence of formal salaries or allowances for monks
prior to the time of the Fifth Dalai Lama,[186] "*spyi so*," the General Management Office (or general fund or officer), is also absent from constitutions before the time of the Fifth Dalai Lama. There is one notable exception:
Tsongkhapa writes in his constitution for the Lhazhöl Hermitage (no. 5) that
"as soon as activities such as weighing and measuring [grains] are complete,
take [them] back to the place of the general fund [*spyi sa skor*]."[187] It is not
entirely clear *what* is to be taken back to the General Management Office—
probably either the scales used to measure the grains received or the grain
itself[188]—but the reference to the "place of the general fund" points to an
emphasis on the collectivization or centralization of resources. However,
Tsongkhapa does not elaborate on how this "general fund" might be struc-
tured or managed.

Likewise, absent from constitutions prior to the time of the Fifth Dalai
Lama are references to "monastery teas" (T. *grwa ja*). The closest analogue

might be the "regular teas" (T. *dus ja*) mentioned by the head of the Sakya school in the constitution for his personal temple (no. 31), although those are specifically said to "come from my hand," that is, from the Sakya hierarch himself.[189] Thus, this was not a depersonalized financial arrangement separate from the whims of the head of the monastery like a monastery tea is understood to be. Newly discovered sources may prove otherwise, but the conclusion that can be drawn from the available sources is that the Gelukpa systematically addressed the issue of how to finance a large-scale monastery by popularizing and promoting, if not inventing, new instruments of administration and finance.

## Epilogue: The Geluk Territorialization of the Tibetan Plateau

In this chapter, I have attempted to illustrate the myriad ways in which the Gelukpa made *the monastery* the foundation of their Buddhist enterprise. What that means is a *corporation*, an entity that has its own internal structure and integrity and can exist apart from, or at least not overly dependent on, any guru or lama or other powerful and charismatic individual. The Gelukpa saw the future of their school and of Buddhism as dependent on maintaining such institutions. This meant an emphasis on impartial offices and dispassionate individuals who could fill those offices and execute the prescribed norms and procedures. Codified in their monastic constitutions are the various, specialized offices and tasks needed to run such an institution. These offices had separate jurisdictions, including separate financial obligations and separately specified incomes.

Routines, including the redistribution of wealth, were standardized. Moreover, all of this was made transparent, or at least *more* transparent: the monastic constitutions were at least read by each new abbot and disciplinarian, and other officers may have had some working knowledge of the contents of the constitutions (the authors of many constitutions describe having consulted with the monasteries' officers and elders during or before the process of composing the constitutions).[190] In addition, the constitutions, or at least parts of them, were regularly read or sermonized on during the periodic disciplinary sermons (T. *tshogs gtam*) that took place throughout the year. Likewise, we have seen how the schedule of the special *Namshak* redistributions was required knowledge of all monks at Gönlung Monastery.

These administrative techniques and organizational strategies were found in Geluk monasteries across the Tibetan Plateau and beyond. In fact, it is perhaps no coincidence that the "general management office" or "general funds" (T. *spyi sa*) of Geluk monasteries were first studied by Western scholars at Mongol monasteries.[191] On the frontier between the major centers of wealth and power (i.e., between Lhasa and Beijing), the Gelukpa may have seen more of a need and more opportunity for such innovations. Robert Miller, writing about the "general funds" of Mongol monasteries, once wrote, "The *jisa* [T. *spyi sa*] serves still another purpose, an even more important one, namely, that of preserving the Sangha, of enabling it to survive periods of economic scarcity or loss of lay support."[192]

This chapter has focused almost exclusively on the internal administration of Geluk monasteries. What has not been discussed, except in passing,[193] is the role of laity. Together with the abbot and the General Management Office, lay patrons made up the triumvirate responsible for financing Gönlung and many other Geluk monasteries.[194] Far less is said in monastic constitutions about the laity, however. Usually, the behavior of laity is governed by the monastery only when they are on monastery grounds.[195] In general, the laity matter because the sangha has to look good in their eyes and because the monastery must maintain a harmonious relationship with the surrounding laity and other potential patrons. As one Geluk constitution puts it (no. 56), "Given that this monastery was newly established as the field for receiving offerings for all [T. *spyi*] in this region, the officers[196] must be universally upright, not succumbing to one's personal favorites or partiality."[197] Or, as Ter Ellingson observed long ago,

> The principle underlying such requirements [of aesthetics in religious practice] is that the life of the monastic community should embody a *spyod-lam mdzes-pa*, or "beautiful path of practice," a concept cited in *bca'-yig* for at least five hundred years . . . , and shared with Buddhist Vinaya traditions in other countries (for example from Thai Theravāda Buddhism . . .). It provides an unusual and potentially instructive example of one way in which a soteriological concept (the religious community as an object of refuge and field of merit) can give rise to a normative concept ("beautiful" practice as a source of religious inspiration), which in turn generates a set of specific laws governing many practical aspects of daily life in the monastic community.[198]

Jansen, too, discusses well the importance of the laity and the concern expressed in monastic constitutions for maintaining a good relationship with the laity.[199]

As a sort of epilogue to this chapter and segue into the next, I would like to describe another way in which Gelukpa expressed their overriding preoccupation with the laity; namely, their desire to maintain a *clear distinction* between laity and monastics. Although this relates to some of the subject matter found in this chapter—that is, the Gelukpa's recourse to administrative measures and legal authority in building and maintaining the integrity of the monastery as an entity—it also relates to the following chapter, in which I discuss how Geluk hierarchs strove to *fix monastic practices in place.*

Buddhism, as it is universally understood, is a three-legged stool, one leg being the sangha or monastic community. The sangha, to have definition, must have rules that draw it in (i.e., give it form) and separate it from everything else. The sequence of provisions that pertain to lay-cleric relations in Jikmé Yeshé Drakpa's constitution for Gönlung are quite revealing: rules requiring that proper attire be worn when outside the monastery, prohibiting the raising of large numbers of livestock, prohibiting the unseemly drying of grass on roofs, and prohibiting yelling and arguing within the monastery are followed by instructions regarding how to calmly and properly file into and out of the assembly hall for services. As one constitution (a Nyingma constitution clearly influenced by the constitutions of the Fifth Dalai Lama) puts it, "As it is said, 'committing acts that cause faithlessness in the world, / And asking, "did [someone] see?" This should be abandoned.' If renouncers cannot do this, who will do it?"[200] In short, such rules that help to distinguish and uphold a positive image of the sangha help to guarantee that monks and monasteries will continue to be the recipient of donors' generosity. This concern, as Jansen has clearly shown, is one that can be traced back to the Vinayic concern over annoying laity and causing them to lose faith and thus desist from their donations.[201] Much of what is found in Geluk constitutions concerning laity, then, is typical of all constitutions and all schools of Tibetan Buddhism. What the Gelukpa have done differently is to *embed in their legislation an even greater concern for controlling the boundaries* between the monastic world and the lay one. This is because a large-scale monastery with hundreds or thousands of monks had a lot more to lose if order was not maintained and because greater devastation could be inflicted on the neighboring countryside by such a large congregation of men.

In his constitution for Gönlung, Jikmé Yeshé Drakpa goes to great lengths to spell out the boundaries of the monastery. Earlier constitutions, beginning with Tsongkhapa's constitution for retreatants at his favorite hermitage of Lhazhöl (no. 5) as well as his disciple Lodrö Gyeltsen's constitution (no. 6) give a great deal of attention to the importance of maintaining the monastery's "*tsam*" (T. *mtshams*), the sacrosanct boundary of practitioners in retreat. The term comes from the Vinaya (S. *sīmā*) to refer to the boundary within which official, sanctioned business of the sangha can take place.[202] Other constitutions make passing reference to the "*tō*" (T. *tho*), the markers that indicate a monastery's or a hermitage's boundary. In the Gönlung constitution and other related historical materials, one finds reference to a "*naktō*" (T. *nag tho*),[203] which could be interpreted as "woman [lit. black] marker" (as in "*nag mo'i tho*"), although the boundary it marks does more than just keep women out.[204] It keeps others, such as merchants, out; it keeps monks in; and, should individuals on one side pass onto the other, then their behavior and dress were to be different, too.

The constitution by Özer Gyatso for a monastery in Amdo (no. 24) refers to such boundary markers by various names. After warning against participating in village rituals alongside lay *mantrins*, he writes, "As for the limits of the monastery, whatever marker one has—royal marker [T. *rgyal tho*], horn marker [T. *ru tho*], beggar marker [T. *sprang tho*], wheat marker [T. *gro tho*]—must be definitively made. If they are not maintained there is punishment. All must remember this without fail."[205] Jikmé Yeshé Drakpa goes even further than this in his constitution for Gönlung, spelling out the precise boundaries of the monastery with reference to nearby natural and manmade features:[206] "The livestock of the Monguor (Hor) nomads are not allowed on [the monastery's] restricted pastures be it winter, spring, summer, or fall, from the Chugo Kari [lit. White Mountain with the Head of the River] [and] the Khekya Shortcut,[207] down to the Khoré Ridge, Kyerkhé and Lake Mountain,[208] Putung Letsé,[209] and within the Muṇi Ridge."[210] Jikmé Yeshé Drakpa also specifies the consequences for anyone caught herding or collecting wood on monastery lands: "Other than wolves, no other animals such as wild herbivores are to be harmed. Villagers are not to take grass or wood from the restricted pastures. Whether someone from the monastery or a villager, if one steals from the forest on the sunny and shady side of Tsher Valley or the forest of Front Mountain then, if a monk, one hundred prostrations, if a layperson, a mass tea and so forth are exacted as punishment."[211] In addition, business and conflicts arising within the monastery and those arising in the neighboring villages are to remain separate and distinct:

> If someone encroaches on [the monastery's] land or something like this, then a strict punishment is by all means to be met out with all of one's ability. If one is a monk from here [prone to getting involved in extra-monastic affairs] and a villager were to kill someone close to him, including even his parents or siblings, and then he does some sort of violent action [in retaliation], then he is not to enter [i.e., reside at] the monastery. No matter what sort of lawsuit arises in the villages, not even *verbal* abuse should be directed toward the monks here. If they are, a thorough investigation must be strictly carried out. Except for the genuine rights of a resident [monk] of this monastery, one must never abuse their power and engage in illicit sales, vie for and plunder possessions, or do other such acts.[212]

The attempt to specify in its legislation as well as in contracts with locals the specific boundaries of the monastery's land and its rights to that land signals the Gelukpa's understanding of the power of the written word and legal institutions. This is as much a reflection of the Gelukpa's own tendencies toward bureaucratization as it is an acknowledgment of the other legal orders operating within the Tibetan cultural sphere. Jikmé Yeshé Drakpa (constitution no. 66) speaks of these orders when describing how to deal with particularly heinous crimes, such as fomenting fighting and factionalism within the monastery: "Certainly [they] may be handed over to the Chinese and Oirat authorities[213] for sentences of corporal and capital punishment."[214]

Such efforts to use the written word and legal system to protect the "genuine rights" of a monastery were not, moreover, abstract speculations on the part of authors such as Jikmé Yeshé Drakpa. Wes Chaney's 2016 dissertation colorfully illustrates how, in the 1820s, one of Gönlung's subsidiary monasteries laid exclusive claim to the forest of a nearby mountain. Local subjects of the nearby Monguor headman (Ch. *tusi* 土司) sought to contest this claim. Having formed a posse of nineteen angry villagers, the ringleader later testified about what happened next: "If we ran into the monastery's monks trying to stop us we would all beat them—let them know fear, so they would not try to stop us again."[215] Deaths ensued, guilty verdicts were handed down by Qing officials, and the mountain in question

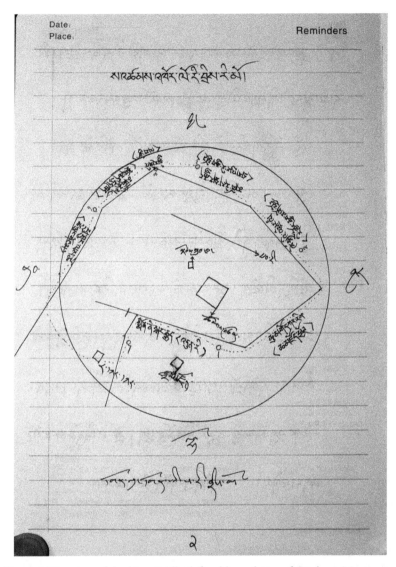

Figure 8. Drawing of the historically defined boundaries of Gönlung Monastery.
North is at the top of the drawing. In the east, the two lines that appear at right
angles to each other are the Khekya Shortcut (to the north) and Chugo Kari (to
the south), which are visible in Figure 9.
Drawing by Mönlam Gyatso, March 2011.

Figure 9. Facing east, this photo shows the Gyelsé Hermitage that is above (and part of) Gönlung Monastery, approximately two kilometers east-northeast from Gönlung. The Khekya Shortcut is located on the backside of the ridge on the left; the ridge descends to the mountain pass and rock cairn (T. *la rtse*) behind Gönlung. The ridge on the right is Chugo Kari.
Photo by the author, July 2016.

was opened for "communal logging" to all the parties in question (i.e., to the monastery, to its Tibetan lay supporters, *and* to the subjects of the local Monguor headman).

Such disputes over land only increased as the eighteenth and nineteenth centuries proceeded, and mass emigration ensued.[216] Geluk monasteries in the region adapted to this changing environment not just through using brute force, on which it certainly had no monopoly, but by mastering and exploiting its own bureaucratic and legalistic networks and those of the Qing empire.[217] We might refer to this as the Geluk *territorialization* of the Tibetan Plateau. That is, Geluk lamas made use of land deeds, the Qing courts, and boundary-making to legitimize and reinforce privileged access to resources.[218]

In the next chapter, we shall look at other ways in which the Geluk mega monastery "took shape." Similar to the way that boundaries were drawn around the monastery and its property to protect its interests, within the monastery new structures called "colleges" (T. *grwa tshang*) became the primary places for socializing, training, and feeding its many monks. In particular, tantra, the collection of esoteric teachings and practices transmitted from guru to disciple, were given a new institutional home in the service of the monastery and the Geluk school, the "tantric college" (T. *rgyud pa grwa tshang*).

# Chapter 3

# Institutionalizing Tantra

In a constitution he penned for three of his satellite monasteries, Sumpa Khenpo Yeshé Peljor (1704–1788) bemoaned the handicaps of monastic practice in peripheral lands:

> As for the regular liturgy, the philosophical monasteries and colleges [T. *grwa tshang*] of Central Tibet take the sutra side of things as most important. To this end they never go beyond the practice of "Sitātapatra,"[1] the "Praises of Tārā,"[2] and the generation stage of the Lion-faced One.[3] Otherwise, they do not recite anything from the mantra side. They recite liturgical collections of praises, aspiration prayers, the *Entrance* [*to Madhyamaka*], and the *Ornament* [*of Realization*], and take the study of the five scriptures as the foundation.
>
> The philosophical colleges [T. *mtshad nyid grwa tshang*] of Amdo, Kham, China, and Mongolia, in order to have the combination of sutra and mantra practice, must also recite esoteric rituals. Because of this, if they have the [exoteric] collections of prayers, numerous great exoteric and esoteric rituals, and a great deal of restoration rituals, the study of philosophy is inhibited.[4]

Sumpa Khenpo is drawing attention to the Geluk school's need for *separate places that specialize in one or another facet of Buddhist practice, specifically the study of doctrine and the practice of tantric rituals*. While the major monasteries in Central Tibet could afford to do this, the more peripheral monasteries were compelled to conflate the two kinds of institutions. One gathers from the above passage that Sumpa Khenpo was most concerned with ensuring separate places for the study of Buddhist doctrine ("philosophy"). What is also implied, however, is that tantra ("the mantra side") was programmatically dealt with in Central Tibet by separate institutions, which is something that also has great benefits.

Tsongkhapa, the founder of the Geluk school, is said to have bequeathed to Tokden Jampel Gyatso (1356–1428)[5] the "Great Miraculous Scripture,"[6] a secret and invisible book given by the bodhisattva Mañjuśrī exclusively to Tsongkhapa and which is said to contain all the most quintessential teachings of both the sutras and the tantras.[7] This transmission was the first[8] in an exclusive lineage of Buddhist masters who make up what is called the Ganden (or Geluk) Oral Lineage.[9] This lineage was so exclusive that only one or two major master-to-disciple streams are recognized within the lineage.[10]

Such exclusivity and wrangling over who should be considered the legitimate heir and successor to an important master has a long tradition in Tibet.[11] Tibetan literature is replete with expressions like "heart son"[12] and "filling a vase [i.e., a disciple] to the brim [with teachings],"[13] expressions that emphasize a unique relationship between a master and disciple. A unique development in the religious history of Tibet was the establishment of institutions for the formalized study, practice, and performance of ritual (as well as scholastic) traditions. These were centers for efficiently training whole cadres of monks knowledgeable in the unique tantric traditions of those places. The story of the Geluk school's rise to power and the concomitant rise of mega monasteries is also one about institutionalizing, making public, and exporting those traditions unique to the school and its monasteries. The transmission of powerful, esoteric knowledge was no longer just between a master and his select disciple(s) but between monastery and student and between monastery and monastery.

## Monastic Groups (T. *dratsang*) and Commentary Classes (T. *shedra*)

The 1644 *History of Amdo* tells us that "the Collection Leader of Drati, Sherap Drak,[14] invited [Gyelsé Dönyö Chökyi Gyatso], and he came to Pari. In 1604, he founded Gönlung Monastery and established a new monastic group [for the study of philosophy, a *grwa tshang*]. He established the customs of a practice group [T. *sgrub sde*] at the Fortress of the Hidden White Land."[15] Thus, from the very beginning of Gönlung's history, the monastery had specialized groups focused on the study of philosophy and meditation, respectively, or so it seems. The actual form of these groups is a little unclear. At first, Gönlung is said to have comprised only a main shrine hall,[16] the quarters of the founder, Gyelsé, and small huts for a hundred or so monks.[17] A short time later, the Collection Leader of Setsa—one of the original patrons of the monastery—built an assembly hall, the kind of structure that, nowadays, is most associated with the practice of scholasticism and debate in Geluk monasteries. It was expanded a few years later to accommodate the growing number of monks.

The "practice group" was situated two or three kilometers up the valley at the Fortress of the Hidden White Land,[18] which was also known as Jangchup Ling[19] or just "The Gönlung Hermitage."[20] Although this hermitage was obviously tied to Gönlung proper—later, it would serve as center of the monastery's Medicine Buddha Ritual—there is no indication that it carried out the functions of a so-called tantric college (T. *rgyud pa grwa tshang, sngags pa grwa tshang*) that nowadays one finds as an integral component of all major Geluk monasteries. When an important Central Tibetan lama was sought out by the monks of Gönlung in the 1630s, they comprised "meditators"[21] from the Gönlung Hermitage and numerous "great lamas" from Gönlung's "philosophical commentary school" (T. *mtshad nyid kyi bshad grwa*). To the former, this lama gave "meditative instructions"[22] and to the latter he gave empowerments, ritual transmissions, and permission-blessings (i.e., tantric ritual authorizations).[23] The hermitage, it would seem, was just that—a secluded place where hermits could individually focus on meditative practices. We do not find mention of the regular performance of institution-wide rituals performed for the monastery's patron deities or its protector deities. Also noticeably absent from this lama's interaction with the Gönlung monks is any mention of debate or "recitation lessons," those features of Geluk philosophical colleges (T. *mtshan nyid grwa tshang*) most conspicuous today.

These scholastic practices (i.e., debate, recitation lessons, curriculums, formalized exams) cohered into an integrated system within a monastery and came to be housed within a "philosophical college" only later in the seventeenth century. Likewise, the formation of "tantric colleges" dedicated to the study and performance of monastery-specific rituals probably occurred around the same time. At Gönlung, it was not until 1710 that a formal "tantric college" was established.

Part of the confusion that surrounds the history of these institutions stems from our rendering of Tibetan terms into English. "*Dratsang*" (T. *grwa tshang*) is usually translated as "college," as in Oxford University's Exeter

College. This conjures up notions of a relatively independent institution complete with housing, a refectory, chapels, and so forth. It seems, however, that the sixteenth-century use of the term referred more simply to a "group of monks" who followed specific teachers. For instance, the 1529 history of the "Old and New Kadampa" (i.e., the Kadampa and the Gelukpa) uses "*dratsang*" in referring to the "monastic groups of philosophical studies" (T. *mtshad nyid grwa tshang*) at Ganden Monastery. These four groups are named after the teachers who either founded or maintained lineages of teachings.[24] These later merged and became the well-known *dratsang* of Jangtsé[25] and Shartsé.[26] During this time, when the *dratsang* of Ganden Monastery were in flux and still forming, they were not so much identified with particular places as they were with particular traditions of teachings.[27]

This semi-uprooted nature of *dratsang* at that time may be the result of their relative independence from local patrons and clans. Sangpu Monastery,[28] for instance, was not sponsored or owned by any single patron, which may have given the monastery the flexibility needed to navigate the social and political turmoil of the fifteenth and sixteenth centuries.[29] Similarly, when Tsongkhapa's disciple Khedrup had a disagreement with a patron in Gyantsé[30] over the settlement of several *dratsang*, he could simply depart for a hermitage, where he freed himself to work on his compositions.[31]

This is not to say that there were *no* fixed abodes for the *dratsang* of the fifteenth and sixteenth centuries. In the *History of the Kadam Dharma* from 1494,[32] we read of "six philosophical *dratsang* and one mantrin *dratsang*"[33] connected with the Drepung Seat[34] at the time of the founder's death. When the Drepung founder passed away, his disciples inherited the leadership posts of these groups.[35] However, there is no indication that these *dratsang* offered anything resembling a regular system of practice. Drepung itself had "teaching halls,"[36] but there is no indication that the *dratsang* themselves had such an infrastructure.

Occasionally, the early heads of these *dratsang* would establish "commentary classes" or "commentary schools," called *shedra* in Tibetan,[37] which incidentally is the same term found in one of the earliest epithets of Gönlung: "the chief of all the *shedra* in Domé."[38] These may have been like the *shedra* of non-Geluk monasteries in more recent centuries that consisted of short-term and irregular study sessions.[39] A *dratsang* would have such classes if a qualified teacher were able to establish and maintain them. This is a far cry from the fully formed curriculum of later "philosophical colleges," a curriculum that includes upward of ten hours of debate practice each day.

The name given to these early scholastic communities—"commentarial schools"—also suggests a different study method than the one that ultimately becomes standard. Georges Dreyfus writes,

> In describing the monastery of Gaden, the text [i.e., the same, aforementioned 1494 *History of the Kadam Dharma*] makes it clear that it was not originally founded by Tsong Khapa as a scholastic center but that it was only transformed into one by [his disciple] Kaydrub. The text then adds that Kaydrub "established a philosophical commentarial school at Gaden" (*dga' ldan du mtshan nyid ki bshad grwa btsugs*).
>
> This description of Gaden as a commentarial school is quite revealing, for it shows that there was no division at that time between commentarial and debating institutions. An institution such as Gaden did not understand itself to be very different from other scholastic institutions, despite its allegiance to Tsong Khapa. Even in the second half of the fifteenth century, there was a fluid and informal scholastic tradition present in various monasteries where monks would come to study particular texts with teachers who were renowned for their mastery of these texts.[40]

In other words, there was not the emphasis on debate as compared with Geluk monasteries today, hence the name "commentary schools."

Thus, what we have at Gönlung in the early seventeenth century, a *shedra*, was likely more akin to these early Central Tibetan *shedra* than to the "philosophical colleges" of later times. By the mid-seventeenth century, however, *debate* at Gönlung's neighbor, Kumbum Monastery, inspired one monk to go on to become a philosopher of the highest standing.[41] Likewise, near the end of the seventeenth century at Gönlung, the Second Changkya gave formal "recitation lessons" (T. *brtsi bzhag*) to the monks there during the "winter dharma session." Thus, by century's end, scholastic training at Gönlung was fully institutionalized. But what of its tantric practices?

## Tantric Colleges

The "practice group" established early on at Gönlung does not appear to be similar in any way to the institutionalized systems of tantric practice epitomized by the "tantric college" or "mantrin college" of later times. During the first half century of Gönlung's existence, there existed a contingent of monks thirsty for meditative experiences and spiritual accomplishments. This phenomenon is perhaps best exemplified by the Great Adept of Denma, to whom we shall turn momentarily. Despite claims to the contrary, tantric colleges appear to be a rather late development. Dreyfus writes that the tantric college of Drepung Monastery dates back to the monastery's founding in 1416.[42] "Hence," he writes "contrary to the other colleges, which were created later, the Tantric Monastic College [T. *sngags khang*] was part of the original plan, though it may at first not have been conceived as a separate college."[43]

Kün'ga Gyeltsen's 1492 history does indeed make reference to Drepung's "mantrin college" [T. *sngags pa'i grwa tshang*].[44] However, the points I made above regarding the danger of translating "*dratsang*" as "college" apply equally well here. Again, "mantrin monastic group" is probably a more fitting translation (and a more literal one). There is no indication that the earliest mantrin of Drepung had anything like the rich, ritual calendar found at today's tantric colleges, nor do we know whether it had any infrastructure or formalized classes. Moreover, it is not clear that it existed *for* the monastery or that it was tightly integrated into a greater monastic program or system. Instead, it is likely that Drepung's mantrin college was like its philosophical ones. That is, the monks there would have focused on studying and practicing the texts and teachings that a particular teacher thought important.

The Lower Tantric College in Lhasa, founded by Sherap Sengé[45] in 1433, may have had more structure to it. It is said that he "established the exegesis of the [*Four-Part*] *Commentary on the* [*Guhyasamāja*] *Tantra* during the summer retreat[46] and, in the autumn, direct instructions on the Five Stages [of Guhyasamāja],[47] instructions on the Six Limbs of Practice,[48] instructions on the Six Yogas of Nāropa, instructions on [the traditions of] Lūipa and Gaṇṭāpa,[49] and instructions on the tutelary deities."[50] However, even this calendar of teachings appears to have largely depended on the presence of Sherap Sengé and not a system carried on by his successors. More important, there is no indication that these tantric traditions were actually practiced or performed within a formalized framework like that of tantric colleges today.

If one is looking for models in Central Tibet for the pattern that emerges across Tibet and Mongolia, Sera Monastery's tantric college may be the best example. As José Cabezón has written, the tantric college at Sera is the youngest of Sera's three *dratsang*, being founded in the early eighteenth century as the "personal ritual college" of the Oirat ruler of Tibet, Lhazang Khan.[51] This temple was established with the explicit purpose of performing protective rites on behalf of the ruler. The establishment of Gönlung's tantric college in 1710 had the support of none other than the Qing emperor, although it is not clear whether the institution performed prayers on his behalf. In any case, both were created as *institutions explicitly dedicated to the regular practice of tantric ritual*, and so they represent the mature formation of the Geluk tendency toward standardization and specialization.

## The Sé and Wensa Secret Lineages

The ritual practices that came to be enshrined in Gönlung's tantric college had a long history of a thoroughly *non*institutionalized transmission before they ever wound their way to Gönlung. In addition to a panoply of practices said to be modeled on the Lower Tantric College in Lhasa, two tantric traditions in particular make up the practices of Gönlung's tantric college: Sé (T. Srad) and Wensa (T. Dben sa). These tantric traditions are the two major Geluk Oral or Mouth-to-Ear traditions,[52] meaning that their most esoteric and complete instructions are not written down and often are transmitted only to a single disciple.[53]

Both of these traditions are said to stretch back to the founder of the Geluk sect, Tsongkhapa. The teachings of the Sé tradition are said to consist of the tantric generation and completion stages of the deity Guhyasamāja. It is named after the region in Tsang (western Central Tibet) where Sherap Sengé (the same one who later founded the Lower Tantric College in Lhasa) established a monastic community focused on the study of Tsongkhapa's *Four-Part Commentary on Guhyasamāja*.[54] Sherap Sengé had been among those present when Tsongkhapa asked if anyone was fit to master his commentary. The question was posed two or three times with no reply, at which point Sherap Sengé held up his hand and volunteered. Later, remembering a vow he had made to Tsongkhapa to propagate the tantric teachings, he went to Sé and established a *shedra* there.[55] This became known as the Sé tantric tradition or the "Tsang tradition."[56]

The Sé tradition found its way to Gönlung through the Second Changkya and his disciple the First Jamyang Zhepa. Both received initiation into the Sé tradition in Tsang from Könchok Yarpel (b. 1602),[57] whom Changkya

calls the "The Preceptor of the Sé Lineage, the All-Pervasive Lord, Unshake-
able Vajra, He Who Reveals Himself Gloriously in the Form of the Vajra
Preceptor."[58] Apparently, Könchok Yarpel had not found a suitable disciple
to whom he was willing to transmit these teachings until Jamyang Zhepa
visited him in 1681 and Chankgya did so in 1682.[59] As founder of the Gönlung's tantric college, it is Jamyang Zhepa who is credited with introducing
its teachings at Gönlung.

The Wensa tradition has a more sublime origin. Tsongkhapa is said to
have received it directly from the bodhisattva Mañjuśrī via revelation. This,
anyway, is the "short lineage."[60] The "long lineage" includes a whole host of
legendary and historical figures who are said to have preceeded Tsongkhapa
in the transmission.[61] The most important teaching in this tradition consists of Geluk Mahāmudrā practices, which entail a specialized *guru yoga* and
advanced tantric techniques centered on the three deities of Guhyasamāja,
Cakrasaṃvara, and Vajrabhairava.[62] The tradition was transmitted through
oral teachings, through divine revelation, and sometimes through the transmission of the "Great Miraculous Scripture," as was the case when Tsongkhapa gave the teachings to Tokden Jampel Gyatso. The Miraculous Scripture
is said to be invisible and of the nature of light, and, according to one tradition, its last recipient was the Paṇchen Lama Lozang Chökyi Gyeltsen (1567–
1662), who returned it to the patron deities of the Geluk school for
safekeeping.[63] The Paṇchen Lama is said to have transmitted the tradition
(though not the Miraculous Scripture) to two of his major disciples, Druchen
Gendün Gyeltsen[64] and Lozang Tsöndrü Gyeltsen,[65] and from that point the
tradition continued in two streams until the twentieth century when they
were once again united.[66]

That, at least, is one idealized portrait of this lineage that survives today.
The Wensa tradition arrived at Gönlung by means of the Second Changkya.
In 1674, Changkya traveled to Tsang and met the young Paṇchen Lama (i.e.,
the Fifth). From the Fourth Paṇchen Lama's disciple Drungwa Rinpoché
Lozang Gyeltsen (1567–1650)[67] (i.e., most likely the aforementioned disciple
Lozang Tsöndrü Gyeltsen) he received a collection of writings comprising
the "uncommon"[68] instructions on the Path and the View of the Wensa tradition.[69] The Seventh Dalai Lama further notes how Changkya passed these
teachings on to his own master, the Ganden Sertri Ngawang Lodrö Gyatso
(see Chapter 2), who in turn passed them on to "numerous, fortunate disciples."[70] Jamyang Zhepa, too, is said to have received directly and indirectly
teachings of the Wensa Tradition from Changkya:

In the biography of the former Omniscient One [i.e., Jamyang Zhepa], it says: "In Jukgo Tsel[71] and in Lhodruk Ralungpa[72] the Sixty Great Ritual Cake Offering to [the deity] Bhairava:[73] from the feet of the Veritable Varja-holder Lodrö Gyatso [i.e., Ganden Sertri] and the *heruka* incarnation of the Supreme Changkya, Lozang Chöden, the master himself received all the Foremost Instructions [T. *man ngag*] on drawing the maṇḍala, the liturgical singing, the drumming pattern, both the sky- and earth-maṇḍalas,[74] and the [making of] *tsampa* effigies[75] and paper effigies." Thus, [one can see that] from this point in time the Lord Jamyang Zhepa was the lord [T. *bdag po*] of the Foremost Instructions of the Sé Oral Tradition and [Changkya] was that of Wensa Tradition.[76]

Note that the Foremost Instructions also include recipes for constructing ritual cakes and practicing the material arts in addition to offering the more abstract teachings on "correct view" and so forth.

Jamyang Zhepa and Changkya were now happily laden with new tantric teachings, teachings that had compelled previous lineage holders to flee from society and monasteries to undertake serious spiritual practice in remote places.[77] As such, these two along with another lineage holder[78] all decided to go to a completely isolated spot somewhere between Tibet and Nepal to practice. The three presented their plan to another one of the Paṇchen Lama's disciples,[79] who ridiculed them: "Are you going to throw away the teachings of the Victor Tsongkhapa? Are you able to independently go your own way? This is not fitting for great scholars who desire to maintain the correct [philosophical] viewpoint such as yourselves."[80] They thus abandoned their flighty dreams and instead became organization men (at the Amdo monasteries of Gönlung, Labrang, and Yershong,[81] respectively).

We shall look momentarily at how these arcane and exclusive traditions came to be institutionalized and accessible to all. First, however, I want to introduce one final layer related to the Wensa tradition. As we have seen, the Paṇchen Lama Lozang Chökyi Gyeltsen is said to have transmitted the Wensa tradition to only one[82] or two disciples, and he may have returned the Miraculous Scripture to the Geluk school's patron deities. However, other sources indicate that the Great Adept from Denma Tsültrim Gyatso (1578–1663/65), a most influential figure from Pari, also received *both* the Wensa tradition and the related Miraculous Scripture from the Paṇchen Lama.[83]

Denma was the principal teacher to a number of important lamas in Amdo, including the Great Adept of Rongwo Kelden Gyatso (1607–1677, also known as Shar Kelden Gyatso, the author of the 1652 *A mdo'i chos 'byung*),[84] and the Great Adept of Meditative Pacification Gendün Zangpo,[85] the founder of an important branch monastery of Gönlung.[86] Later in his career, he served as abbot of Gönlung, and he founded both Chöten Tang[87] and Kenchen Monasteries,[88] important branches of Gönlung. Most of his life, however, was dedicated to the pursuit of scholastic and, especially, contemplative instruction. Kelden Gyatso writes that "nowadays, here in this land of Amdo there are many who engage in spiritual practice.[89] However, among them are the sun and moon: the Dharma King Without Peer Lozang Tenpé Gyeltsen (1581–1659)[90] and the Dharma King Ascetic of Gönlung Denma Tsültrim Gyatso."[91]

While in Central Tibet, Denma studied philosophy at some of the most respected monastic centers and earned acclaim when he was selected to participate in the newly established "academic circuit" debates of the Great Prayer Festival in Lhasa. He is said to have arisen as "the debater without peer."[92] However, as his epithet suggests, he was equally accomplished in the realm of spiritual attainment. Most of Denma's contemplative training and practice took place in western Central Tibet (Tsang), where Denma took on the appearance and habits of a Kagyü "madman."[93] There, according to one later tradition, Denma became one of the "four heart-sons" of the Paṇchen Lama.[94] Once, while he was visiting the Paṇchen Lama, one of the Paṇchen Lama's disciples[95] asked the Paṇchen lama about and received instructions on the Ganden Mahāmudrā; that is, the Wensa Oral Tradition. Denma heard about this and went to inquire. The Paṇchen then gave him transmission of "the root text and commentary of the Mahāmudrā."[96] Denma also expressed his wish to learn the actual practices of this tradition, to which the Paṇchen responded, "You don't have a need for this. There is nothing here that surpasses the view of the Middle Way [i.e., Madhyamaka]."[97] Later, however, the Paṇchen Lama is said to have placed the Miraculous Scripture on Denma's head, thereby blessing him and consummating the transmission of the tradition.[98]

We have seen that Gönlung's most important tantric practices originated in Tsang, west of Lhasa and the center of Geluk power in Central Tibet. In addition, many of the early, powerful abbots and lamas associated with Gönlung had strong ties to the Paṇchen Lama and Tsang, and on occasion they even had trouble getting along with the Dalai Lama's establishment in

Lhasa.[99] This bespeaks both the great influence of the Paṇchen Lama[100] and the social and political turmoil of Central Tibet in the early seventeenth century. Whatever the cause may have been, the Geluk tantric traditions, such as the Sé and Wensa traditions, were not the uncontested, supreme practices of seventeenth-century Tsang. There were numerous other traditions, particularly Kagyü ones, that competed with these Geluk traditions. Thus, when Denma later spoke of the "short lineage" of the Wensa tradition (i.e., the lineage that originated with the Buddha, Mañjuśrī, and Tsongkhapa), some people expressed skepticism: How could a genuine lineage not have human forebears? To this, Denma had a witty reply: "The origin of [this] dharma is Tsongkhapa, Mañjuśrī, and Vajradhāra. In contrast, those who find purer [those teachings] whose origin is in the earth, rocks, or cliffs are merely parochial."[101]

The reference to those who dig their teachings out of the earth, rocks, and so on, is a not-so-veiled criticism of Nyingmapas and others who made use of "hidden treasures,"[102] religious teachings embedded in physical objects (as well as the minds of certain individuals) and revealed at a later time. On another occasion, Denma taught a certain Kagyüpa, whose body was depleted from his own spiritual practice, the methods for retaining the proper tantric visualizations. The Kagyüpa exclaimed, "I did not know that the Geluk [school] had spiritual advice of this sort!" He and others like him were thus converted to the Geluk school.[103]

These are important examples of Geluk luminaries who competed in the arena of tantra and spiritual accomplishment against those of other traditions. However, as far as the hierarchs of the later Geluk school was concerned, these exploits were best kept in the past as sources of inspiration. There is a tension that exists between such stories and later attempts to institutionalize monastic practice, including tantra. Despite Denma's tantric exploits, there is no indication that he was part of any coordinated effort to institutionalize the practices back at Gönlung. He gave "direct instructions" on meditation to numerous disciples, who went on to have great meditative achievements. However, their histories are basically unknown. At one point, Denma was driven away from Gönlung by gossip and slander, after which he founded the nearby monastery of Chöten Tang. However, he did not wish to lead that congregation for long, so he bequeathed the institution to another lama,[104] traveled a short distance to the northwest, and established Kenchen Monastery.[105] There he enshrined the skull of Gönlung's founder, Gyelsé, which he had acquired while in Central Tibet. It seems that Denma was not an "organization man" after all, preferring to retire in more remote places, unfettered by the prattle of mega monasteries.

## Gönlung's Tantric College

In 1710, the Second Changkya and the First Jamyang Zhepa, master and disciple, established a Tantric College (T. *rgyud grwa*) at Gönlung.[106] This coincided with Changkya's final visit to the monastery in 1710. As the biography (and, in less detail, the autobiography) of Changkya explains, the First Jamyang Zhepa, Ngawang Tsöndrü (1648–1721),[107] had previously told Chankgya that "at Gönlung there is [already] a source for the development of the teaching of sutra. You should establish one for the teaching of mantra." Changkya then sent Jamyang Zhepa a letter explaining that he wished to do just that. Changkya, however, was unable to do it himself because of other commitments, so he sent a messenger to invite Jamyang Zhepa to Gönlung to build the tantric college.

Jamyang Zhepa apparently reserved doubts concerning the seriousness of the plan; he said to the messenger, "If you all can build the tantric college, then I will go. If you [cannot] build it, then I do not have time." Jamyang Zhepa was in fact busy with the construction of his own, new monastery of Labrang. The messenger, thinking of the uniqueness of the connection and the serendipity of the moment, replied, "If your lordship were to go, then the tantric college will be built." Jamyang Zhepa was pleased and acquiesced. They met up at Gönlung, where Changkya ordered him to establish the college, which he accepted.[108]

Changkya and others at Gönlung requested Jamyang Zhepa to give the scriptural transmission and exegesis of Tsongkhapa's *Four-Part Commentary on Guhyasamāja*[109] as well as a black protection cord of the Sé lineage Vajraholder to the abbot (i.e., Tuken III), the former abbot (the Second Denma Ngawang Tendzin Trinlé, 1666–1723),[110] and other elders at the monastery. The Second Denma was appointed as the head of the tantric college, and the *Kachen* scholar Lodrö Gyatso[111] was made its lama-cantor (ritual head).[112]

Clearly there exists in this account some continuity with past lore and lines of transmission. The exegesis of Tsongkhapa's *Four-Part Commentary*, which becomes a part of the annual curriculum of Gönlung's tantric college, indicates that the tantric college was seen as embodying the traditions initiated by Tsongkhapa's disciple Sherap Sengé and transmitted from individual to individual up to Könchok Yarpel and, through him, to Jamyang Zhepa and the Second Changkya. But then we see an interesting and ironic twist: the transmission and exegesis of the tantric scripture and the protection cord of the holder of the Sé lineage were given to monastic *officers*, not to "heart-disciples." Moreover, the rebirth of the Great Adept of Denma—that holder of rare tantric traditions who largely eschewed institutional life—was chosen as the first throne-holder (T. *khri pa*) or head master (T. *slob dpon*; S. *ācārya*) of the tantric college.

The Second Denma was just the first in a long line of masters of this new institution. As we saw in Chapter 2, the master of the tantric college had a higher status (as reflected by the number of typical shares accorded him) than every other officer or functionary in the monastery other than the abbot.[113] The second highest officer within the tantric college—the lama-cantor—had a status equivalent to the monastery's disciplinarians, cantor, and head of the Accomplishment Offerings to the monastery's principal deities. This institution was also a *place*. It had its own assembly hall (T. *'du khang*) and courtyard (T. *chos grwa*; *chos ra*) for carrying out its elaborate, scripted program of rituals and training.[114]

Constitutions for tantric colleges are not as readily available to the interested scholar as are constitutions composed for monasteries or for philosophical colleges. This is probably due to their association with tantra and thus secrecy. In fact, I have only been able to locate and read one such constitution, that composed by the Seventh Dalai Lama for Kumbum's tantric college (no. 61).[115] The college was founded in 1649,[116] but it was not until 1726, not long after the Seventh Dalai Lama's stay at Kumbum, that this Dalai Lama composed a constitution for the college.[117] What stands out most is just how *similar* the constitution for this college is to constitutions composed for other monasteries and philosophical colleges. Vinaya and discipline are stressed. Entrance requirements and restrictions are given for the college. A brief history of the monastery is provided, along with a description of how assembly is supposed to convene, carry out its business, and disperse. In addition, specific instructions regarding the roles of the officers and functionaries for carrying out the college's ritual program are given. It is also remarkable how the routinized behavior of those enrolled in the tantric college contrasts with the image of earlier "mouth-to-ear" transmissions and impromptu lessons in tantric scriptures given by one's guru.

The Kumbum Tantric College constitution describes an institution that was nearly a mirror image of the monastery's other major institution, the

Philosophical College. It had its own courtyard, kitchen, and hall for assembling.[118] According to the constitution, the officers and functionaries of the college, besides the lama (the head of the college) and lama-cantor, included a disciplinarian (T. *dge skos*), cantor (T. *byang 'dren*), "manager" (T. *zhal ta ba*), cleaners (T. *khrus chab pa*),[119] caretaker (T. *dkon gnyer*),[120] conch-horn blowers (T. *dung mkhan*), and assistants to the disciplinarian (T. *chab ril ba*).

The Kumbum Tantric College constitution also provides an elaborate and exacting routine of ritual and worship. The most extensive section describes the all-day affair that is the climax of the Ritual Cake Offering for Geluk patron deity Guhyasamāja. Assembly begins as it does in philosophical colleges: monks gather at the portico of the Tantric College assembly hall dressed in the proper attire; the lama-cantor leads them in reciting certain texts as part of the ritual of confession and expiation of sins and defilements; then, they enter the hall and sit in rows. The roles of each officer and functionary are scripted: the caretaker hands the cymbals to the cantor (T. *byang 'dren*), who initiates the recitations; the disciplinarian shuts the door. Thanks are offered, as prescribed in the Vinaya.[121] Dishes for eating are to be distributed during the empowerment of the "inner offerings," which are set aside for the gods. The request for food, specifically, a "monastery tea" (T. *gra ja*), is to be made while one is visualizing oneself as the deity. And the food is finally eaten while monks are visualizing themselves within the protective circle (T. *srung 'khor*) of the deity. As is the case in nearly every other monastic constitution, the monks are warned not to make unseemly munching noises while eating, although, in this case, the reason given is that their bodies at that moment are the maṇḍala of the deity, and the food they are consuming is the ritual offering to the deity—this is one of the rare but novel ways in which this constitution is distinguished from other (nontantric) constitutions.[122] The disciplinarian is instructed to eat in the kitchen once the rest of the monks have reassembled.

The entire sequence of events from morning to evening is precisely programmed. Individual meditation is kept to a minimum: in the morning, when the disciplinarian wakes them, they are to visualize a maṇḍala from the clear light of their sleep and to dress the deities for the day before dressing themselves. No more detail is given.[123] This is in contrast to the earlier Kagyü constitutions that give just as much attention to what one does in his own quarters as to what is to be done in assembly. This is not to say that more individual, tantric meditation does not happen at Geluk monasteries. The Kumbum Tantric College constitution makes a passing reference to this:

"Because going on retreat to approach [the tutelary deity] in accordance with the foremost instructions [T. *man ngag*] of one's guru is very important, therefore people who are engaged in authentic approach [to the deity] are given a special dispensation even though the time to assemble in the courtyard has arisen."[124] For everyone else, however, tantra has come to mean the collective ritual and collective worship focused on the deities most central to the Geluk school and to the monastery. The instruction that one receives when in assembly is formalized and adheres to a specified curriculum in the same way that it does in a philosophical college (see Chapter 4). According to the Kumbum constitution, the head of the college (the lama) is to give "recitation lessons" (T. *[b]rtsi bzhag*), a pedagogical technique used in philosophical colleges (see Chapter 4), on the *Guhyasamāja Tantra*, which he gives from his throne.[125] The head of the tantric college also gives sermons and explanations on the *Four-Part Commentary on the Guhyasamāja Tantra* by Tsongkhapa.[126]

The Kumbum Tantric College constitution also provides a calendar—albeit a partial one—for the college. The "self-entering" [T. *bdag 'jug*] initiation of the patron deity Bhairava is on the eighth of each month, and that of Guhyasamāja is on the fifteenth.[127] Restoration rituals for Mahākāla[128] are done between the twenty-fifth and twenty-ninth of the month. The constitution even specifies that the tantric college is to have "monastery teas" and salaries (T. *phogs*), which, as discussed in Chapter 2, were some of the innovative financial arrangements of Geluk mega monasteries. "When assembling in the courtyard, regardless of whether it is a month-long ritual session or not, the general manager [T. *spyi gnyer*] gives a salary . . . to each monk as has been done before."[129]

I have not been able to see the constitution for the tantric college at Gönlung Monastery. A nineteenth-century history, however, provides an overview of the monastery and of the tantric college in particular:

At the end of the year, [there are] the Great Ritual Cake Offering to Mahākāla[130] along with ritual dancing [T. *'cham*],[131] the New Year [First] Day Ritual Cake Offering [to Pelden Lhamo],[132] and fifteen days of the Great Prayer Festival of Magical Displays.[133] Afterwards, there is also the Iron Castle Ritual Dance of the Wensa Tradition,[134] although it is said to be the ritual dance of Chamdo.[135] The Vajra Preceptor always recites the root mantra ten million [times], and the successive tradition of mouth[-to-ear instructions on] visualizations[136] flourishes there. Also, during the main stage [of the ritual], the water-bearers must watch over their speech, and other such actions must be punctilious. Also, the schedule and order of the liturgical calendar of the seven days of the Great Prayer Festival of the [Turning of] the Dharma Wheel[137] are permanently established.

At Gönlung's tantric college, the [study of the *Four-Part] Commentary* must be completed [at least] one time. As for Accomplishment Offerings [T. *sgrub mchod*], there is a Great Ritual Cake Offering, the quarterly throwing of ritual cakes, an "Alms Bowl Offering,"[138] tantric offerings[139] and so forth like at the Lower Tantric College [in Lhasa]. [The monks there] must memorize the disciplinary sermon said to be composed by the former Omniscient One [i.e., Jamyang Zhepa].[140] There is also a commemoration day[141] for this lord. The lama-cantor must be one who has spent a long time in the Tantric College, and [he] must have unbroken [attendance] at assemblies and dharma sessions.[142]

The performance of "private assemblies"[143] is to be strictly monitored [i.e., kept to a minimum][144] [at all times] except during the [First] Day Ritual Cake Offering and the Twenty-Ninth Ritual Cake Offering.[145] The contour-tone and melodious [chants] and techniques[146] of [the following] are pure [and] pleasing to the mind: The Four Hundred [Offerings],[147] the Flaming Mouth Queen,[148] the Ritual Cake Offering for Repelling [Obstacles] by Lord [Tuken III] Chökyi Nyima, and whatever other exorcistic type rituals[149] there are, as well as the Fire Offering of the Four Activities.[150]

Mention is made in this passage to the Iron Castle Ritual Dance of the Wensa Tradition. This ritual dance is integrated with the Offering of Sixty Great Ritual Cakes to Vajrabhairava.[151] According to the Vajrabhairava tantras on which this ritual is based, this celebrates Vajrabhairava's victory over Yama, the lord of death, although it might also be understood as a ritual program for trapping and eliminating enemies.[152] This is one of the most important ritual occasions at Gönlung. Those responsible for preparing the ritual cakes undergo a seven-day retreat leading up to the climax of the ritual on the fourteenth.[153] The masked ritual dancing is performed by dancers from the Great Assembly Hall as well as some from the Protectors Hall (T. *gtsan khang*) and would have been a public spectacle well attended by local laity.[154] It is in this highly orchestrated and semi-public space that the "vajra preceptor" performs this ritual and thus maintains "the successive tradition of mouth[-to-ear instructions on] visualizations" of the Wensa tradition.

Although the above passage does not state the specific role of the Gönlung Tantric College in the Iron Castle Ritual Dance and Ritual Cake Offering to Vajrabhairava, it is safe to assume that the college played an important role in this monastery-wide event. As the constitution for Kumbum's tantric college instructs its members, "During the three prayer festivals [of the year], as an example, assemble together in the Great Assembly Hall."[155] In any case, the point is that these major ritual occasions were events that called upon the services of all sectors of the monastery and integrated them into a coordinated program in service of the monastery. During the Great Prayer Festival of Miraculous Displays (of the first month), monks associated with the Medicine Buddha Ritual, based up the valley at the Gyelsé Hermitage, came to Gönlung's Maitreya Hall to perform an extensive Medicine Buddha Ritual (which was based on the Fifth Dalai Lama's own manuals for the ritual).[156] Another group of monks, known as the "propitiators of the protector gods" (elsewhere referred to as the "Mantrins College" monks), perform restoration rituals up through the fifteenth day of the month.[157] All of these—the Medicine Buddha Ritual monks, the restoration ritual monks, those assigned to preparing and empowering the ritual cakes, and the ritual dancers—were part of an orchestrated, *monastery-wide* program. Each specialized corps of monks was assigned a specific role at specific times and places. No group, including the Tantric College, existed in complete isolation, and likewise no group existed solely for itself. In this case, the groups served a higher purpose through their roles of worshipping and invoking the powers of the principal deities of the monastery and of the Geluk school.

The above description of the Gönlung Tantric College also provides a picture of the *domestication* of hitherto untethered, esoteric transmissions. What were once visualized solely in terms of streams of transmission are now incorporated in institutional structures. A vajra preceptor of the college recites the root mantra of the deity in and for the institution that dictates the time, place, and manner of its performance. The founder of the college—Jamyang Zhepa—is ritually commemorated because now the institution is

Figure 10. Performance of the Iron Castle Ritual Dance
of the Wensa Tradition at Gönlung.
Photo by the author, February 2011.

just as important as are the practices it embodies. The head ritual officiant
of the college, the lama-cantor, is chosen based on his attendance and loyalty to the system. And ritual masked dances were instituted as important
parts of the entire monastery's program. Dancers began training early in the
year for these public events to which local laity would turn out in droves.

Lineage and transmission are still important, but now what matters most
are the lineages of *monastic institutions.* At Gönlung, the study of the *Four-
Part Commentary* and the performance of rituals such as the "Alms Bowl
Offering"[158] are to be done *"like at the Lower Tantric College"* in Lhasa.[159]
Similarly, the program of the tantric college at Kumbum is said to be "based
on the sequence of rules and procedures of the Lower Tantric College [in
Lhasa] with suitable additions made for the ethics of the [local] place and
time."[160] The same is true of Labrang and other monasteries throughout
Amdo and Mongolia. These *institutional connections* were facilitated by the
movement of Geluk lamas between Central Tibet and the periphery. For ex-

ample, when the Second Changkya was at Gönlung at some point in the final years of the seventeenth century, he reported that the ritual techniques of the Ritual Cake Offering to Mahākāla there were incorrect. Although the specialist in charge of the ritual[161] and others ignored Changkya, the abbot at that time[162] interceded, and the ritual techniques were corrected. Auspicious connections are said to have been thereby established.[163] This story illustrates the particular attention given to the details of ritual procedures. Moreover, Changkya had recently completed more than twenty years of training in Central Tibet, and it is likely that he was especially attentive to practices in Amdo that depart from the "orthopraxy" with which he was familiar.[164] At the same time that such efforts were made to maintain the institutional connections with monasteries in Central Tibet, Geluk hierarchs at Gönlung and other monasteries in Amdo were exporting their practices and institutions to places even farther afield.

## Exporting Traditions Among Gönlung's Branch Monasteries

Semnyi Monastery was a branch monastery of Gönlung located to the north, along the Datong River in present-day Menyuan County 門源縣. The history of its founding parallels precisely that of Gönlung, though on a smaller scale. The Third Dalai Lama prophesied the founding of a monastery in Semnyi. A local leader traveled to Tibet, became a "Collection Leader" for the Dalai Lama's government, and then returned with a lama[165] from Central Tibet to help establish the monastery. Later, when that lama was on his deathbed (ca. 1626), he took Sumpa *lopön* Damchö Gyeltsen[166] by the hand and told him that the future success of Semnyi depended on him. He thus became the second abbot of Semnyi. Sumpa *lopön* was the younger brother of Sumpa Damchö Gyatso (d. 1651), the figure who Gyelsé Rinpoché installed as Gönlung's abbot before returning to Central Tibet.[167] This seems to be one of the many ties that collectively make Semnyi a "branch monastery" (T. *dgon lag*) of Gönlung.

Sumpa *lopön* studied at Gönlung[168] and he, too, later served as its abbot from 1633 to 1637.[169] He is said to have served as Semnyi's abbot for twenty years altogether, which suggests that this abbacy overlapped with his abbacy at Gönlung. Holding concurrent abbacies is one of the ways that Geluk hierarchs established and maintained consistency across its vast system of monasteries.[170] In 1626, he established a main shrine hall for Semnyi, and the number of renouncers grew to the point that there were about a hundred monks there. He established a philosophical college and introduced scholastic debate. Significantly, in 1632 he built a sixteen-pillared assembly hall for the monastery, and then the cantor of Gönlung[171] arrived and taught the Semnyi monks the contour-tone and melodious chants of the liturgy,[172] including tempo changes, the manner in which to play music that accompanies the liturgy,[173] ritual dancing [T. 'chams], and so on. Here we see the unique liturgical and ritual components of the larger monastery being exported to a smaller institution, constituting yet another tie between these two monasteries.

Toward the end of the seventeenth century, an important lama from Semnyi, known as Semnyi Tendzin Trinlé Gyatso (b. 1655),[174] assumed the throne of Tetung Gönchen, another branch monastery of Gönlung that later came to house as many as 500 monks.[175] Semnyi Trülku had taken his novice vows from the rebirth of Gönlung's founder, Gyelsé Lozang Tendzin, in 1666 when the latter was visiting the area. From Gyelsé he also "memorized all the rituals of the tantric class as well as the restoration rituals[176] for the protector deities, and he completed most of the approach [rituals needed for commencing tantric practice]."[177] Then, beginning in 1670, he entered the philosophical dharma classes of Gönlung and studied hard for eight years, at the end of which he attained Gönlung's highest rank of lingsé kaju scholar.[178] Later, he also took his full monastic vows from the reigning abbot of Gönlung.[179]

Having received ample training from Gönlung's lord lama and at the monastery itself, Semnyi made known his wishes to travel to Central Tibet to further his studies. However, his home monastery was in a state of disrepair and, in 1678, he was asked to serve as its abbot. He accepted and quickly went to work restoring Semnyi Monastery to its former glory. This included restoring the practice of the "Three Foundations" of a monastery.[180] In addition, the tradition of the Ritual Cake Offering for Mahākāla had been broken, so he acted as the Vajra Preceptor and reestablished it. At the end of the year, he performed an extensive restoration ritual and the throwing of the ritual cake, thereby attracting the presence of numerous patrons. He built an assembly hall for the monastery and had made a large Maitreya tapestry. In 1684, he undertook the prestigious role of leading the Great Prayer Festival at Gönlung, further strengthening the ties between his home monastery of Semnyi and Gönlung.

In 1696, at the age of forty-two, he approached the Monguor headman, Lu Tusi 魯土司, asking him for a copy of the Kanjur [i.e., the canon of Buddhist sutras and tantras] for his home monastery. It was at this time that Semnyi Trülku was made abbot of Tethung Gönchen, a monastery closely tied to the Lu Tusi.[181] Perhaps the Monguor headman wished to secure some of Semnyi's institution-building skills for his own monasteries.[182] As he had done at his own monastery of Semnyi, at Tethung Gönchen Semnyi Trülku promoted the ritual practices he had acquired at Gönlung. Shortly after becoming Tethung Gönchen's abbot, he "there established the [First] Day Ritual Cake Offering for [Pelden] Lhamo *like at Gönlung.*"[183] In 1701, he attempted to resign from his abbatial post,[184] but the monastery's dharma protector would not let him. When, in 1705, he prepared to resign, the local monks and laity successfully petitioned him to stay on to serve in a teaching capacity. He thereupon installed a statue of Maitreya in the assembly hall and built a stupa on the north side of the monastery in accordance with instructions given to him by Gönlung's lord lama, Gyelsé Rinpoché. In short, he is said to have "taught and restored" at Tethung Gönchen the following:[185] "the debate of dharma classes; its rituals, liturgy, consecrations, and burnt offerings; its contour-tone and melodious chants, including tempo changes, for restoration rites; its [manner of] making of ritual cakes, and its [manner of] playing of music all in accordance with the practices at Gönlung and the [manner in which they were] recited by the Omniscient Changkya."[186]

His institution-building at his home monastery of Semnyi seems to have resumed again after 1707, for we read "at his own monastery . . . from 1707 onward the liturgical schedule was made to expand year after year."[187] In 1724, he built a "fifteen-room, three-story mantrin hall [T. *sngags khang*]," among other things. Unfortunately, all of the institutions and practices that Semnyi Trülku had helped establish there were lost later that year. In the third month (T. *nag zla*) of 1724, "hundreds of thousands" of Qing troops are said to have descended on the monastery as part of the Qing reponse to the Oirat Lubsang-Danzin Rebellion.[188]

Semnyi Trülku continued to play an instrumental role in resurrecting Buddhism in the region of Pari after the rebellion. After the rebellion, we find him leading his congregation of monks at the nearby Gyadok Monastery, itself a branch monastery of Semnyi.[189] There he established an assembly hall, the Offerings of the [Twenty-]Fifth, the Great Prayer Festival, and the Spring Dharma Session, some of the essential components of a successful Geluk monastery. When permission came from the Qing officials in Xining to reestablish the Semnyi Monastery, Semnyi Trülku was there to rebuild, too.

The same nineteenth-century Tibetan history that provides us with an overview of the Gönlung Monastery and its tantric college similarly provides an overview of the ritual calendar at the Semnyi Monastery:

> The Spring Dharma Session was two months long, and there was a one-month Dharma Session each in summer, fall, and winter. There are seven holy days [T. *dus bzang*] during the *Saga* [T. *sa ga*; i.e., fourth] Month. There is a dharma session during the Summer Retreat. On the eighth day of the ninth month there is a Prayer Festival during which the Wensa tradition of ritual dance [T. *'chams*] and Iron Castle ritual are performed. On the sixteenth day [of that month] there is a seven-day Prayer Festival and Offering to Śākyamuni.[190] The Offerings of the [Twenty-]fifth lasts for seven days, and at the end the ritual cake is thrown. During the twelfth month there is the "approach and realization" of Mahākāla.[191] During the New Year, there is a Ritual Cake Offering [to Mahākāla] and a [First] Day Ritual Cake Offering.[192]

Particularly noteworthy in this passage is the reference to the Wensa tradition of ritual dance and Iron Castle Ritual. Although there is no way of knowing whether Gönlung monks and lamas were responsible for introducing this tradition at Semnyi, it is very likely, especially given the fact that Sumpa *lopön* is said to have previously established a ritual dance tradition there. Similarly, it is possible that the chanting and music techniques said to have been introduced by Gönlung's cantor informed the performance at Semnyi of several universal Geluk rituals, including the Mahākāla Ritual Cake Offering, the First Day Ritual Cake Offering, and the Offerings of the Twenty-fifth.[193]

Throughout the literature, we see a common concern among Geluk hierarchs for maintaining orthodoxy and orthopraxy *along institutional lines.* The practices introduced at Semnyi Monastery and Tetung Gönchen were explicitly modeled on those at Gönlung Monastery. Gönlung, in turn, was modeled on the more centrally located institutions. For its tantric college, this meant the Lower Tantric College in Lhasa. The impetus behind this process of institutional integrity is partially explained by the more general proclivity for rationalization described in the Introduction to this book. In the case of tantra, there is likely another motivation, too. The quotation at the beginning of this chapter shows the dismay of Sumba Kanbo—a prolific lama from Gönlung Monastery—concerning the lack of separate places and specialization at monasteries on the periphery of the Tibetan Plateau. "Those with bad memories and [even] those with good memories cannot with assurance retain all of that, and so there is study in name only. In short, it has become like the metaphor of "if it is too big, it will burst in the middle," Sumba Kanbo explains.[194] The image evoked by this metaphor is of one attempting to carry a heavy load on a sheet of paper, which rips under the pressure.[195] Moreover, Sumba Kanbo expresses a concern for the consequences of approaching the practice of tantra outside an orderly and proper institutional context:

> In addition, the practice of secret mantra rituals requires at a minimum that one has renounced and that one has at least begun to perceive the mind of enlightenment, and, in particular, that one have a complete [intellectual] understanding of emptiness. If one does not have these [qualifications], then although it looks as though one is practicing the meditation of mantra yoga, [in fact] it is like Lord Drom[196] writes, "though he conquers the mantra of that renowned as the Profound Dharma, [I] fear [he] is making an anchor for samsara."[197]

> Likewise, even though there are those who, despite having not completed the preliminaries and other steps, casually act as if practicing the rituals, although they claim to be yogis, not only is there little meaning in [their practice], but also the benefit or harm [to others] is [in fact measured] according to whether or not they uphold [their] spiritual commitments [T. *dam tshig*]. [They] are like the snake trapped in the bamboo tube: either they come out through the top [i.e., attain enlightenment] or they drop down to the depths [of hell].

> Thus, it would look best if, in the Great Assembly Hall, rituals [T. *cho ga*] were kept to a very few [and] sacrificial cake offerings and supplications to protector deities were abridged. Moreover, it would look better if rituals, restoration rites, and so forth done for such purposes as the obstacle-clearing rituals [T. *rim gro*] of the patrons of each college were done on the side [only].[198]

What is being prescribed here is a system of separation, specialization, and prioritization. The Gelukpa could not very well do without tantra. It represents the third "tier," or "wing," of Buddhism: that of practice or realization. Reginald Ray has argued that, although this tier is largely ignored by those Buddhists (as well as scholars) who most closely identify with the other two tiers of Buddhism—that of discipline and purity and that of scholasticism and wisdom—it is a fundamental and powerful component that Buddhists have never been able to do without.[199] The Geluk school, in becoming the predominant religious power across Tibet and Mongolia, therefore institutionalized this tier of Buddhism, making it safer. The powers of tantra were channeled into the service of the monastery and the Geluk school as a whole, and other forms of meditation and tantric practice were assigned either to the distant past or to the rare elite who managed to first pass through a system of monastic socialization and education designed by the school's hierarchs.

Chapter 4

# The Systematization of Doctrine
# and Education

How does one get the multiple components of a far-flung enterprise to toe the company line? Doctrine. Or, more specifically, scholasticism. As José Cabezón has written in his overview of Indo-Tibetan scholasticism, "There is no better way to ensure that what an adept experiences is particularly Christian or Buddhist, or that the way in which an adept behaves is particularly Confucian or Jewish, than to ensure that the 'experiencer' has had a strong foundation in his or her respective intellectual tradition."[1] Or, as another scholar puts it, "Monastic education plays a crucial role in consolidating and continuing religious traditions by means of systematically indoctrinating the next generation of religious specialists."[2]

The most common refrain running throughout the Geluk school's promotional and organizational literature—its constitutions—is that "discipline" and "purity" are the foundation of the sangha, which in turn is the lifeblood of the Buddha's Teachings. But the Gelukpa also presented themselves as being the most philosophical. Recall the Fifth Dalai Lama's insistence upon attaining "the qualities of realization" *through "properly listening to and thinking about the precious dharma of the scriptures."*[3] Geluk constitutions that have anything to say about the benefits of meditation are far fewer.[4]

By "scholasticism," I mean the monastic program of curricula, textbooks, memorization, recitation checks or quizzes, sermons, debates, exams, degrees, networks of "study abroad," and other practices focused on understanding the tradition of knowledge to which one belongs so as to establish or reaffirm correct knowledge and refute incorrect knowledge.[5] All Tibetan Buddhists engage in scholasticism, and, as Georges Dreyfus has shown, the subject matter of the Geluk curricula and the non-Geluk curricula are quite similar.[6] Today, however, the Gelukpa are often perceived as the *most* scholastic. Part of the reason for this is that the Geluk school's presentation of itself as the most philosophical has been a very public one. Their preferred method of engaging with the tradition's scriptures is through lively and often public debate performances rather than through writing and commentary. Another reason for this perception is that the Gelukpa ultimately *formalized* and *standardized* their scholastic program across the Tibetan Plateau and Mongolia such that, for example, the famous monastery of Labrang Tashi Khyil[7] in Amdo (northeastern Tibetan cultural sphere), shortly after its founding in 1710, followed the same scholastic program as that of Drepung Monastery in Lhasa and, in particular, Drepung's Gomang College.[8] Thus, the tradition presents itself as one concerned with maintaining and disseminating structures and practices of right knowledge across the expanse of Inner Asia.

This process of formalization and standardization took place relatively late. It would be a mistake to assume that the picture of the Three Seats of Geluk monasticism in Lhasa—Sera, Drepung, and Ganden—as they exist today or in the twentieth century reflects the early years of these monasteries. As explained at the beginning of Chapter 3, in the fifteenth century and probably throughout most of the sixteenth century, these monasteries were probably much closer to the "encampments" described in the Introduction than to the rigid standards of tradition that they became in later centuries.[9] That is, the content of what was studied and the manner in which it was studied was more flexible and open to the influence of whatever abbot or teacher was present. The reification of a formalized *system* of scholasticism took place principally during the time of inter-regional and inter-sectarian conflict, which is described in Chapter 1, and, in particular, under the influence of the Fifth Dalai Lama and his followers.

## Early Rationalization of Scholasticism

One way in which the Gelukpa first began to systematize their school's scholasticism was through the production and use of "textbooks" or "debate manuals," known as *yikcha* in Tibetan.[10] These are a sort of sub-commentary, summaries of the important points found in the scriptural commentaries written by Tsongkhapa and his two "spiritual sons," Gyeltsap Jé (1364–143) and Khedrup Jé (1385–1438).[11] They first began to appear in the fifteenth century, and the philosophical colleges of Geluk monasteries would adopt one or another of the authoritative manuals. Although the doctrinal differences between these textbooks were minor, they came to distinguish each major Geluk monastic college (T. *grwa tshang*) and its loyal members from the other colleges and monks.

This narrowing of focus—from the Indian scriptures and canonical Tibetan commentaries to a particular textbook—is one of the features of a developing "high scholasticism" that Dreyfus has suggested was the result of the prolonged conflict that took place between the Karma Kagyü school and its patrons in Tsang and the Geluk school and its patrons in Ü. One of the last sets of textbooks to be composed and accepted as authoritative was that composed for Drepung Monastery's Gomang College, a place that came to maintain numerous connections with monasteries in Amdo and Mongolia. The Gomang textbooks are said to have been delivered orally by Gungru Chöjung (sixteenth to seventeenth centuries)[12] around the time he became the college's abbot in 1611.[13] This was on the eve of the Rat-Ox Years War (1612–1613) during which the king of Tsang invaded and destroyed much of Lhasa, including Drepung and Sera Monasteries.[14] The history of scholasticism in Tibet and especially the Geluk systemization of it cannot be separated from the history of sectarianism in Tibet.

It is no coincidence, then, that we find in one of the constitutions composed by the Ninth Karmapa (no. 22) in the late sixteenth or very early seventeenth century a warning to his readers: "Except for the textbooks [T. *yig cha*] and authentic [texts] *of our own tradition, especially Karma commentaries,* there is no place for [other] recitations[15] or memorization."[16] With the Dalai Lama's consolidation of power in the mid-seventeenth century came a consolidation of scholastic priorities, and we find the authoritative Geluk textbooks being enshrined at new monasteries established across Tibet. By the 1690s, at Gönlung Monastery along the Tibet-China frontier, we read: "Now, the abbot is Kün'ga Gyatso,[17] who teaches Madhyamaka and Perfection of Wisdom in accordance with the textbooks of Drepung Monastery's Gomang College, and Vinaya based on Kyilkhangpa's textbook, and who teaches [Abhidharmakoṣa] based on the Lord Lama's composition of the *Jewel of Metaphysics: The Chariot of the Guide*."[18] A nineteenth-century history informs us that the Fifth Dalai Lama himself composed a constitution for Gönlung's Philosophical College and was thus responsible for codifying the monastery's selection of textbooks and other aspects of its scholastic program.[19] While

he specified Gungru Chöjung's Drepung Gomang textbooks for use in the
Madhyamaka and Perfection of Wisdom classes, "Kyilkhangpa" refers to one
of Trashi Lhünpo Monastery's three exoteric colleges, and the eponymous
textbook was composed by Trashi Lhünpo's sixteenth-century abbot, Sang-
gyé Gyatso.[20] The "Lord Lama" is the Fifth Dalai Lama himself.[21] All of
these were later replaced by the "new textbooks" of the influential Amdowa
the First Jamyang Zhepa (1648–1721), who served as abbot of Drepung Gomang from 1700 through 1707.[22]

The Fifth Dalai Lama himself wrote several monastic textbooks. Efforts
to have those instituted in the curricula of major monastic centers largely
failed,[23] notwithstanding the presence of his *Jewel of Metaphysics* in the early
Gönlung curriculum. Note, though, that while his textbooks may have been
somewhat ignored, what was not ignored was the desire to promote a system of Geluk scholasticism that valued and adhered to orthodoxy, an orthodoxy that included textbooks associated with the major Geluk centers of
learning. The above description of Gönlung's textbooks comes from a comprehensive, seventeenth-century catalog of Geluk monasteries. In that catalog, each monastery is summarized in anywhere from one to a dozen or so
lines, and there one can perceive a consistent effort to record the curriculum
of each monastery whenever one is present. It is thus apparent that, at least
from the perspective of that author, *what* one studied was considered a significant, defining feature of a monastic institution.

The same cannot be said about the scholasticism of the Gelukpa's major
competitor of the sixteenth and seventeenth centuries, the Karma Kagyü.
Admittedly, little is known about Karma Kagyü scholasticism. It seems likely,
though, that the (Ninth) Karmapa's insistence that Karma Kagyü monks adhere to "my own *yikcha*"[24] reflected his tradition's relatively greater depen-
dence upon its major reincarnate lama as compared with the Gelukpa.

The Ninth Karmapa, in some of his constitutions, refers to many of the
features of the kind of scholastic program that ultimately would come to be
the hallmark of Geluk monasteries. These features include a basic curriculum,[25] a daily schedule of assembly and debate indistinguishable from a typical
Geluk one,[26] regular tests to ensure texts are being thoroughly memorized,[27]
and admonitions that one should not simultaneously study philosophy and
mantra (which is said to be like "sewing with two needles").[28] However, despite
the Karmapa's prolific composition of constitutions, he does not appear to have
directed his attention (or have had the opportunity to do so) at instituting
scholastic practices far away on the Tibetan frontier with China and Mongolia.

The Fifth Dalai Lama's constitutions in which he gives greatest attention to scholasticism are, aside from his constitution for Drepung Monastery, for monasteries in Kham ("Eastern Tibet"). In his constitution for Ganden Pendé Ling in Ba (no. 49) he emphasizes the importance of separating those engaged in the study of philosophy (lit. sutra) from those who, because of either a lack of intelligence or a lack of interest, choose to engage in the other major monastic enterprise: worshipping the monastery's protector and tutelary/meditation deities.[29] In his constitution for Litang's Thupten Jamchen, the major Geluk outpost in Kham founded by the Third Dalai Lama, the Great Fifth goes even further, specifying the curriculum for two separate groups: the "sutrikas" (T. *mdo grwa ba*) and the "mantrikas" (T. *sngags grwa ba*). Regarding the former, he writes:

> The philosophers [lit. sutra monks] [are to study] the new textbooks for Madhyamaka, Perfection of Wisdom, and [Abhidharma] koṣa and whichever Vinaya textbook is appropriate. Maintain the tradition of Upper Rawa [College][30] for the *Pramāṇavārttika*.[31] Emphasize especially recitation lessons[32] and debate.[33] After that [lit. beneath that] memorize and practice the breviary[34] and aspiration prayers, the "White Umbrella," the *Heart Sūtra*, the "Tārā," the *dhāraṇī* of the [Buddha of Infinite] Life, and so forth. Apart from emphasizing [these] melodies and so forth, as for that which pertains to the mantra side, except for just the ritual-cake offering rite of [the goddess] Makzorma, do not engage in it.[35]

Here the Dalai Lama both insists upon the need for separation and specialization and provides a basic curriculum and liturgy for the monks.

This insistence on separation and specialization reminds one of the quotation that opens Chapter 3. There the eighteenth-century Geluk luminary Sumba Kanbo—an Oirat Mongol from Kökenuur whose seat is at Gönlung Monastery—alludes to the difficulties he encounters when trying to establish and promote Geluk monasticism along the periphery of the Tibetan cultural sphere. There, due to a shortage of monks or a lack of space or perhaps to sheer ignorance, the monks engaged in the study of philosophy have to split their time worshipping and invoking the monastery's deities. This lack of separation and specialization is seen as a problem.

When Sumba Kanbo writes of the "philosophical monasteries and colleges of Central Tibet" that "take the sutra side of things as most important," he no doubt has in mind Drepung Gomang, a place the Fifth Dalai Lama designated as a "philosophical monastery" and specifically of "the class of Madhyamaka and Perfection of Wisdom."[36] The Dalai Lama's Drepung constitution (no. 51) is clearly his magnum opus as far as his constitutions are concerned.[37] It's the last constitution he wrote and, as such, it's also the longest and most detailed of his constitutions. He writes, "Because this monastery is one that principally recites philosophical explanations, aside from the abbot's palace and the Mantra Hall, music with accompanying cymbals for morning rituals and [protector deity] restoration rites is prohibited."[38] In fact, as Jansen has shown in her study of this constitution, this late and lengthy constitution of the Great Fifth reflects a concern for the growing number of monks at Drepung, many of whom were coming from Mongolia and far-off places.[39] He laments the growing use of music in many parts of the monastery, hence his prohibition.[40] He laments that attendance at the Summer and Winter Dharma Sessions, where debate is promoted, has been waning, and so describes the need to institute "disciplinary sermons" for ensuring full attendance.[41] Like his first constitution for the Great Prayer Festival (no. 37), he provides instructions on who can participate in the monastery's debates and the duration of the debates.[42] And he proscribes the use of bribery and influence, irrespective of an individual's intellectual virtues, in conferring praise in the monastery's formal inter-monastery debates.[43]

## Philosophical Colleges and Scholasticism in Amdo

When this influx of "foreign" monks at Drepung and other centrally located monasteries began to make its way back home, the most outstanding among them took with them the same concerns and monastic regimens. Among these individuals was the architect of Drepung Gomang's "new" textbooks and the founder of what would later become the largest and most influential Geluk monastery outside central Tibet, the First Jamyang Zhepa, Ngawang Tsöndrü (1648–1721). The constitution he wrote (no. 60) for his monastery of Labrang Tashi Khyil in 1719 along with the constitution composed for Gönlung in 1737 stand out among the first wave of constitutions that followed the death of the Fifth Dalai Lama. In particular, both of these constitutions give considerable attention to three of the most pronounced features of a large-scale monastic institution, namely, finances (see Chapter 2), ritual (see Chapter 5), and scholasticism.

In his discussion of scholasticism at his monastery, the First Jamyang Zhepa alludes both to the uncoordinated nature of the monastery's procedures and practices in the first decade of the monastery's existence and to his motivation for penning the constitution: "As for classes, mass tea services, tips, and so forth of the two Colleges [i.e., Philosophical and Tantric], previously each of the two did as it pleases according to whatever came to mind. Thinking about this, henceforth, everyone must do [as follows] while taking responsibility for ways to bring benefits to the Teachings and to the happiness of wandering beings and while bearing firmly in mind the like of this constitution."[44] He proceeds to paint a picture for his reader of what a proper Geluka dharma class should look like. The lama abbot (i.e., the Jamyang Zhepa himself) and the disciplinarians are expected to hold regular classes. Classes entail debate practice, which is not to be too easy or too hard but to attend to the different capacities and levels of the students. The disciplinarians are to monitor the debate and performance of each individual as the disciplinarians make three circles around the entire courtyard. The First Jamyang Zhepa instructs that the "general customs of all philosophers," such as the custom of reciting the seed syllable of the Bodhisattva of Wisdom Mañjuśrī[45] and that of clapping hands together during debate, are required.[46]

These and other features of a Geluk philosophical college are elaborated in Ön Gyelsé Jikmé Yeshé Drakpa's constitution for Gönlung. In fact, among the constitutions composed up to that time, Gyelsé's Gönlung constitution is the most detailed with regard to scholastic expectations. This is probably the result of the later stage of institutionalization as well as the needs and opportunities that were presented upon reestablishing Gönlung in the aftermath of its destruction. Recall that Gönlung was implicated in the Lubsang-Danzin Rebellion of 1723–1724 and that it was not rebuilt until 1729 when the Yongzheng Emperor agreed to allow it. Thus, the constitution contains within it a blueprint for building a major scholastic center from scratch and for returning the monastery to its onetime glory.

Gyelsé's constitution provides us with a bird's-eye view of the life and operation of a Geluk monastery as monasteries became more formalized than ever and as the Gelukpa standardized monastic life and practice across the Tibetan Plateau and Mongolia. Each year, the constitution explains, the monastery (specifically, the Philosophical College) is to hold at least four and as many as six dharma sessions during which scholastic practice, especially debate, was most intense. Of these, four are monthlong sessions and two are "intermediary sessions,"[47] lasting only two weeks.[48] Gyelsé lists these in the following order: The Great Winter Dharma Session lasts from the eighth day of the eleventh month until the eighth day of the twelfth month. The Great Spring Dharma Session lasts from the fifteenth of the third month until the fifteenth of the fourth month. The "intermediary session" of the spring, otherwise known as the Post-Spring Assembly,[49] runs from the first of the fifth month to the twentieth of that month. The Summer Dharma Session actually lasts a month and half, coinciding with the Summer Rains Retreat, lasting from the fifteenth of the sixth month to the first of the eighth month. The Great Autumn Dharma Session runs from the fifteenth of the eighth month to the fifteenth of the following month. The autumn "intermediary session," or Second Autumn Dharma Session, runs from the first of the tenth month to the fifteenth of that month.[50] Altogether this amounts to 170 days, or almost six months, of scholastic practice.

The constitution also informs us of the intensity of the daily schedule during these dharma sessions. It consists of three periods of the day: morning, noon, and evening. During each period an assembly is held, at which prayers and hymns are recited (see Chapter 5), and afterward the monks congregate in the debate courtyard[51] for their lessons. Soup and tea are served at the assemblies, usually in the form of a "mass tea,"[52] which is a donation of food and drink made by an individual (usually a layperson) for the entire present assembly. However, "monastery teas" are also provided at the monastery's expense (hence the name) so as to maintain enthusiasm among the monks and to encourage the growth of monks engaged in the study of philosophy.[53] Attendance was also required of every monk who was not elderly or infirm.[54]

Once in the courtyard, dharma class begins with a series of prayers. According to Gönlung's later, nineteenth-century, constitution, these were to be capped by the ritual invocation of the Bodhisattva of Wisdom as was the case for Jamyang Zhepa's Labrang Monastery.[55] Monks then go to their respective classes and pair up with a partner[56] for debate practice.[57] Judging from present-day performances, during which partners alternate positions—challenger/questioner and defender—these were boisterous occasions. The "claps" or "hand slaps" that Jamyang Zhepa expected of his monks would punctuate the challenger's attack on the seated defendant's command of the day's lesson. Anthropologist Michael Lempert describes the combative nature of debate as practiced today at Sera Mé in India:

Asked to recount their first impressions of debate, my interlocutors often laughed, then confessed that they were shocked at first. "It looked sort of strange," one admitted. "I sort of thought to myself, 'Why are they fighting?'" Another said that debate initially "looked strange" and that "if [you] talk to outside[rs], [they'd say] a fight has broken out, right?" . . . Warnings about taking debate's martial idiom literally were conveyed to me with some urgency when I first visited Sera Mey. I was cautioned about the 'bad words' (*tshig nyen*) I might hear in the debating courtyard, like 'idiot' (*lkugs pa*) and 'donkey' (*bong gu*). Technically, such words are not permitted but slip out (*shor ba*) anyway, one monk explained. Doctrinally, [the challenger's method of drawing out the] consequences [of the defendant's position] catalyze learning in defendants, but the kinesic accompaniments iconically figurate this method as a kind of violence.[58]

Debate practice would continue until a class's turn for "recitation lessons." During recitation lessons, the abbot recites the relevant section from the text being learned to the class rehearsal leader (T. *skyor dpon*), who repeats, in turn, what the abbot recites.[59] The class rehearsal leader subsequently goes through the text with the rest of his class. These exercises were important because they were one of the many series of checks and tests that a monk had to pass in order to advance in his studies. Ön Gyelsé Jikmé Yeshé Drakpa's constitution for Gönlung (no. 66) explains, "Every effort must be made to perform recitation lessons uninterruptedly except for occasions that arise in which the abbot has to perform a special village ritual for the good of society. When there are not obligatory recitation lessons, alternate practicing singing recitations,[60] formal debating,[61] and [reciting] the *Ornament* and *Entrance*."[62] Testing was a regular part of the dharma sessions, and failure to perform adequately could result in demotion or repeating a class.[63]

According to Jikmé Yeshé Drakpa's constitution, before a monk could even participate in these dharma session debate classes, he had to prove he was qualified. This meant studying under a personal teacher[64] to learn the monastery's rules[65] and procedures, its system of distributing offerings,[66] and, most important, its litany of hymns and prayers, some of which—like the above-mentioned *Ornament* and *Entrance*—were also relevant debate materials:

Figure 11. Monks debating at Rongwo Gönchen in Amdo.
Photo by the author, March 2011.

In addition, if one is not a Collected Topics [level] student, he
must [first] memorize the Refuges, Giving Rise [to the Mind of
Enlightenment], the Tārā, and the *Heart Sutra*. As soon as he is
just able to read and has truly internalized [these], he can [go on
to] the years-long retreat[67] for studying the Collected Topics,
including the [properties of things and their attributes, such as]
the colors white and red. After that is completed, the abbot and
the disciplinarians exam him by questioning him in debate in the
middle of the class. If the student doesn't get the Collected
Topics, then he is deemed one who must repeat it, and he cannot
enter the Treatise classes. If he has done Collected Topics before
and is capable of doing formal debate, then, if he passes the
*Ornament* and *Entrance* exam, he may enter the Beginning
Treatise class.[68]

Testing such as this occurs at every stage of the scholastic program, and its
prescription here (as well as the record of it from ethnographic observations

and oral histories) contradicts what some have suggested about the lax standards of large-scale Geluk monasteries: "New monks had no exams to pass in order to remain in the monastery, and monks who had no interest in studying or meditating were as welcome as the dedicated scholar monks," according to one rather standard account.[69] While this may have been true for the monastery as a whole, membership in any one of the "colleges" within a mega monastery *did* have exams.[70]

The curriculum that Jikmé Yeshé Drakpa specifies for Gönlung is what had become *the standard Dge lugs curriculum*. He writes, "Apart from studying the old or new monastic manuals (*yig cha*)—whichever is suitable—for Beginning and Advanced Collected Topics, Types of Mind, Types of Evidence, Seventy Topics, Madhyamaka and Perfection of Wisdom, the *Abhidharmakoṣa* and Vinaya, one is not to follow whatever he desires nor succumb to partiality."[71] A nineteenth-century source, drawing on earlier materials, elaborates on this:

> The constitution of the philosophical college [of Gönlung] was written by the Great Fifth, and it [has] thirteen classes:[72] [1] Beginning and [2] Advanced Collected Topics,[73] both [3] Types of Mind and [4] Types of Evidence classes,[74] the [5] Seventy Points,[75] [6] Beginning Treatises, the [7] Mind of Enlightenment,[76] the [8] Dharma Wheel,[77] the [9] Fourth Section [of the *Ornament of Realization*], [10] Madhyamaka, [11] Abdhidharmakośa, [12] Pramāṇavārttika, and [13] Vinaya. Their studies of the Five Scriptures are unmatched, as they follow the old textbook of Gomang for both Madyamaka and Perfection of Wisdom, Kyilkhangpa['s textbook][78] for Vinaya, [the Fifth Dalai Lama's] *Jewel of Metaphysics: The Chariot of the Guide*[79] for Abhidharmakośa, and Changkya Rölpé Dorjé's writings [*gsung*] for Pramāṇavārttika.[80]

Unfortunately, we do not have the Fifth Dalai Lama's constitution for Gönlung itself. Nonetheless, we still see evidence of his influence in the mention of the Dalai Lama's own text for studying monastic discipline.

The above curriculum starts with the Beginning and Advanced Collected Topics, which introduces students to the methods and terminology of Geluk debate.[81] Then one advances to the Types of Mind and Types of Evidence classes. These classes, which treat epistemology and logic, respectively, are still considered preliminary studies and fall under the rubric of Collected Topics in the wider sense of that term.[82] Next comes the Seventy Topics, which is a summary of a treatise important to the Geluk curriculum, *The Ornament of Realization*. These, then, are the first five classes of Gönlung's scholastic curriculum.

*The Ornament of Realization* (S. *Abhisamayālankāra*), which is attributed to the Future Buddha Maitreya, is understood as a commentary on the Perfection of Wisdom sutras and is studied in classes six ("Beginning Treatises") through nine ("Fourth Section of the *Ornament of Realization*"). This treatise is the first of the "five scriptures"[83] that form the foundation of the Geluk curriculum. Classes ten through thirteen correspond to the remaining four scriptures.[84] Altogether, the curriculum takes monks fifteen to twenty years to complete.[85]

As was the case at other Geluk monasteries, certain times of the year were designated for specific subjects.[86] In addition, Jikmé Yeshé Drakpa specifies the subject matter of the abbot's sermons.[87] Monks were also instructed to periodically hold "formal debates," which are distinguished from ordinary debate practice by the fact that a single debate becomes the main spectacle and the roles of questioner/challenger and defendant are formalized or fixed for the duration of the debate.[88] "From time to time, each group gets together in its respective place and practices formal debate. At midday, up until the time of the [recitation lesson] test for the First Section [class of the Treatise/Perfection of Wisdom class], they debate both the 'Twenty Bhikṣus' and 'Dependent Origination.' Up until [the tests for] the Advanced Treatise class they debate 'Distinguishing Conventional and Ultimate [Realities]' and 'Thought and Form.'"[89]


## Debate Circuits and Scholastic Degrees

The scholastic program outlined by Gyelsé is intense. Multiple periods each day and multiple sessions each year filled much of the time of the monks enrolled in such a philosophical college. Entrance exams, recitation lesson exams, and written exams,[90] were required of all its members. The reason for this level of scrutiny is no doubt the same one given for the expectation that even advanced scholars and elderly monks attend dharma classes: "It is a great service to the Teachings."[91] Apart from this, however, there was also an anxiety fueled by the fact that monks were constantly moving among and between monasteries. There was always the fear that the way of doing things would be upset by newcomers unless steps were taken to ensure the monastery's integrity. Moreover, if a monastery lapsed in its standards, word could travel with those same monks. Monastic constitutions constantly warn against the "disgrace"[92] that results from impropriety. Disgrace could mean that the stream of monks coming to study there dries up.[93]

One precaution built into the system was to limit study abroad to qualified monks. From Gönlung, monks would travel to other major monasteries in Amdo and in Central Tibet to further their studies and, eventually, to test themselves in the annual formal debates of prestigious monasteries, a practice known as "monastic circuit" or "debate circuit." Jikmé Yeshé Drakpa, for instance, required that only monks who have been in the First Section Perfection of Wisdom class were permitted to travel to Central Tibet for further studies,[94] where they were expected to strictly follow the rules of the monastery, the college, and the dormitory where they stayed.[95] The successful ones who earned the scholastic degree or title of Kachu or Rapjam Scholar[96] were expected to participate in formal debate upon their return to Gönlung as a means to inspire earnest study among the rest of the congregation.[97]

Back at Gönlung, monks who were enrolled in the Philosophical College were exhorted to focus exclusively on the study of the "four scriptures" (i.e., the five scriptures minus the study of the Vinaya) and not to be distracted by other pursuits, such as painting and medicine.[98] All monks in the college were required to take exams at every dharma session.[99] Those unable to pass the Treatise-level exam were held back in the preliminary, Collected Topics classes or made to do chores, such as carrying water during assembly and sweeping.

In the early eighteenth century, one of the monasteries closely associated with and near to Gönlung,[100] having improved the practice of debate there, petitioned the Dalai Lama's government and was granted the privilege of awarding Kaju degrees.[101] "Kaju" means "Master of the Ten Difficulties" or Texts, the texts being the five Indian scriptures fundamental to the Geluk curriculum and their respective commentaries.

Gönlung appears to have awarded the degree of Kaju, or Lingsé Kaju,[102] as early as the 1670s.[103] This may have made it a destination for monks from smaller monasteries in the region and from farther away in Inner Mongolia. This meant precautions had to be taken to maintain the integrity of this institution. First, an individual was required to demonstrate a high level of knowledge and fluency with the Geluk scriptures. Jikmé Yeshé Drakpa writes:

"Those who wish to participate in the debate circuit of this place must test on the 'Chain of Consequences'[104] of both Madhyamaka and Perfection of Wisdom in front of the abbot, disciplinarians, the director of studies, etc. who have gathered together. Afterwards, no matter what [they] question him on—be it all of the Special Topics of both Madhyamaka and Perfection of Wisdom, Vinaya, Abhidharmakośa, etc.—he must never refuse, saying 'I haven't studied that!'"[105] Such scrutiny of potential candidates is to begin a full year and a half in advance: "Next year's Lingsé [degree candidates] are to participate in formal debate at the dharma sessions beginning with this year's Great Prayer Festival."[106] According to the later, nineteenth-century, constitution of Gönlung, a potential candidate was required to participate in a "Standing Assembly Debate"[107] at the Great Spring Dharma Session of the third and fourth months. This was an occasion for two individuals to square off and debate in front of the entire assembly, while the abbot and disciplinarians were to give "the strictest and most exhortative attention to [those who may qualify for] new [degree exams]."[108]

The degree exams, or defenses, did not take place at Gönlung until the Summer Dharma Session, the period that coincides with the commemoration of Śākyamuni Buddha's first teaching or "turning of the wheel of dharma." A candidate for degree at Gönlung was referred to as Lingsewa, as one who completes the "debate circuit," and simply as "degree candidate,"[109] and his formal debate at the summer session was also regulated so as to maintain a certain protocol and reputation:

> Only one monk [is examined] at a time, and the formal debate is to last up to three days. As for those doing the questioning,[110] except for a few particular [cases of] elders who are in poor health, every single one of the Kachu and Rapjam scholars on the monastery's roster are to inspire intelligent debate. Moreover, they are not to employ any covert deceit, any misleading strategies, or spurious topics in their questioning. Even if they do employ these, they are not to do improper acts that destroy the Teachings. The disciplinarians are to distinguish the good from the bad [debate]. After the Kachu and Rapjam scholars have finished, the classes go each in turn [in questioning the candidate].[111]

The overriding concern here is for a decent, intellectual debate that rises above personal enmity and base invectives. The constitution explains,

Whenever there is a formal debate, great or small, being attached to the desire for one's own victory, having anger that wishes the debasement of one's opponent, as well as the defendant focusing primarily on [proposing] deceptive arguments;[112] having a smiling appearance while speaking quickly, arguing in factions, having conspiratorial talk[113] of one's own distaste for debate; in short, an intention marked by the wrongful behavior of degrading [others], ridiculing, [saying] hurtful words, [speaking] querulous words,[114] speaking of others' faults, revealing others' weaknesses, etc.—[all of this] should not to be done.

Meanwhile, one should have a reverence that desires the realization of truth.[115] One should have a compassion that desires to dispel the misconceptions of others. One should have a kindness that desires to make one's opponents understand truth. While having such an intention and emphasizing scripture and reason,[116] to analyze and refute [one's opponent] in the proper fashion based on such things as the *Seven Treatises on Valid Cognition*[117] is a great delight. This is pure happiness.[118]

It is known that, despite such provisions, debates offered opportunities for monks to display their wit as well as their literary acumen. A nineteenth-century Tibet history recounts one such exchange that took place between a hitherto renowned and peerless Gönlung *geshé* and an individual from the younger, ascendant Labrang Monastery. The Gönlung *geshé*, one Pari Khaykho,[119] initiates the exchange:

Pari Khaykho stood up and ridiculed [the Labrang monk Tendzin Gyayuma[120]], saying, "So![121] You have three unnecessary things— on your mouth you have an unnecessary beard; in your hands you have an unnecessary rosary;[122] in your mind you have an unnecessary fabrication.[123] . . ."

[Tendzin Gyayuma] stood up, motioned three circles [in the direction of Pari Khaykho],[124] and retorted: "As for me, although I have all necessary things, I also have three unnecessary things. As for you, you are missing three necessary things! The meat that your body needs you don't have! The debate[125] your tongue needs you don't have! The clap your hands need you don't have!"

[Pari Khyakho] replied, "It is said that this is the kind of baseless talk one makes up at Sera, Drepung, and Ganden Monasteries."

Someone else [said], "He is fond of verbiage, but his assertion is that there is no omniscience in the individual's mind-stream!" [Everyone] roared with laughter.

He [i.e., Tendzin Gyayuma] stood up [and stated], "It follows from this that there is omniscience in an individual's mind-stream."

"Agreed," [replied Pari Khyakho].

"Well, then it follows that an individual wears monastic robes[126] on his upper body."

"Agreed."

"It follows that an individual wears pants."

"Agreed."

[Tendzin Gyayuma] retorted and established the implication: "Then it follows that an individual wears monastic robes on his upper body *together with* pants on his lower body!"[127]

Pari Khyakho's defeat and humiliation also signaled a shift in Gönlung's and Labrang's respective fortunes and reputations.

In addition to addressing such "querulous" or "bad" words, Jikmé Yeshé Drakpa is also concerned with the problem of frivolously doling out degrees: "The [practice of] wise one's leading debate and so forth must not be departed from such that 'only a little talk is done' [and one earns a degree]. [Such] bad customs of awarding degrees must not be established." Despite his warnings against such "bad customs," Jikmé Yeshé Drakpa was also cognizant of the reality on the ground. As the Fifth Dalai Lama did in his constitution for Drepung, Jikmé Yeshé Drakpa acknowledges the practices of awarding "honorary degrees"[128] but restricts their use. These were degrees that an individual might, under exceptional circumstances, "purchase" without going through the normal performance of formal debate in front of the entire monastic assembly: "For the study-abroad monks residing here [who come] for the purpose of [acquiring] a title, if they suddenly have to leave, then [there is] a system of the master granting [them titles] according to the circumstances. Also, except for cases in which a subsidiary monastery's own monks[129] need to leave suddenly for China or the periphery of Mongolia for very important matters, honorary degrees are never to be given to monks residing here."[130] In other words, we see certain concessions made in cases of title-seeking monks who are not from Gönlung itself and who have other important business to attend to back East. This likely had to do with the ties Gönlung was continuing to form with wealthy patrons in Mongolia, since the process of awarding honorary degrees was one that brought significant wealth to the monastery in exchange for the monastery's name and prestige: "As for the process of [awarding] honorary titles, [they] do not need to engage in formal debate. On top of giving five mass teas, they must speak from between the pillars [in the assembly hall][131] as if they were doing Standing Assembly Debate.

"[Honorary] degree [seekers] must offer a minimum of one horse to the abbot. To the congregation of monks [they must give] two mass teas and a mid-morning meal.[132] They must give an Extensive *Namshak* offering. [Finally, they should give] to [the monastery's] Beneficial Endowment[133] an ounce[134] of silver." This exception aside, the goal of the degree and debate system was to showcase high-level debate so as to stimulate the next generation of scholar-monks. Thus, as Jikmé Yeshé Drakpa's constitution explains, "If there are no individuals seeking a normal [i.e., not an honorary] degree, then the Kachu and Rapjam scholars and so forth are to engage in a great formal debate[135] as is traditionally done."[136]

## Exporting to Inner Mongolia

Aside from issuing honorary degrees to eligible (and wealthy) monks from Mongolia, how else did the Geluk school exert its influence and its particular system of organizing monasticism in Mongolia? This was done mostly through the missionizing activity of homegrown lamas from Amdo, such as Gönlung's Sumba. Sumba Kanbo records in his autobiography how he established a new philosophical college in Inner Mongolia[137] and initiated "the start of the Domé [i.e., Amdo]-Mongolia [study-abroad] monk-stream."[138]

Sumba Kanbo was not the only Gönlung lama proselytizing and instituting Geluk scholasticism in Mongolia. One of Gönlung's less well-known incarnate lamas, the Fourth Wang Khutugtu (1846–1906),[139] penned a constitution for a certain Eren Monastery in Inner Mongolia.[140] Not coincidentally, he is also the author of Gönlung's other extant constitution.[141] He clearly had an organizing as well as a proselytizing mind, having spent years traveling around Inner Mongolia, printing Tsongkhapa's scriptures, and establishing Geluk systems of practice.

The Wang lineage had ties with Inner Mongolia stretching back to the second of this series (Skal bzang ye shes dar rgyas, 1739–1804) and possibly even farther.[142] The ties between the Wang lineage and Inner Mongolia coincide with a renewed interest among Gelukpas from Amdo in building networks of monasteries and patrons in Inner Mongolia in the aftermath of the 1723–1724 Lubsang-Danzing Rebellion and the destruction of the Oirat Mongols' rule in Kökenuur.

When the Fourth Wang composed his constitution for the Eren Monastery in Inner Mongolia in 1898, he had been traveling in those areas that had recently been devastated by the Jindan Massacre of 1891.[143] So, his activity there mirrored in some ways that of Jikmé Yeshé Drakpa a century and a half earlier: both were seeking to revitalize and standardize Geluk practice in the way of its destruction. The constitution that the Fourth Wang left to us, "The Mirror That Illuminates [What Is to Be] Accepted and Rejected," is short but exhibits many of the same concerns for Geluk scholasticism as found in Jikmé Yeshé Drakpa's constitution for Gönlung. Wang explains that it was written on the occasion of "the establishment of the new degree of Dorampa."[144] Thus, the system of rewarding accomplished scholar-monks with degrees, which drew its authority from the major monasteries of Central Tibet, found its way here, too. The name of the degree is different from that of Gönlung—Dorampa[145] rather than Kachupa—but this is just an artifact of the time. When Gönlung established its system of conferring Kachu degrees, the custom of awarding Dorampa degrees did not yet exist.[146]

This difference aside, the protocol for preparing for the defense or formal debate was the same at Eren as was that laid out by Jikmé Yeshé Drakpa for Gönlung 150 years earlier. The potential candidates are nominated by officers of the monastery or the philosophical college and are evaluated on Perfection of Wisdom ("Treatise") material up through the topic known as "Naturally Abiding Lineage" and on Madhyamaka material up through "Establishment and Refutation."[147] If the candidate passes, then, on the third day of the first month, coinciding with the Great Prayer Festival, the disciplinarian announces that the candidate may proceed by participating in formal debates. As we have seen, Jikmé Yeshé Drakpa, too, required Gönlung candidates to begin regularly participating in formal debates at the Great Prayer Festival of the first month. At Gönlung, additional vetting and scrutiny took place at the Great Spring Dharma Session of the third and fourth months, and similarly at Eren, on a day at the end of the fourth month, the candidate's standing is reviewed by the officers of the monastery and the college, after which the candidate is invited to present himself before the abbot. A final decision is made. If the candidate is deemed qualified, then in the sixth month he will participate in the Great Formal Debate, his degree defense: "As for debating, for periods of three days in both the first and sixth months, debate from the colors of red and white [i.e., from the beginning Collected Topics material] to Vinaya [i.e., the most advanced material]. While this is being done, it is permissable for the upper-classmen to drill [the examinee]. During the Great Formal Debate, custom is that the upper-classmen lead [in questioning the examiners]."[148]

Like Jikmé Yeshé Drakpa before him, Wang insists that the language used in debate stick to the formalistic vocabulary and language of debate lest the occasion be marred by informal or personalistic language: "No matter which of the five treatises one is reasoning over,[149] other than the words 'the reasoning is [or is not] connected,'[150] when debating, no other interruptions to the assembly are allowed. The questioners team up;[151] however, other than establishing points of scripture and reason, other responses are not to be made at any time. [The examinees] must debate [lit. "say 'there is' [or 'there is not'] any connection"] on each of the five treatises."[152] Wang adds, in closing, that the objective of these debates should be the propagation of the Buddha's dharma, not one's own fame and glory: "[One] should not transgress the objective of the Teachings and the Buddhist Vinaya."[153]

## Conclusion

As the monopoly of the Geluk school grew in Amdo and Mongolia, a priority was placed on scholasticism. But orthodoxy meant more than just adherence to some set of creeds. It meant adherence to a *system* of learning and socialization. There were proper ways of debating—permissible and formulaic language, systems for awarding scholastic degrees, and so on. Such codified *ways of learning* both facilitated the growth of connections between more centrally located monasteries and more peripheral ones and were facilitated by these connections. Geluk legitimacy extended because there was scholastic consistency and predictability built on the promise of reason and truth. Benefits included the increased mobility (of monks), and the prestige of the Geluk school as a whole benefited as a result.

In the next chapter, we will examine a similar process of expansionism and rationalization. The ideas and systems being promoted, however, were liturgical ones. The daily litany of prayers and hymns, which composed the other half of the monastic life, was orchestrated by Geluk hierarchs, giving rise to a remarkable level of consistency to the Geluk school even as it expanded across greater distances.

# Chapter 5

# Singing Together in One Voice

In the spring of 2011, I made a trip north from the city of Xining, past Gön-lung and across the Qilian Mountains toward the Hexi Corridor of the ancient Silk Road. Approximately 60 kilometers south of the city of Zhangye—historically known as Ganzhou and an important stop along the Hexi Corridor—one finds the monastery known as Mati si 馬蹄寺,[1] literally "Horse Hoof Monastery." It is a Tibetan Buddhist monastery named after an impression found on the ceiling of one of its many cliffside grottoes and formed, so the saying goes, by the steed of the epic Tibetan hero Gesar.

I made this long drive because Mati is said to have been a "child" or "branch" monastery of Gönlung or, more precisely, of one of Gönlung's principal incarnate lamas, until at least the early twentieth century. One missionary to the region in the early twentieth century writes that Mati si would annually pay to this lama the interest on the land that the lama had bought for the branch monastery.

On my visit, I asked the resident monks if they possessed a monastic constitution. I hoped to compare it to the constitutions of Gönlung and thereby find similarities and relationships between the liturgical calendars and the internal administration of the two monasteries. Unfortunately, as is often the case in China today, particularly in this region, whatever documents had managed to survive into the twentieth century were burned or otherwise destroyed during the "Democratic Reforms" of 1958 and the Cultural Revolution. Upon pressing further, however, I was led by one monk to his room where he revealed to me the monastery's "Rules and Procedures" (T. *grig lam*) together with its "Arrangement of the Recitations" (T. *'don bsgrigs*), texts that together are nearly identical to the monastic constitution (T. *bca' yig*) genre of literature: the compilation of the two

Figure 12. The rock-grotto Mati Monastery, a branch monastery of Gönlung.
The indentation of the divine steed of Gesar can be found inside these grottoes.
Photo by the author, April 2011.

begins with quotations from canonical literature regarding the importance
of proper conduct for the achievement of salvation; rules are given defining
what kind of clothes can be worn, when one can leave the monastery, and
so on; fines and punishments for breaking these rules are specified; then a
calendar for rituals to be performed and texts and prayers to be recited,
including an indication of which are to be specially sung rather than simply
chanted, is provided; the procedures for installing new monastic officials
are given; and so on.[2]

   This, however, was not an old text. It was written in 1999 by an incarnate lama from the renowned and influential Labrang Tashi Khyil Monastery, several hours south and east from Mati Monastery.[3] This lama's master
was one of the most renowned *geshés*, or scholar-monks, at Labrang, and most
of the monks at Mati are also reportedly disciples of this *geshé*. A third individual from Labrang, the cantor of one of Labrang's colleges, is said to have
taught the monks of Mati the manner in which to actually chant and sing
the liturgy.[4]

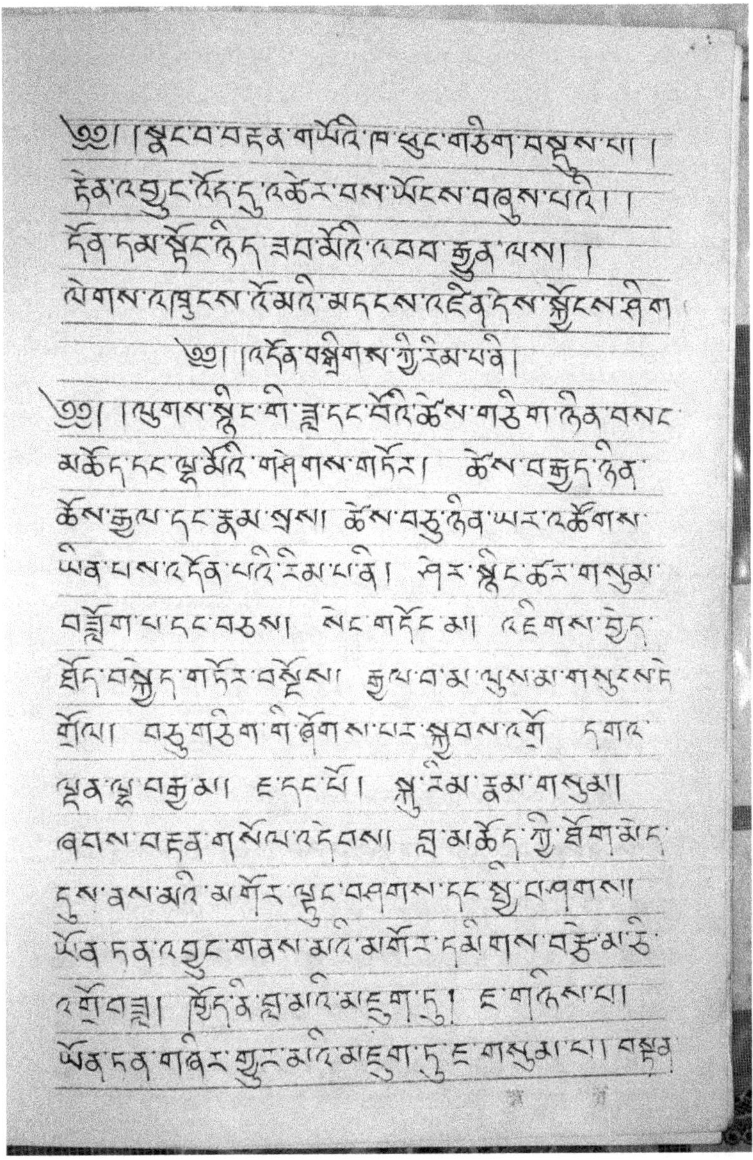

༄༅། །སྐྱང་བ་བརྟན་གཡཕའི་ཁ་ཕྱུང་གཅིག་བསྲས་པ། །
རྟེན་འབྱུང་དོད་དུ་འཆེར་བས་ཡོངས་བཞུས་པའོ། །
དོན་དམ་སྟོང་ཉིད་ཟབ་མོའི་འབབ་རྒྱུན་ལས། །
ཡེ་གས་འཕྲུངས་དོ་མའི་མདངས་འཛིན་དེས་སྐྱིངས་ཤེག །

༄༅། །འདིན་བསྐྱིགས་ཀྱི་རིམ་པ་ནི། །

༄༅། །ལྷགས་སྐྱུང་གི་ཟྲུང་དང་ཕོའི་ཚེས་གཅིག་ག་ཉེན་བསང་
མཆོད་དང་ལུ་མོའི་གཤིགས་གཏོ། ཚེས་བཅུད་ཉེན་
ཚེས་རྒྱལ་དང་རྫམ་སྲས། ཚེས་བཅུ་ཉེན་ཡར་འཚོགས་
ཡན་པས་འདོན་པའི་རིམ་པ་ནེ། ཤེར་སྟོང་ཆོ་གསུམ་
བརྒྱག་པ་དང་བཅུས། ཤེང་གདོང་མ། འཇིགས་བྱེད་
སྟོད་བརྒྱུད་གཏོར་བསོས། རྒྱལ་བ་མ་ལུས་མ་གསུར་འཏེ
གོལ། བཅུ་གཅིག་གི་ཞོགས་པར་སྐྱབས་འགྲོ དགའ
ལྡན་ལྷ་བརྒྱ། ཇ་དང་ཕོ། སྐུ་རིམ་རྣམ་གསུམ།
ཞབས་བརྟན་གསོལ་འདེབས། ཧྲ་མཆོད་ཀྱི་ཐོག་མེད་
དུས་ནས་མའི་མགོར་ལྱུང་བཤགས་དང་སྲུ་བཤགས།
ཡོན་དན་འབྱུང་གནས་མའི་མགོར་དགེ་གས་བརྗ་མ་རྩེ
འགོབ་ཛྲ། ཕྱེད་ན་སྲ་མའ་མཇུག་དུ། ཇ་གདིས་པ།
ཡོན་དན་གཞར་གྱུང་མའ་མཇུག་དུ་ཇ་གསུམ་པ། བརྒྱ

Figure 13. Closing verses of the "Rules and Procedures" and opening of the
"Arrangement of the Recitations" of Mati Monastery.
Photo by the author, April 2011.

A similar example of such inter-institutional connections can be found at a Mongol temple in present-day Xinjiang Region. The temple, two thousand kilometers west from Gönlung, follows the "Assembly Recitations" (T. *tshogs 'don*) written by the previous Chuzang Lama—that is, one of the major incarnate lamas of Gönlung. The one-page, handwritten text sits on the main altar and reminds the monks of what they are to recite each day. Similarly, the abbot from Chuzang Monastery[5] explained to me that other monasteries—including Gönlung in 2010, Chöten Thang in 2010, and a monastery two thousand kilometers to the east in Liaoning Province—all learned and employed the liturgy and chanting style of Chuzang Monastery for certain "eye-opening" (i.e., consecration) ceremonies at their respective monasteries. A monastery cannot casually modify its unique chanting style, he informed me, and when such a tradition is lost, one must try to restore it as best one can. Hence, this instance of Gönlung and these other monasteries turning to their close relative, Chuzang Monastery, to reclaim their lost traditions.

It seems, then, that even though a Chinese law from 2010 forbids monasteries from having "parent" or "child" monasteries, Labrang has, nonetheless, in many ways subsumed Mati under its supervision, and Chuzang, nominally a branch monastery of Gönlung, maintains some degree of control over the ritual program at temples located thousands of miles away. This is not a recent phenomenon. The historical record demonstrates the importance of liturgical connections for the spread and uniformity of the Geluk school. In fact, liturgy may be the realm of monastic life where conscious efforts of Geluk hierarchs to mold a common identity are most conspicuous. Hierarchs of the Geluk school, beginning with the Fifth Dalai Lama, stand out above earlier and non-Geluk lamas from the same period in encoding elaborate liturgies for monasteries across Tibet and Mongolia.[6]

## Liturgies Before the Fifth Dalai Lama

In the Christian world, "liturgy" designates "service to God." It stands for collective worship as well as the entire schedule or system of worship services.[7] It is nearly a perfect synonym for the Tibetan *chöjö* (T. *chos spyod*), or "service [to the] dharma." The latter term designates the complex of regularly occurring (usually daily) prayers and hymns recited collectively by residents of a monastery, and, as such, it can also refer to the collection of prayers

Figure 14. The main shrine hall of a branch monastery of Gönlung located in present-day Xinjiang Region. The framed document on the altar includes handwritten instructions for the performance of the branch's liturgy (T. *tshogs 'don*) composed by one of Gönlung's incarnate lamas.
Photo by the author, April 2011.

and hymns—the "breviary"—of a monastery or school. However, *chöjö* is a bit more restrictive than "liturgy," since it can be distinguished from "ritual" proper (T. *cho ga*). Rituals are less frequent (scheduled, but not all daily) periods of heightened religious activity (usually tantric) directed at a particular god or set of gods or one's guru with a specific, stated aim of some kind.[8] My use of the word *liturgy* in this chapter, then, is more akin to the English (and Christian) use insofar as I wish to discuss all types and levels of the ritual program at monasteries, from the "regular recitations" (T. *rgyun gyi tshogs 'don; rgyun pa'i chos spyod;* etc.) to the less frequent and more major ritual occasions that involve propitiating and otherwise more directly interacting with the gods.[9]

Most Tibetan Buddhists share a common framework for servicing the dharma.[10] This is partly a result of the common Indian Buddhist heritage they share. So, for instance, the liturgical year is marked by the major events of Śākyamuni Buddha's life, such as his birth, enlightenment, and death (celebrated together in the fourth month); his first teaching (for Gelukpa, in the sixth month) and, often, his descent from Tuṣita Heaven (ninth month); as well as the Summer Rains Retreat (T. *dbyar gnas*; S. *varṣā*), the release from the Summer Rains Retreat (T. *dgag dbye*; S. *pravāraṇā*), and the fortnightly confession of sins and restoration of vows (T. *gso sbyong*)—the last three making up the so-called Three Foundations (T. *gzhi gsum*) that all Buddhists everywhere acknowledge in some fashion. Tibetan Buddhists also single out many of the same days each month for heightened ritual activity.[11] Finally, as part of the "regular liturgy" that Tibetan Buddhists share, we find the following: taking of refuge in the Three Jewels ("Refuges"), Giving Rise to the Mind of Enlightenment, homages to the Sixteen Arhats, the Seven-Branch Offering, the Maṇḍala Offering, the recitation of the *Heart Sutra* and its accompanying apotropaic rite, the Tārā, the One Hundred Ritual Cake Offerings [T. *brgya rtsa*], guru yoga and supplication prayers, the Litany of Names of Mañjuśrī,[12] aspiration prayers (T. *smon lam*) to certain bodhisattvas such as Samantabhadra or to the Western Pure Land of Amitabha Buddha, and the mantra of Amitabha, among others.

A review of the liturgical elements of monastic constitutions alone cannot give us a complete history of Tibetan liturgies, nor is this an attempt to write one. Such a history would require the time-consuming and intensive work of identifying individual ritual texts and, whenever possible, the institution or location for which they were composed, and then piecing together the various components of a location's overall ritual program, not to mention the study of "breviaries" (T. *chos spyod*) or collections of liturgies used by particular monasteries.[13] Nonetheless, the prescriptions of liturgical programs found in monastic constitutions provide us with a rare, bird's-eye view of how Geluk lamas envisioned the rhythm of prayers, hymns, and rituals that constitute what one scholar has called "the ultimate function" of monastic life.[14]

The earliest monastic constitution to address liturgy is Tsongkhapa's constitution for the general sangha (no. 4). It is rather short and consists entirely of elements of the stock, pan-sectarian formulas for worshipping the dharma (see "regular liturgy" above).[15] Liturgy does not surface in a constitution again until the Eighth Karmapa's constitution for the "Holders of Varja Awareness" (T. *rdo rje rig pa 'dzin pa*) of the Dakini Section (T. Mkha' spyod gling) of his Great Encampment (no. 8) and his constitution for Tsurpu Monastery (no. 9). Here we begin to see a degree of specificity and sectarianism that comes to characterize later Geluk constitutions. The Karmapa specifies the periods of the day and what is to be performed when. Monks are also tested on their memorization of the liturgy.[16]

Although the makeup of the Karmapa's liturgy largely consists of the same stock formulas mentioned above, the Karmapa does introduce a sectarian dimension by instructing monks, having arranged the ritual cakes and visualized the offerings, to "properly offer ritual cakes to the lamas, patron deities, and protector deities of the Kar[ma] tradition."[17] In addition, the Karmapa designates himself as the primary ritual officiant, which is not surprising given that his constitutions were composed for his encampment and what had by that time become his primary monastery, Tsurpu. As we shall see, Geluk constitutions associated with monasteries founded by a Dalai Lama similarly give central importance to the Dalai Lama in the liturgy. However, this is *not* the case for other, later, Geluk constitutions.

Finally, the collective aspect of the Karmapa's liturgy is rivaled by the private worship that is insisted upon therein. Although the monks are to meet throughout the day at the Great Encampment's White Tent (T. *kur dkar*; *dkar gur*; *gung* [sic] *dkar*), this is sandwiched between a detailed schedule of meditation and tantric practice that is specified to take place in the morning, at night, and in one's sleep.[18] Meanwhile, in his Tsurpu constitution (no. 9), he warns against growing too attached to the others with whom one lives.[19] That is, he explicitly challenges the collective aspect of monastic life even while trying to maintain it in his competition with the rising Geluk school.

The Ninth Karmapa's constitutions (nos. 13–23) are quite disappointing for our understanding of Karma Kagyü liturgy. Scattered throughout the various, collected constitutions (five, to be exact) one finds isolated liturgical elements that, when taken together, are characteristic of later Geluk constitutions—for example, an emphasis on the importance of recitations and their memorization, a list of the prayers and hymns to be recited, a breakdown of the day into sessions, and a specification of the gods to be worshipped. No doubt, this relative paucity of liturgical subject matter is due in part to the existence of earlier constitutions that elaborated on this but which are no longer available. Nonetheless, it is telling that in none of his eleven constitutions written for monasteries and monastic communities across the Plateau do we find a full, multidimensional discussion of the liturgy as we find in later Geluk constitutions. This suggests that either a common liturgy was not important to the Karmapa or that he did not care to codify it, which often amounts to the same thing when an organization expands over greater and greater distances.

The First Drukpa Zhapdrung, Ngawang Namgyel,[20] wrote his constitution for the central monastery of his Drukpa Kagyü school just two years before he fled from Tibet and established the state of Bhutan due to a disagreement with the king of Tsang.[21] His constitution fits the pattern of a high lama from a school composing a constitution for his own, personal monastery. Furthermore, although this constitution does include a breakdown of the daily sessions and the liturgy to be performed, as well as mentioning tests on the liturgy, it is relatively short and stops short of detailing a fuller, multidimensional liturgy that includes a calendar of the major ritual occasions or a schedule of the important monthly rituals to be carried out.

It is only with Sakya Trichen Ngawang Künga Sönam's[22] constitution for his own personal retreat at Geding (no. 31) that we find the elaborate liturgy characteristic of later Geluk constitutions. Likewise, the importance of the liturgy is underscored in the constitution: the cantor is instructed to be attentive and apply himself, while everyone else is to try hard, be faithful, and "sing together in one voice."[23] Sakya Trichen even instructs his monks to correct "any lapses in this regular liturgy . . . at whatever monastery one is at."[24] Aspects of Sakya Trichen's liturgy also influenced later Sakya constitutions.[25] Nonetheless, we do not have evidence that he wrote constitutions for any other monasteries. In addition, this constitution is unapologetically tied to praising and worshipping the author and his family, which may have limited the wider impact of his constitution on monasteries other than that which was his own retreat.

## Conversion by the Fifth Dalai Lama

This all changed after the Fifth Dalai Lama assumed power and began to use liturgy as a mechanism for the expansion of the Geluk school. It was my reading of a passage concerning liturgy in Zahiruddhin Ahmad's translation of the biography of the Fifth Dalai Lama that first alerted me to the importance of monastic constitutions for the success of the Geluk school:

> In the year Earth Sheep [11 February 1679–31 January 1680], within the jurisdiction of the 13 government districts and estates in the administrative divisions of Do-Kham, there were 657 monasteries with monk-pupils, of which those of the Gelukpa sect were in a majority, with 31,947 monk-pupils. In the Gelukpa monasteries, the White Umbrella and the Names of Mañjuśrī were recited. All monasteries regardless of sect performed "firm feet" services on behalf of the Lord-Lama [i.e., the Dalai Lama] by reciting both "The Protector Amitāyus" and the Brahman of the White Conch Headdress Offering Amitabha Residing in [His] Realm." Those Nyingmapa monasteries which harbored no resentment [toward us] *should have [performed], unimpairedly, the special rites and rituals of [our] important acts of worship.* But some among them did not take into consideration the establishment of our Gelukpa monasteries in their areas. . . . *An edict was issued to the Sakyapa and the Nyingmapa [saying that] they should read [and act according to] what had been decided by the "clear and powerful" sealed edicts [T.* gtan tshigs*] of the Lord-Lama,* the great crest-ornament of Saṁsāra and Nirvāṇa. *The other objects of worship [i.e., monasteries] should read [and act according to], principally, the Gelukpa rules.* Together [with the edict], disciplinary rules [T. *bca' yig*], suited to the country, time, state-of-affairs and individuals were issued [saying] that whatever was not in those [rules] would not be right.[26]

This was an act of conversion of Sakya and Nyingma Monasteries in Kham (Eastern Tibet), and it centered on redirecting the arrangement and performance of the liturgy.

Similarly, compiled alongside a constitution that the Fifth Dalai Lama composed for a monastery in Kham (no. 49)[27] is another text in which he responds to a request to provide a name and to identify the proper protector deity for a newly established monastery in Amdo. He gives it the Geluk-infused name of Ganden Gyetsel (T. Dga' ldan skyed tshal; "Pleasure Grove of Tuṣita Heaven) and named the Six-armed Mahākāla and

Yama (T. Las gshin)—two principal Geluk protector deities—as the monastery's protectors.[28]

Another example of fixing the identity of a monastery by making changes to its system of worship is that of the Nyingma Monastery, known as Ngesang Dorjé Ling in Gongra, western Central Tibet (constitution no. 43). As James Gentry has discussed, this monastery was the base of Gongra Zhenpen Dorjé,[29] a disciple of Sokdokpa,[30] who the Fifth Dalai Lama despised and whose teachings the Dalai Lama rejected because of Sokdokpa's long-term alliance with the Geluk school's erstwhile opponent, the king of Tsang. As a result, in his constitution for the monastery, the Dalai Lama proscribed the use of texts and practices associated with these two figures and with Sokdokpa's own master, Nangtsewa:[31]

> [These] fabricated and corrupted false Treasures [of Nangtsewa, Sokdokpa, and Gongra Zhenpen Dorjé] here are rejected, and so as to avoid opposing the Geluk Teachings and government, the Protector of the Earth, Treasurer Sönam Rapten[32] commanded and Tratsangpa, the Great Scholar-Adept, Lodrö Chökyi Dorjé,[33] was appointed abbot. Also, because those who clinged to the bad traditions of old did not act appropriately, the teachings and individuals tainted by sectarianism were expelled. For the Teachings in general and for the Obstacle-clearing Rites and so forth of the government in particular, these are the sequences to be accepted and rejected for renewing the flourishing of this monastery of Gongra ngesang dorjé ling.[34]

In the name of his government and anti-sectarianism, the Dalai Lama imposed a sectarian liturgical agenda for explicitly political purposes.


## The Fifth Dalai Lama's Program

The Fifth Dalai Lama at times directly intervened in the liturgical and administrative programs of monasteries that fell within his immediate domain of influence. This included naming the Nyingma Monastery of Ngesang Dorjé Ling as treasonous[35] and directly appointing a new and more loyal abbot.[36] Apart from that, however, the Dalai Lama also attempted to foster a Geluk liturgy in a more indirect fashion, through the numerous constitutions he composed and which later Geluk hierarchs would follow. In his constitutions, the Dalai Lama would frequently include prayers and hymns written by or for Tsongkhapa and the Dalai Lamas; he would provide long and detailed liturgies that address what is to be performed on daily, monthly, and annual bases; he encouraged the worship of Geluk patron and protector deities; and he made explicit calls for modeling a monastery's liturgy on other, more centrally located monasteries.

One of the first constitutions that the Fifth Dalai Lama composed after assuming power was his 1645 constitution for Chökhorgyel (no. 34) in southern Central Tibet. In some ways, Chökhorgyel is unique and represents an outlier: the Second Dalai Lama founded the monastery, and, as such, it is recognized as the personal monastery of the Dalai Lamas.[37] However, the constitution reveals the full breadth of the Fifth Dalai Lama's efforts to fashion a Geluk liturgy and, through that, a unique Geluk identity. Looking closely at it can help us to understand the various aspects of the comprehensive Geluk liturgy that appear in subsequent Geluk constitutions. The constitution includes a short litany of prayers and hymns for the regular "assembly recitations"—that is, the recitations for daily (at least two or three times a day) assemblies, each service lasting one to two hours. These consist mostly of stock recitations and rituals found in earlier and non-Geluk liturgies, although two stand out as Geluk additions: the recitation of the "two great scriptures," which refers to the *Ornament of Realization* (T. *Mngon rtogs rgyan*) and the *Entrance to the Middle Way* (T. *Dbu ma 'jug pa*; on these scriptures, see Chapter 4); and, the "Glorious Three Realms" (T. *Sa gsum ma*), a praise of Tsongkhapa by one of his foremost disciples, Khedrup Jé.[38] Monks were expected to memorize all the prayers and hymns, the process of maṇḍala visualizations of the Geluk trinity of patron deities, and the restoration rites dedicated to the school's protector deities within six months of arriving at the monastery, at which point a test was given.[39]

Six years later, when the Fifth Dalai Lama composed his revision to the Chökhorgyel constitution (no. 40), the liturgical section was expanded immensely and moved to the front of the constitution. In the intervening years, the Dalai Lama had given much thought to and written about the rituals to be performed at the monastery. The monastery's protectors were the protectors of the Dalai Lamas and, beginning with the Fifth Dalai Lama, the Dalai Lama's government.[40] The Fifth Dalai Lama designed a program that would all but guarantee that these deities were properly worshipped and that every other aspect of the liturgical program at the monastery was complete.

The Fifth Dalai Lama writes about liturgy in two sections. The first is the "arrangement of required recitations for regular assembly" and the second provides a calendar for the annual and monthly worship of the monastery's principal deities through such major rituals as Accomplishment Offerings (T. *sgrub mchod*, the "great ceremonies"; the visualization and offering of all of one's virtues and merit to specified buddhas),[41] the offering of periodic ritual cakes (T. *dus gtor*), and regular (daily) ritual cake offerings.

The litany of recitations that make up the first section comprise at least sixteen prayers and hymns that are tied to Tsongkhapa, the Dalai Lamas, and, to a lesser extent, the Panchen Lamas. Their inclusion indicates a conscious effort by the Dalai Lama to codify a uniquely Geluk liturgy:

1. "[The Chief Accomplished One among] the Gods" (T. *Skabs gsum ma*),[42] which is a praise of Śākyamuni by Tsongkhapa;
2. "The Complete Liberation of the Omniscient One [The First Dalai Lama]—[His] Twelve Miraculous Deeds" (T. *Thams cad mkhyen pas mdzad pa'i* [sic] *mdzad bcu*);[43]
3. "Limitless Light" (T. *Snang ba mtha' yas ma*),[44] praises of Atiśa by the Second Dalai Lama;
4. "Praises of Drom, [Teacher of Wandering Beings] Including the Gods" (T. *'Brom gyi bstod pa lha bcas ma*),[45] also by the Second Dalai Lama;
5. "Praises of the First Dalai Lama" (T. *Thub dbang bstan sgron ma*),[46] by the First Dalai Lama's disciple Lodrö Bepa;[47]
6. the Second Dalai Lama's praises of himself (T. *Rab dkar dge tshogs ma*);[48]
7. the Third Dalai Lama's praises of himself (T. *Rgya chen bsod nams ma*);[49]
8. the Fourth Panchen Lama's praises of the Fourth Dalai Lama (T. *Phun tshogs yon tan ma*);[50]
9. the Fifth Dalai Lama's praises of himself (T. *Blo bzang rgyal ba ma*);[51]
10. the "Protector of the *Rapjam* Scholars" (T. *Rab 'byams skyob pa ma*),[52] by the Fourth Panchen Lama;
11. the "Spontaneous Accomplishment of the Land of Bliss" (T. *Bde chen lhun grub ma*),[53] by the Second Dalai Lama;
12. "The Body of Maitreya" (T. *Byams pa'i sku gzugs ma*),[54] by the First Dalai Lama;

13. "Brahma's Crown" (T. *Tshangs pa'i cod pan ma*),[55] a praise of Maitreya by Tsongkhapa;

14. "Clouds on the Face of the Precious Mountains at Sunset" (T. *Mtshams sprin ma*),[56] praises of and prayers for Tsongkhapa and his teachings by Khedrup Jé;

15. "The Vast and Deep [Knowledge]" (T. *Zab yangs ma*),[57] a praise of Maitreya by Tsongkhapa;

16. "Aspirational Prayers for Past, Present, and Future" (T. *Thog mtha' bar gyi smon lam*),[58] by Tsongkhapa."

In addition, one finds as part of the regular liturgy aspirational prayers to the Geluk patron deity Guhyasamāja[59] and ritual cake offerings to some of the quintessential Geluk protector deities, Pelden Makzorma (a form of Pelden Lhamo), Mahākāla, Bektsé and Sister-Spouse (T. *Zhal lcam sring*),[60] and more. We will see how some of these and other such prayers and hymns regularly appear in Geluk constitutions in the decades following the Fifth Dalai Lama's death. Moreover, nearly all of these can be found today in widely available breviaries or "collected liturgies" of the Geluk school (collated in much the same order), which speaks to the lasting influence of these early efforts to codify a Geluk liturgy.[61]

The second section of the Fifth Dalai Lama's constitution consists of a description and schedule of the major tantric visualizations and offerings directed to the monastery's most important deities. It begins with a discussion of the Summer Prayer Festival (T. *dbyar ka'i smon lam*), during which deity yoga and empowerments of the Geluk trinity of patron deities—Guhyasamāja, Vajrabhairava, and Cakrasaṃvara—are performed. The Dalai Lama also instructs the monks to revive the practice of Accomplishment Offerings (T. *sgrub mchod*) for the buddha Kalacakra in accordance with the manual of the fourteenth-century luminary Butön (1290–1364), the scholar-monk closely with Zhalu Monastery in Tsang. In addition, the major protector deities of the Geluk school are to be worshipped through ritual offering cakes: Six-armed Mahākāla, Vaiśravaṇa, Yama, Pelden Lhamo, Panjara ("Lord of the Tent") Mahākāla, and Four-faced Mahākāla.[62] Following that is mention of the Twenty-fifth Offering (T. *lnga mchod*), the ritual commemorating the death of Tsongkhapa. The Winter Session at the monastery begins on the first of November and entails offerings to all the eight classes of worldly deities and demons and exams on this, including fines for those who fail to pass these exams.[63]

At this point, the annual calendar breaks to specify the periodic ritual cake offerings and other monthly rituals. These take place at five different chapels at the monastery on specified days.[64] So, for instance, Bektsé is worshipped in the Cool Grove on the fifth of each month,[65] Panjara Mahākāla and Four-faced Mahākāla are worshipped in the Cool Grove of the eighth and twenty-third of each month, the Makzorma Glorious Goddess (Pelden Lhamo) is worshipped at the Goddess Palace on the fifteenth and twenty-fifth of each month,[66] the Four-armed Mahākāla and several other deities, including Vaiśravaṇa and Pehar are worshipped at the Protector Palace on the ninth and nineteenth of each month,[67] and so on.

After this, the annual calendar resumes, specifying that the Great Ritual Cake Offering of the first day of the new year (to Pelden Lhamo, what is often called the *tshes gtor*, or "Day Ritual Cake Offering") takes place in the Goddess Palace. Apart from the monthly worship of the protector deities, the ninth month is designated as the time for the annual, "extended" Ritual Cake Offering to the protectors. The twenty-ninth of the tenth month is the Ritual Cake Offering (T. *bcu pa'i dgu gtor*) for Pelden Lhamo, and that of the twenty-ninth of the twelfth month is for Bektsé.

The importance of maintaining this ritual calendar, particularly the second section dealing with rituals proper (T. *cho ga*), which are directed toward the monastery's deities, is made explicit at the end of the section: "Establishing Accomplishment Offerings twice each year for each [of the principal deities] is beneficial to the conditions of the Teachings and for clearing obstacles[68] [of the monastery]."[69] Moreover, in this constitution the Dalai Lama codifies the daily, monthly, and annual rhythms of the monastery such that all the monastery's monks participate in a predictable schedule of worship of the principal patron and protector deities of the Geluk school. The regular (daily) liturgy is replete with reminders of the school's founder, Tsongkhapa, and the succession of Dalai Lamas who, up to and including the Fifth Dalai Lama, played a crucial role in the development of Chökhor-gyel and of the Geluk school in general.

The Fifth Dalai Lama's other constitutions do not contain such an elaborate liturgy. Nonetheless, several of them do represent similar efforts at codifying and fashioning a Geluk liturgy. The Dalai Lama's constitution for the tantric monastery[70] of Ganden Tupden Rabgyé (no. 42) tells us that it takes Tsongkhapa's own constitutions as its base,[71] and, in addition, directs the monks to adhere to specified tantric instructions by Tsongkhapa, a disciple of Tsongkhapa,[72] the Second Dalai Lama, the Second Dalai Lama's disciple,[73] and others for the worship and visualization of the three principle patron deities of the Geluk school as well as Vairocana, Amitāyus, Six-armed Mahākāla, Yama, and the Makzorma Glorious Goddess.[74] This same list of liturgical texts to be followed is found more or less unchanged in the Dalai Lama's constitutions for Litang Tupden Jamchen (no. 48) and Ba Ganden Pende Ling in Kham (no. 49).

The daily liturgy of the Litang Monastery constitution also includes the Secret Biography of Tsongkhapa[75] and the Ritual Cake Offering to the Lady of the Desire Realm (Pelden Lhamo).[76] The daily liturgy at the Ba Monastery is left unspecified but does say that it is to follow unchanged the liturgy of the main assembly of Drepung Monastery in Lhasa plus the Medicine Buddha Sutra ritual, which itself is quite revealing: first, the Dalai Lama specifies an *institutional relationship* for the liturgy of the Ba Monastery that is akin to the study-abroad relationships (T. *grwa rgyun*) taking shape between philosophical colleges at the same time. Second, as Stacey van Vleet has recently shown, the Medicine Buddha Sutra ritual was one of the liturgical components that the Fifth Dalai Lama promoted with zeal. Through the constitution he composed for the medical institute known as the Sanctuary of Assembled Sages (no. 46) in Tsang and a new ritual manual for the Medicine Buddha Sutra, the Fifth Dalai Lama coopted the tradition of medical practice that had been associated with the Kagyü school by reframing its teachings within a liturgical framework drawn up and approved by the Dalai Lama himself.[77] Moreover, van Vleet argues, the Dalai Lama presents his program for the medical institute and medicine in general as "undefiled by and unfamiliar with the demon of sectarianism" and as capable of "benefiting enemies, too, and making enemies into friends."[78] The Dalai Lama's promotion of the Medicine Buddha ritual, then, is paradigmatic of the larger push to present the Geluk school as nonsectarian and as the only legitimate option for those interested in spiritual liberation.

## The Formation of the Geluk Liturgy
## After the Fifth Dalai Lama

The constitutions by Ön Gyelsé Jikmé Yeshé Drakpa, particularly that for Nartang Monastery (no. 62) and his constitution for Gönlung (no. 66), are some of the first to carry on the Fifth Dalai Lama's zeal for elaborating a Geluk liturgy. Before that, there is the constitution for Tawang Monastery

in what is today Arunachal Pradesh (no. 55) and Jamyang Zhepa's constitution for his Labrang Monastery in Amdo. The latter specifies that the assemblies for the prayer festival(s) are to be done "roughly in accordance with
Glorious Drepung Monastery" in Lhasa. Its procedures and recitations of
the dharma classes must be like Drepung's Gomang College, and the procedures and rituals carried out by Labrang's Tantric College must be "bound
to the tradition of contour-tones and melodic chants at the Glorious Lower
Mé Monastery" in Lhasa. Unfortunately, it is not entirely clear what the liturgies were of these Lhasa institutions at that point in time. A later breviary of Drepung and Drepung's Gomang College was compiled by the
Seventh Dalai Lama (1708–1757). Almost all the prayers and hymns that he
compiled there are either by or for the founder of the Geluk school, Tsongkhapa. As such, the breviary shares a great deal in common with the Geluk
liturgy first formulated by the Fifth Dalai Lama. Moreover, the existence of
the Seventh Dalai Lama's breviary also speaks to the ongoing role of the successive Dalai Lamas in defining the Geluk liturgy.[79]

The constitution for Tawang Monastery (no. 55) shares numerous similarities with the Fifth Dalai Lama's constitutions, although this might be
explained by the monastery's intimate connection with the Dalai Lama, its
founder. Thus, the constitution gives great importance to the practice of the
Medicine Buddha Sutra Ritual,[80] a very detailed month-by-month calendar
that includes the First Day Ritual Cake Offering to Pelden Lhamo, the Great
Prayer Festival of Miraculous Displays, the Twenty-fifth Offering of the
Tenth Month for Tsongkhapa, restoration rituals to the major Geluk protector deities at the end of the eleventh month and beginning of the twelfth,
and the Iron Castle Ritual to Vajrabhairava (see Chapter 3).[81] The regular
recitations at Tawang include, besides the stock prayers and hymns, the
"Lion-faced One" by the Fourth Panchen Lama,[82] Tsongkhapa's "The Chief
Accomplished One Among the Gods," and praises (T. bstod pa) to the Dalai
and Panchen Lamas. In fact, each Dalai Lama is given his own day of worship, and on each day the Medicine Buddha ritual is also performed. Such a
schedule of commemoration days for the Dalai Lamas is also found, more
or less unchanged, in the Seventh Dalai Lama's breviary for Drepung and
Drepung Gomang.[83]

The monks of Gönlung in Amdo also claim a special relationship with
the Dalai Lamas—the Fourth, in particular—but the monastery was in fact
founded by another Central Tibetan hierarch, Ön Gyelsé. So, the relationship with the Dalai Lamas is more indirect, which allows us to begin to trace

the development of the Geluk liturgy beyond the long shadow cast by the Fifth Dalai Lama. In his constitution for Gönlung (no. 66), Jikmé Yeshé Drakpa repeatedly underscores the importance of properly performing the liturgy. New monks are required to memorize the basic liturgy comprising the Refuges, Giving Rise to the Mind of Enlightenment, the Tārā, and *Heart Sutra* before they can participate in the philosophical college's dharma session assemblies that fill the annual calendar. As discussed in Chapter 3, we no longer have the "disciplinary sermon document" (T. *tshogs gtam gyi yi ge*) composed by the founder of the Gönlung Tantric College (Jamyang Zhepa), but monks enrolled there were required to memorize this instructional document, thereby preparing them to carry out the college's liturgical calendar "like at the Lower Tantric College" in Lhasa.[84]

Once a monk was admitted to Gönlung's main assembly, he must continue the process of memorization: "One must study well the breaks in the recitations [i.e., where to start and stop], the manner in which to recite mantras, the custom of worshipping past lamas [i.e., abbots], and the inerrant contour-tones, music, words, and practices of the restoration rituals."[85] Moreover, during assembly, "unseemly behavior" (T. *mi mdzes pa'i spyod lam*) is to be rejected, the cantor and the "voice types" (T. *skad gral*) are to sit in the center aisle alongside the scholar-monks, and, "all are to follow whatever elegant melodies and tempo changes [T. *gdangs 'dur*], singing together in one sonorous voice without wavering and without falling into separate divisions. In so doing, the cantor chooses what to recite and what not to recite according to whatever occurs to him."[86] And, "everyone, having accepted this, except for the deafening sound of reciting [scripture], they must never engage in jealous and harmful behavior, and they must exert themselves single-mindedly on the Teachings in general and on gathering [merit] and purifying [sin] and the clearing the obstacles [T. *sku rim*] of those beyond oneself [i.e., other than oneself]."[87] This emphasis on obedience and the pageantry of the recitations at assembly, although mentioned in earlier and non-Geluk constitutions, becomes a refrain in Geluk constitutions beginning with the Fifth Dalai Lama and subsequent Geluk hierarchs. This speaks to the observation Ter Ellingson made long ago that, according to monastic constitutions, "the life of the monastic community should embody a *spyod-lam mdzes-pa*, or 'beautiful path of practice.'"[88] What is more, this emphasis reflects some recognition of the power of collective ritual to increase shared identity, loyalty, and cooperation. We shall return to this subject at the end of the chapter.

The annual liturgical calendar prescribed by Jikmé Yeshé Drakpa for
Gönlung is what we have now come to expect of a Geluk monastery: the
Ritual Cake Offering to the Glorious Goddess on the first day of the new
year; the Great Prayer Festival of Miraculous Displays in the first month,
modeled on the main festival in Lhasa; five periodic ritual cake offerings (T.
*dus gtor*) each month; a Twenty-fifth Offering for Tsongkhapa on the twenty-
fifth of the tenth month; an autumn period of homage to the protector
Pehar (T. *lha mjal*);[89] and, a Twenty-ninth Ritual Cake Offering at the end
of the last month of the year for the protector Mahākāla, among other major ritual occasions.[90]

In addition, the Medicine Buddha Sutra Ritual (T. *sman bla chog*; *sman
chog*) that the Fifth Dalai Lama worked so hard to promote was part of Gönlung's liturgical calendar. This likely happened around the same time as or
shortly after the Second Changkya instituted this ritual at Gönlung's erstwhile branch monastery of Kenchen in 1685.[91] The ritual took place in Gönlung's Medicine Buddha Ritual Hall (T. Sman chog khang), which was
located a few kilometers farther up the valley from Gönlung at the "Gyelsé
Hermitage," otherwise known as Jangchup Ling.[92]

The "regular recitations" (T. *zhal 'don dkyus ma*) at Gönlung consist of
many of the stock prayers and hymns—the Refuges, Giving Rise to the Mind
of Enlightenment, the *Heart Sutra*, and so forth. However, like the earlier
constitutions of the Dalai Lama, we find here the recitation of the *Ornament of Realization* (T. *mngon rtogs rgyan*); the "Indra [and One Hundred
Gods]" (T. *Legs bris ma*),[93] a praise of Tārā by the First Dalai Lama; and the
"Non-conceptual Loving One" (T. *Dmigs brtse ma*), one of the most well-
known and important praises of Tsongkhapa.[94] In addition, there are particular aspects of the evening "obstacle-clearing" assembly (T. *sku rim*) that
we find as a recurrent part of the developing Geluk liturgy. The obstacle-
clearing assembly, which Georges Dreyfus has described as "the main ritual
of the day," invariably falls in the evening and comprises a lengthy liturgy of
prayers and hymns.[95] Jikmé Yeshé Drakpa's constitution for Gönlung makes
it clear that monks who for some reason fail to attend an earlier assembly
must appear at this evening assembly to perform the *Heart Sutra* and its apotropaic rite. The main function of the assembly appears to be protecting the
well-being and integrity of the monastery as well as the health of its monks.[96]

During the obstacle-clearing assembly each evening, the monks were
also to recite the Tārā, or "Homage to Twenty-one Tārās," as Stephan Beyer
has translated it,[97] between twenty-one and fifty times.[98] The nineteenth-

century, supplementary constitution for Gönlung elaborates, saying that at the evening assembly the Tārā is to be recited "more and more, and when an important occasion arises, it is most important to recite it eighty or fifty times."[99] In yet another constitution from the late nineteenth century composed for a monastery in Mongolia[100] by the fifty-ninth abbot of Drepung Gomang, it is explained that, whereas the "Tārā" is normally to be recited two times during a particular service,[101] on special occasions its recitation is to increase daily by fours. So, during that monastery's evening obstacle-clearing assembly, we read:

> Recite the "Tārā" like during assembly. The recitation of the
> "Tārā" is initially done thirty-one times. From the third day [of
> the dharma session] on the recitation of the "Tārā" is to grow by
> fours up to the middle of the month-long dharma session, [when]
> the "Tārā" is recited seventy-five times. Then, [the recitations are
> to be gradually reduced by fours until thirty-one recitations are
> [again] arrived at, and from there reduce the recitations down [by
> twos?] to twenty-one. This is said to be like [a grain of] barley
> [i.e., fat in the middle and skinny on the ends].[102]

For dharma sessions lasting only half of a month or one lasting twenty days, the specified apogees of recitations are fifty-one and fifty-nine, respectively.[103] The same process of "growing" and "shrinking" the number of Tārā recitations—"like a grain of barley"—is also attested in the liturgy of Drepung Monastery as we know it today: in fact, it is clear from comparing the obstacle-clearing assembly liturgy of Drepung with that of the Mongol monastery that the Drepung liturgy was directly exported to this Mongol monastery.[104] Moreover, we see the remarkable consistency of liturgical practices stretching from Lhasa to Gönlung to Mongolia.

## Exporting Liturgies

In the aftermath of the repression of the Lubsang-Danzin Rebellion in 1724, which decimated the power of the Oirat Mongols in Amdo, Geluk monasteries in Amdo turned with greater frequency to Inner Mongolia for patronage and for promoting the Geluk school. By that time, monasteries such as Gönlung had grown in size and organizational sophistication, and they became centers in their own right for exporting Geluk liturgical traditions. Furthermore, the appearance of homegrown incarnate lamas at Gönlung and elsewhere in Amdo had major consequences for the dissemination of Geluk traditions in Mongolia. The monasteries in Amdo, where these lamas were based, were frequently visited by Mongol pilgrims, patrons, and, eventually, aspiring monks. In addition, these lamas continued the practice of peregrination and helped to extend Geluk influence through their proselytism.

The Third Tuken, Lozang Chökyi Nyima (1737–1802), is one such example. His *Collected Works* contain four constitutions that he wrote for communities in Amdo and Mongolia.[105] We do not know much about Tuken's motivation for composing these texts beyond what the colophons to his constitutions tell us, although the biography of Tuken does reveal the circumstances that gave rise to his constitution for the monastery known as Lapchok Ling (T. Bslab mchog gling) in the Sönid Banner of Inner Mongolia:

> A messenger of the Sönid Left Banner Prince, the Da Lama Lozang Jungné [T. dA bla ma Blo bang 'byung gnas] and servants as well as the Bhikṣu Gyeltsen Drakpa [T. Rgyal mtshan grags pa] from the Wing [T. *shog*] of the Oirat Prince Domta and servants arrived in succession [to Gönlung where Tuken was staying]. Thereupon, the Da Lama, with the petition of the nobles and commoners [of Sönid] and the Prince at their head, made offerings of religious objects. He [Tuken] gave each of them an Avalokiteśvara empowerment, a permission-blessing of Tārā of the Acacia Forest [T. Seng ldeng nags sgrol], and so forth. The petition of eight communities [T. *sde brgyad*], the Da Lama, and so forth urged, requesting that [he] "please make the wealth of the patron prince flourish," whereupon, he composed the constitution for Lapchok Ling.[106]

It is interesting to note that this direct appeal for help in "increasing the riches" of the Mongolian ruler are absent in the constitution itself, which gives only minimal information. This reference demonstrates that the acquisition of a constitution from a major incarnate lama associated with a major Amdowa monastery was an important matter for this Mongol monastery.

Tuken's penning of constitutions for monasteries in Inner Mongolia was not an isolated event. Gungtang Könchok Tenpé Drönmé (T. Gung thang Dkon mchog bstan pa'i sgron me, 1762–1823), one of the major incarnate lama's from Labrang Monastery, composed a constitution for a monastery in Inner Mongolia.[107] The other major hierarchs of Tuken's home monastery of Gönlung also composed constitutions for monasteries in Inner Mongolia. The Third Changkya, Lcang skya Rol pa'i rdo rje, composed a constitution for the Alashaa monastery known locally as Baruun Kheid ("South Monastery"), discussed in more detail below.[108] As mentioned in Chapter 4, Gönlung's Wang Khutugtu composed a constitution for a monastery in Inner Mongolia in 1898;[109] and, as discussed at the outset of this chapter, the late Chuzang (d. 2000) composed a constitution for a small, Oirat temple in Xinjiang. Moreover, if we consider the overwhelming number of ritual manuals and hymns composed by such figures as the Third Thu'u bkwan and the Second Changkya for individuals and monasteries in Inner Mongolia, it is evident that Tuken's composition of Mongol constitutions is part of a much larger and ongoing effort to export a Geluk liturgy.

Tuken's constitution for Lapchok Ling provides an overview of how the Mongols' requesting the constitution should appropriately run their monastery. The first section pertains to the "daily" or "continuous recitations (T. *rgyun kyi zhal 'don*), which is divided into the Morning Tea and Service (T. *zhog ja*), the Midday Tea and Service (T. *nyin gung*), and the Evening Tea and Service (T. *dgung ja*). The second section advises that on the twenty-ninth of each month, after having recited the General Confession,[110] monks are to propitiate the Geluk protector deity Yama.[111] The third section pertains to the Prayer Festival of the Sixth Month. The fourth section pertains to the Prayer Festival of the First Month. The fifth section discusses the "Three Foundations" of fortnightly confession, Summer Rains Retreat, and Release from the Rains Retreat. And the final, sixth, section discusses the restoration rituals (T. *bskang gso*) to be performed for Geluk protector deities. By way of illustration, I here translate section 1:

> As for the assemblies to be carried out each year, their liturgy and
> the order of the liturgy, [first,] the continuous recitations are
> every day. At the morning tea there are offerings to the lineage of
> masters [T. *bla mchod*], the One Hundred [Ritual Cake Offerings]
> [T. *brgya rtsa*], the Ritual Cake Offering to the Serpent Deities [T.
> *klu gtor*], [purifying] smoke offerings [T. *bsangs*], and so forth.
>
> At midday there are petitions and offerings [T. *gsol mchod*] to the
> Sole Hero Vajrabhairava [T. *'Jigs byed dpa' gcig*] and the Twelve

Steadfast [Protector] Goddesses [T. bstan ma gcu gnyis], and
whatever restoration ritual that is appropriate. At evening tea one
recites the White Umbrella [T. Gdugs dkar; S. Sitātapatra], Tārā,
the *Heart Sutra*, the Lion-faced One, and the Torch of the
Teachings [T. *Bstan 'bar ma*].

The midday and evening assemblies stand out in particular as representative
of a now typical, Geluk liturgy. The high patron deity Vajrabhairava is worshipped, as are the twelve protector goddesses who often figure as part of the
entourage of the Glorious Goddess Pelden Lhamo.[112] Likewise, the evening
assembly includes the worship of White Umbrella and Tārā, who both serve
to ward off evil and harm to the monastery and its inhabitants. It includes the
recitation of the *Heart Sutra*, which is also regularly used for its apotropaic
powers. And it includes the recitation of the Fourth Paṇchen Lama's Lion-
Faced One, which is similarly used for its apotropaic function, and the "Flame
of the Teachings." For Gelukpas, the "Flame of the Teachings" can sometimes
refer to the "Prayer for Flourishing of the Well-being of the Geluk Sect" (T.
*Dge ldan lugs bzang rgyas pa'i smon lam*) by the Labrang hierarch Gungtang
Tenpé[113] rather than the nonsectarian hymn to the Buddha's teachings. Every
one of these prayers and recitations prescribed in the Mongol monastery's
constitution appear in the same place in the evening liturgy at Gönlung Monastery. Moreover, although the evening assembly in this Mongol constitution
is not referred to as an obstacle-clearing assembly (T. *sku rim*), it is clear from
the content of the evening liturgy that it serves that same function.

Tuken's constitution for the Mongol monastery of Tenpa Dargyé Ling
(T. Bstan pa dar rgyas gling) of the Üüshin Banner (present-day Wushen qi
乌审旗) also came about due to an extravagant request by various Mongol
figures: "There being a need for such [a text], Abbot Lozang Özer [T.
Mkhan po Blo bzang 'od zer], *Rapjam* Scholar Dharma King Ngawang Rinchen [T. Rab 'byams pa chos rje Ngag dbang rin chen], and Dharma King
Lodrö Dargyé [T. Chos rje Blo gros dar rgyas] all petitioned together with
money, mandalas [T. *maN*] and silk scarves [T. *lha rdzas*] that a manual for
dharma sessions, assembly recitations, and so on [be written]."[114] Tuken responded accordingly, insisting that "the essential must be firmly established: reading and writing, rituals [T. *cho ga*], and the liturgy [T. *chos spyod*]
as well as the order of recitations at assembly. One must be a great absorber of
the exoteric and esoteric scriptures that accord with his intellectual capacities,

and he must exert himself in practices that load his mind-stream with the meaning of these scriptures. . . . In particular, the manner of sitting during assembly, the manner of taking mass tea, the manner of reciting/chanting all *must accord with the conduct found in a large monastery*."[115] The final line regarding being in "accord with the conduct found in a large monastery" reflects the concern lamas such as Tuken had for monastic practice at places on "the periphery" of the Tibetan Buddhist world. A "large monastery" might refer to Lhasa's Drepung, but it might as easily refer to Tuken's own monastery of Gönlung in Amdo.

Next, Tuken provides an overview of the liturgy to be performed at Tenpa Dargyé Ling during the busy time of the Great Prayer Festival of the first month:

From the eighth day onward, every day there is a series of five assemblies. During the first assembly, recite the "Refuges," the "Mind of Enlightenment," make offerings to the lineage of masters [T. *bla mchod*], do the "Confession of Downfalls" [T. *ltung bshags*] and "General Confession," alternate Praises to the [various] buddhas and bodhisattvas, True Words for Long Life of the Victorious Father and Son *[and] me*,[116] and the five kinds of aspiration prayers.[117]

For the second assembly, the Recite the "Litany of Names of Mañjuśri" and the *Medicine Buddha Sutra Ritual*.

For the third and fourth assemblies, recite the *Kanjur*[118] and the "White Umbrella."

For the fifth assembly, the "Twenty-one Tārās and prostrations," the "White Umbrella," the "Indra [and One Hundred Gods]," the *Heart Sutra*, the apotropaic rite of the "Lion-faced One,"[119] a "Three-part [Ritual Cake Offering],"[120] the Ritual Cake Offerings to the dharma protectors, the Ritual Cake Offerings for the landlord deities, the "Torch of the Teachings," including the Verses of Good Fortune [T. *shis brjod*]. In addition, do the deity evocation [T. *sgrub thabs*] and self-initiation [T. *bdag 'jug*] of Guhyasamāja, Cakrasaṃvara, and Vajrabhairava; rituals of the Omniscient One [Vairocana], the Medicine [Buddha], and the [Sixteen] Arhats; and,

restoration rituals for the major dharma protectors, the Five
[Royal] Bodies [i.e., Pehar and four members of his retinue],[121]
together with the Keeper of Oaths [T. Dam can].

It is noteworthy that Tuken manages to include prayers of long life for himself in the liturgy while still maintaining a rather standard Geluk liturgy. This reflects the role of peregrinating lamas in the promotion of an otherwise uniform system of monastic administration and practice. This liturgy of the Great Prayer Festival of the First Month, moreover, includes what is likely the Fifth Dalai Lama's Medicine Buddha Ritual and rituals dedicated to the patron deities and protector deities of the Geluk school. Tuken further prescribes the performance of ritual dancing [T. 'chams] and the throwing of a sacrificial cake on the fourteenth day and the circumambulation of Maitreya (probably the monastery's large tapestry of Maitreya) on the fifteenth day, the same as at Gönlung Monastery.[122]

Tuken's constitution for Tenpé Dargyé Ling, moreover, has sections dedicated to the Prayer Festival of the Fourth Month (dedicated to Śākyamuni Buddha), to bathing and worshipping the image of Maitreya at the monastery in the seventh month, to the Twenty-fifth Offering to Tsongkhapa in the tenth month, to the restoration rituals for the monastery's protectors at the end of the year, and to the First Day Ritual Cake Offering to Pelden Lhamo at the start of the new year. The annual calendar he prescribes is thus in line with the liturgical year found at more centrally located Geluk monasteries, such as Gönlung.

A final example should suffice to demonstrate the role of Amdo lamas in promoting Geluk liturgy in Mongolia. The Third Changkya, Rölpé Dorje (1717–1786), composed a constitution for Baruun Kheid in Alashaa sometime after that monastery was founded in 1757 by the rebirth of the famous Tibetan prime minister Sangyé Gyatso (T. Sde srid Sangs rgyas rgya mtsho), Darji Nom-un Khan.[123] The constitution contains what is probably one of the earliest attestations of the cult of the Sixth Dalai Lama in Inner Mongolia and of the cult of the Dalai Lama's teacher, Prime Minister Sangyé Gyatso.

The section of the Baruun Kheid constitution that prescribes the daily routine of assembling in the assembly hall to perform the monastery's regular liturgy begins as follows: "Assemble, with the cantor (T. byang 'dren) urging [all] to recite and so forth."[124] The fact that the word "byang 'dren" is used rather than "dbu mdzad" to refer to the chant-leader is the first clue that this monastery is best understood as a tantric monastery without a formal Geluk scholastic structure in place. The constitution continues: "If it is the morning assembly, [recite] the 'Refuges' and the 'Giving Rise to the Mind of Enlightenment;' the 'Confession of Downfalls' and the 'General Confession;' the 'One Hundred Ganden Gods'[125] and the 'Non-Conceptual Loving One;' the 'Pledge to Maitreya *dhāraṇī;*'[126] the 'Supreme Sacred Site of Ganden;'[127] the extended or abbreviated ritual for the Thirteen of Vajrabhairava [i.e., Vajrabhairava and his twelve-member retinue] according to circumstances; and, do the self-empowerment [as Vajrabhairava] and worship of Yama."[128] Here Changkya prescribes a rather standard liturgy for the morning assembly, but it is one that also includes the praise and guru yoga of Tsongkhapa by the Second Jamyang Zhepa, known as the One Hundred Ganden Gods, as well as the prayer to Tsongkhapa, The Non-Conceptual Loving One. It also includes a praise of the Dalai Lama's residence, the Potala Palace (the "Supreme Sacred Site of Ganden"), and the invocation and worship of the Geluk patron deity Vajrabhairava and the protector deity Yama.

> At midday,[129] if no additional mass tea is provided,[130] then first [just] perform the Water Offering to Jambhala,[131] and the "One Hundred Ritual Cake Offerings." After that, recite the *Heart Sutra* together with its apotropaic rite. After practicing the offering of the ritual cake to Lhamo, assembly disperses. Afterwards, newcomers practice reading and writing and so forth at the door to the assembly hall.

> If there is a mass tea at midday then, in addition to the assembly procedure from before [in the morning]: perform the guru yoga, the "Realms," "Path," and "The Gods"—all three[132]—and so forth from the liturgy [T. *chos spyod*] as appropriate. Perform the "[Six] teen Arhats" [T. *gnas bcu*], the "Water Offering" [T. *chu sbyin*], the "One Hundred [Ritual Cake Offerings]," and the *Heart Sutra* and its apotropaic rite three times; throw the ritual cake. If at midday there is bread or soup, then offer the shares to the arhats beginning with the performance of the seven-fold offering;[133] do the "One Hundred [Ritual Cake Offerings]" as many times as appropriate, and the midday meal is taken.

The three prayers referred to collectively as the "Realms," "Path," and "The Gods" are the "Glorious Three Realms" praise of Tsongkhapa by Khedrup,

Tsongkhapa's "Condensed Meaning of the Stages of the Path," and Tsong-khapa's praises of Śākyamuni, the "Chief Accomplished One among the Gods." The Baruun Kheid regular liturgy concludes as follows: "At the obstacle-clearing rite of the evening tea, in addition to the assembly proce-dures from before: recite the 'Buddha, Dharma, and Sangha'[134] three times; after that, recite the 'Tārā' seven times, the 'White Tārā' three times, the 'White Umbrella,' the *Heart Sutra* and the 'Lion-faced One' together with their apotropaic rites, the *dhāraṇī* of the '[Goddess] Adorned in Leaves' [T. *Lo ma gyon ma*], and throw the ritual cake. After that, assembly disperses."[135] This evening, obstacle-clearing assembly contains the same litany of recitations as seen in the Geluk constitutions described above. The *dhāraṇī* of the Goddess Adorned in Leaves (S. Parṇaśabarī), which is useful for warding off or curing sickness, is also found in the liturgy for the obstacle-clearing assembly at Gönlung, at Tawang Monastery, and the Kumbum Tantric College.[136]

The largest portion of Changkya's constitution for Baruun Kheid is ded-icated to the tantric rituals to be performed on behalf of the monastery's protector and patron deities. After describing the restoration rites to be per-formed for Geluk protectors on a daily basis (to Pelden Lhamo) or monthly basis (to Pelden Lhamo and other protectors), the constitution outlines in great detail the liturgical year: in the first month, the Great Prayers Festival of Miraculous Display (which includes, among many other things, the cir-cumambulation of the Maitreya tapestry around the monastery for the aus-piciousness of the place and the monastery,[137] as is also prescribed in Tuken's constitution for Tenpé Dargyé Ling); in the second month, a ritual cake of-fering to either Mahākāla or Pelden Lhamo; in the third month, a periodic sacrificial cake offering (T. *dus gtor*) to the protector Mahākāla; in the fourth month, ritual dancing (T. *'chams*) and the visualization and invocation of the major Geluk patron deities; in the fifth month, visualization and invocation of the major Geluk patron deities and ritual dances associated with the cre-ation of and offerings within the maṇḍalas (T. *sa chog*; *mchod gar*); in the sixth month, offerings of accomplishment (T. *sgrub mchod*) for the Great Prayer Festival of the Turning of the Wheel of the Dharma; in the seventh month, offerings to the local deities (T. *yul lha*); in the eighth month, offer-ings of accomplishment for the Geluk patron deities Guhyasamāja and Akṣobhyavajra; in the tenth month, the Twenty-fifth Offering for Tsong-khapa; and, in the twelfth month, the Iron Castle Ritual of Vajrabhairava and the throwing of the sacrificial cake on the twenty-ninth day of the month. Clearly, we see here a robust liturgical year that overlaps with the ritual calendar of other monasteries (regarding the Iron Castle Ritual of Vajrabhairava, see Chapter 3).

The detailed instructions that Changkya provides seek to establish a complete program of worship and visualization of the major Geluk deities based on scriptures, practices, and institutional connections that can be traced back to Central Tibet. So, for example, for the fourth month, Changkya writes, "From the first of the fourth month through the new moon: listen respectfully to words of a knowledgeable master [T. *slob dpon*] and carefully train in[, one,] the garland dance [T. *'phreng ba'i gar*] according to Lama Sönam Drup's[138] supplement to Butön Rinchen Drup's Treatise on the Vajra Garland Dance,[139] and[, two,] the offering dance to the Vajra Space [T. *rdor dbyings kyi mchod pa'i gar*] according to Dawa Pelrin[140] and Lama Samdrup's[141] supplements to Butön's Offering Dance to the Vajra Space." Here Changkya is instituting practices of tantra and ritual dance based on traditions associated with the fourteenth-century master Butön and his monastery of Zhalu in Tsang. Changkya's constitution continues, "Also, practice without allowing to decline[, one,] the custom of the garland dance that was created by Düldzin Rinpoché[142] based on the tradition of the Omniscient Lord Tsongkhapa and[, two,] Butön's custom of the offering dance to Cakrasaṃvara [T. *Bde mchog gi mchod pa'i gar*]." Düldzin Rinpoché is Tsongkhapa's close disciple Drakpa Gyeltsen (T. Grags pa rgyal mtshan, 1374–1434). Changkya again: "You must carefully do the correct mudras [T. *phyag rgya 'ching tshul*], ritual sequences, and moments between mudras [? T. *'chings mtshams*] based on careful analysis of[, one,] the cycles composed by Butön, such as his *Great Yoga Commentary: The Wish-fulfilling Jewel*,[143] and[, two,] the elegant writings of numerous scholars such as Düldzin Rinpoché's ritual [manuals] on the Vajra Space and on Vairocana." In his constitutions for Chökhorgyel (no. 40), Ganden Tupten Rabgyé (no. 42), and Litang (no. 48), the Fifth Dalai Lama likewise prescribes Düldzin Rinpoché's ritual manuals for Vairocana (and, in two of those constitutions, for the Nine-deity maṇḍala of Amitāyus).

Changkya continues:

> Study well [how to draw] the lines of mandalas and auxiliary practices based on Lord Tsongkhapa's commentary in his [*Great Exposition of*] *The Stages of the [Path of] Mantra*[144] on the [description of how to draw] lines in Master Abhyāgara[gupta]'s[145] *Vajra Garland*[146] and on the manuals of other authentic scholars.

In this way, do principally the contour-tones of both Guhyasamāja
and Vajrabhairava according to the Glorious Lower Tantric
College and those of the Vajra Space according to Zhalu. Practice
and do not let decline the previously established cycles of the
contour-tones of Cakrasaṃvara and Vairocana.

Here Changkya makes explicit the two Central Tibetan monastic institutions on which this Mongol monastery, Baruun Kheid, is to base its own
tantric practices down to and including the manner in which the liturgy is
intoned: The Lower Tantric College in Lhasa and Zhalu in Tsang.

The final section on the liturgical instructions for the fourth month:
"In short, examine well the practices of the good holy ones, particularly non-
killing. Since one cannot be knowledgeable from merely reading about the
three—dancing, drawing lines [of maṇḍalas], and contour-tones—in depen-
dence on the verbal and manual instructions of a learned master and with
consideration for the continuity of the Precious Teachings, one must study
carefully and not make guesses." Here Changkya is expressing the same mis-
givings about the careless study of tantra on the "periphery" as had been
expressed by Sumba Kanbo in his constitution for branch monasteries in
Amdo (see Chapter 3). His remedy is the traditional emphasis on learning
tantra from a qualified master; here, however, it is to be done in the context
of the highly orchestrated and collective rituals of the monastery.


## The Power of Collective Ritual


Why would Geluk hierarchs dedicate so much detail and attention to pre-
scribing and instituting a systematic liturgical program? Although such a
world in which days are punctuated by regular assemblies and the recitation
of a common program of prayers and hymns and one in which the energy of
the year rises and falls according to the phases of the moon seems alien to
most moderns, it was the most important aspect of the lives of many in the
pre-modern world, especially of monastics. Ritual is the most crucial yet most
overlooked element of monastic life and monastic administration. It is the
engine that fires the monastery as well as the blueprint for its inner architecture. In her overview of Tibetan consecration rituals, Yael Bentor writes,
"In the majority of Tibetan monasteries the performance of rituals is the
principal undertaking of most monks. Even in monastic educational insti-

tutions monks devote part of their time to rituals. It should be emphasized that almost all forms of Tibetan meditation are highly ritualized and therefore fall within this category as well."[147] Beyer, another scholar who has made the rare contribution to the study of Tibetan Buddhist ritual, refers to the performance of rituals as "the ultimate function of their [monks'] monastic life." Beyer continues,

> From the time a young man passed through the gates of the monastery, whether as an incarnate lama or as an ordinary monk, he was surrounded by the constant sound and excitement of the rituals; every time he was initiated into the evocation of a deity, he committed himself to so much time spent in private ritual contemplation, to so many hundreds of prostrations when he awoke in the morning. Each monk owed a duty to the monastery, to the lay community and the king that supported it, and, by the strength of his vows as a Bodhisattva, to the entire realm of sentient beings, all of whom, at one time or another in his past lives, had borne him as his mother; his debt was paid by the performance of ritual, by the study of ritual techniques, and by his increase of understanding in the monastic college.[148]

Beyond the past work of these two scholars, however, it is difficult to locate a scholarly monograph on the place of ritual in Tibet.[149] Although the study of ritual has a venerable history in anthropology and in religion, dating back at least to the nineteenth-century and early twentieth-century preoccupation with sacrifice, and although it attracted renewed interest over the past thirty to forty years, giving rise to the subfield of Ritual Studies, still, Ritual Studies has yet to penetrate Tibetan Studies, a field more generally concerned with philosophy and the biographies of religious saints.

A certain disdain for ritual as well as outright misunderstandings of the importance of ritual date back to some of the earliest, systematic observations of Tibetan monasticism. These early explorers and missionaries saw in Tibetan Buddhism, or "Lamaism," a suspect "popish ritualism."[150] L. Austine Waddell, writing at the close of the nineteenth century, referred to the "contemptible mummery" of the Tibetan form of Buddhism.[151] And the Catholic missionary Louis Schram, who spent several years in Mongolia and Northeastern Tibet in the first half of the twentieth century, concludes that "at the present time . . . [t]he lamas . . . except for attendance at the morning convention, which lasts *only an hour*, have to kill time making their own living."[152] Tibetan monks are doubly condemned, first for participating in mindless and purposeless acts of imitation, and then for not participating in them enough.

Although the level of participation likely ebbed and flowed over the centuries, the account given in this chapter demonstrates that the life of the monk was anything but idle. First, just getting access to the main assemblies of a monastery required anywhere from a year to several years of preparation followed by exams in the presence of the monastery's abbot before admission was granted. Then, once a monk was officially on the monastery's roster, a *very full* liturgical calendar kept monks extremely busy. Reading through the two constitutions of Gönlung Monastery (the earlier one by Gyelsé Jikmé Yeshé Drakpa and the late nineteenth-century supplement by the Fourth Wang) we find that *nearly every day is accounted for* when specifying the liturgical calendar of the monastery. Even if we exclude the rituals to be carried out by smaller temples and colleges at Gönlung (distinguished in Table 1 by parentheses around the number of days for the performance of the ritual) and focus only on the major ritual occasions that those enrolled in the Philosophical College would attend (nearly half the monastic population),[153] we still arrive at an estimated 235 days, or eight months, during which time the monks are to be engaged in ritual activity, normally consisting of a minimum of three assemblies each day. This, of course, is about the same amount of time that college students today spend each year doing coursework.

What is the consequence of this level of ritualization? What happens when certain powerful hierarchs impose extensive liturgies for monasteries across the Tibetan Plateau and in Mongolia and when the hundreds and thousands of monks at these monasteries collectively participate in chanting the same hymns and worshipping the same gods all explicitly linked to a particular sectarian identity? New empirical evidence from cognitive science and cognitive anthropology suggest that one of the primary functions of collective ritual is to foster group cohesion.

A 2000 study by Richard Sosis found that *religious* communes in early American history had an average survival rate of 25.3 years compared to 6.4 years for their secular counterparts.[154] In addition, the odds of a secular commune dissolving within any given year were up to four times greater than those for religious communes.[155] A 2003 study by Sosis and Eric Bressler considered the same data, this time asking whether the relative success of the

Table 1. Ritual calendar for Gönlung Monastery based on its two constitutions of 1737 and 1885

| Ritual Occasion | Number of Days for Performance |
|---|---|
| First Ritual Cake Offering to Pelden Lhamo, 1/1 (i.e., the first day of the first Hor month) | 1 |
| Greater Prayer Festival, 1/2–1/16 (i.e., the second day through the sixteenth day of the first Hor Month) | 15 |
| Quarterly Ritual Cake Offering (T. *dus bzhi'i gtor rgyag*), 1/10[1] | (1) |
| Dharma Protectors Day, 2/2 | 1 |
| Memorial Offering for Monastery Founder and His Reincarnations, 2/14–2/15 | 2 |
| First Spring Dharma Session, 2/16–3/1 | 15 |
| Great Spring Dharma Session, 3/15–4/15 | 30 |
| Quarterly Ritual Cake Offering, 4/10 | (1) |
| "Book Retreat," 4/16–4/30 | 15 |
| Post-Spring Assembly, 5/1–5/20 | 20 |
| Prayer Festival for the Turning of the Wheel of the Dharma, 6/2–6/8 | 7 |
| Summer Retreat and Summer Dharma Session, 6/15–8/1 | 45 |
| Practice for Courtyard Ritual Masked Dance, 7/1–7/21 | (21) |
| Quarterly Ritual Cake Offering, 7/10 | (1) |
| Great Autumn Dharma Session, 8/15–9/15 | 30 |
| Visitation of the Oracle's Deity, 9/1 | (1) |
| Second Autumn Dharma Session, 10/1–10/15 | 15 |
| Twenty-fifth Offerings Commemorating Tsongkhapa's Death, 10/22–10/25 | 4 |
| Great Winter Dharma Session, 11/8–12/8 | 30 |
| Quarterly Ritual Cake Offering, 12/25 | (1) |
| Great Ritual Cake Offering for Mahākāla, 12/25–12/29 | 5 |
| Each Month: Five periodic Ritual Cake Offerings (T. *dus gtor*) | (60) |
| Each Month, 2nd day: Restoration Rites to protector deities[2] | (12) |
| Each Month, 3rd day: worship of protector deity Damchen Dorjé Lekpa | (12) |

Table 1. *(Continued)*

| Ritual Occasion | Number of Days for Performance |
|---|---|
| Each Month, 8th day: worship of local protector deity, Vaiśravaṇa, and Nechung | (12) |
| Each Month, 15th day: worship of Nechung | (12) |

[1] The exact date of this ritual occasion and that of the following Quarterly Ritual Cake Offerings at Dgon lung are unknown. These dates are borrowed from the *bca' yig* for a branch monastery of one of Dgon lung's incarnate lamas, Thu'u bkwan, known as Bde chen chos gling and as Chos bzang ri khrod. Thu'u bkwan III Blo bzang cho kyi nyi ma, "Dben gnas bde chen chos gling gi bsam gtan pa rnams kyi bca' khrims," 697/12a.4–5.

[2] Wang IV's constitution describes the "*lha tshes*" for the second day of the second month, and it seems to involve at least the disciplinarians and the Protectors Hall (T. Btsan khang) if not the entire congregation of the monastery. Nonetheless, I do not count this toward the total of 235 days, hence the parentheses. Wang IV Blo bzang 'jam pa'i tshul khrims, "Bstan bcos sgo brgya 'byed pa'i zab zing gser gyi sde mig," 2b.3. An informant at Dgon lung tells me that the second day of each month there are "restoration rites" (T. *bskang gso*), reciting Thu'u bkwan III's "incense offering" text (T. *bsang mchod*), i.e., his "Rgyal gsol gyi cho ga phrin las lhun grub" in the cycle of deity evocation texts for Hayagriva (*rta mgrin gsang sgrub kyi chos skor*). See BDRC W21506. On the third day of each month, they recite a ritual text by Lcang skya III for the worship of Dam can rdo rje legs pa. On the eighth of each month, an incense offering text by the Fifth Dalai Lama is recited for the worship of the local protector deity (T. *gnas bdag*), Rnam sras (S. Vaiśravaṇa), and Gnas chung (i.e., an emanation of Pe har). Finally, on the fifteenth of each month, the ritual text "Bsang rnam dag ma," composed by Bsod nams ye shes dbang po, is recited for the worship of Gnas chung. My version of the text is a xylograph given to me by a Dgon lung monk. It can also be found at BDRC W00KG06. Dgon lung also has separate halls for the worship of Dpal ldan lha mo and the local protector deity (T. *gnas bdag*).

religious communes could be explained by what is known as costly signaling theory. Briefly, the theory, drawn from research in ethology and evolutionary biology, suggests that certain handicaps (such as the extravagant tail feathers of a peacock or stotting in gazelles) have evolved for organisms to *reliably signal* to conspecifics that they possess some other ideal trait (such as biological fitness or speed and strength).[156] Some scholars have suggested that this theory could be applied to certain behaviors typical of (though not necessarily unique to) religious groups, such as membership costs or costly rituals, wherein they signal genuine commitment to the group, its success, its ideology, and so on. Sosis and Bressler confirmed that, at least for religious groups,[157] higher costs (such as celibacy and dietary restrictions) did correlate with greater longevity of the groups in question. Such a finding could help to explain how the Geluk school's ostensibly greater (i.e., more widespread and persistent) concern with ritual orthopraxy, doctrinal orthodoxy, and monastic discipline (principally celibacy[158]) did not diminish the group's success and growth but actually helped it.[159]

It remains to be seen whether a Geluk monastery exacts *more* from its residents than a Sakya or Nyingma monastery, for example. In terms of time devoted to participating in monastic activities, however, we can say for sure that belonging to a Geluk monastery was not a free ride. Whatever food, leisure, or other perks might have allured individuals to monasteries or kept them there[160] came at a significant cost.

Even more relevant to the study of Geluk monasteries is Sosis and Bradley Ruffle's 2003 study on Israeli *kibbutzim*, both secular and religious. Subjects from successful *kibbutzim*[161] were asked to play a particular type of economic game used to measure one's willingness to share resources and, by extension, one's willingness to cooperate with others. The results were striking: First, members of religious *kibbutzim* exhibit higher levels of cooperation than do members of secular ones. Second, religious males will exhibit higher levels of cooperation than religious females because of their greater participation in collective ritual, particularly daily prayer. And, significantly, third, the *frequency* of participation in collective ritual is positively correlated with cooperativeness. So it is that religious males, who happen to participate in communal prayer and other forms of collective ritual more often, behave more cooperatively with fellow members of their *kibbutz*. Note, too, that these religious males also *perceive* their *kibbutz* as more cooperative. That is, this correlational data suggests (though the direction of causality is not proven here) that frequent participation in collective ritual leads to changes in behavior and perception such that these participants are more willing to work cooperatively with co-residents and are more likely to perceive their co-residents as cooperative themselves.

Although the conclusions reached in the Sosis and Ruffle study are similar to those in the costly signaling theory tested by Sosis and Bressler, there are other ways of interpreting this correlation between frequency of collective ritual and cooperation. It may be that there is something going on physiologically or psychologically during collective ritual that makes an individual more likely to cooperate. Scott Wiltermuth and Chip Heath's 2009 controlled study attempts to identify causality. In it, test subjects were asked to perform a series of actions together with other test subjects. In one group, they sang together synchronously. In another, they both sang and moved together synchronously. In a third, they sang and moved together asynchronously (each subject was listening to a different version of the same song through headphones). And in the control group, the subjects did not sing or move together in time. The results demonstrate that both the synchronous singing group and the synchronous singing-and-moving group cooperated significantly more in follow-up economic games aimed at measuring cooperation. These two groups also displayed a significant increase in self-reported identification with their fellow test subjects (the extent to which they "felt as if they were on the same team"). Moreover, the willingness these subjects had to cooperate with one another was at least partially mediated by this instilled sense of being "on the same team."[162]

The fact that acting together in time can boost an individual's sense of belonging to a group is significant when we also consider the explicit attempts by Geluk hierarchs to demarcate the boundaries of their school and to distance themselves from other schools. Sumba Kanbo writes in one of his monastic constitutions, "If he is of a different school [T. *grub mtha'*], or if he has any other flaws; if his limbs or sense organs are extremely unsightly, then he [can] not reside [here]."[163] Similarly, Jikmé Yeshé Drakpa classifies mantrins of other traditions alongside merchants and profiteers when he writes that "Nyingma or Bön practitioners who perform exorcism type rituals [T. *gto rigs*] and thread cross rituals [T. *mngos rigs*] . . . are not allowed."[164] In other words, at the same time that Geluk hierarchs were promoting a ritual program that instilled camaraderie among Geluk monks, they were also making very public pronouncements—doctrine—concerning the boundaries of their group.

One of the best attempts to understand the cognitive and neurological mechanisms explaining the impact of ritual on group dynamics is Uffe Schjoedt et al.'s 2013 "Cognitive Resource Depletion in Religious Interactions." In it, the authors draw on a series of experiments in order to examine the impact of ritualized behavior[165] and charismatic authority on subjects' experiences. Two common characteristics of ritualized behavior—goal demotion and causal opaqueness—are found to divert the subject's attention away from interpretation (i.e., the generation of a model that makes sense of the ritual action being performed) and toward lower-level action parsing, the sensorial-motor skills that often make up more complex, goal-oriented actions.[166] Others have described this as a momentary "swamping of working memory."[167] Without recourse to their *own* interpretations and memories of the ritual, subjects, it is suggested, are left more susceptible to the authoritative exegesis introduced by religious experts.

If we were to look at a highly developed and regularized system of frequent ritual practice, such as that devised by the Gelukpa, we should expect to see an increased and a persistent attention to low-level actions among the ritual participants. This diversion of executive cognitive resources, these authors argue, is likely to hamper the brain's attempt to generate and update its own model (that is, its own interpretation) of what is transpiring.[168] Such "depletion leaves participants with an inferential gap, which amplifies a search for meaningful interpretations of the ritual after the event. Thus, we propose that ritualized behavior, unlike ordinary instrumental actions, may use obscurity to increase participants' susceptibility to authoritative interpretations by religious experts."[169] Therefore, we should not be surprised that an enormous body of exegetical and doctrinal literature pertaining to ritual was amassed in Tibet at the same time that ritual programs were being standardized across the Plateau.[170]

So, what does this mean for explanation of the Geluk school's success? A top-down, systematic approach to designing a Geluk liturgy and orthopraxy that complemented Geluk orthodoxy helped pave the way for the school's success. Of course, as discussed at the outset of this book, the Fifth Dalai Lama's charisma deserves the scholarly attention it has attracted, as does the craft of his prime minister, Sangyé Gyatso. Likewise, the military support provided by the Oirat Mongols was indispensable to the Geluk's rise, and the financial support later provided by the Qing Court was also instrumental. But we must not stop here. We must look at how the Gelukpa themselves used these resources, which they did effectively by crafting and institutionalizing the practices for the most important institutions in Tibetan society, namely, their monasteries. This *ritualization* led to greater *socialization* of the group's members. Being a member of a group requires that members be socialized into its norms and practices, and often this is done without members' conscious consent.

Geluk lamas, such as the Fifth Dalai Lama, Ön Gyelsé Jikmé Drakpa, Tuken, Changkya, and numerous others, crafted and insisted upon a common Geluk liturgy for their monasteries in Central Tibet, in Amdo, and beyond in Mongolia. This liturgy included a similar calendar of holy days (e.g., commemorating Tsongkhapa on the twenty-fifth day of the tenth month), a common litany of prayers and hymns associated with Tsongkhapa and the Dalai Lamas, and rituals associated with a relatively narrow set of important protector and patron deities of the Geluk school. Much as early modern states discovered that forcing a battalion to march together in formation contributed to the group's cohesion and group identity,[171] Geluk lamas fashioned an extensive liturgy that was practiced in common by hundreds of thousands of monks. This contributed to the integrity of the Geluk school even as it extended farther and farther across the Tibetan Plateau and Mongolia.

# Conclusion

What might explain the lack of scholarly attention devoted to the creation of such liturgies as those discussed in the last chapter and, more generally, to the institutionalization of monastic life? Unlike Christianity, in which monasticism is a phenomenon that developed two centuries after the time of Jesus, monasticism in Buddhism dates back to the time of the founding figure himself, Śākyamuni Buddha. However, just what that monasticism looked like is unclear. Was it a more itinerant, ascetic tradition, akin to the forest-dwelling monks of twentieth-century Thailand,[1] or was it a more settled, institutional arrangement? We may never know for sure because, as the historian of Indian Buddhism Gregory Schopen has noted, whatever itinerant renunciants might have existed in the early days of Buddhism did not, by their very nature, leave us with any historical or archaeological records of their lifestyle. Nonetheless, the *ideal* of the itinerant ascetic is a powerful one, and it is one that has existed in productive tension with settled monastic life in nearly all times and places in which Buddhism has flourished.[2] The sociologist Max Weber might have referred to this as the tension between a "this-worldly" orientation and an "other-worldly" one, something that arguably goes back to the very beginning of Buddhism when, following his enlightenment, the Buddha hesitated to go forth and teach others rather than remain alone, enjoying his emancipation.[3]

This dichotomy is paralleled by a second one made in Buddhism as early as the fifth century[4] between the study of scripture and realization through the practice of meditation. This same distinction is made in other parts of Asia in later centuries, such as in the Song Dynasty in China (960–1279), where certain monasteries are deemed *chan*, or "meditation," monasteries by the Song Court and others *jiao*, or "teaching," monasteries. In Tibet, the tantric adept Padmasambhava and the scholar-monk Kalamaśīla become the paradigmatic representatives of these two tendencies, ideal types that get redeployed polemically in later centuries by such figures as the author of the hagiography of Milarepa.[5]

Early Western accounts of Buddhism in Tibet set up a third dichotomy with regard to the different ways of being a Buddhist monastic, what one scholar calls the dichotomy between the "pristine" and the "polluted."[6] These are the two edges of the knife of Orientalism, which glorifies the Orient at the same time as it demonizes it. An early Jesuit account of Tibetan Buddhism is quite sympathetic and even full of praise. Referring to the monks, which he calls "priests" and "lamas," the author writes, "They discharge the largest part of the day with prayer, which they do at least two hours in the morning and just as long in the evening. They sing like us in a quiet tone, just as we sing the cantus firmus. . . . The lamas seem to me a very gentle people."[7] Later religious "seekers" saw in Tibetan Buddhism (and in Tibet more generally) a tradition that has been isolated from the rest of the world and therefore left untainted by it. This spawned the myth of Shangri-la, which was forever seared into the Western imagination by James Hilton's novel *Lost Horizon* and Frank Capra's adaptation of the novel to film.[8]

Protestant missionary accounts were often less sympathetic to what they found in Tibet. The well-traveled and prolific Robert Ekvall, writes: "Tibet, where every breeze is freighted with the voiceless supplication of flapping prayer flags, where streams and rivers turn the mills of prayer, where prayer wheels spin by pilgrim effort, and where the matter of an endless petition punctuates all of human activity—Tibet, the citadel of evil and the land of false prayer, will only yield as we—missionaries and readers of this urgent cry—learn truly to pray. Soldiers of Christ pray on."[9] Here we see that the same disciplined or regular attention to prayer and ritual activity that excited the earlier Jesuit account is now pointed to as justification for a more militant, Christian attitude toward missionary work in Tibet. Donald Lopez describes how such contempt for the "formalistic" or "rote" practices of knowledge and ritual within and outside the monasteries of Tibet was indebted to a similar Protestant and modernist critique of Roman Catholicism, or "Papism," that was prevalent in the West at that time.[10]

The critiques of Tibetan Buddhism were not limited to the important place accorded to ritual but included also the wealth and corruption that was understood to inevitably occur whenever a religion becomes overly institutionalized, a "Church." Writing about the renowned and massive monastery of Labrang Trashi Khyil, Ekvall says, "Labrang is more than the greatest visible symbol in the building and organization of lamaism in north-east Tibet. It is an effective and despotic power of rule controlling not only the worship but the actions and livelihood of thousands. . . . In all things it has well-nigh absolute power over the people of the district."[11]

I introduce these three dichotomies—this worldly vs. otherworldly, scholasticism or philosophy vs. meditation and realization, and pristine vs. polluted—to help isolate the presumptions and motivations that may determine scholarly focus. The previous chapters have focused on the growth in size and complexity of monastic institutions in Tibet and the geographic expansion of a network of these institutions in the latter half of the seventeenth and eighteenth centuries. Labrang Trashi Khyil Monastery, situated halfway between Central Tibet and Mongolia, is exemplary of this growth. It was founded in 1709 by a scholar who belonged to the Geluk school of Tibetan Buddhism. His own scholastic treatises were very important for philosophy and scholastic curricula in many of the monasteries that belonged to his school. He was also an institution-builder, establishing new, specialized facilities dedicated to the study of philosophy and tantra at his own monastery and elsewhere,[12] and his successors established further facilities for the study of astrology and medicine, among other things.[13] "In addition to these major structures," writes Paul Nietupski in his comprehensive study of the monastery, "Labrang had some forty-eight other temples, and extensive monastic residences to house at least three thousand and five hundred monks."[14] Nietupski also traces the extensive network of donor communities that further characterize the network of large-scale monasteries that developed during the period under consideration.

For the critics introduced above, such a monastery falls short of the ideal of a Buddhist monastery, be that the ideal of being alone "like the horn of a rhinoceros," the ideal of practice and spiritual accomplishment, or the romance harbored by some modern Westerners of an untarnished wisdom that is free from the trappings of society and institutions. Such a monastery as Labrang is clearly "this-worldly." It had extensive interactions with the other spheres of society: political, economic, and even military. Most of the monks resident at such a monastery would be focused on the memorization and recitation of prayers and the performance of rituals, which left little time for sustained and focused contemplative practice. Some of these monasteries were the size of small cities, and many of the Western explorers and seekers escaping the modernization and massive social change of late-nineteenth-century and twentieth-century Europe and America were certainly not seeking massive institutions that boasted schedules and classes, not to mention financial assets such as endowments and serfs.[15] Such places have struck many Westerners and moderns[16] as degenerate and polluted, thus earning the name "Lamaseries" or "mass monasteries" to distinguish them from "normal" Buddhist monasteries found elsewhere in time, space, or the imagination. In short, these monastic institutions fall on the "wrong" side of each of the three dichotomies introduced above, and this in part helps to explain the inadequate attention given to the development of the most important institution for religious life across Tibet and Mongolia: the monastery.

This book is an argument for the importance of considering the mechanisms that Buddhist hierarchs stipulated for the administration of their vast system of monastic institutions and for the rhythm of the lives of those institutions' residents. Earlier chapters considered the various dimensions of the Geluk system of monastic life and administration as it took shape in the period following the military conquest by the Gelukpa's Oirat allies until the mid-eighteenth century. One major point I have sought to make is that the success of the Geluk school and its very identity—its longevity and its relatively uniform agreement on the manner in which every facet of the monastery and monastic life is organized—is as much a result of the efforts of prolific, peregrinating lamas as it was any martial and financial boons granted the school by political allies or patrons.

To be sure, without the decision in 1637 by the Oirat Khoshud ruler Güüshi Khan to lead his troops to Tibet, where he settled once and for all the violence between the major religious and political powers in Central Tibet, there is no guarantee that the Gelukpa or any single school would have become the hegemonic power on the Tibetan Plateau. However, the Khanate of Güüshi did not last forever, nor did it stretch to include the many lands and peoples where even today one can find Geluk monasteries. The Geluk school outlasted its erstwhile patron. It also spread from its early center of power in the Lhasa Valley to establish a religious monopoly across much of the Tibetan Plateau and Mongolia. It was the codified body of practices—scholastic, liturgical, administrative, and those pertaining to the cult of its high gods—that bound together this extensive religious network.

Such a process was not unprecedented in history. For instance, Peter Heather has provocatively argued that the Western Christian Church of the medieval period developed over several hundred years into an "ecclesiastical empire" capable of governing itself and its own interests across a civilizational realm—"Christendom"—comprising a multitude of different peoples and polities.[17] The Holy Roman emperor Charlemagne provided an enormous financial stimulus to the Holy See. In addition, he and his churchmen launched a series of monastic and ecclesiastical reforms (what Heather refers to as "*correctio*"), which included producing "correct" versions of a curated body of texts that would provide the foundation for a more "accurate" and uniform understanding of Christian teachings.[18] As Heather writes, "The long-term effect of Charlemagne's religious reforms generated a Latin Church with strong enough institutional roots in cathedrals and larger monasteries to form and maintain a continuous (though not unchanging) religious identity and reform programme, whatever the surrounding political situation. In contrast to what happened after the fall of the old Roman West, therefore, the collapse of Charlemagne's empire did not cause Western Christendom to fragment into its constituent parts."[19] In addition, a clear and uncompromising vision of the supremacy of the papacy over the Western Church—including all other bishops as well as any divinely appointed monarch—gradually developed during this period. Finally, a momentous legal development of the twelfth and thirteenth centuries—the creation and distribution of an organized and authoritative body of canon law at the top of which sat papal decretals (decrees)—provided the practical mechanisms for the papacy to become the unrivaled ruler over a vast, uniform Christendom.[20] The study of Christian monasticism and "church history" has not been sidelined by the same series of dichotomies laid out above as has Buddhist monasticism; as a result, we know far more about the development of the former.

Of course, there are differences between the case of the Geluk school and that of the medieval Western Christian Church. The divinely appointed emperor, Charlemagne, was the primary driver of the program of reforming and standardizing Christian learning and devotion, whereas in our story it is the figure of the Geluk lama (with the Fifth Dalai Lama being arguably the most active representative) who drove the process of systematizing monastic practice.[21] Also, although it is clear that the presence of large-scale Geluk monasteries did indeed impact the arrangement of and life within lay communities (recall that monastic constitutions did bear on laity as well as monastics), we still know too little about the day-to-day religiosity of laity living on the Tibetan Plateau during this period to speculate much about the impact the Geluk revolution may have had on lay life.

Finally, as many commentators regularly point out, Buddhists, including Tibetan Buddhists, have no single pontiff who alone decides orthodoxy and orthopraxy. Neither the Dalai Lama nor the throne-holder of Tsongkhapa's own monastery, Ganden, exercises the same sort of authority over the whole of the Geluk system of monasticism and religious practice. Nor were there any regular church councils or synods for establishing church doctrine, law, or practice. Certainly there were monasteries and lamas that were more central and important than others, such as the Three Seats in Ü, Tashi Lhünpo in Tsang, Labrang in Amdo, the Dalai Lama and the Panchen Lama, the Ganden throne-holder, and so on, and these did exert a disproportional influence on the decision-making of Gelukpa from across Tibet and Mongolia. For instance, the contested and political process of identifying the rebirth of an incarnate lama often included asking for the input of the Dalai and Panchen Lamas, among others. Likewise, the formal debates of the Great Prayer Festival in Lhasa each year could be seen as a "synod" of sorts, where the best and brightest of the major monasteries would compete in debate. This, however, did not result in new rulings or legislation.

Such differences aside, there is a remarkable similarity between the processes by which a uniform Christendom and a Tibetan Buddhist cultural sphere took shape. In the case of Tibetan Buddhism, the rulings and legislation that instituted this process come in the form of the monastic constitutions discussed throughout this book. Precedents established by Tsongkhapa and the Fifth Dalai Lama were emulated and built upon, resulting in hundreds or perhaps even thousands of texts dedicated to codifying a correct way of being a monk and running a monastery. Moreover, these were disseminated across often vast distances to monasteries, resulting in a web of monasteries adhering to a relatively uniform set of monastic norms.

The lamas who composed the constitutions for monasteries near and far would train at the same major monasteries, usually in Central Tibet, although in the eighteenth and nineteenth centuries new "local centers"[22] along the periphery came to serve a similar albeit less prestigious role. These lamas traveled regularly between Central Tibet and their home monasteries, but they also traveled to various other monasteries and communities to which they were invited, penning constitutions along the way and otherwise taking measures to ensure a consistency in monastic forms between monasteries and across the Tibetan Buddhist cultural sphere.

Authority was more distributed throughout the system and governed by the bureaucratic principles and mechanisms prescribed in the monastic constitutions and other texts devised for Buddhist learning, worship, and ritual. Polities would rise and fall, including the Oirat Khoshud Khanate and even its successor, the Manchu Qing Empire (1644–1911), but the religious empire of the Gelukpa lived on. Indeed, even after Geluk monasteries in the twentieth century were deprived of the material base for their might and rule—their landed estates, subject populations, courts and jails, and ability to exercise legitimate force to ensure their rights and property—these monasteries continued to command the respect and even the financial support of lay populations.[23] And today its "ideological force" commands a global audience.[24] Whatever material impetus may have ushered the Geluk school to power in the seventeenth century is not the force that perpetuates it today. That, rather, is the result of the consistent messaging of Geluk lamas, who have devised and maintained an extensive yet uniform body of monks and monastic practices rooted in tradition.

# Appendix

# Monastic Constitutions to the Mid-Eighteenth Century

| Number | Date | Title | Author |
|--------|------|-------|--------|
| 1 | ca. 1060s–1136 | Rong zom chos bzang gis rang slob dam tshig pa rnams la gsungs pa'i rwa ba brgyad pa'i bca' yig[1] | Rong zom chos kyi bzang po (1042–1136) |
| 2 | ca. 1210–1217 | Gdan sa nyams dmas su gyur skabs mdzad pa'i bca' yig[2] | 'Jig rten mgon po (1143–1217) |
| 3 | ca. 1200–1255 | Mag+ha d+ha rdo rje gdan 'bri gung byang chub gling gi bca' khrims[3] | 'Bri gung Grags pa 'byung gnas (1175–1255) |
| 4 | 1405? | Dge 'dun gyi khrims su bca' ba[4] | Tsong kha pa Blo bzang grags pa (1357–1419) |
| 5 | 1405? | Byams pa gling na bzhugs pa'i dge 'dun rnams kyi spyi'i khrims su bya ba'i bca' yig chung ngu[5] | Tsong kha pa Blo bzang grags pa (1357–1419) |
| 6 | 1449 | Theg chen rtse'i bca' yig[6] | Spyan snga Blo gros rgyal mtshan (1402–1472) |
| 7 | ca. 1478–1507 | Thub bstan gser mdog can gyi lo rgyus dkar chag[7] | ShAkya mchog ldan (1428–1507) |
| 8 | ca. 1520s–1554 | Bstan pa mtha' dag yongs su rdzogs pa'i Karma sgar chen gyi rdo rje'i rig pa 'dzin pa mkha' spyod gling gi bya ba'i rim pa[8] | Karma pa VIII Mi skyod rdo rje (1507–1554) |

| Number | Date | Title | Author |
|--------|------|-------|--------|
| 9 | ca. 1520s–1554 | Dga' tshal karma gzhung lugs gling dang por sgar chen 'dzam gling rgyan du bzhugs dus kyi 'phral gyi bca' yig[9] | Karma pa VIII Mi skyod rdo rje (1507–1554) |
| 10 | ca. 1520s–1554 | Lam gcig chod kyi khrid[10] | Karma pa VIII Mi skyod rdo rje (1507–1554) |
| 11 | ca. 1520s–1557 | Ra bsgreng 'od 'jo gdan sa ba bshes rab nyi ma la gdams pa'i rdor dkar gyi phan yon bzhugs[11] | Rin chen phun tshogs (1509–1557) |
| 12 | ca. 1540s–1584 | Grwa tshang gi bca' yig bstan pa'i nyi 'od[12] | Shes rab 'od zer (1518–1584) |
| 13 | 1575 | TsA ri mtsho dkar dben pa la bzhugs nas sgar sogs mi gnang bar byas thag bcad skabs rgyal mtshab rin po che sogs grwa rigs sbyin bdag thams cad kyis nan cher spyan drangs dus 'phral bder gnang ba'i bca' yig[13] | Karma pa IX Dbang phyug rdo rje (1556–1601/1603)[14] |
| 14 | 1579 | Mtshur phu grwa tshang gi bca' yig[15] | Karma pa IX Dbang phyug rdo rje (1556–1601/1603) |
| 15 | 1585 | Spa rnam dga' ba gdong gi bca' yig[16] | Karma pa IX Dbang phyug rdo rje (1556–1601/1603) |
| 16 | 1588 | Kon ting gu'i shri[17] si tu sprul pa'i sku rin po che dpon slob la gnang ba'i bca' yig[18] | Karma pa IX Dbang phyug rdo rje (1556–1601/1603) |
| 17 | 1600 | Sgar chen 'dzam gling rgyan gyi bca' yig chen mo[19] | Karma pa IX Dbang phyug rdo rje (1556–1601/1603) |
| 18 | ca. 1570s–1603 | Karma dar rgyas gling gi dge 'dun rnams la 'phral dgos kyi bca' ba khrims su bkod pa[20] | Karma pa IX Dbang phyug rdo rje (1556–1601/1603)[21] |
| 19 | ca. 1570s–1603 | Re dga' gra tshang rab rgyas kun dga' gling rtse lha sgang bsgrub sder 'jog pa gnang ba slar pho brang nyid du spos te dar rgyas su byas pa'i bca' yig[22] | Karma pa IX Dbang phyug rdo rje (1556–1601/1603) |

| Number | Date | Title | Author |
|--------|------|-------|--------|
| 20 | ca. 1570s–1603 | Thob rgyal 'dul gra gling gi bca' yig[23] | Karma pa IX Dbang phyug rdo rje (1556–1601/1603) |
| 21 | ca. 1570s–1603 | Thob rgyal bkra shis khri bstan bshad gra dang bkra shis khri skor sngags gra gnyis thun mong gi bca' yig las khri skor gyi khyad par rnams mchen bu byas pa[24] | Karma pa IX Dbang phyug rdo rje (1556–1601/1603) |
| 22 | ca. 1570s–1603 | Rtses thang do sngon gra tshang thub bstan dar rgyas gi bca' yig[25] | Karma pa IX Dbang phyug rdo rje (1556–1601/1603) |
| 23 | ca. 1570s–1603 | Dwags por karma bshad sgrub gling gi 'dus sde chen mo'i bca' yig[26] | Karma pa IX Dbang phyug rdo rje (1556–1601/1603) |
| 24 | 1586 | Dpal se ra theg chen chos 'khor gling gi dge 'dun spyi la khrims su bca' ba'i yi ge[27] | 'Od zer rgya mtsho (1557–1623) |
| 25 | 1601? | 'Dul ba ba'i bcas khrims slar spang bsdam pa'o[28] | 'Od zer rgya mtsho (1557–1623) |
| 26 | ca. 1580s–1623 | Skyi bsrung bsnyung gnas bca' yig[29] | 'Od zer rgya mtsho (1557–1623) |
| 27 | ca. 1580s–1623 | Bsgrub grwa ba rnams kyi bca' yig[30] | 'Od zer rgya mtsho (1557–1623) |
| 28 | ca. 1580s–1623 | Dbyar gnas kyi skabs dang dbrel bar khrims su bca' ba'i yi ge[31] | 'Od zer rgya mtsho (1557–1623) |
| 29 | ca. 1590s–1662 | Thar pa don du gnyer ba'i ri khrod pa rnams la khrims su bca' ba sku gsum gzhal med khang du 'dzegs pa bai DUrya'i them skas[32] | Panchen Lama IV Blo bzang chos kyi rgyal mtshan (1570–1662) |
| 30 | 1614 | Ra lung thel gyi bca' yig chen mo[33] | Ngag dbang bstan 'dzin rnam rgyal 'jigs med grags pa (1594–1651) |
| 31 | 1624 | Dpal ldan Sa skya'i gdan sa bar pa Dge sding 'dra 'dri chos rdzong bkra shis bsam 'grub kyi chos sde bstan pa'i lhun po'i bca' yig bsam don kun 'grub[34] | Sa skya *khri chen* Ngag dbang kun dga' bsod nams (1597–1660) |

| Number | Date | Title | Author |
|--------|------|-------|--------|
| 32 | 1642 | Khrig se dgon gi bca' yig[35] | Dalai Lama V Ngag dbang blo bzang rgya mtsho (1617–1682) |
| 33 | 1644 | Gdan sa chen po rwa sgreng rgyal ba'i dben gnas kyi bca' yig gong sa mchog nas bstsal ba'i zhal bshus 'khrul med[36] | Dalai Lama V Ngag dbang blo bzang rgya mtsho (1617–1682) |
| 34 | 1645 | Chos 'khor rgyal gyi khrims ldan 'dus sde rnams kyi khrims su bca' ba'i rim pa[37] | Dalai Lama V Ngag dbang blo bzang rgya mtsho (1617–1682) |
| 35 | 1645? | Gso rig 'gro phan gling gi bca' yig[38] | Dalai Lama V Ngag dbang blo bzang rgya mtsho (1617–1682) |
| 36 | 1646, sixth month, eleventh day | Chos grwa chen po dpal snar thang gi rab 'byams grwa skor gyi bca' tshe shel dkar me long[39] | Dalai Lama V Ngag dbang blo bzang rgya mtsho (1617–1682) |
| 37 | 1646, sixth month, eleventh day | Smon lam chen mo'i mtshan rtags skor la bstsal ba'i dran tho[40] | Dalai Lama V Ngag dbang blo bzang rgya mtsho (1617–1682) |
| 38 | 1646, tenth month, fifteenth day | Ri khrod dga' ldan pa'i spyi khrims kyi bca' tshe shel dkar me long[41] | Dalai Lama V Ngag dbang blo bzang rgya mtsho (1617–1682) |
| 39 | 1647 | Chos grwa chen po dpal rtses thang gi rab 'byams grwa skor gyi bca' tshe shel dkar me long[42] | Dalai Lama V Ngag dbang blo bzang rgya mtsho (1617–1682) |
| 40 | 1651 | Chos 'khor rgyal gyi 'dus sde'i khrims su bca' ba sngar shing bya lo bris par bzo bcos bgyis pa shu shel dbang po[43] | Dalai Lama V Ngag dbang blo bzang rgya mtsho (1617–1682) |
| 41 | 1653 | Sku 'bum byams pa gling la bstsal ba'i bca' yig[44] | Dalai Lama V Ngag dbang blo bzang rgya mtsho (1617–1682) |

| Number | Date | Title | Author |
|--------|------|-------|--------|
| 42 | 1664 | Dga' ldan thub bstan rab rgyas kyi dge 'dun spyi'i khrims su bca' ba dran pa'i lcags kyu[45] | Dalai Lama V Ngag dbang blo bzang rgya mtsho (1617–1682) |
| 43 | 1664 | Gong ra nges gsang rdo rje gling gi khrims su bca' ba'i rim pa[46] | Dalai Lama V Ngag dbang blo bzang rgya mtsho (1617–1682) |
| 44 | 1675 | Lha ldan cho 'phrul smon lam chen mo'i tshogs bzhugs dge 'dun spyi la bstsal ba'i bca' yig[47] | Dalai Lama V Ngag dbang blo bzang rgya mtsho (1617–1682) |
| 45 | 1676 | Chos sde chen po zha lu'u sgrub mchod bco lnga gsar tshugs skabs bstsal ba'i bca' yig shes dkar me long[48] | Dalai Lama V Ngag dbang blo bzang rgya mtsho (1617–1682) |
| 46 | 1676 | Nyang smad bsam don lhun gyis grub pa'i rdzong chen du tshe'i rig byed gso ba rig pa'i grwa tshang drang srong 'dus pa'i gling gi bca' yig[49] | Dalai Lama V Ngag dbang blo bzang rgya mtsho (1617–1682) |
| 47 | 1679 | Pho brang po ta la'i sum skas mgo'i bca' yig[50] | Dalai Lama V Ngag dbang blo bzang rgya mtsho (1617–1682) |
| 48 | 1680?[51] | Li thang thub bstan byams chen phyogs thams cad las rnam par rgyal ba'i sde'i khrims su bca' ba'i skor[52] | Dalai Lama V Ngag dbang blo bzang rgya mtsho (1617–1682) |
| 49 | 1680?[53] | 'Ba' dga' ldan phan bde gling pa'i khrims su bca' ba'i rim pa blang dor gsal ba'i zla ba sogs[54] | Dalai Lama V Ngag dbang blo bzang rgya mtsho (1617–1682) |
| 50 | 1680 | 'Bri gdan byang chub gling gi bca' yig nyes brgya kun grol[55] | 'Bri gung che tshang Dkon mchog 'phrin las bzang po (1656–1718) |

| Number | Date | Title | Author |
|--------|------|-------|--------|
| 51 | 1682 | Chos sde chen po Dpal ldan 'bras spungs kyi khrims su bca' ba'i rim pa tshul 'chal sa srungs 'dul ba'i lcags kyo kun gsal me long[56] | Dalai Lama V Ngag dbang blo bzang rgya mtsho (1617–1682) |
| 52 | 1687 | Rtse bar sku zhabs grwa tshang chung ba gsar 'dzugs kyi bca' yig[57] | 'Bri gung che tshang Dkon mchog 'phrin las bzang po (1656–1718) |
| 53 | 1689 | O rgyan smin grol gling gi 'dus sde'i bca' khrims kyi yi ge blang dor gsal bar byed pa'i nyi ma[58] | Gter bdag gling pa 'Gyur med rdo rje (1646–1714) |
| 54 | 1689 | Bca' yig ma mo las 'phros pa'i zur bkod dum dum khrigs kyi skor[59] | Gter bdag gling pa 'Gyur med rdo rje (1646–1714) |
| 55 | 1698 | Rta wang dga' ldan rnam rgyal lha rtse'i bca' yig mdor bsdus[60] | 'Phyong rgyas pa Ngag dbang rnam rgyal (17th c.) |
| 56 | ca. 1698 | Dga' ldan byang chub gling gi dge 'dun rnams kyi khrims su bca' ba mdor bsdus blang dor gsal ba'i me long[61] | Lcang skya II Ngag dbang blo bzang chos ldan (1642–1714) |
| 57 | ca. 1698 | Rong po re skong g.yer gshong gi dben gnas bsam gtan gling gi bca' yig[62] | Lcang skya II Ngag dbang blo bzang chos ldan (1642–1714) |
| 58 | 1709 | Phun tshogs dar rgyas gling gi dge 'dun spyi'i bcas khrims sbrang rtsi'i rgyal mtshan thar 'dod bung ba'i dga' ston[63] | Brag dkar *sngags rams pa* Blo bzang bstan pa rab rgyas (ca. 1647–1727) |
| 59 | 1711 | Mang spro chos 'khor shar gling Skyid mang Gog mig bcas kyi dgon ma lag dang bcas pa'i dgon bca' yig[64] | Nyi ma rnam rgyal (the king of Ladakh) |
| 60 | 1719[65] | Dga' ldan bshad sgrub dar rgyas bkra shis chos gling gi bca' yig phan bde kun 'byung[66] | 'Jam dbyangs bzhad pa I Ngag dbang brtson 'grus (1648–1721) |

| Number | Date | Title | Author |
|--------|------|-------|--------|
| 61 | 1726, first month(?), seventh day | Sku 'bum rgyud pa grwa tshang gi bca' yig/ yid kyis srung 'dul ba'i bca' yig dran pa'i lcags kyo[67] | Dalai Lama VII Skal bzang rgya mtsho (1708–1757) |
| 62 | 1726, second month, fifteenth day | Chos grwa chen po dpal snar thang gi dge dun gyi sde rnams kyi khrims su bca' ba'i rim pa[68] | 'On rgyal sras 'Jigs med ye shes grags pa (ca. 1696–1750) |
| 63 | 1726, third month, eleventh day | Rnam rgyal grwa tshang la bstsal ba'i bca' yig gser gyi gnya' shing[69] | Dalai Lama VII Skal bzang rgya mtsho (1708–1757) |
| 64 | ca. 1727[70] | Ra sgreng gi khims su bca' ba gdul bya'i kun+da bzhad pa'i zla[71] | 'On rgyal sras 'Jigs med ye shes grags pa (ca. 1696–1750) |
| 65 | 1727[72] | Dben gnas lha ri bsam gtan gling gi ri khod pa rnams la khrims su bca' ba'i yi ge phan bde'i 'byung gnas[73] | Brag dkar *sngags rams pa* Blo bzang bstan pa rab rgyas (ca. 1647–1727)[74] |
| 66 | 1737, second month, twenty-seventh day | Dgon lung byams pa gling gi mtshon dgon ma lag dang bcas pa'i bca' khrims phan bde'i 'dab rgya bzhad ba'i snang byed[75] | 'On rgyal sras 'Jigs med ye shes grags pa (ca. 1696–1750) |
| 67 | 1737, fifth month, fourteenth day | Dben gnas lhag bsam bkra shis 'khyil gyi dge 'dun pa rnams la khrims su bca' ba mdor bsdus blang dor rab tu gsal ba'i nyi ma[76] | Blo bzang bsam gtan (1687–1749) |
| 68 | 1737, tenth month, fifteenth day | Chos sde chen po se ra theg chen gling la bstsal ba'i bca' yig gser tham chen mo 'byar ma[77] | Dalai Lama VII Skal bzang rgya mtsho (1708–1757) |
| 69 | ca. 1737[78] | Steng sgang bkra shis thos bsam gling gi dge 'dun pa rnams la khrims su bca' ba thub bstan rgyas byed[79] | Blo bzang bsam gtan (1687–1749)[80] |

# Notes

## INTRODUCTION

1. I borrow this phrase from Donald Lopez, who uses it to describe what the current, Fourteenth, Dalai Lama and other Dge lugs hierarchs are doing today in promoting Tibetan Buddhism around the globe. Lopez, *Prisoners of Shangri-La*, 206–7. Note that I am using "colonialism" here in a broad and provocative sense, not in a theoretically informed sense. Certainly there are features of colonialism as scholars have defined it that are applicable to the case of the Dge lug pa (e.g., reliance on a civilizing project to exercise dominion). As I will discuss below, I find "bureaucracy" and even "empire" to be more readily applicable to the case of the Dge lug pa. See Osterhammel, *Colonialism: A Theoretical Overview*. For an application of Osterhammel's definition of "colonialism" to the Manchu Qing, see Oidtmann, *Forging the Golden Urn*, 40–44.

2. Aris, *Hidden Treasures and Secret Lives*, 9. Cited in Chou, "Reimagining the Buddhist Universe," 437n28.

3. See, for instance, Shakabpa's discussion of the "Pelden Döndrup affair." Shakabpa, *One Hundred Thousand Moons*, 609–14.

4. Tsyrempilov, "Dge lugs pa Divided."

5. See, for instance, Oidtmann, "Between Patron and Priest," 437–56.

6. Gorski, "Protestant Ethic and Bureaucratic Revolution," 269.

7. McNeill, *Keeping Together in Time*.

8. Scott, *Art of Not Being Governed*, 294.

9. Among scholars, Robert Thurman has been one of the most vocal proselytizers of this view. See, for instance, his contributions to Bstan-'dzin-rgya-mtsho et al., *MindScience*; Kraft, *Inner Peace, World Peace*. These orientalist assumptions were also prevalent in the Orient. Max Oidtmann notes that Qing officials and rulers also saw Tibet as a unique Buddhist polity quite unlike Mongolia or the Muslim regions. Oidtmann, *Forging the Golden Urn*, 23.

10. Dreyfus, "Proto-Nationalism in Tibet"; Dreyfus, "Tibetan Religious Nationalism"; Kapstein, "A Pilgrimage of Rebirth Reborn."

11. Goldstein, *A History of Modern Tibet, 1913–1951*, 21; Goldstein, "Bouddhisme tibétain et monachisme de masse" [Tibetan Buddhism and mass monasticism]; Cassinelli and Ekvall, *A Tibetan Principality*, 311, citing Carrasco; Carrasco Pizana, *Land and Polity in Tibet*, 121 who, in turn, is citing Das; Das, "The Monasteries of Tibet," 106; Das, *Narrative of a Journey*, 89–100.

12. Samuel, *Civilized Shamans*, 582.

13. Spiro, *Buddhism and Society*, 284; Tambiah, *World Conqueror and World Renouncer*, 266–67.

14. Stein, *Tibetan Civilization*, 139. Stein does not cite his source.

15. Sangs rgyas rgya mtsho composed the text between 1692 and 1698.

16. Dung dkar Blo bzang 'phrin las, *Bod kyi chos srid zung 'brel skor bshad pa* [The merging of religious and secular rule in Tibet], 1982 (1981), 102. Dung dkar writes 95,538 monks on page 98 of the same text. In any case, Dungkar (Dung dkar) appears to be the source of scholars today, such as Goldstein and Kapstein. Goldstein, *A History of Modern Tibet, 1913–1951*, 21; Kapstein, *The Tibetans*, 142. Interestingly, I do not know whether anyone has ever tried to independently recalculate these figures in order to "check the math" of Dungkar.

17. This is based on the *Sheng wu ji*, originally written in 1842. Therein it says that the Lifanyuan carried out a census in 1737 (Qianlong 2). Wei Yuan 魏源 (1794–1857), *Sheng wu ji* 聖武記, 226. And Shi Shouyi's 守一 *Lama suyuan* 剌麻溯源 of circa 1890, gives the same figures as the *Sheng wu ji*: 302,500 for Dbus and 13,700 for Gtsang. http://tripitaka.cbeta.org /X88n1668_001. These figures are cited by such scholars as Rockhill and Stein: Rockhill, "Tibet," 13–14; Stein, *La civilisation tibétaine*, 111; Stein, *Tibetan Civilization*, 139–40. Dpal bzang bdang bdus at the Tibetan Academy of Social Sciences has suggested to me that the Lifanyuan statistics would have been provided by the Tibetan *bka' shag* (the Tibetan government's council of ministers). Personal communication, October 2012. Strangely, Dung dkar gives 342,560 for Dbus and 13,670 for Gtsang for the year 1733. Dung dkar Blo bzang 'phrin las, *Bod kyi chos srid zung 'brel skor bshad pa*, 102; this is a reprint of the 1981 Beijing edition. This must be a reference to the census of 1737 referred to above, although it is not clear why these discrepancies exist (the answer is probably arithmetic error or a typographical error introduced between the multiple printings and translations of Dung dkar's text). Present-day scholars have reproduced Dung dkar's figures, although a proliferation of slightly different and confusing totals abound. Goldstein, "Tibetan Buddhism and Mass Monasticism"; Kapstein, *The Tibetans*, 142; Goldstein, *A History of Modern Tibet, 1913–1951*, 21; McCleary and van der Kuijp, "Market Approach," 174–75.

18. T. *spyil po*. Thu'u bkwan III Blo bzang chos kyi nyi ma, "Bshad sgrub bstan pa'i byung gnas chos sde chen po dgon lung byams pa gling gi dkar chag" (hereafter "Dgon lung gi dkar chag"), 646/7b.4. The number before the slash is the page number introduced by a later editor of the volume (using Arabic numerals) in which this work of Thu'u bkwan's (the "Dgon lung gi dkar chag") is found. The number after the slash corresponds to the page number of the work, carved into the wood blocks in Tibetan script. The "b" indicates *verso* (an "a," conversely, would indicate *recto*), and the "4" following the period is the line number.

19. Sde srid Sangs rgyas rgya mtsho, *Dga' ldan chos 'byung baiDUrya ser po*, 340.

20. Brag dgon zhabs drung Dkon mchog bstan pa rab rgyas, *Mdo smad chos 'byung*, 117.8; Schram, who may be relying on Chinese sources, says that Dgon lung had 2,500 monks in the lead-up to the Lubsang-Danzin Rebellion. *Monguors of the Kansu-Tibetan Border*, 283, 323.

21. T. *a mdo*.

22. Tuttle, "Building Up the Dge lugs pa Base in A mdo," 128.

23. Tuttle writes that the first half of the seventeenth century, which led to the establishment of the Dalai Lama's rule in Central Tibet, "saw the greatest expansion of Gelukpa massive monasteries in A mdo's history." However, the size and complexity (including consistency) of these newly founded monasteries, such as Dgon lung, took longer to take shape. Tuttle, "Building Up the Dge lugs pa Base in A mdo," 135.

24. Although in Mongolia the Manchu Qing Empire also exerted great influence. Charleux, *Temples et monastères de Mongolie-Intérieure*, 69–70.

25. Wei Yuan 魏源 (1794–1857), *Sheng wu ji* 聖武記, 226; this is an increase from the figure given by Dung dkar for the year 1694 (this being a reference to Sde srid Sangs rgyas rgya mtsho's history of the Dge lugs school compiled between 1692 and 1698): 1,807 monasteries across Central, Eastern, and Western Tibet. Dung dkar Blo bzang 'phrin las, *Bod kyi chos srid zung 'brel skor bshad pa*, 102.

26. Of course, what is presumed here is that the vast majority of the monasteries recorded in 1737 as under the dominion of the Dalai Lama and Panchen Lama belonged to the Dge lugs school, which is a reasonable presumption. Sarat Chandra Das claimed in 1896 to have received official statistics for 1882 during his stay in Lhasa.

27. McCleary and van der Kuijp, "Market Approach," 175.

28. Indeed, Gray Tuttle has informed me that, based on his own calculations, the number of monasteries did in fact go up over this period.

29. Goldstein, "Tibetan Buddhism and Mass Monasticism." I have relied principally on this English version of the paper, which is available for download at the author's website. It has been published in French as "Bouddhisme tibétain et monachisme de masse" [Tibetan Buddhism and mass monasticism]. This article is largely a reiteration of material found in Goldstein's earlier article on modern Drepung Monastery in China. "Revival of Monastic Life in Drepung Monastery." He introduced some of these ideas earlier still in Goldstein, *A History of Modern Tibet, 1913–1951*, 21–24.

30. Goldstein, "Revival of Monastic Life in Drepung Monastery," 15.

31. Tucci, *Tibetan Painted Scrolls*, 69.

32. Blo bzang 'phrin las, Dung dkar, *Merging of Religious and Secular Rule*, 73; the corresponding Tibetan original is found in Dung dkar Blo bzang 'phrin las, *Bod kyi chos srid zung 'brel skor bshad pa*, 97.

33. Blo bzang 'phrin las, Dung dkar, *Merging of Religious and Secular Rule*, 77; Dung dkar Blo bzang 'phrin las, *Bod kyi chos srid zung 'brel skor bshad pa*, 104.

34. Gray Tuttle has numerous essays that look at Dge lugs activity in A mdo. One example is his "Building up the Dge lugs pa Base in A mdo." See also BAN Shinichiro, "Darai rama seiken seiritsu zen'ya ni okeru geruku-ha no amudo fukyō: Geruku-ha sōryo depa choje no katsudō o chūshin ni mita." The expansion of the Dge lugs school into Mongolia and Mongolia's "second conversion" is, of course, well known, and both the early relationship struck between the Third Dalai Lama and Altan Khan as well as the later Qing patronage of monasteries in Mongolia are recognized as factors for explaining Dge lugs success there. However, as other scholars have pointed out, we still do not know for sure what made the Dge lugs school rather than another school attractive to these patrons (especially to Altan Khan).

35. McCleary and van der Kuijp, "Market Approach," 151.

36. Goldstein, "Bouddhisme tibétain et monachisme de masse" [Tibetan Buddhism and mass monasticism]. Goldstein, "Revival of Monastic Life in Drepung Monastery," 17–19.

37. Dreyfus, *Sound of Two Hands Clapping*, 39–40.

38. Yijing 義淨 (635–713), *Buddhist Monastic Traditions of Southern Asia*, 63. This corresponds to the Taishō edition of the canon, T2125, 213a–214a.

39. A colleague pointed out to me that Goldstein's notion of "mass monasticism" does not mean "monasteries with masses of monks at them" so much as an *overall*, massive population of monks. Be that as it may, the criticism inherent in the concept (i.e., of valuing

quantity over quality in recruiting monks) is the same criticism that is made of massive monasteries (i.e., that there are many monks at the monastery who are idle or even taking part in violence and mischief).

40. Kapstein, *The Tibetans*, 120–21; cited in DiValerio, *Holy Madmen of Tibet*, 122. My thanks to DiValerio for drawing my attention to this passage and for sharing his own insights into the rise of the Dge lugs school. Kapstein makes a similar point regarding the introduction of Buddhism into Tibet and the accommodation and naturalization of Buddhism in Tibet in the post-imperial period. Kapstein, *Tibetan Assimilation of Buddhism*, 54–58. DiValerio has also written a compelling summary of the rise and success of the Dge lugs school. DiValerio, *Holy Madmen of Tibet*, 121–27. He points to the founding of numerous Dge lugs monasteries in the century following the death of Tsong kha pa as reflecting the unique institutional features of the Dge lugs school and as indicating the school's success. I would draw a distinction, however, between the founding of monasteries and the growth in size and complexity of monastic institutions, not to mention the development of the monastic networks that both resulted from and ensured a high degree of institutional consistency. I attribute the latter to the administrative efforts of the Fifth Dalai Lama and later to Dge lugs pa.

41. Philip Gorski, in discussing the history of bureaucracy in early modern Europe, suggests that "revolution can catalyze bureaucratization by demolishing distributional coalitions that can stand in the way of reform." Gorski, "Protestant Ethic and Bureaucratic Revolution," 288.

42. Smith, *Among Tibetan Texts*, 41.

43. The Tibetan term for "bureaucrat" is *dpon ngan*, literally "bad official" or "bad lord." Goldstein, Shelling, and Surkhang, *The New Tibetan-English Dictionary*, 652. "*Dpon ngan*" is said to refer to "bad functionaries and officials in a feudal or capitalist state." Zhang Yisun 张 怡荪, *Bod rgya tshig mdzod chen mo*, 1641. "*Dpon*," which is generally and adequately translated as "official," "lord," or "headman," is also given the definition of "the name given to one who has acquired a definite position within the military or an office of a state run by the exploiting class. They are the ones who possess power in a government of the exploiting class, and they are the servants of the reactionary ruling class." Tshan chung, *Dag yig gsar bsgrigs*, 464. The *Bod rgya tshigs mdzod chen mo* and *Dag yig gsar bsgrigs*, from which these latter two definitions come, are two of the most commonly used, modern Tibetan dictionaries, and both, unsurprisingly, are published in the People's Republic of China. There is no word in Tibetan for "bureaucrat" completely distinct from the word used for "officials" in "pre-liberation" Tibet. Both concepts are heavily influenced by Marxist and communist theory. It is worth pointing out that the Chinese term for bureaucrat, *guanliao* 官僚, is also one of the terms used through the centuries to refer to state "officials" in China.

44. U, *Disorganizing China*, 15–20.

45. Weber, "Social Psychology of the World Religions," 299.

46. Weber, *Economy and Society*, 1:223.

47. Weber, *The Protestant Ethic*, 123–24.

48. Weber, "Social Psychology of the World Religions," 281.

49. Swidler, "Foreword," xiv.

50. Weber, "Social Psychology of the World Religions," 277–78.

51. Note that Weber does not reduce the religious impulse to mere psychology. If Weber is anything, he is anti-reductionistic in the sense that he draws attention to the variety of mutually interacting forces, social status, historical circumstance, ideal interests, and so on.

52. Weber, "Social Psychology of the World Religions," 275; Kapstein has noted that the Buddhist notions of karma and saṃsāra fit with and may have even contributed to legal rationalization in Tibet. Kapstein, *Tibetan Assimilation of Buddhism*, 54.

53. Weber, *The Sociology of Religion*, 35–36; see also Weber, "Social Psychology of the World Religions," 293–94.

54. U, *Disorganizing China*, 10–11, citing the essay by Roberto Antonio, "The Contradiction of Domination and Production in Bureaucracy: The Contribution of Organizational Efficiency to the Decline of the Roman Empire," in *American Sociological Review* 44, no. 6 (1979): 895–912. See also Weber, "Social Psychology of the World Religions," 293.

55. Elsewhere, Weber suggests that "to judge the level of rationalization [that] a religion represents we may use two primary yardsticks which are in many ways interrelated. One is the degree to which the religion has divested itself of magic; the other is the degree to which it has systematically unified the relation between God and the world and therewith its own ethical relationship to the world." Weber, *The Religion of China*, 226. As discussed below, the Geluk suspicion of charismatic authority and its attempts to control it as well as the Geluk program of disciplining and organizing its body of monks reflect this characterization of rationalization, too.

56. Weber, *The Protestant Ethic*; Gorski, "Protestant Ethic and Bureaucratic Revolution."

57. Weber, "Social Psychology of the World Religions," 281–82; Weber, *The Sociology of Religion*, 181ff.

58. Weber, *The Sociology of Religion*, 181.

59. Ibid., 181.

60. Gellner, *Anthropology of Buddhism and Hinduism*, 37. In defending Weber against the charge of mistaking doctrinal portrayals of Hinduism for the "real thing," Gellner writes that Weber "was attempting to analyze South Asian religion in order to find out what its effects on the actions of its adherents would be *if and when* they attempted to act systematically in accordance with their religious doctrines or prescribed practices" (90; emphasis added).

61. Weber, *The Sociology of Religion*, 181–82.

62. Schopen, *Bones, Stones, and Buddhist Monks*; Schopen, *Buddhist Monks and Business Matters*; Schopen, *Figments and Fragments of Mahayana Buddhism*; Schopen, *Buddhist Nuns, Monks, and Other Worldly Matters*.

63. Stein, *Tibetan Civilization*, 138.

64. Weber, "Social Psychology of the World Religions," 294, 288.

65. Ibid., 288.

66. The phrase "prophetic assault" comes from Gorski, "The Return of the Repressed," 179; see also Weber, *The Sociology of Religion*, 68–69.

67. Weber, "Social Psychology of the World Religions," 295.

68. U, *Disorganizing China*, 7.

69. Weber, "Social Psychology of the World Religions," 294–95.

70. U, *Disorganizing China*, 6.

71. Ibid., 11. As Weber puts it, "Orders are given in the name of the impersonal norm, rather than in the name of a personal authority; and even the giving of a command constitutes obedience toward a norm rather than an arbitrary freedom, favor, or privilege." Weber, "Social Psychology of the World Religions," 294–95.

72. U, *Disorganizing China*, 11. For another useful summary of the attributes of bureaucracy according to Weber, see Gorski, "Protestant Ethic and Bureaucratic Revolution," 268.

73. Graeber, *Utopia of Rules on Technology*, 27.

74. Anthropologist David Graeber writes provocatively about the allure of bureaucracy and its basis in our fear of uncertainty. Graeber, *Utopia of Rules on Technology*, 190–93. Loyalty is a desired outcome of bureaucratic regimes ranging from early modern Sweden to the High Qing. Gorski, "Protestant Ethic and Bureaucratic Revolution," 286; Guy, "Who Were the Manchus?," 157, 161.

75. Weber, "Social Psychology of the World Religions," 299–300.

76. Gorski, "Protestant Ethic and Bureaucratic Revolution," 271–74.

77. Weber, "Social Psychology of the World Religions," 280.

78. Schaeffer, "The Beginnings of the Gandenpa School," 507–8.

79. For an introduction to Tsong kha pa's life, see Powers, *Introduction to Tibetan Buddhism*, 467–75; Ary, *Authorized Lives*.

80. James Apple's introduction to Tsong kha pa's hermeneutical strategy for his interpretation of the topic of the Twenty Saṃghas provides a clear overview of the subject. Apple, *Stairway to Nirvāṇa*, 10–20.

81. T. *Gnam rtse ldeng, Gnam rtser ldeng, Gnam rtseng ldeng, Gnam rtseng lding.*

82. T. *Dga' ldan rnam par rgyal ba'i gling.*

83. Schaeffer, "The Beginnings of the Gandenpa School," 507.

84. Gorski, "Protestant Ethic and Bureaucratic Revolution," 288.

85. Two important new contributions to our understanding of this period are Schwieger, *The Dalai Lama and the Emperor of China*, and Oidtmann, *Forging the Golden Urn*.

86. Ishihama Yumiko 石濱裕美子, "On the Dissemination of the Belief in the Dalai Lama as a Manifestation of the Bodhisattva Avalokiteśvara."

87. Schaeffer, "Ritual, Festival and Authority"; see also the essays in Pommaret, *Lhasa in the Seventeenth Century.*

88. Schaeffer, "Indian Intellectuals." My thanks to Schaeffer for sharing with me and other students in his Dalai Lamas graduate seminar a copy of this and other research he had completed on the Fifth Dalai Lama. Schaeffer, "Fifth Dalai Lama Ngawang Lopsang Gyatso," 70.

89. The biography of Altan Khan and his immediate descendants describes the prophecies and aspirations regarding the Dge lugs conversion of the Mongols. Elverskog, *The Jewel Translucent Sūtra*, 151.

90. Elverskog, *The Jewel Translucent Sūtra*,158–59. According to Elverskog, this was likely composed in early 1607.

91. The meeting is said to have taken place alongside Lake Kökenuur in a place called Cabciyal, which corresponds to the Tibetan Chab chi ya la or Chab tsha. Charleux, *Temples et monastères de Mongolie-Intérieure*, 42n133. As Charleux suggests, this could correspond to today's Chab cha (Ch. Gonghe County 共和).

92. Ye shes rgyal mtshan, "Rgyal ba Bsod nams rgya mtsho'i rnam thar," 463. The biography of Altan Khan and his descendants, composed circa 1607, is probably the earliest account of the interactions between the Third Dalai Lama and Altan Khan.

93. Elverskog, *The Jewel Translucent Sūtra*, 158–9n287; Elverskog, "Tibetocentrism," 71–73; Charleux, *Temples et monastères de Mongolie-Intérieure*, 43n145.

94. Sullivan, "The Manner in Which I Went to Worship Mañjuśrī's Realm," 91–92.

95. Ultimately, the argument I put forward in this book does not rest on identifying Tsong kha pa's influence as a "cause" or an "inspiration" of what came next. What matters is the trail of documents that clearly display the Dge lugs school's unprecedented interest in rationalizing the life within and operation of its monasteries.

96. Doyle, *Empires*, 12, see also 45.

97. Burbank and Cooper, *Empires in World History*, 61–92.

98. Ibid., 8.

99. Doyle, *Empires*, 45; Burbank and Cooper, *Empires in World History*, 2–3. Rulers of empires also "sent out agents—governors, generals, tax collectors—to take charge of territories they incorporated," which took the form among the Dge lugs pa of lamas founding monasteries and of monks as tax and alms collectors. The peregrinating corps of Dge lugs prelates as well as its system of "study abroad" and "debate circuits" also maintained influence on peripheral monasteries and communities. It may even be appropriate to speak of a Dge lugs "logic of enrichment through expansion" in the form of the school's missionizing and petitioning of patrons among the Mongols, the Oirat, the Manchus, and other Inner Asian peoples. Burbank and Cooper, *Empires in World History*, 13, 10.

100. Doyle, *Empires*, 31n27.

101. Heather, *The Restoration of Rome*, 408.

102. This is not to say that Geluk control over its religious doctrines and practices was uncontested or that it reached the extent of the papacy's control over the Western Christian Church, for instance. Max Oidtmann has argued convincingly that Manchu colonialism in Tibet also significantly influenced Buddhist doctrine and practice there. Oidtmann, *Forging the Golden Urn*; Oidtmann, "Between Patron and Priest."

103. For certain readers, the term "organization men" may call to mind the title of William Whyte's 1956 study of the American ethic, *The Organization Man*. Whyte's organization man bears little resemblance to the organization men of Tibet described in this book—the architects and administrators of Tibet's large-scale monastic institutions. Whyte's criteria of the "social ethic" to which America's organization men are said to cling—belief in group as the source of creativity, a positive valuation of "belongingness", and a belief in the ability of science to affect such belongingness—have no analogues in pre-modern Tibet. However, if we accept the more general similarities between the two groups, the use of the term "organization men" to describe both modern American workers and premodern Tibetan monks is justifiable. In both cases, the *organization* (the company, the monastery) supplants the prestige of individual success (as an entrepreneur or as a lone, spiritual adept). Moreover, both see the success of the organization itself as essential to achieving greater goals (social progress; the growth of the Buddha's Teachings). In any case, I do not want to attach too much importance to the term "organization men" or to Whyte's view. I use "organization" and "institution" more or less interchangeably. My use of "organization men" is meant to merely draw attention to the surprisingly overlooked fact that educated Geluk monks were as much bureaucrats (planners) and administrators (executors of plans) as they ever were scholars or spiritual adepts.


CHAPTER 1


1. Kökenuur is traditionally considered the region immediately around the great lake of the same name on the northeastern edge of the Tibetan Plateau. Today it is understood to be part of the cultural region of Amdo (T. a mdo), although historical understandings of these place names and their relationship to each other were not static and are still not entirely understood. For more on Chagan Nom-un Khan (Cagan Nomunhan), see ch. 5 of Oidtmann, "Between Patron and Priest."

2. Aris, *Hidden Treasures and Secret Lives*, 9.

3. T. *spyi so*. Ordinarily, I would translate this as the "General Office" or "Public Office" of the monastery in charge of finances and certain administrative tasks. In other constitutions, however, we see a similar sentiment being expressed (i.e., that the welfare of *all people* depends on the Teachings of the Buddha), and so it makes more sense to interpret *spyi so* here as *spyi tshogs*, or society. This manuscript has numerous other misspellings, chief of which is "mi spyod rdo rje" for the Eighth Karmapa Mi *skyod* rdo rje.

4. Constitution no. 13, p. 18a.2–3.

5. Chayet, "The Potala," 45.

6. Of course, his "palace" was initially located at Drepung Monastery, and that special relationship persisted (e.g., he gave priority to the monks from 'Bras spungs for seating at the Great Prayer Festival in Lhasa). However, he was no longer thought of as simply Drepung's lama.

7. As a reviewer of this book commented, Dga' ldan Monastery has a claim to being the primary seat of the Dge lugs school. It is often pointed out that it was founded by Tsong kha pa and, thus, the successor to his throne at the monastery is recognized as the highest religious authority of the school. It may be that Dga' ldan Monastery thereby exercised some greater powers within the Dalai Lama's Dga' ldan pho brang government than other monasteries. For instance, Melvyn Goldstein reports that regents for the Dalai Lama were often chosen from among the current or former Dga' ldan throne-holders. Goldstein, *A History of Modern Tibet, 1913–1951*, 186. Apart from this, however, it is not at all clear how or if the monastery and its throne-holder's greater respect translated into greater authority and power in other dimensions of the Geluk school (such as the internal administration of other monasteries, especially those founded by or associated with the other major "seats" in Central Tibet).

8. They can go by different names, too, particularly *bca' khrims*.

9. For a useful summary of this genre of literature, see Jansen, *The Monastery Rules*, 14–30; Ellingson, "Tibetan Monastic Constitutions."

10. Jansen, *The Monastery Rules*, 17.

11. T. *tshogs gtam*.

12. Many constitutions include a short history of the monastery and place it within the history of the development of Buddhism in Tibet. Constitutions were "foundational" in providing the monastery a sense of history and identity, although they were not alone in doing that (other documents, such as "chronicles" or *dkar chag*, did this, too).

13. Rong zom Chos kyi bzang po, "Rong zom chos bzang gis rang slob dam tshig pa rnams la gsungs pa'i rwa ba brgyad pa'i bca' yig" (constitution no. 1).

14. A text by the fifteenth-century Lo dgon pa Bsod nams lha'i dbang po (1423–1496) refers to several Bka' gdams constitutions that appear to be no longer extant. Vetturini, "The bKa' gdams pa School of Tibetan Buddhism," 165–66; cited in Jansen, *The Monastery Rules*, 15.

15. Although this number is not exhaustive, it is close to the total number of extant constitutions that I am aware of. The sample of constitutions is limited to the nineteenth century and earlier both because of the particular historical focus of this book and so as to remove any possible distorting influence of the prolific Dge lugs hierarchs from later periods: the Thirteenth Dalai Lama and offices associated with his government composed over two dozen customaries, more than any other individual. All of this is likely a function of the state-building efforts of the Thirteenth Dalai Lama as well as a result of the Dalai Lama's

forced travels through various parts of Tibet and Mongolia. For gathering constitutions, I have relied principally upon (1) published compilations of constitutions (e.g., Rdo sbis Tshe ring rdo rje and O rgyan chos 'phel, *Bca' yig phyogs bsgrigs*, 2011), (2) manuscripts I have collected in A mdo (e.g., both of the constitutions for Dgon lung Monastery, a 1758 constitution for Dgon lung's erstwhile branch monastery, Kan chen, etc.), and (3) the Buddhist Digital Resource Center (www.tbrc.org; previously, the Tibetan Buddhist Resource Center; hereafter BDRC). Thus, my attempt at gathering every extant constitution was not exhaustive. Nonetheless, the general picture of the production and historical development of constitutions presented here is not likely to change unless new archives within the People's Republic of China suddenly become accessible and, contrary to the pattern that has emerged so far, a large number of earlier and substantially more complex, non–Dge lugs constitutions emerges.

16. Berthe Jansen has argued reasonably that we cannot assume that the relative preponderance of Dge lugs constitutions represents more compositional output. It could, rather, reflect editorial and preservation methods: most extant constitutions come to us in the "collected works" (T. *gsung 'bum*) of reputed scholar-monks and writer-monks. Jansen, *The Monastery Rules*, 6–7. If this were true, however, one might expect the *ratio* of constitutions to collected works to be the same for the Dge lugs school as for other schools, which does not appear to be the case. An early and rudimentary calculation I attempted using data, which was available at the Buddhist Digital Resource Center (www.tbrc.org), found that Dge lugs *bca' yig* account for approximately 79 percent of all *bca' yig* (183 of 233), while Dge lugs *gsung 'bum* account for approximately 24 percent of all *gsung 'bum* (66 of 272). That ratio decreases significantly when we look at the *bca' yig* and *gsung 'bum* of other schools. The next highest ratio in that calculation was that of the Bka' brgyud: approximately 9 percent of all *bca' yig* (21 of 233), and approximately 40 percent of all *gsung 'bum* (108 of 272). It is possible that non–Dge lugs schools just have chosen not to include constitutions in their volumes at the rate that the Dge lugs school has, but that, too, arguably would tell us something about the differing priorities of these schools. One might reasonably ask why the Dge lugs pa were so keen on cataloging and preserving these constitutions (which are often found alongside other compositions pertaining to the *identity* and *structure* of monasteries, such as chronicles (T. *dkar chag*) and breviaries (T. *mchod brjod*). We also have evidence of the overwhelming Dge lugs preoccupation with orthodoxy and orthopraxy from other sources, such as biographies. It is certain that more constitutions—including non–Dge lugs ones—will continue to be unearthed in the future, but it is unlikely that the sectarian picture I describe here will be drastically altered. In any case, as I discuss below, the argument presented here regarding the innovative utilization of monastic constitutions by the Dge lugs pa rests less on the number of constitutions produced than on the content of their constitutions and the manner in which they disseminated them.

17. Tuttle, "Building Up the Dge lugs pa Base in A mdo," 138. Gene Smith makes a similar point about the particular case of Dgon lung Monastery. Smith, *Among Tibetan Texts*.

18. Charleux, *Temples et monastères de Mongolie-Intérieure*, 127.

19. In volume 4 of Jibzundamba I Lubsang-Danbi-Jaltsan (Rje btsun dam pa Blo bzang bstan pa'i rgyal mtshan) et al., *Khal kha rje btsun dam pa sku phreng rim byon gyi gsung 'bum*. Christopher Atwood has also shared with me a Tibetan-language constitution composed by a certain Dge slong Blo bzang dbyig gnyen on the occasion of the reestablishment of the Kalacakra college of the Bkra shis dkon brtsegs gling Monastery in 1894 (*Dus 'khor bkra shis*

*dar rgyas bshad sgrub gling gi grwa tshang gi dge ʼdun rnams kyi thun mong ma yin paʼi ʼgrigs lam kun spyod kyi rim pa bcaʼ khrims mi ʼgyur rdo rjeʼi*), which was published in Ulaanbaatar in 2007. This appears to be a Mongol monastery. Atwood has also found Mongolian-language constitutions. Atwood, personal communication, 23 August 2017.

20. T. *gsung ʼbum*. See Kim, "A mdo, Collected Works (gSung ʼbum), and Prosopography."

21. Tuttle, "Pattern Recognition"; Tuttle, "The Role of Mongol Elite."

22. On the Dge lugs' use of printing technology to expand and institutionalize Dge lugs power, particularly in Amdo, see Nourse, "Revolutions of the Dharma Wheel."

23. Elverskog, *The Jewel Translucent Sūtra*, 138.

24. This number includes all extant constitutions I have been able to collect and to reliably assign to a particular date or time period.

25. The year 1750 was also one of several key turning points in the history of Tibet and Sino-Tibetan relations. ʼGyur med rnam rgyal, the son of Pho lha nas and Qing-recognized "king" of Tibet, took steps to rebel against Qing rule in Tibet, going so far as to collude with the Zünghars. He was thus killed by the two Qing ambans in Lhasa, who, in turn, were killed by an angry mob. The Qing imperial response included the reorganization of the Tibetan political administration. Luciano Petech writes that this left "the field clear for the natural factors of Tibetan politics in the 18th century: the spiritual power of the dGe-lugs-pa sect and the military force of the Manchu emperors. In that moment and for a long time afterwards they needed each other, and the result was the curious and unique form of dual government, which lasted without serious challenge till the crisis of 1904–1912." Petech, *China and Tibet in the Early 18th Century*, 235.

26. Constitution no. 2 by ʼJig rten mgon po also fits this pattern. See the relevant note in the Appendix.

27. This includes a concern that health care be provided to all regardless of their ability to pay, a disdain toward sophistry in philosophical exchanges, and especially a concern for the integrity of the community. See Sur, "Constituting Canon and Community," 40.

28. Sur, "Constituting Canon and Community," 26.

29. Ibid., 17, 20, 23, 24–25, passim.

30. T. *theg pa chen por gsungs paʼi bslab paʼi gzhi lnga*.

31. Rong zom Chos kyi bzang po, "Rang slob dam tshig pa rnams la gsungs paʼi rwa ba brgyad paʼi bcaʼ yig," 393.

32. Ibid., 398.

33. Sur, "Constituting Canon and Community," 26.

34. For a translation of the corresponding rules in the Tibetan text, see Vidyabhusana, "So-Sor-Thar-Pa; or, a Code of Buddhist Monastic Laws," 42–43. For a translation of the corresponding rules in the Sanskrit text, see Prebish, *Buddhist Monastic Discipline*, 57–58.

35. Sur, "Constituting Canon and Community," 21–22.

36. Rdo sbis Tshe ring rdo rje and O rgyan chos ʼphel, *Bcaʼ yig phyogs bsgrigs*, 431.

37. Constitution no. 11, p. 414/2b.6.

38. Ibid., pp. 418–20/4b–5b.

39. T. *sdzogs chen* [sic].

40. For a brief discussion of *khregs chod* and *thod rgal*, see Germano, "Food, Clothes, Dreams, and Karmic Propensities," 294–95. For more on *gcod*, see Sorensen, "Making the Old New Again and Again."

41. For a recent study of the early history of Rwa sgreng, see ʼBrom Shes rab me lce, *History of Rwa sgreng Monastery*, edited by Maho Iuchi.

42. Constitution no. 11, p. 415/3a.2.

43. The title of the constitution is "Instructions for Sherap Nyima, Throne-holder of the Beacon of Light, Reting: Benefits of Vegetarianism" (*ra bsgreng 'od 'jo gdan sa ba bshes rab nyi ma la gdams pa'i rdor dkar gyi phan yon bzhugs*). Of course, the Vinaya does not insist on vegetarianism. However, a concern with "white foods" rather than the "red," bloody ones reflects, like the Vinaya, an ethical rationalism that transcends any individual or interpersonal bonds.

44. Constitution no. 11, p. 416/3b.1–4.

45. T. [*chos*] *khrims pa*.

46. T. *zhal ta*. Nornang, "Monastic Organization and Economy," 253. For a thorough discussion of the ambiguity of this term, see Jansen, *The Monastery Rules*, 72–74.

47. T. *dge bskos*.

48. T. *zhal ta ba*.

49. T. *spyi las byed pa'i dge bsnyen*. This constitution and his other constitution may have been composed in 1405. They were both written in a Bird (T. *bya*) year. However, the colophon to one of the texts informs us that it was composed at (and for) his favorite hermitage, the Lha zhol Hermitage at Mount 'o de gung rgyal. Tsong kha pa went on retreat here in 1394 and 1397 or 1398. Thurman, *The Life and Teachings of Tsong Khapa*, 105, 203. Thus, it is probable that he wrote these texts in the years after his stay there and possibly not long after his sermons on *bhikṣu* precepts delivered at Gnam rtse ldeng Temple in 1402. Tsongkhapa, *Tantric Ethics*, 1–2.

50. Constitution no. 5, p. 699/251a.2–4.

51. Ibid., p. 698–99/250b–251a. Tsong kha pa also writes about winter and summer as designated meditation periods in his other constitution (no. 4, p. 692/249b).

52. See his discussion of the requirements for renouncing and for full ordination in constitution no. 4, p. 690/246b.

53. Thurman, *The Life and Teachings of Tsong Khapa*, 23; Tsongkhapa, *Tantric Ethics*, 1–2.

54. See note 49 above.

55. Jansen has also made this point. "How to Tame a Wild Monastic Elephant."

56. Cf. Śāntideva, *The Bodhicaryāvatāra*, 143.

57. "May the monasteries be well appointed, humming with recitation and study. May the *Saṅgha* always remain undivided and may the purpose of the *Saṅgha* be fulfilled," Śāntideva writes. *The Bodhicaryāvatāra*, 142.

58. This corresponds to Louis de La Vallée Poussin's translation of the Chinese version of this text. Vasubandhu, *L'Abhidharmakośa de Vasubandhu*, 218 (ch. 8, v. 39a–b).

59. T. *rang re'i grwa na gnas pa rnams*.

60. The liturgical formula and list of basic, monastic rules that are recited collectively every fortnight by members of the sangha.

61. Vidyabhusana, "So-Sor-Thar-Pa; or, a Code of Buddhist Monastic Laws," 37, 73. This is a paraphrase of the first paragraph of part 6 of the *Mahāparinibbāna Sutta*, which has the Buddha explaining that his Dharma and Discipline will serve as one's Teacher in the Buddha's absence.

62. Rgyal sras 'Jigs med ye shes grags pa, "Dgon lung byams pa gling gi mtshon dgon ma lag dang bcas pa'i bca' khrims," (constitution no. 66), 18b–19a.

63. Constitution no. 6, p. 79/5a.7–5b.1.

64. Constitution no. 1, Rong zom Chos kyi bzang po, "Rong zom chos bzang gis rang slob dam tshig pa rnams la gsungs pa'i rwa ba brgyad pa'i bca' yig," 405. Sur, "Constituting Canon and Community," 25.

65. Constitution no. 66, p. 28b.5–29a.1.

66. T. *nad pa byung na gang du byung ba'i sa skor de'i dge bskos kyis brtags nas nad pa nyid la rim gro'i chas 'dug na legs.*

67. Constitution no. 4, pp. 694–95/248b–249a.

68. Constitution no. 42, p. 71.

69. Constitution no. 4, p. 696/249b.

70. Ibid., p. 696/249b.5–6. Indeed, Tsong kha pa's constitution is also the first constitution to emphasize the narrative of present decline of the dharma. He writes,

> Formerly, there were good customs that made flourish widely the Precious Teachings that were a result of pure beings who greatly revered the Precious Teachings, wise ones who understood the essence of the Teachings, who enacted as if in stages the rules of the sangha. At this moment, due to the exigencies of time, [these good customs] have greatly degenerated. I thought, "how wonderful would it be if the great treasury of happiness and benefit for all beings—the Sage's Precious Teachings—were to develop and spread in every manner and in all directions, persisting for all time!" Thereupon, I was motivated to make this constitution. It is a means to establish the customs of the Precious Teachings according to tradition [here] set down as a base for eternity.

Constitution no. 4, pp. 696–97/249b–250a.

71. Tsong kha pa appears to be copying nearly verbatim from the Vinaya here. See the section "Undertaking Acts of Worship for Sick or Dying Fellow Monks" in Schopen, "Deaths, Funerals, and the Division of Property"; cited in Jansen, "The Monastery Rules," 179–80. See also the Buddha's admonishment of a group of monks for not having cared for a monk suffering from dysentery in the Pali Vinaya. Horner, *The Book of the Discipline*, vol. 4 (*Mahāvagga*), 431–34.

72. Also known as the Zhwa nag pa, the "Black Hat" Karmapa.

73. T. *sgar chen.*

74. See constitution no. 20, p. 50b.1.

75. See constitution no. 13. See also the scholarship of Toni Huber, particularly his *Cult of Pure Crystal Mountain.*

76. Tucci, *Tibetan Painted Scrolls*, 62.

77. T. *Zhwa dmar pa*; the "Red Hat" Karmapa.

78. Wylie, "Monastic Patronage in 15th-Century Tibet."

79. Sørensen and Hazod, *Rulers on the Celestial Plain*, 8–9.

80. Thub bstan phun tshogs, "Karma pa'i chos tshogs sgar chen 'dzam gling rgyan zhes pa'i skor mdor bsdus tsam brjod pa," 56.

81. Ibid., 57.

82. T. *khrim yig chen mo.* See constitution no. 8, p. 693/3b.6.

83. Thub bstan phun tshogs, "Karma pa'i chos tshogs sgar chen 'dzam gling rgyan zhes pa'i skor mdor bsdus tsam brjod pa," 57.

84. Ibid., 58.

85. Constitution no. 9, in W8039, pp. 702/2a.6–703/2b.3.

86. Dreyfus, "Where Do Commentarial Schools Come From?"

87. T. *rab 'byams kyi grwa skor.* "*Rab 'byams*," literally "universally learned one," is a title awarded to those who successfully participate in these scholastic competitions.

88. T. *dpe mtshams*. The periods between seasonal sessions when, as the Gelukpa would have it, one is supposed to continue his book learning on his own.

89. Constitution no. 9, pp. 712/7a.5–713/7b.4.

90. DiValerio, *Holy Madmen of Tibet*, 164. DiValerio explains that "it is not the case that the Madman of Tsang really wanted all members of the Kagyü sect to 'Do without food, clothing, and fame,' as Marpa had instructed Milarepa" and so on. "Quite to the contrary, the Madman of Tsang worked to commodify the ideals of meditation and asceticism, as embodied in the story of Milarepa, in order to position the Kagyü sect strategically in the competitive market places of fifteenth- and sixteenth-century Tibet, and beyond."

91. Thub bstan phun tshogs, "Karma pa'i chos tshogs sgar chen 'dzam gling rgyan zhes pa'i skor mdor bsdus tsam brjod pa," 58.

92. See, for example, the opening pages of constitution no. 21.

93. Constitution no. 23, p. 65a.4.

94. These were said to be on the payroll of the Sangs rgyas mnyan pa Lama. Thub bstan phun tshogs, "Karma pa'i chos tshogs sgar chen 'dzam gling rgyan zhes pa'i skor mdor bsdus tsam brjod pa," 60.

95. Thub bstan phun tshogs, "Karma pa'i chos tshogs sgar chen 'dzam gling rgyan zhes pa'i skor mdor bsdus tsam brjod pa," 64. Constitution no. 19, p. 41a.7–41b.1, specifies for the monastic community that had been associated with the practice center of Rtse lha sgang that anyone caught fighting to defend a polity or joining the military is to be expelled "except for cases in which the interests of the Teachings of the Kar[ma] government as headed by Rtse lha sgang need it."

96. See Thub bstan phun tshogs, "Karma pa'i chos tshogs sgar chen 'dzam gling rgyan zhes pa'i skor mdor bsdus tsam brjod pa."

97. Those designated at "Dynastic Preceptors." T. *go shri*, from the Chinese, *guoshi* 國師.

98. T. *khrims dpon*.

99. T. *khrims pa*. Thub bstan phun tshogs, "Karma pa'i chos tshogs sgar chen 'dzam gling rgyan zhes pa'i skor mdor bsdus tsam brjod pa," 58. Constitution no. 8 for the Karma pa's *sgar chen* also makes reference to the roles of *chos khrims pa* and *dge skos*.

100. Thub bstan phun tshogs, "Karma pa'i chos tshogs sgar chen 'dzam gling rgyan zhes pa'i skor mdor bsdus tsam brjod pa," 58–59.

101. Constitution no. 23, p. 73a.1–2.

102. Thub bstan phun tshogs, "Karma pa'i chos tshogs sgar chen 'dzam gling rgyan zhes pa'i skor mdor bsdus tsam brjod pa," 59.

103. For instance, the Fourth Karmapa Rol pa'i rdo rje is credited with taming a noxious serpent deity that made it possible to found Mchod rten thang in A mdo. Rol pa'i rdo rje is also rumored to have resided and left a footprint at Dgon lung Monastery. Similarly, the Fourth Karmapa is said to have tamed a noxious serpent deity at Chos bzang ri khrod (Thu'u bkwan's personal monastery), and the temple is said to have made use of a ritual text composed by him. Brag dgon zhabs drung Dkon mchog bstan pa rab rgyas, *Mdo smad chos 'byung*, 123.14; Thu'u bkwan III Blo bzang chos kyi nyi ma, "Dgon lung gi dkar chag," 644/6b.3, 645/7a.1, 775/67a.2–3; Thu'u bkwan III Blo bzang chos kyi nyi ma, "Dben gnas bde chen chos gling gi bsam gtan pa rnams kyi bca' khrims bstan pa'i pad tshal rgyas pa'i nyin byed sogs bca' yig gi rim pa phyogs gcig tu bkod pa bzhugs so," 679/3a.1–2. My information regarding Rol pa'i rdo rje's influence at Chos bzang ri khrod

comes from informants at the monastery who I spoke with upon visiting the place in May 2012.

104. The early name for followers of Tsong kha pa's tradition was "Dga' ldan pa," "those of Dga' ldan Monastery," the important monastery founded by Tsong kha pa. At some point, this name seems to have been replaced by "Dge ldan pa," "the Virtuous Ones," which itself was largely replaced by "Dge lugs pa." Kapstein, "Buddhism, Schools of," 1228b.

105. Emphasis added. Constitution no. 17, p. 3b.5–6; see also p. 5b.3.

106. The previous rule in this constitution mentions "the three, father and sons." This is reference to the Karmapa and two other major incarnate lamas. Constitution no. 17, p. 6b.2–3.

107. Constitution no. 20, p. 54a.3–4. See also no. 15, p. 30b.1.

108. Analects of Confucius 2:1.

109. To be clear, this is not a strict qualitative difference between the Karma pas and the Dge lugs pas but rather one of degree. The Fifth Dalai Lama traveled a great deal. However, his encampment was not his "seat" nor was it understood to be a regular monastic community to the extent that the Karma pa's *sgar chen* was.

110. Tibetan literature usually uses the phrase *'chad rtsod rtsom gsum*, or "the three: teaching, debate, and composition," in order to refer to scholasticism. Composition, however, is never actually discussed in the constitutions I have read.

111. Constitution no. 42, p. 70.

112. Constitution no. 51, pp. 188–90.

113. Constitution no. 24, p. 683/1a.2–3. The "five scriptures" are the Indian treatises that serve as the foundation of Dge lugs (and Bka' brgyud) scholasticism. See Dreyfus, *Sound of Two Hands Clapping*, ch. 6.

114. See, for example, constitution no. 19, p. 43b.2.

115. T. *Sa skya*.

116. T. *ShAkya mchog ldan*.

117. T. *Gser mdog can*. See Caumanns, "Paṇ chen Shākya mchog ldan's Monastic Seat Thub bstan gser mdog can (Part 1)."

118. T. Kun dga' rgyal mtshan (1182–1251).

119. T. Rngog Legs pa'i shes rab (fl. 1073); an important disciple of Atiśa and founder of the important monastery of Gsang phu.

120. T. *Tshad ma rnam par nges pa*. Dergé Tenjur no. 4211.

121. T. *Rigs pa'i gter*.

122. Caumanns, "Paṇ chen Shākya mchog ldan's Monastic Seat Thub bstan gser mdog can (Part 1)," 67, 82.

123. Ibid., 85. Caumanns is quoting a text by Shākya Mchog ldan.

124. Davidson, *Tibetan Renaissance*, 112.

125. Constitution no. 33, pp. 422, 431; See also Sørensen, "The Dalai Lama Institution"; Sørensen, "The Sacred Junipers of Reting."

126. Constitution no. 33, p. 431.

127. Ibid., pp. 429–31.

128. "Clarify" appears in the constitution (no. 33, p. 426). "Renew" appears in an edict issued by the Dalai Lama in 1648 regarding Reting and which appears to have accompanied this constitution or to have followed the constitution in quick succession. See Dalai Lama V Ngag dbang blo bzang rgya mtsho, "Rwa sgreng dang ri bo bde chen sogs chos sde chung rigs 'gar stsal ba'i bka' yig sogs." In the constitution (no. 33, p. 425), the Dalai Lama explains

that a constitution (*bca' khrims*) had previously been composed by the Paṇchen Lama and that various monastery officials had also taken it upon themselves to write various rules (*bsgrigs lam*). None of these was regularly heeded.

129. Constitution no. 37, p. 2. His constitution for Tsetang Monastery (Rtses thang; Rtsed thang) (no. 39) also discusses the role of the Phag mo gru emperors in supporting Buddhism and associates the monastery with debate competitions. See, especially, no. 39, pp. 26–27.

130. Constitution no. 37, pp. 2–3. See also Kurtis Schaeffer's study of the Dalai Lama's second constitution for the Great Prayer Festival (no. 44). That constitution introduces Tsong kha pa and his disciples as institution-builders, who established the Great Prayer Festival and 'Bras spungs Monastery, among other things. I was initially introduced to this constitution in a seminar taught by Schaeffer in 2007. Schaeffer, Kapstein, and Tuttle, *Sources of Tibetan Tradition*, 543–45.

131. T. *spyi don*. See Dreyfus, *Sound of Two Hands Clapping*, 108.

132. Constitution no. 51, p. 182.

133. See Yi, "History of Monastic Textbooks." I will return to this question in Chapter 4 on scholasticism.

134. Constitution no. 51, p. 185. We see the same separation and specialization of tasks in the constitution he wrote for 'Ba' dga' ldan phan bde'i gling in Khams (no. 49), pp. 89–90.

135. T. Zhwa lu.

136. T. Dga' ldan thub bstan rab rgyas.

137. Heller, "The Great Protector Deities," 90; Heller, "Protective Deities Srung-Ma Dmar-Nag," 479.

138. The terms here are *tho btsun* and *dad btsun*. I am not entirely sure what the meaning of these are, although on a similar pair of terms, *khral btsun* and *dad btsun*, see Cassinelli and Ekvall, *A Tibetan Principality*, 295.

139. T. *chos spyod thogs 'don*.

140. This is a reference to the *Rgyan 'jug*, the Ornament of Realization (*Mngon rtogs rgyan*) and the Entrance to the Middle Way (*Dbu ma 'jug pa*).

141. T. *Sa gsum ma*.

142. T. *lam gnyis*. Unidentified.

143. T. *rim gro*.

144. Constitution no. 34, p. 10.

145. Heller, "Étude sur le développement de l'iconographie," 252. Heller refers in her bibliography to the following text: *Chos 'khor rgyal ba'i srung ma rang bzhin gyis bzhugs gans* [sic: *gnas*] *lhun grub dga' ba'i tshal gyi chos srung 'ga' zhig gi mchod gtor 'bul tshul las bzhi lhun grub*. My thanks, too, go to Chris Bell for sharing with me his knowledge of this ritual corpus.

146. T. Nag po skor gsum. My translation of this is tentative. Alternatively, *kha btags* offering texts in the Fifth Dalai Lama's Collected Works suggests that "*nag po skor gsum*" refers to Vajrabhairava ('Jigs byed), Mahākāla (Mgon po phyag drug pa), and Yama (Las gshin). Dalai Lama V Ngag dbang blo bzang rgya mtsho, *Rgyal dbang lnga pa ngag dbang blo bzang rgya mtsho'i gsung 'bum*, 21 (zha): 170–71, 174–75, 188–89.

147. T. Dpal ldan lha mo mag zor ma. Heller translates her title as "The Glorious Goddess Who Holds the Magic Offering of War." Heller, "The Great Protector Deities," 83.

148. See Nebesky-Wojkowitz, *Oracles and Demons of Tibet*, 50.

149. Constitution no. 40, p. 45.

150. Dreyfus, *Sound of Two Hands Clapping*, 249.

151. Bell, "The Nechung Record"; Bell, "Nechung."

152. Known locally as Baruun Heid. For more on this monastery, see Chapter 5.

153. This is Thar shul Monastery in Mtsho lho Prefecture, Qinghai Province.

154. A khu Bkra shis (scholar-monk and teacher at the monastery's school for young monks), personal communication, 23 July 2016.

155. Sde srid Sangs rgyas rgya mtsho, *Life of the Fifth Dalai Lama*, 310–11; Sde srid Sangs rgyas rgya mtsho, *Drin can rtsa ba'i bla ma Ngag dbang blo bzang rgya mtsho'i thun mong phyi'i rnam thar du kU la'i gos bzang*, 180b.5.

156. Constitution no. 49, p. 89.

157. See the Fifth Dalai Lama's account of the Third Dalai Lama's personal connection to Dpal ldan lha mo as translated in Heller, "The Great Protector Deities," 86–87.

158. Constitution no. 49, p. 87. See also no. 38 for Ri khrod Dga' ldan, p. 13.

159. van Vleet, "Medicine as Impartial Knowledge," 287. Furthermore, van Vleet writes, "the Fifth Dalai Lama himself assumed the role of the highest arbiter of impartiality" (p. 288).

160. See constitution no. 43 for Nges gsang rdo rje gling in Gong ra.

161. See constitution no. 51 for 'Bras spungs, p. 191; Schuh and Phukhang, *Urkunden und Sendschreiben aus Zentraltibet, Ladakh und Zanskar*, 2:68, line 7.

162. T. Gong ra nges gsang rdo rje gling.

163. T. Snang Sogs [*sic*: Sog] Gong.

164. T. Bsod nams rab brtan.

165. T. Khra tshang pa *mkhas grub chen po* Blo gros mchog gi rdo rje.

166. Constitution no. 43, p. 60. See also Gentry, *Power Objects in Tibetan Buddhism*, 379–408.

167. This is the case in, for example, 'Jigs med ye shes grags pa's constitution for Dgon lung (no. 66) and Sumba Kanbo's (T. Sum pa mkhan po) constitutions (listed in bibliography).

168. Rwa sgreng Monastery is another example. See the note accompanying the listing of the Fifth Dalai Lama's constitution for Rwa sgreng in the Appendix (no. 33).

169. Graeber, *Utopia of Rules on Technology*, 26–27.

170. The recursion in the name of the monastery suggests the monastery has been there a very long time, long enough for the valley to be named after it and then for the monastery to be (re)named after the valley. The Dge lugs monastery is said to have been built on the remains of a Sa skya monastery.

171. Sullivan, "The Body of Skyid shod sprul sku"; Yon tan rgya mtsho, "Skyid shod sde pa'i skor"; Schwieger, "A Nearly-Forgotten Dge lugs pa Incarnation Line"; BAN Shin-ichiro, "Darai rama seiken seiritsu zen'ya ni okeru geruku-ha no amudo fukyō."

172. T. Dpa' ris. Pronounced "Huari" in local, Amdo Tibetan.

173. The "Monguor" people north of the Huang River 湟水 (T. Tsong kha chu) in today's Qinghai Province are referred to as "Huzhu Monguors" to distinguish them from another group of "Monguors," the "Sanchuan" or "Minhe Monguors," who speak a related but distinct language. (Huzhu, Minhe, and Sanchuan are all local place names). Keith Slater recommends referring to the Huzhu Monguors as "Mongghuls" and the Minhe Monguors as "Mangghuers." Because my discussion of Monguors is limited to the Huzhu Monguors (the Mongghuls), I will continue to simply use "Monguor." Slater, *A Grammar of Mangghuer*, 9–10. Tibetan literature refers to them as "Hor," which is the same term used historically to

refer to the Mongols, that is, the noble descendants of Chinggis Khan (and so to be distin-guished from other "Mongols," such as the Oirat (T. Sog)). Modern Chinese literature refers to all Monguors and some who arguably should not be classified as "Monguors" as Tuzu 土族.

174. On the correlation between minority status and multilingualism on the Tibetan Plateau, see Roche, "The Vitality of Tibet's Minority Languages."

175. The date of this Rgyal sras' death is disputed. Bstan pa bstan 'dzin, *Chos sde chen po dpal ldan 'bras spungs sgo mang grwa tshangs gi chos 'byung*, 1: 523.

176. Rgyal sras 'Jigs med ye shes grags pa's *Collected Works* are found at the Library of the Research Institute for Ethnology and Anthropology, Chinese Academy of Social Sci-ences, on the campus of Minzu University, Beijing. A scan of the same is held at the China Tibetology Research Center in Beijing. My thanks to Professor Rin chen sgrol ma for shar-ing this with me.

177. Bstan pa bstan 'dzin, *Chos sde chen po dpal ldan 'bras spungs sgo mang grwa tshangs gi chos 'byung*, 1:522. An eighteenth-century source describes 'On Rgyal sras as becoming the *mkhan po* of Se ra and 'Bras spungs Monasteries at this time. Ye shes dpal 'byor, Sum pa mkhan po, *Chronology of Tibet*, 107, 202.

178. Constitution no. 66, p. 38a.3–4.

179. Sullivan, "Administering Tibet."

180. Smith, *Among Tibetan Texts*, 159; Tuttle, "Pattern Recognition."

181. Lcang skya III Rol pa'i rdo rje (1717–1786) was raised at the Qing Court and was childhood friends with Prince Hongli 弘曆, the future Qianlong emperor. His predecessor had been very intimate with the Kangxi emperor, and the priest-patron relationship that they developed continued in the eighteenth century with Qianlong and Lcang skya III. There is an extensive body of secondary literature on Lcang skya III. Illich, "Imperial Stooge or Emisary to the Dge Lugs Throne?," 17n2. Thu'u bkwan III Blo bzang chos kyi nyi ma (1737–1802) was also an influential figure at the Qing Court and is perhaps best known for his *Grub mtha' shel gyi me long*, translated as Thuken Losang chökyi nyima, *The Crystal Mir-ror of Philosophical Systems*. Sum pa mkhan po Ye shes dpal 'byor (1704–1788), or Sumba Kanbo (this spelling reflects how Sumba Kanbo himself may have pronounced his name, based on the dialect of the Upper Mongols), has been referred to as a "polymath" for his prolific writ-ings (running twenty volumes in a new, modern book format edition of his collected works) on topics ranging from Buddhist philosophy and ritual to medicine and geography. He is perhaps best known for his history of Kökenuur as well as his geography of the world, and he was a formidable Buddhist scholar, having participated in and excelling at the monastery-wide debates in Central Tibet, as well as participating in the preeminent Tibetan "academic circuit" debates with monks from other monasteries in Lhasa during the new year Great Prayer Festival. In Mongolia, he is also well-known for his works on medicine and astrology, the latter being the basis for the Mongolian calendar. There is a growing body of scholarship on Sum pa mkhan po. In particular, two recent dissertations by Hanung Kim and Rachael Griffiths (Oxford University) help to fill out our picture of him. Kim, "Renaissance Man from Amdo;" Griffiths, "A Polymath from Amdo." See also Sullivan, "The Manner in Which I Went to Worship Mañjuśrī's Realm."

182. T. *bla chen lnga*; Ch. *wu da nang [qian]* 五大囊[欠]. Per Nyi ma 'dzin Ngag dbang legs bshad rgya mtsho, *Bshad sgrub bstan pa'i 'byung gnas chos sde chen po dgon lung byams pa gling gi gdan rabs zur rgyan g.yas 'khyil dung gi sgra dbyangs*, 19; Schram, *Monguors of the Kansu-Tibetan Border*, 321.

183. T. Chu bzang.

184. T. Wang.

185. T. Chu bzang blo bzang bstan pa'i rgyal mtshan (1652–1723); T. Chu bzang ngag dbang thub bstan dbang phyug (1725–1796).

186. The Seventh Dalai Lama was apparently quite fond of the young Chu bzang III, since the latter's predecessor had served as the Dalai Lama's own master. Brag dgon zhabs drung Dkon mchog bstan pa rab rgyas, *Mdo smad chos 'byung*, 91.

187. T. *bla chung dgu*. Schram says there were eleven in his day. Schram, *Monguors of the Kansu-Tibetan Border*, 335.

188. They are Li kyA (Ch. Li jia 李家), Bde rgu (Ch. Dugu 杜固), Sgo mang (Ch. Guomang 郭莽), Wushi 五十 (which gives T. ul shri/ul shi), Khyung tsha (Ch. Qiongcha 琼察), Rgya tig (Ch. Jiading 加定), Hor skyong (Ch. Huo'erjiang 霍尔姜), Lin kyA (Ch. Lin jia 林家), and Ser lding (Ch. Se'erdang 色尔当). The Chinese renderings of these names are not standardized. The Sgo mang lineage appears to have commenced with the former abbot of 'Bras spungs Monastery's Sgo mang College (r. 1792–1798), Har chin *tho yon* Mthu stobs nyi ma, who served as Dgon lung's forty-eighth abbot.

189. Louis Schram writes that "according to the superiors of the monastery, and the general testimony in the country, forty-two branches proceeded from Erh-ku-lung." *Monguors of the Kansu-Tibetan Border*, 2006, 337, 358, passim. Today, monks and scholars regularly speak of forty-eight or forty-nine branch monasteries of Gönlung.

190. "*Huang bei zhu si zhi mu*" 湟北諸寺之母. Han Rulin 韓儒林, "Qinghai Youning si ji qi ming seng 青海佑寧寺及其名僧 [Qinghai's Youning Monastery and its famous monks]," 45.

191. Thu'u bkwan III Blo bzang chos kyi nyi ma, "Dgon lung gi dkar chag," 647/8a.2; Lcang skya II Ngag dbang blo bzang chos ldan (1642–1714), "Rnam thar bka' rtsom (Peking ed.)," 5a.1.

192. Dbal mang paN+Di ta Dkon mchog rgyal mtshan, "'Jam dbyangs bla ma rje btsun bstan pa'i sgron me'i rnam par thar pa brjod pa'i gtam," 691/70a.1.

193. Sku 'bum Monastery might be a contender for this status, and, of course, there were other important centers of Buddhist scholasticism and practice in Amdo at that time, such as Rong bo dgon chen, Bya khyung, and Thang ring, to name a few.

194. Rong po grub chen I Skal ldan rgya mtsho, "Sde ba chos rje Bstan 'dzin blo bzang rgya mtsho'i rnam thar dad pa'i sgo 'byed," 248, 250.

195. These included the First Lcang skya Grags pa 'od zer (d. 1641), 'Dan ma grub chen Tshul khrims rgya mtsho (1587–1663/1665), and Kwa ring dka' bcu Phun tshogs rnam rgyal (fl. 1612–1624).

196. T. *phyi mo*.

197. Oidtmann, "Overlapping Empires"; Oidtmann, "A 'Dog-Eat-Dog' World"; Oidtmann, "Between Patron and Priest"; Sullivan, "The Qing Regulation of the Sangha in Amdo."

198. Tsyrempilov, "Dge Lugs Pa Divided."


CHAPTER 2

1. Constitution no. 66, pp. 28b.5–29a.5.

2. Constitution no. 1, p. 405. Sur, "Constituting Canon and Community," 25.

3. Aside from the general Geluk orientation toward bureaucratization examined in this chapter, another reason for this may be Tsong kha pa's own familiarity with and dedication

to the Vinaya. In fact, Tsong kha pa's passage comes more or less directly from the Vinaya. See note 71 in Chapter 1.

4. Welch, *The Practice of Chinese Buddhism, 1900–1950*; Nonomura, *Eat Sleep Sit*; Foulk, "The 'Ch'an School.'"

5. See the beginning of "The Types of Legitimate Domination," in Weber, *Economy and Society*, 1:212–55.

6. T. *dge skul*. Literally "one who exhorts [others] in virtue." A regional spelling. It appears also in Wang Khutugtu's later constitution for Dgon lung.

7. Smin grol III Ngag dbang 'phrin las rgya mtsho, "Theg chen thar pa gling gi bca' yig mu tig gi phreng mdzes." The Tibetan reads: *dge skul gyi las 'bras dpang bzhag gi sgo nas ngo 'dzin nye ring med par che 'bring chung gsum la rang rang la skabs su babs pa'i thugs dam dge sbyor tshogs chos ra 'dzin gshar sbyang sogs la lteng skul dang de dang 'gal ba dag la nye pa che chung gi tshad dang bstun pa'i tshogs gtam dbyug bltungs mar me snyan dar tshogs shing tshogs chu brgya phyag gnas dbyung 'og nas 'byung bzhin bya.*

8. T. *Legs bshad gling*. Sde srid Sangs rgyas rgya mtsho refers to the monastery as "Chos 'khor rgyal legs bshad sgrog pa'i dga' tshal." Sde srid Sangs rgyas rgya mtsho, *Dga' ldan chos 'byung baiDUrya ser po*, 196. Cited in Ehrhard, "A 'Hidden Land,'" 495n5. Comparing the two Chos 'khor rgyal constitutions, we can also see that the term "*bla ma*" in the earlier constitution (no. 34, pp. 9, 10) is replaced by "Legs bshad gling" in the later constitution (no. 40, pp. 42, 47), suggesting that it also served as the name of the palace of the *bla ma*, which I interpret here to mean the abbot.

9. Constitution no. 40, p. 47.

10. T. *zhal ta*.

11. T. *chab ril*. Literally "water-bearers."

12. Constitution no. 48, p. 84.

13. Jansen, "How to Tame a Wild Monastic Elephant," 134.

14. Constitution no. 37, p. 3.

15. Constitution no. 23, pp. 72b.7–73a.1. The Eighth Karmapa, too, refers to the "public tasks" (T. *spyi las*) to be completed by the disciplinarian no matter whether he be of high or low status. Constitution no. 8, p. 693/3b.1.

16. Constitution no. 66, p. 38a.1–2. The protector deities of the respective monastery are also often called upon to "partake of the heart blood" or otherwise deal trenchantly with offenders of this norm. For example, constitution no. 66, p. 38a.4; constitution no. 60, p. 4a.5–6. This parallels the sense of loyalty and duty that Lauran Hartley finds in the autobiography of Mdo mkhar ba Tshe ring dbang rgyal. Hartley, "Self as a Faithful Public Servant."

17. Sum pa mkhan po Ye shes dpal 'byor, "Dgon sde 'ga' zhig gi bca' yig blang dor snyan sgron," 129/13a.3–5.

18. Ellingson makes a strong case that the *dbu mdzad* is second to the *bla ma*, at least at many monasteries. Ellingson, "The Mandala of Sound," 320.

19. Constitution no. 66, p. 28a.2–3.

20. See Lempert, *Discipline and Debate*, ch. 4.

21. Asad, *Genealogies of Religion*, 161.

22. Gorski, *The Disciplinary Revolution*, xvi.

23. Graeber, *Utopia of Rules on Technology*, 174–81. The other two primary components of the state, Graeber argues, are sovereignty (principally the monopoly on the legitimate use of violence) and politics (the contest between aristocratic big men in redistributive, feasting

systems, in which they compete for allegiance from allies and subjects). The Gelukpa and their allies (the Oirat Mongols and the Qing) certainly shared to some extent these characteristics.

24. Constitution no. 61, p. 276/13b.1–2. The latter is a quote from the *Śīlasamyuktasūtra* (T. *Tshul khrims yang dag par ldan pa'i mdo*), D303, P969 ("D" and "P" stand, respectively, for the numbers of the Dergé and Peking editions of the the Kanjur (T. *Bka' 'gyur*). Another relevant quote regarding discipline that frequently appears in Geluk constitutions reminds us that, "the discipline of some is happiness; / the discipline of others is suffering. / Possessing discipline is happiness; / Disregarding discipline is suffering." This appears in the 'Bras spungs constitution (no. 51), p. 175, and is cited by Jansen, "How to Tame a Wild Monastic Elephant," 115. It also appears in a constitution by Rgyal mtshan seng+ge for Stag tshang lha mo in Amdo (founded in 1748) and in Gter bdag gling pa's constitution for Smin grol gling (no. 54). Rgyal mtshan seng+ge, "Zha ser cod paN 'dzin pa'i 'dus sde chen po dge ldan bshad sgrub gling gi bca' yig blang dor gsal ba'i me long," 7b.

25. Constitution no. 66, p. 37b.2.

26. Ibid.

27. Ibid., p. 37b.6.

28. Ibid., p. 37b.5.

29. Ibid., p. 37b.4–5.

30. See Graeber, Utopia *of Rules on Technology*, ch. 3. Such a fear was not entirely concocted or misplaced. Sumba Kanbo recounts a raid on Dgon lung's wealth by a posse of its monks in 1743. Sum pa mkhan po Ye shes dpal 'byor, *PaN+Di ta Sum pa Ye shes dpal 'byor mchog gi spyod tshul brjod pa sgra 'dzin bcud len*, 342.

31. It was common in Western publications from the early twentieth century and before and remains common in Chinese-language publications to refer to *all* Tibetan monks as "lamas." This is not in keeping with Tibetan usage or with the most current scholarly norms.

32. T. Sum pa Dam chos rgya mtsho (d. 1651).

33. Rong po grub chen I Skal ldan rgya mtsho, "Sde ba chos rje Bstan 'dzin blo bzang rgya mtsho'i rnam thar dad pa'i sgo 'byed," 200.

34. This was Dpal ldan rgya mtsho, who served from 1665–1672. The *Mdo smad chos 'byung / Deb ther rgya mtsho* gives him the title of "the Degu the Elder" (T. *bde rgu che ba*).

35. T. *dbu chos*. Short for *dbu mdzad* and *chos khrims pa*.

36. T. *spyi ba*.

37. T. *sgar sgom sde*. "*Sgar*" is short for "*sgar ba*," "encampment." Here it refers to a type of settled, monastic estate overseen in succession by a lama and his chosen apprentice, often a nephew. See Schram, *Monguors of the Kansu-Tibetan Border*, 308–9.

38. T. *dge 'dun bgres ba rnams*. At Dgon lung, at least, this appears to have been a select group of six or seven elders.

39. Modifying "*kher du*" to "*khyer du*."

40. Constitution no. 66, p. 28b.2–4. Scholars who have studied the concept of the "public" and "private" in the context of traditional Japan and China caution us against interpreting the indigenous terms (Ch. *gong* 公; Japanese *kōgi*) as "public," as we understand it today in modern Western societies. They are better understood not along an axis of public/visible to private/personal/hidden but of public/peace to private/partiality and turmoil. In this regard, Tibetan "*spyi*" bears some resemblance to these other Asian language concepts. Berry, "Public Peace and Private Attachment"; Berry, "Public Life in Authoritarian Japan"; Wakeman, "Boundaries of the Public Sphere."

41. It is clear from the context that the "*bla brang*" here does not refer to 'Jam dbyangs bzhad pa's palace and estate but rather to that of the abbot of the philosophical college. The constitution speaks of two "*bla ma*," suggesting that the other lama, then, is the head of the newly established Lower Tantric College.

42. Constitution no. 60, p. 821/3a.5–6. Emphasis added.

43. "The lama palace [i.e., the residence of the abbot] must, from the third to the seventh, provide good service to the three: the lama in charge of sacrificial cake offering rituals and his [two] assistants. It must [also] provide [to them] twelve[-colored paper] for drawing *ling ga* [effigies], whatever colored sand is needed, and three arm-spans of black cloth for a cushion for the *ling ga*. It must [also] provide a silk offering scarf to the painting of [the deity] Yama and thirteen extra [scarves; T. *kha yol bcu gsum*]. On the thirteenth, [he] gives a block of tea, two [bolts of] cloth, assorted foods, and a saddle to each of the Court-yard Ritual Dancers [T. *thang 'chams pa*]." Constitution no. 66, p. 33a.2. This passage is prefaced by the phrase "When there is a *rnam gzhag* [i.e., a type of offering]," which sug-gests that what follows is the *rnam gzhag* itself and that the abbot is responsible for it, or, alternatively, that what follows coincides with the distribution of the *rnam gzhag*. Also, the passage begins with "*bla brang gi tshes gsum nas*," which I have amended to "*bla brang gis tshes gsum nas*."

44. Constitution no. 66, p. 31b.5.

45. Fires would be lit at the heads of the assembly rows to help keep the monks warm on the cold, winter mornings. Constitution no. 66, p. 33b.2–4.

46. Constitution no. 66, pp. 33b.4–34a.1.

47. Ibid., p. 22b.2.

48. Ibid., p. 22b.4.

49. The abbot on this occasion was Sumpa Dharma King Phuntsok Namgyel (Sum pa chos rjes phun tshogs rnam rgyal, r. 1729–1734). Sum pa mkhan po Ye shes dpal 'byor, *PaN+Di ta sum pa ye shes dpal 'byor mchog gi spyod tshul brjod pa sgra 'dzin bcud len*, 149–50.

50. I shall have more to say about the "intendant" below. Schram, *Monguors of the Kansu-Tibetan Border*, 340.

51. T. *gnyer ba*.

52. T. "*tshab ra*," "*tshab ra*," "*tshabs ra*," and so on, appear in several customaries I have read from Dgon lung and surrounding monasteries. A Dgon lung informant explained to me that it means "bread." A passage from the *Mdo smad chos 'byung / Theb ther rgya mtsho* indi-cates that it is a type of cake. Brag dgon zhabs drung Dkon mchog bstan pa rab rgyas, *Mdo smad chos byung*, 92.3–8; Zhiguanba•Gongquehudanbaraoji, *Anduo zhengjiao shi*, 93–94.

53. Constitution no. 66, p. 22a.5.

54. Ibid., p. 22b.6.

55. Ibid. p. 32b.4–5.

56. For more on *rnam gzhag*, see below. Constitution no. 66, pp. 32a.3–5, 32b.6–33a.1, 37a.3–6.

57. Thu'u bkwan III Blo bzang chos kyi nyi ma, "Dben gnas bde chen chos gling gi bsam gtan pa rnams kyi bca' khrims bstan pa'i pad tshal rgyas pa'i nyin byed sogs bca' yig gi rim pa phyogs gcig tu bkod pa bzhugs so," 691/9a.1–2.

58. T. *Rtse nya*.

59. Constitution no. 64, p. 16b.5–6.

60. Constitution no. 33, p. 427.

61. Constitution no. 64, p. 11a.3.

62. Rgyal mtshan seng+ge, "Zha ser cod paN 'dzin pa'i 'dus sde chen po dge ldan bshad sgrub gling gi bca' yig blang dor gsal ba'i me long."

63. Jansen, "How to Tame a Wild Monastic Elephant."

64. Jansen, "The Monastery Rules," 114–16.

65. T. *gtor sgrub bla ma.*

66. T. *rgyud pa'i bla ma dbu mdzad.*

67. T. *chos khrims pa.*

68. T. *dbu mdzad chen mo*; i.e., the cantor of the Great Assembly Hall or the monastery as a whole. At Dgon lung, this may have been the cantor of the Philosophical College.

69. T. *rnam gzhag che kha.*

70. T. *rgyud pa'i byang 'dren.*

71. T. *sku gnyer.*

72. T. *zhal lta ba.*

73. I am assuming that the "*rgyud pa'i*" of "*rgyud pa'i byang 'bren* actually applies to all four of these position types. This would explain why we find "*sku gnyer*" twice in this passage.

74. T. *bskang gso dbu'i mdzad.*

75. T. *gtor sgrub dbu mdzad.*

76. T. *sman chog dbu mdzad.*

77. T. *mchod dbyangs dbu mdzad.*

78. T. *bla brang gnyer pa.*

79. T. *ri khrod gnyer pa.*

80. T. *sku rten pa.*

81. T. *sku rim pa gsum.*

82. T. *chab skad pa.*

83. T. *chab bril pa*, from "*chab ril pa.*"

84. T. *ja ma.*

85. T. *chu len.*

86. It is not clear which two cantors are being addressed here. Perhaps they are the *tshogs chen dbu mdzad* and the *rgyud pa'i byang 'bren.*

87. T. *rnam gshag rang ga ba.*

88. T. *mchog dbyangs.* I have amended this to *mchod dbyangs [dbu mdzad].*

89. T. *byams pa'i sku gnyer.*

90. T. *rkang gling pa.*

91. T. *rgya gling pa.*

92. T. *spos phor ba.*

93. T. *gdugs 'dzin pa.*

94. T. *gtan cha ba gnyis.*

95. T. *gtor bzo ba gnyis.*

96. T. *smon lam dge rgan.*

97. Constitution no. 66, pp. 32b.3–33a.2.

98. This was conveyed to me by the *mchod dbyangs dbu mdzad* of Dgon lung in March 2011.

99. Ellingson, "Don rta dbyangs gsum," 144. The information regarding the number of liturgies (T. *chos spyod*) that he recites, for example, comes from the *mchod dbyangs dbu mdzad* of Dgon lung in March 2011. One of the liturgies he was required to memorize was ti- tled *Chos spyod gsol 'debs khrus gsol sogs kyi dbyangs yig kun bzang mchod sprin rgya mtsho.*

100. T. *skad gral.* Constitution no. 66, p. 21a.2.

101. Ellingson, "The Mandala of Sound," 339. The *mchod dbyangs dbu mdzad* at Dgon lung described a long process of listening and imitating at the feet of a former cantor.

102. For example, Constitution no. 48, p. 84. Jansen provides a succinct overview of job qualifications. Jansen, *The Monastery Rules*, 65–67.

103. Jansen, *The Monastery Rules*, 65. Jansen speculates that this may be the result of a new intended audience for constitutions (officers, rather than the monastic congregation as a whole) as well as the growing number of monks.

104. Constitution no. 66, p. 22b.1–2.

105. Jansen, *The Monastery Rules*, 91–92.

106. T. *sku rim*.

107. Constitution no. 66, p. 34b.4.

108. T. *gnyer ba*. I am taking this here to be synonymous with "*spyi gnyer*," see the section on "The General Management Office" below.

109. Constitution no. 66, p. 22a.6.

110. T. *zhabs drung*.

111. T. *las bye pa*.

112. Constitution no. 66, pp. 22a.6–22b.1.

113. T. *dka' rams*; T. *chos grwa ba*.

114. Constitution no. 66, pp. 32a.6–32b.1. The later constitution for Dgon lung by Wang IV makes a slight change: "Moreover, only two shares are given to those 'revered ones' [T. *sku zhabs*], former abbots, and dharma class students on the 'privately compiled' roster only; otherwise, no extra shares are given." Wang IV Blo bzang 'jam pa'i tshul khrims, "Bstan bcos sgo brgya 'byed pa'i zab zing gser gyi sde mig," 7a.1.

115. Constitution no. 66, p. 19b.4.

116. Ibid., p. 32a.5.

117. Ibid., p. 37a.3–4.

118. Ibid., pp. 32b.6–33a.1.

119. T. *rgya ma*. It is not clear to me what the actual amount of this unit is.

120. Constitution no. 66, p. 22b.4–5.

121. Constitution no. 68. The relevant passage is translated in Jansen, *The Monastery Rules*, 125. Jansen's translation of this passage helped me make better sense of the analogous passage found in the Dgon lung constitution.

122. Jansen, "How to Tame a Wild Monastic Elephant," 125–26. The Pali "Illīsa-jātaka" likewise advises monks to be "as the bee when it sucks the nectar from the flower" in their dealings with donors. Cowell, *The Jātaka*, 195–201.

123. Constitution no. 66, p. 37a.3.

124. Sum pa mkhan po Ye shes dpal 'byor, *PaN+Di ta Sum pa Ye shes dpal 'byor mchog gi spyod tshul brjod pa sgra 'dzin bcud len*, 566.

125. Tuttle, "Pattern Recognition."

126. Smith, *Among Tibetan Texts*, 159. Even in the early 1700s (before 1714), when Lcang skya II Ngag dbang blo bzang chos ldan (1642–1714) finished his autobiography, his seat of Dgon lung Monastery was referred to as "the throne of Rgyal sras, rebirth of Śāntideva" (Dgon klung *gi* Rgyal sras Zhi ba lha *yi gdan sa*). Lcang skya II Ngag dbang blo bzang chos ldan, "Rnam thar bka' rtsom," 13a.1.

127. T. *bla spyi sogs khag bzhi*.

128. T. *bla brang che kha rnams*.

129. T. *'bul pa thob zhin pa gnyis re re*. My interpretation of this is tentative.

130. T. *bla brang chung kha gsum res re.*

131. T. *dge 'dun mang.*

132. Wang IV Blo bzang 'jam pa'i tshul khrims, "Bstan bcos sgo brgya 'byed pa'i zab zing gser gyi sde mig," 3a.2. Emphasis added.

133. These are oblique references to "*sku skye.*" Constitution no. 66, pp. 30b.2, 33b.4.

134. Lattimore, "Introduction," 86; Hendrickx, "Louis J. M. Schram, CICM, 54–55."

135. Schram refers to him as the "supreme chief of the lamasery"—i.e., of the physical monastery.

136. Schram refers to him as the "supreme chief of the community of lamas"—i.e., the body of monks at the monastery.

137. Hendrickx, "Louis J. M. Schram, CICM," 372–74.

138. Schram glosses the "intendant" as "*Tsuordzi*" in Tibetan and "*Hsiang tso*" in Chinese (*xiangzuo* 襄佐), which is a rendering of the Tibetan *phyag mdzod.* This is more commonly translated as "treasurer" or "steward." For the Chinese rendering of this term, see Qinghai sheng bianji zu, *Qinghai Tuzu shehui lishi diaocha,* 48. This source does not mention a "supreme chief of the lamasery," nor does it place the power of the "intendant" above all others. Instead, it places the abbot (Ch. *fatai*) at the top of the hierarchy, after which comes the power of the major incarnate lamas. In either case, the power of the major incarnate lamas is great when compared to their complete absence in the 1737 constitution of Gönlung.

139. Schram, *Monguors of the Kansu-Tibetan Border,* 339.

140. Ibid., 341.

141. "Nirwa," a transcription of T. *gnyer ba?*; Ch. "Takuan-chia," a transcription of *da guanjia* 大管家?

142. Schram, *Monguors of the Kansu-Tibetan Border,* 341.

143. Approximately 2,467 hectares, or 6,096 acres.

144. That is, the property of the *zhongseng* 众僧. Another 160–70 *mu* are said to have been property of the *jiwa ang* 吉哇昂 (T. *spyi ba nang* [*chen*]?). It is not entirely clear what the distinction between these two groups of property is supposed to be. Qinghai sheng bianji zu, *Qinghai Tuzu shehui lishi diaocha,* 52. Another source suggests that Dgon lung and its incarnate lamas may have possessed up to 49,000 *mu* of land. Pu Wencheng 蒲文成, *Gan Qing Zangchuan fojiao siyuan,* 77. Unfortunately, it is not clear what Pu's source is for these figures.

145. On this incarnation's visit to Gönlung, see Vostrikov, *Tibetan Historical Literature,* 219n636; Thu'u bkwan III Blo bzang chos kyi nyi ma, "Dgon lung gi dkar chag," 706/32b.5.

146. T. Dpal ldan rgya mtsho.

147. Thu'u bkwan III Blo bzang chos kyi nyi ma, "Dgon lung gi dkar chag," 707/33a.4.

148. Ibid., 706/32b.4.

149. In other contexts, it might be more appropriately understood as the "general fund" of the monastery or even as the person responsible for overseeing the management of the monastery, the "general manager."

150. We read in one constitution (Se ra theg chen chos 'khor gling), for instance, that officers of the monastery are to "care for the common wealth more than their own [wealth]." Constitution no. 24, p. 686/2b. An informant at Dgon lung Monastery told me that another monastery, Mang 'dus (also spelled "Mang 'du and "Man tho'i ri khrod"), used to belong to the *dgon pa'i gzhung* but was later given to Thu'u bkwan.

151. T. *spyi so'i gnyer pa.* The biography of the Second Changkya, however, clearly gives the plural: "*spyi so'i gnyer pa tsho.*" Shes rab dar rgyas, *Rje ngag dbang blo bzang chos ldan dpal bzang po'i rnam par thar pa mu tig 'phreng ba,* 42a.1.

152. Lcang skya II Ngag dbang blo bzang chos ldan (1642–1714), "Rje btsun bla ma ngag dbang blo bzang chos ldan dpal bzang po'i rnam par thar pa dad pa'i rol mtsho (Zhol Edition)," 16b.1–4.

153. T. Mtsho bdun dgon gsar. Also known as "Mtsho bdun gyi lha khang chen mo," it is later given the names Khökhe süme ("Blue Temple") and Huizong si 彙宗寺 ("Monastery that Convenes the Clans").

154. T. spyi 'jog.

155. T. mchod theb.

156. Shes rab dar rgyas, Rje ngag dbang blo bzang chos ldan dpal bzang po'i rnam par thar pa mu tig 'phreng ba, 68a.5–68b.2.

157. Schram, Monguors of the Kansu-Tibetan Border, 339.

158. Per Nyi ma 'dzin Ngag dbang legs bshad rgya mtsho, personal communication, May 2011. See also Qinghai sheng bianji zu, Qinghai Tuzu shehui lishi diaocha, 48.

159. Known as the "jiwaang" 吉哇昂, which appears to be derived from the Tibetan "spyi ba nang [chen]," the "estate of the General Management Office." Qinghai sheng bianji zu, Qinghai Tuzu shehui lishi diaocha, 52. The local incarnate lama and former resident of Dgon lung Monastery, Per Nyi ma 'dzin, referred to the group as "Those Twelve" (T. khong rnam pa bcu gnyis). The mixture of Tibetan and Chinese terms for the members of this group reflects our conversation, which switched regularly between the two languages when confusion arose. Schram writes of four elderly "councilors" at the monastery. Schram, Monguors of the Kansu-Tibetan Border, 375.

160. Schram, Monguors of the Kansu-Tibetan Border, 342–44, 339, 372, passim.

161. T. Dga' ldan shri re thu Ngag dbang blo gros rgya mtsho; Ch. Gaerdan Xiletu 噶爾丹西勒圖. See Ahmad, Sino-Tibetan Relations in the Seventeenth Century, 265–68. He is also known as the Khri chen rgya nag pa, "the Great Throne-holder Revered Chinese." For more on this figure, see Sullivan, "Convincing the Mongols to Join Mañjuśrī's Realm." His rebirth is the renowned Gser khri Blo bzang bstan pa'i nyi ma (1689–1762). For more on this rebirth see Nietupski, "The 'Reverend Chinese'," 197–99.

162. Ngag dbang blo gros rgya mtsho was the abbot of Sgo mang from 1665 through 1673. Dalai Lama VII Skal bzang rgya mtsho, "Khri chen sprul pa'i sku blo bzang stan pa'i nyi ma dpal bzang po'i rnam par thar pa," 357–360/15b.1–17a.3.

163. Note that this could also be translated as the "monastic council" (T. bla spyi). Georges Dreyfus and José Cabezón have both written at www.thlib.org about this institution found at Dge lugs mega monasteries. Nonetheless, there are many cases where "bla spyi" is clearly referring to two separate individuals or offices, that of the lama and that of the spyi. That these combined in some cases to form a single council does not obviate the fact that "bla spyi" is used regularly in monastic constitutions and other texts to refer to two separate entities. Jansen suggests that "bla spyi" is similar to, if not the same as "spyi so/bso/sa," which is not borne out by the evidence. Jansen, The Monastery Rules, 67. In any case, the main point that I am making here—that there were few to no "public" or "common" funds available to the community of monks until new institutional arrangements were made—remains the same no matter how one here translates "bla spyi."

164. Dalai Lama VII Skal bzang rgya mtsho, "Khri chen sprul pa'i sku blo bzang stan pa'i nyi ma dpal bzang po'i rnam par thar pa," 360/17a.1–3.

165. Dgon lung informant, personal communication.

166. Yet another meaning of the term—one that does not seem to apply here—is tea paid out to monks who attend prayers for a recently deceased monk, the tea being purchased

with funds raised by the sale of the deceased monk's possessions. Khenpo Ngawang Dorjee, personal communication, December 2011.

167. For an example of such a fund being established for the explicit purpose of providing "monks' tea," see Wang V Ngag dbang mkhyen rab rgya mtsho, *Dgon lung byams pa gling gi gdan rabs*, 19a.1. For another example, pertaining to the nearby monastery of Yarlung, or Shimen si, see Brag dgon zhabs drung Dkon mchog bstan pa rab rgyas, *Mdo smad chos 'byung*, 132.18.

168. This is a rough estimate. Georges Dreyfus estimates that in the twentieth century Sgo mang College may have housed as many as 20 to 30 percent of 'Bras spungs' 10,000 monks. If we assume that ratio was the same in the seventeenth century, then we get 1,200–1,300 monks at Sgo mang. Dreyfus, "An Introduction to Drepung's Colleges"; accessed 11 September 2012. Goldstein gives an even greater ratio: 3,500–4,000 of 'Bras spungs's 10,000 monks. *A History of Modern Tibet, 1913–1951*, 30n41; cited in Tuttle, "Tsong kha Range," 56n41.

169. T. *bgres pa*. Constitution no. 66, p. 28b.2–3.

170. This expands the definition of this institution given by the Mongolist Robert Miller, who says that the "Jisa," from T. *spyi sa*, here translated as "General Management Office") may refer to (1) a storehouse, or the place where the goods or capital funds donated are stored; (2) the goods or funds so donated, which are liquidated in carrying out the purpose of the donor; and (3) a fund from which the interest is used to pay for a specific recurring monastic function. Miller, *Monasteries and Culture Change*, 427–28; see also Jansen, *The Monastery Rules*, 74–76.

171. Miller explains that the "*jisa*" in Mongolia were also called "*tsang*" (Pinyin "*zàng*" 藏), a term that likewise means "treasury" in the Chinese Buddhist context. In a review of Miller's work, George Murphy refers to "*jisa*" as "primitive banks" and "decentralized treasuries." Murphy, "Buddhist Monastic Economy," 439.

172. Constitution no. 66, p. 35b.2–3.

173. Ibid., p. 33b.1–2.

174. Constitution no. 66, 34a.6; Jansen, *The Monastery Rules*, 76. The exceptional status of the officers of these two offices is also signaled by the fact that only they were permitted to wear sleeves within the bounds of the monastery. Constitution no. 66, p. 36a.4–5. Certain constitutions, particularly ones written for monasteries in colder climates (in neighboring parts of A mdo and Mongolia) extend this privilege to ordinary monks. Additional financial responsibilities of the General Management Office included providing meals and provisions to the disciplinarians and other functionaries during the dharma sessions. It was also responsible for providing a new year's banquet and tea services (T. *nyung ja*) for each of the five monthly "periodic sacrificial cake offerings" (T. *dus gtor*) should the office fail to secure patronage for these events. Constitution no. 66, pp. 34a.1, 34b.4–5. The responsibility of providing for the ritualists during the two-week-long Great Prayer Festival was shared among the General Management Office, the abbot, and the patrons. During the major year-end event—the Twenty-ninth Ritual Cake Offering (T. *dgu gtor*) and the Ritual Cake Offering of the first day of the new year (T. *tshes gtor*)—the General Management Office was tasked with providing for all the monks and lamas in attendance. Constitution no. 66, p. 35b.5.

175. T. *sum the re*. The meaning of "*the*" here is unclear.

176. Constitution no. 66, p. 35b.1–2; see also pp. 35b.5–36a.1.

177. Schram, *Monguors of the Kansu-Tibetan Border*, 346–51. No other financial office appears in the constitution or historic record for Dgon lung. Namri Dagyab, the son of the incarnate lama Daygab Kyabgön (Brag g.yab skyabs mgon), writes in detail about the

diverse financial activity of premodern monasteries, which could be directed by several different responsible offices. Namri Dagyab, "Vergleich von Verwaltungsstrukturen und wirtschaftlichen Entscheidungsprozessen tibetisch- buddhistischer Klöster in der Autonomen Region Tibet, China und Indien," 107–80.

178. For instance, Nawang Nornang has described a system of checks and balances at Dwags po gling in Central Tibet aimed at preventing abuses. One office dealt principally with the monastery's land and its subjects and with providing salaries and meals to the congregation of monks while the other office oversaw herds, grain, cash, other donations, and corvée. Nornang, "Monastic Organization and Economy at Dwags-Po Bshad-Grub-Gling." At Dwags po gling the treasurer (*phyags mdzod*) overseeing the *spyi so/bso* was appointd by the abbot, which shows that the abbot's powers and purview were not always kept separate from those of the *spyi so* and "worldly" matters. Still, in this case, activity of the *spyi so* as well as the other economic office alluded to here (known as the *gnyer tshang*) were also accountable to a monastery-wide council (known as the *lhan rgyas*) composed only of senior monks and the disciplinarians. In fact, one of the responsibilities of this same monastery-wide council was to nominate the abbot.

179. Nornang, "Monastic Organization and Economy, " 256; Namri Dagyab, "Vergleich von Verwaltungsstrukturen und wirtschaftlichen Entscheidungsprozessen tibetisch- buddhistischer Klöster in der Autonomen Region Tibet, China und Indien," 59.

180. T. *gtsug lag khang.*

181. T. *spyi khang*; the storehouse and meeting place of *spyi ba.*

182. Constitution no. 66, p. 36a.1–3.

183. Constitution no. 65, pp. 681/3a.3–682/3b.2.

184. This might also be translated as "general management office."

185. Constitution no. 60, pp. 821/3a.6–822/3b.1.

186. See note 105.

187. Constitution no. 5, p. 699/251a.5–6. Cited in Jansen, *The Monastery Rules,* 89.

188. Jansen interprets this as "goods or money."

189. Constitution no. 31, p. 39/20a.4–5.

190. Sumba Kanpo, for instance, mentions enforcing the monastic constitution of Dgon lung while serving as its abbot, a position he held on three separate occasions. Sum pa mkhan po Ye shes dpal 'byor, *PaN+Di ta Sum pa Ye shes dpal 'byor mchog gi spyod tshul brjod pa sgra 'dzin bcud len,* 271–72, 338.

191. Miller, "Buddhist Monastic Economy."

192. Ibid., 431. It is important to point out that Miller himself drew a distinction between *jisa* and a monastery's "endowment." He saw the former as funds (of which there could be many at a single monastery) that are established for unique, specialized purposes, such as carrying out in perpetuity a ritual requested by a patron. The "Sangha endowment," as he sees it, consists of the monastery's land-holdings and perhaps other wealth that is for the *general* welfare of the monastery's monks. However, Miller also writes about the *Tsogchin jisa,* which clearly comes from the Tibetan "*tshogs chen spyi sa.*" It is not clear how or whether this is different from the "Sangha endowment," but, in any case, this appears to be more analogous to the *spyi sa* I have described above. See also the critique of Miller's article by George Murphy: "But while some treasuries united laymen and monks in fulfilling joint religious ends others were clearly oriented to maintaining the monastic collectivity as such and it seems artificial to make distinctions between the types of treasuries." Murphy, "Buddhist Monastic Economy," 440.

193. See the above discussion of the cost of "mass teas."

194. The Dga' ldan pho brang government also helped finance monasteries in Central Tibet and parts of Khams.

195. One significant exception is found in the constitution for Kan chen Monastery, in which the local "clans" (T. *mtsho ba* [*sic*]) are explicitly mentioned as responsible for financing. Smin grol III Ngag dbang 'phrin las rgya mtsho, "Theg chen thar pa gling gi bca' yig mu tig gi phreng mdzes."

196. T. *sne mo ba rnams.*

197. The constitution for Rta wang Monastery, no. 56, p. 20. Similarly, the Seventh Dalai Lama's constitution for Se ra Monastery (no. 68), specifies that the abbot must be appointed based on a wide reputation of the highest character and that he must not be one known for favoritism (T. *nye dga'*) or partiality (T. *phyogs lhung*), p. 91. As for appointing the disciplinarian of the Great Assembly Hall (T. *tshogs chen*), he warns against compiling lists of potential candidates outside of the prescribed rules by (secretly) asking each of the monastery's colleges as had been done previously under Daichingbaatur (Khang chen nas).

198. Ellingson, "Tibetan Monastic Constitutions," 212–13.

199. See Jansen, *The Monastery Rules,* ch. 6.

200. This appears in constitution no. 54 in the section of the constitution concerning the study and recitation of tantra (p. 103/8b.5). For more on this constitution and its related constitution (no. 53), see Townsend, "How to Constitute a Field of Merit."

201. Jansen, *The Monastery Rules,* 129ff.

202. Kieffer-Pülz, "Rules for the Sīmā Regulation."

203. Constitution no. 66, p. 28a.1.

204. Women are permitted to enter the monastery for religious purposes at specified times.

205. Constitution no. 24, p. 3a.5–6.

206. The Ninth Kar ma pa does the same for one of his monasteries. Constitution no. 20, p. 52b.4–5.

207. This path is said to lead to the county seat. Dgon lung Monastery informant, personal communication, July 2016.

208. Alternatively, this could be rendered as "the Skyer khe Lake Mountain," although the map my informant helped to draw lists these as adjacent but separate markers.

209. Alternatively, this could be "the Putung Mountain Pass [as in *la rtse* or *lab tse*]," although, again, my informant has drawn the *la rtse* in a slightly different location.

210. Constitution no. 66, pp. 36b.6–37a.1. The Tibetan reads: *rtsa bkag chu mgo dkar ris khe skya'i 'phreng lam 'og ma kho re sgang rgyud / skyer khe'i / mtsho ris / phu thung las tshe / smon ne sgang rgyud tshun chad du dgun dbyid / dbyar ston sogs dus nam yang / hor 'brog gi zog dang 'brog tu mi 'jog.*

211. Constitution no. 66, p. 37a.1–3.

212. Ibid., p. 36b.3–5.

213. T. *rgya sog po'i khrims bdag rnams.* This constitution was composed in 1737. Here the word "Oirat" (Sog) is probably a vestige of earlier times (prior to the Lubsang-Danzin Rebellion of 1723–1724 and the Qing conquest of the Khoshud Mongols), although it could be a reference to the local Monguor *tusi* (more often referred to as "Hor").

214. Constitution no. 66, p. 38a.3–4.

215. Chaney, "Land, Trade, and the Law," 243–44.

216. Limusishiden and Jugui's novel (based on their families' histories) provide a candid description of the transitional and often transitory lives of those living in Dpa' ris, around Dgon lung, in the late nineteenth and the twentieth centuries. Limusishiden (Li Dechun 李得春) and Jugui (Lu Wanfang 鲁万芳), "Passions and Colored Sleeves."

217. Schram notes that most villagers were unwilling to fight the monasteries in the courts because of the monasteries' greater resources and connection with Qing officials. *The Monguors of the Kansu-Tibetan Border*, 351. See also *Chinese Legal Documents Series* and the blog post there by Max Oidtmann, as well as the second half of Oidtmann's dissertation, "Between Patron and Priest."

218. Sack, *Human Territoriality*.

CHAPTER 3

1. T. *gtugs dkar*.

2. T. *sgrol bstod*.

3. T. *seng gdong ma*.

4. Sum pa mkhan po Ye shes dpal 'byor, *Dgon sde 'ga ' zhig gi bca' yig*, n.d., 131/14a.3–5.

5. T. Rtogs ldan 'Jam dpal rgya mtsho.

6. T. *sprul pa'i glegs bam chen mo*.

7. Willis, *Enlightened Beings*, 36, 161–62, passim.

8. That is, the first *human-to-human* transmission. Tsong kha pa himself received it from the bodhisattva Mañjuśrī, although the "distant lineage" (T. *ring brgyud*) includes some human predecessors to Tsong kha pa. See Jackson, "The dGe ldan-bKa' brgyud Tradition of Mahāmudrā," 158–60.

9. The "Miraculous Volume" itself was not transmitted to the later generations of this lineage. The teachings of the lineage were transmitted in a variety of ways, however, such as through oral teachings from one's guru or visionary revelations. Willis, *Enlightened Beings*, 161–62n114; see Jackson, "The dGe ldan-bKa' brgyud Tradition of Mahāmudrā," 158–59.

10. The two streams were reunited in the early twentieth century by Pha bong kha Rin po che (1871–1941), such that one might now speak of a single stream. As we shall see, there are others who claim to have received the esoteric teachings of this lineage but who do not appear to belong to this major stream. Jackson, "The dGe ldan-bKa' brgyud Tradition of Mahāmudrā," 158–59; Willis, *Enlightened Beings*, 99–100.

11. See, for instance, Davidson's explanation of the successors to Sa chen Kun dga' rgyal mtshan in the wake of the latter's death. Davidson, *Tibetan Renaissance*, 335–38.

12. T. *thugs zin gyi slob sras* (lit. a disciple whose mind has been grasped).

13. T. *bum pa gang byo ba*.

14. T. Bra rti'i 'bul dpon Shes rab grags.

15. Rong po grub chen I Skal ldan rgya mtsho, "Rje skal ldan rgya mtsho'i gsung las mdo smad a mdo'i phyogs su bstan pa dar tshul" (hereafter "A mdo'i chos 'byung"), 350; see also 341–42.

16. T. *gtsug lag khang*.

17. Thu'u bkwan III Blo bzang chos kyi nyi ma, "Dgon lung gi dkar chag," 646/7b.4–5.

18. T. Sbas yul dkar bo rdzong.

19. T. Byang chub gling. The hermitage went by this name by at least 1665, when Rgyal sras Blo bzang bstan 'dzin, the rebirth of Gönlung's founder, visited Gönlung and composed

his "Praises of the Place of the Hidden White Land." Rgyal sras Blo bzang bstan 'dzin, "Sbas yul dkar po'i ljongs kyi gnas bstod ka la ping ka'i sgra dbyangs," 171. The edition of the text at my disposal incorrectly gives the year as "*sna tshogs zhes pa chu mo sbrul lo.*" It should read "*sna tshogs dbyig zhes pa shing sbrul lo.*" See also Vostrikov, *Tibetan Historical Literature*, 219.

20. T. Dgon lung gi ri khrod, Dgon lung gi ri khrod chen mo. Rong po grub chen I Skal ldan rgya mtsho, "Sde ba chos rje Bstan 'dzin blo bzang rgya mtsho'i rnam thar dad pa'i sgo 'byed," 224, 247.

21. T. *sgom chen pa rnams.*

22. T. *sgom khrid.*

23. T. *dbang lung rjes gnang.* Rong po grub chen I Skal ldan rgya mtsho, "Sde ba chos rje Bstan 'dzin blo bzang rgya mtsho'i rnam thar dad pa'i sgo 'byed," 224.

24. Their names are PaN chen pa, Snon pa, Yar 'brog pa, and Grags pa dpal pa. Pan chen Bsod nams grags pa, *Bka' gdams gsar rnying gi chos 'byung*, 98. Another possible etymology for "*grwa tshang*" is "pure monks" (T. *grwa gtsang*). This would indicate an establishment that upholds celibacy, and it may even be a marker of a specific identity. Sde srid Sangs rgyas rgya mtsho, *Dga' ldan chos 'byung baiDUrya ser po*, 102 and passim.

25. T. Byang rtse (lit. northern peak). Also known simply as "*rtse*" (lit. the peak).

26. T. Shar rtse (lit. eastern peak).

27. See the (terse) histories of Nyag rong grwa tshang and Cha dkar grag tshang which moved about due to social unrest; they ultimately came to be affiliated with Ganden Monastery. Sde srid Sangs rgyas rgya mtsho, *Dga' ldan chos 'byung baiDUrya ser po*, 102–3; Dreyfus, Everding, and others have also made the related point that there were no strict sectarian obstacles to movement between monasteries and *grwa tshang* in the early history of the Dge lugs pa. Monks could and did travel from teacher to teacher, from *grwa tshang* to *grwa tshang* to acquire the instruction they needed regardless of "sect." Dreyfus, "Where Do Commentarial Schools Come From?," 293–96; Everding, "gSang phu Ne'u thog, Tibet's Earliest Monastic School (1073)," 140–41.

28. T. Gsang phu.

29. Everding, "gSang phu Ne'u thog, Tibet's Earliest Monastic School (1073)," 143–46.

30. The patron's name is Rgyal rtse bdag po Rab brtan kun bzang 'phags.

31. Sde srid Sangs rgyas rgya mtsho, *Dga' ldan chos 'byung baiDUrya ser po*, 75.

32. Regarding the date of composition, see Martin, "Tibetan Histories: Addenda & Corrigenda," entry no. 148.

33. T. *sngags pa'i grwa tshang.*

34. T. *gdan sa.*

35. Las chen Kun dga' rgyal mtshan, *Bka' gdams kyi rnam par thar pa bka' gdams chos 'byung gsal ba'i sgron me*, 375.3–376.1.

36. T. *'chad nyan khang.* Pan chen Bsod nams grags pa, *Bka' gdams gsar rnying gi chos 'byung*, 110.

37. T. *bshad grwa.*

38. Rong po grub chen I Skal ldan rgya mtsho, "Sde ba chos rje Bstan 'dzin blo bzang rgya mtsho'i rnam thar dad pa'i sgo 'byed," 248.

39. Ronis, "Celibacy, Revelations, and Reincarnated Lamas," 206.

40. Dreyfus, "Where Do Commentarial Schools Come From?," 295–96; citing Las chen Kun dga' rgyal mtshan, *Bka' gdams kyi rnam par thar pa bka' gdams chos 'byung gsal ba'i sgron me*, 370b.1; see also 375b.4–5.

41. This was the first Ganden Shiretu Ngag dbang blo gros rgya mtsho (1635–1688). Dalai Lama VII Skal bzang rgya mtsho, "Khri chen sprul pa'i sku blo bzang stan pa'i nyi ma dpal bzang po'i rnam par thar pa," 340/7a.1–6.

42. Dreyfus, "An Introduction to Drepung's Colleges."

43. Ibid.

44. Las chen Kun dga' rgyal mtshan, *Bka' gdams kyi rnam par thar pa bka' gdams chos 'byung gsal ba'i sgron me*, 375b.6–376a.1.

45. T. Shes rab seng ge.

46. T. *Rgyud 'grel gyi bshad pa*.

47. T. *Rim lnga dmar khrid*.

48. T. *Sbyor ba yan lag drug gi khrid*.

49. T. *LU dril gnyis kyi khrid*.

50. T. *yi dam gyi khrid*. Pan chen Bsod nams grags pa, *Bka' gdams gsar rnying gi chos 'byung*, 99; cf. Thuken Losang chökyi nyima, *The Crystal Mirror of Philosophical Systems*, 288.

51. Cabezón, "An Introduction to Sera's Colleges," accessed 28 July 2010.

52. T. Snyan brgyud.

53. Jackson, "The dGe ldan-bKa' brgyud Tradition of Mahāmudrā," 183n4.

54. Bsod nams grags pa says that Shes rab seng+ge established the community and then handed it over to his disciple, 'Dul nag pa, although later tradition holds that 'Dul nag pa himself founded it. Paṇchen Bsod nams grags pa, *Bka' gdam gsar rnying gi chos 'byung*, 99. Alexander Berzin also made this point earlier: Berzin, "A Brief History of Gyumay and Gyuto Lower and Upper Tantric Colleges."

55. Thu'u bkwan III gives an elaborate portrayal of this history. Bsod nams grags pa's older account is much more bare bones, and there exist some differences in details. Thuken Losang chökyi nyima, *The Crystal Mirror of Philosophical Systems*, 286–88.

56. T. Gtsang rgyud. The Mé (Smad) tradition of the Lower Tantric College in Lhasa became known as the Ü tradition (Dbus *rgyud*). Bsod nams grags pa, *Bka' gdams gsar rnying gi chos 'byung*, 99–100.

57. T. Dkon mchog yar 'phel.

58. T. Srad rgyud pa'i dpon slob khyab bdag mi bskyod rdo rje nyid/ /rdo rje slob dpon gzugs su legs bstan pa/ /rje btsun dam pa Dkon mchog yar 'phel. Lcang skya II Ngag dbang blo bzang chos ldan, "Rje btsun bla ma ngag dbang blo bzang chos ldan dpal bzang po'i rnam par thar pa dad pa'i rol mtsho," 10b.4–5.

59. Lcang skya II Ngag dbang blo bzang chos ldan, "Rje btsun bla ma ngag dbang blo bzang chos ldan dpal bzang po'i rnam par thar pa dad pa'i rol mtsho," 10b.4–11a.5; Thu'u bkwan III mentions a third individual who received these teachings at the same time as Lcang skya II: Thang sag pa Dngos grub rgya mtsho. Thuken Losang chökyi nyima, *The Crystal Mirror of Philosophical Systems*, 289; Maher, "Knowledge and Authority," 107.

60. T. *nye brgyud*.

61. Jackson, "The dGe ldan-bKa' brgyud Tradition of Mahāmudrā," 158–59.

62. Willis, *Enlightened Beings*, xiv–xv; Jackson, "The dGe ldan-bKa' brgyud Tradition of Mahāmudrā," 156.

63. Willis, *Enlightened Beings*, 161–62n114.

64. T. Grub chen Dge 'dun rgyal mtshan.

65. T. Blo bzang brtson 'grus rgyal mtshan.

66. Jackson, "The dGe ldan-bKa' brgyud Tradition of Mahāmudrā," 158–59.

67. T. Drung ba rin po che Blo bzang rgyal mtshan.

68. T. *thun mong min pa.*

69. Lcang skya II Ngag dbang blo bzang chos ldan, "Rnam thar bka' rtsom," 8a.1–2.

70. It is unclear what is meant by "the combined streams of advice coming from the lineage [*brgyud*] and Wensapa's Oral Tradition [Dben sa pa'i snyan rgyud]." Dalai Lama VII Skal bzang rgya mtsho, "Khri chen sprul pa'i sku blo bzang stan pa'i nyi ma dpal bzang po'i rnam par thar pa," 361/17b.2–3.

71. T. 'Jug sgo tshal.

72. T. Lho 'brug ra long ba. One informant suggested this was along the border between Nepal and Tibet. A more likely possibility, I think, is Ra lung Monastery and vicinity in present-day Rgyal rtse County (Ch. Jiangzi 江孜), Tibetan Autonomous Region. Ra lung Monastery is the principal seat of the 'Brug pa Bka' brgyud school. Dorje, *Footprint Tibet Handbook*, 305. BDRC (formerly TBRC) and the Tibetan and Himalayan Library (www .thlib.org) both were also helpful in searching this (and many other) place name(s).

73. T. 'Jigs byed grags po'i gtor chen drug cu ba.

74. T. *gnam dang sa'i 'khor lo.*

75. T. *zan ling* (lit. "*tsampa* enemy").

76. Brag dgon zhabs drung Dkon mchog bstan pa rab rgyas, *Mdo smad chos 'byung*, 59.3–8. I am particularly indebted to Khenpo Ngawang Dorjee for help interpreting parts of this passage. Cited in Per Nyi ma 'dzin Ngag dbang legs bshad rgya mtsho, *Bshad sgrub bstan pa'i 'byung gnas chos sde chen po dgon lung byams pa gling gi gdan rabs*, 128–29.

77. For example, after Dben sa pa blo bzang don yod—after whom the tradition is named—received the Miraculous Scripture from his master, he went to numerous solitary places to practice. Willis, *Enlightened Beings*, 65.

78. I.e., G.yer gshong sngags rams pa 'Jam dbyangs blo gros (1651–1733), who received transmission of the "Lineage of Zhalu" (Zhwa lu phyogs brgyud). See 'Brug thar and Sangs rgyas tshe ring, *Mdo smad rma khug tsha 'gram rong 'brog yul gru'i sngon byung mes po'i ngag gi lo rgyus deb ther chen mo*, 593–94.

79. I.e., Rta phug pa Dam chos rgyal mtshan.

80. Brag dgon zhabs drung Dkon mchog bstan pa rab rgyas, *Mdo smad chos 'byung*, 59.

81. T. G.yer gshong bsam gtan chos gling.

82. In the lineage studied by Willis, there is only a single heir to the tradition. *Enlightened Beings.*

83. Sullivan, "The First Generation of Dge lugs Evangelists in Amdo."

84. T. Rong bo grub chen Skal ldan rgya mtsho, Shar Skal ldan rgya mtsho.

85. T. Sgom zhis grub chen Dge 'dun bzang po; also known as Dge 'dun blo gros.

86. I.e., Stong shags bkra shis chos gling. Ch. Yangguan si 羊官寺.

87. T. Mchod rten thang. Ch. Tiantang si 天堂寺。

88. T. Kan chen dgon.

89. T. *sgrub pa mdzad mkhan.*

90. T. Blo bzang bstan pa'i rgyal mtshan.

91. Rong po grub chen I Skal ldan rgya mtsho, "A mdo'i chos 'byung," 343.

92. Thu'u bkwan III bzang chos kyi nyi ma, "Dgon lung gi dkar chag," 670/19b.5–671/20a.5.

93. On Tibetan *smyon pa*, see DiValerio, *The Holy Madmen of Tibet.*

94. Brag dgon zhabs drung Dkon mchog bstan pa rab rgyas, *Mdo smad chos 'byung*, 108.4.

95. I.e. Dge 'dun rgyal mtshan, who was mentioned above.

96. T. *phyag chen rtsa grel gyi lung.*

97. The Paṇchen Lama argued that Mahāmudrā could be found within *both* exoteric (i.e., Madhyamaka) and tantric levels of practice, although he did maintain that the tantric system was separate and superior. It is not clear why the Paṇchen Lama may have withheld the tantric Mahāmudrā teachings from 'Dan ma. Jackson, "The dGe ldan-bKa' brgyud Tradition of Mahāmudrā," 172–74.

98. Thu'u bkwan III Blo bzang chos kyi nyi ma, "Dgon lung gi dkar chag," 24b.3–25a.1.

99. For example, the First Chu bzang Rnam rgyal dpal 'byor (1578–1651) took his monastic vows from the Paṇchen Lama. Sde ba chos rje Bstan 'dzin blo bzang rgya mtsho appears to have had a priest-patron relationship with the ruler of Gtsang, and he was a close disciple of the Paṇchen Lama. Thu'u bkwan III's chronicle of Dgon lung explains that Btsan po "the Stern," the founder of Gser khok Monastery, may have had a falling out with the Dalai Lama's establishment.

100. Brag dgon zhabs drung Dkon mchog bstan pa rab rgyas, *Mdo smad chos 'byung*, 70.

101. Ibid., 108.24–28.

102. T. *gter ma.*

103. Brag dgon zhabs drung Dkon mchog bstan pa rab rgyas, *Mdo smad chos byung*, 109.9–11.

104. I.e., Stong 'khor Mdo rgyud rgya mtsho (1621–1683).

105. Other traditions hold that Stong 'khor himself established the monastery. Thu'u bkwan III Blo bzang chos kyi nyi ma, "Dgon lung gi dkar chag," 682/25b.4–5; Brag dgon zhabs drung Dkon mchog bstan pa rab rgyas, *Mdo smad chos 'byung*, 123.11–24.

106. Lcang skya II Ngag dbang blo bzang chos ldan, "Rnam thar bka' rtsom," 31a.5–31b.1.

107. T. 'Jam dbyangs bzhad pa Ngag dbang brtson 'grus.

108. Shes rab dar rgyas, *Rje ngag dbang blo bzang chos ldan dpal bzang po'i rnam par thar pa mu tig 'phreng ba*, 76b.5–77b.3. Schram suggests that Emperor Kangxi financed the construction. I have not yet been able to corroborate this. Schram, *Monguors of the Kansu-Tibetan Border*, 326–27n299. He is citing Heissig, *Die Pekinger lamaistischen Blockdrucke in mongolischer Sprache Materialien zur mongolischen Literaturgeschichte*, 27, who himself is citing a late nineteenth-century Mongolian biography of Lcang skya.

109. T. *'Grel ba bzhi sbrags kyi lung dang zab bshad.*

110. T. 'Dan ma Ngag dbang bstan 'dzin 'phrin las.

111. T. Ka chen Blo rgyam bla ma ("Ka chen" should be "Dka' chen"). Also known as Slob dpon rin po che Ka chen Blo gros rgya mtsho bla ma. See Shes rab dar rgyas, *Rje ngag dbang blo bzang chos ldan dpal bzang po'i rnam par thar pa mu tig 'phreng ba*, 77b.4.

112. Lcang skya II Ngag dbang blo bzang chos ldan, "Rnam thar bka' rtsom," 31a.6–31b.1. The inclusion of the black protection cord of the Sé lineage Vajra-holder (T. *Sras 'rdo rje 'chang gi phyag mdud nag po*) in this exchange is found in the later, *Ocean Annals*. Brag dgon zhabs drung Dkon mchog bstan pa rab rgyas, *Mdo smad chos 'byung*, 70.

113. Actually, we saw that he also shared this status with retired abbots.

114. The *Mdo smad chos 'byung* mentions the rebuilding of the assembly hall of Dgon lung's tantric college twice. Brag dgon zhabs drung Dkon mchog bstan pa rab rgyas, *Mdo smad chos 'byung*, 70, 111.

115. Apart from this, we have the Fifth Dalai Lama's constitution for Dga' ldan thub bstan rab rgyas (no. 42), a "tantric monastery."

116. Karsten, "A Study on the Sku-'bum/T'a-Erh Ssu Monastery," 104.

117. Karsten refers to some regulations being written for the college during the Fifth Dalai Lama's stay at the monastery in 1653. Unfortunately, I have not seen or heard of their present-day existence. Karsten, "A Study on the Sku-'bum/T'a-Erh Ssu Monastery,"187.

118. The college's *gtsug lag khang* is mentioned on more than one occasion. Reference is also made to the college's assembly hall (*'du khang*). It is not clear whether this was a separate hall from the *gtsug lag khang*.

119. Among other tasks they might have, they are responsible for sweeping and cleaning the *gtsug lag khang* following morning and midday assemblies.

120. Among other tasks, he is responsible for giving the cymbals (T. *sil gnyan*) to the *byang 'dren* at the appropriate time. Thus, he is probably responsible for the ritual implements and objects within the assembly hall.

121. T. *'dul ba bzhin byin len gtod 'jog byed*.

122. Another example is the transition from the discussion of discipline and conduct at the beginning of the constitution to the discussion of tantra. The author explains that one must internalize and make habitual such good conduct (T. *sgom pa gshis lugs su byas*). To do so, one must practice tantra. Constitution no. 61, p. 276/13b.4–6.

123. Constitution no. 61, p. 274/14a.4.

124. Ibid., p. 277/14a.1–2

125. Ibid., p. 279/15a.4–6.

126. Ibid., p. 281/16a.3–4.

127. Ibid., p. 282/16b.3–4. Beyer suggests that *bdag 'jug* are typically done by Dge lugs monks in private. Beyer, *The Cult of Tārā*, 401–2. Nonetheless, the constitution at this point describes procedures for what is done during assembly (T. *tshogs dus*).

128. T. Nag po skor gsum. Constitution no. 61, 282/16b.3–4. As previously noted, *bka' rtags* offering texts in the Fifth Dalai Lama's *Collected Works* suggest, alternatively, that "Nag po skor gsum" refers to Vajrabhairava, Mahākāla, and Yama.

129. Constitution no. 61, p. 284/17b.2–3. The ellipses stand for a word I do not understand: *shin ce* or perhaps *shin co*. The entire passage reads: *chos ra tshogs skabs zla chos yin min la ma bltos pa'i [sic] spyi gnyer nas gra rer phogs shin ce gsum re sngar rgyun ltar brgyag*.

130. T. Mgon po'i gtor chen.

131. T. *'cham*.

132. T. Lo sar tshes gtor.

133. T. Cho 'phrul smon lam.

134. T. Dben sa lugs kyi lcags mkhar 'cham.

135. T. Chab mdo. I do not know for sure why this tradition may have been called "the *'cham* of Chamdo." One possibility is that it came to be associated with the Iron Castle *'cham* tradition established at nearby Mchod rten thang by Stong 'khor V Bsod nams rgya mtsho (1684–1752), who was active in Khams, perhaps including Chab mdo. However, this is just conjecture.

136. T. *zhal shes dmigs rnam*.

137. T. Chos 'khor smon lam. This is carried out in the sixth month.

138. T. Lhung bzed mchod pa.

139. T. *rgyud mchod*.

140. Lempert has translated "*tshogs gtam*" ("disciplinary sermon") as "public reprimand." See Lempert, *Discipline and Debate*, 107–26, 143–50.

141. T. *'das mchod*.

142. T. *tshogs chos*.

143. T. *sger 'tshogs.*

144. T. *'grig khrims dam.*

145. T. Dgu gtor.

146. T. *dbyangs rta phyag len.*

147. T. Brgya bzhi.

148. T. 'Bar ma, short for Kha 'bar ma.

149. T. *mdos rigs.*

150. T. Las bzhi'i sbyin sreg. Brag dgon zhabs drung Dkon mchog bstan pa rab rgyas, *Mdo smad chos 'byung,* 71.

151. T. Rdo rje 'jigs byed gtor sgrub chen mo drug cu ba. Per Nyi ma 'dzin Ngag dbang legs bshad rgya mtsho, *Bshad sgrub bstan pa'i 'byung gnas chos sde chen po dgon lung byams pa gling gi gdan rabs zur rgyan,* 130, 133.

152. Cuevas, "Sorcerer of the Iron Castle," 12.

153. Per Nyi ma 'dzin Ngag dbang legs bshad rgya mtsho, *Bshad sgrub bstan pa'i 'byung gnas chos sde chen po dgon lung byams pa gling gi gdan rabs zur rgyan,* 129–30.

154. I was able to attend this masked ritual dancing there in February 2011.

155. Constitution no. 61, p. 284/17b.3–4. Actually, at Dgon lung, members of the tantric college may have divided their time between the Tantric College assembly hall and the Great Assembly Hall. 'Jigs med ye shes grags pa's constitution for Dgon lung explains: "As for the ritual monks of the time of the Great Prayer Festival, aside from those of the Tantric College, the Propitiators of Protectors [T. *bskang gso*], the Empowerers of Ritual Cakes [T. *gtor sgrub pa*], and the ritual monks of the Medicine Buddha [T. *sman bla chog grwa*], everyone had to go to the Great Assembly Hall [for services]." Constitution no. 64, p. 32b.3.

156. Per Nyi ma 'dzin Ngag dbang legs bshad rgya mtsho, *Bshad sgrub bstan pa'i 'byung gnas chos sde chen po dgon lung byams pa gling gi gdan rabs zur rgyan,* 136. Lcang skya II promoted the Fifth Dalai Lama's Medicine Buddha Ritual in various A mdo monasteries. Lcang skya II Ngag dbang blo bzang chos ldan, "Rnam thar bka' rtsom," 12a.3–6; Shes rab dar rgyas, *Rje ngag dbang blo bzang chos ldan dpal bzang po'i rnam par thar pa mu tig 'phreng ba,* 35b.1; see also van Vleet, "Medicine as Impartial Knowledge." The biography of Lcang skya II also makes reference to Dgon lung's "Medicine Buddha Chapel." Shes rab dar rgyas, *Rje ngag dbang blo bzang chos ldan dpal bzang po'i rnam par thar pa mu tig 'phreng ba,* 31b.5–32a.1.

157. Per Nyi ma 'dzin Ngag dbang legs bshad rgya mtsho, *Bshad sgrub bstan pa'i 'byung gnas chos sde chen po dgon lung byams pa gling gi gdan rabs zur rgyan,* 137. Nyi ma 'dzin writes that the "*sngags pa grwa tshang rnams*" perform restoration rituals in the "*bskangs gso khang.*" This "Hall of Restoration Rituals" is probably what is today known as the Protectors Hall (T. *btsan khang*).

158. T. Lhung bzed mchod pa. On the sequence of this ritual at Rgyud smad, see Ser gtsug nang bstan dpe rnying 'tshol bsdu phyogs sgrig khang, *Rgyud smad chos thog khag gi lo rgyus,* 218–26.

159. That the practices of Dgon lung's Tantric College were modeled on those of the Lower Tantric College in Lhasa is corroborated in perhaps the earliest available source for information on the college, the biography of the Second Changkya. Shes rab dar rgyas, *Rje ngag dbang blo bzang chos ldan dpal bzang po'i rnam par thar pa mu tig 'phreng ba,* 77b.4–5.

160. Constitution no. 61, p. 286/18b.5–6

161. T. *gtor sgrub bla ma.* The specialist's name was Phar skyang bzod pa.

162. I.e., Degu Zhapdrung. This is likely Degu Zhapdrung Kün'ga Gyelsten (Bde rgu zhabs drung pa kun dga' rgyal mtshan), abbot from 1693 through 1701.

163. Per Nyi ma 'dzin Ngag dbang legs bshad rgya mtsho, *Bshad sgrub bstan pa'i 'byung gnas chos sde chen po dgon lung byams pa gling gi gdan rabs zur rgyan*, 130.

164. For instance, colophons to two texts in his *Collected Works* indicate that he was troubled by ritual manuals being published by the Phun tshogs gling printery, since it was apparently producing mass quantities of certain texts that were inaccurate or that gave inadequate attention to the ritual procedures that were to accompany the ritual recitations. See the colophons to the texts titled "'Jigs byed kyi sgrub thabs za ma tog ngag 'don bya tshul go bde bar bsgrigs pa 'jam dpal dgongs rgyan," "'Jigs byed chen po'i sgrub thabs ngag 'don gyi chog khrigs 'khrul spongs mkhas pa dgyes byed," and "'Khor lo sdom pa'i sgrub thabs bde chen gsal ba ngag 'don du bsgrigs pa bde chen rab rgyas" in Lcang skya II Ngag dbang blo bzang chos ldan, *Gsung 'bum*, vol. 4 (nga). Similarly, Thu'u bkwan III composed a manual for the First Day Ritual Cake Offering at Dgon lung due to the proliferation of laxity, ignorance, and mistakes. Thu'u bkwan III Blo bzang chos kyi nyi ma, "Dpal ldan lha mo la tshes gtor 'bul tshul gyi lag len khrigs chags su bkod pa 'gag med rdo rje'i sgra dbyangs," 2a.3–2b.2.

165. I.e., Yer ba/pa lha ri'i gdan sa pa Tshe brtan don grub.

166. T. Sum pa slob dpon dam chos rgyal mtshan. This is the previous incarnation twice removed of the illustrious Sumba Kanbo.

167. Brag dgon zhabs drung Dkon mchog bstan pa rab rgyas, *Mdo smad chos byung*, 57.27–8.

168. Thu'u bkwan III Blo bzang chos kyi nyi ma, "Dgon lung gi dkar chag," 667/18a.4.

169. Smith, *Among Tibetan Texts*, 161.

170. Another example of a Dge lugs hierarch holding concurrent abbacies is Gung thang III Dkon mchog bstan pa'i sgron me (1762–1823), who was simultaneously abbot of Bla brang bkra shis 'khyil and Dgon lung. Wang V Ngag dbang mkhyen rab rgya mtsho, *Dgon lung byams pa gling gi gdan rabs*, 20a.3; Brag dgon zhabs drung Dkon mchog bstan pa rab rgyas, *Mdo smad chos 'byung*, 68.

171. His name was bang kyA, suggesting he may have been related to the Wang Tusi 王土司.

172. T. *dbyangs*; *rta*; *'dur*. For a fuller and more exact discussion of these terms, see Ellingson, "Don rta dbyangs gsum."

173. T. *rol mo 'bud dkrol*.

174. T. Sems nyid Bstan 'dzin 'phrin las rgya mtsho. Semnyi is an interesting lama not only because he is one of the earliest indigenous incarnation lineages in Tibet, but also because he appears to have been Chinese: He was born as the son to a certain Chöpa of the Sun family (T. Sun kya Gcod pa) in Zhuanglang City (T. Grong lang mkhar) in the Wood-Sheep year of the eleventh rapjung (1655). After a few months, he said "I am Tibetan. There are 'such and such' a monk, monastery, and holy objects." Several Chinese said, "Such talk is an evil omen!" He washed his body with impure things, made [? *byin*] offerings of dog meat and blood, [and said,] "May molten metal be poured on your gossipy tongues!" The local lord, however, must have read these signs differently, because sometime thereafter he recognized the boy as the incarnation of the previous Semnyi! His rebirth was born in 1762. Brag dgon zhabs drung Dkon mchog bstan pa rab rgyas, *Mdo smad chos 'byung*, 115, 119. The following highlights from Semnyi's life come from the *Mdo smad chos 'byung* unless otherwise noted.

175. "Tianzhu Songshan Dalong si jieshao," accessed 28 April 2012. This site cites the gazetteer of Pingfan County 平番县志. This information may also be found in the following, although I do not have it available to check at the time of writing. Miaozhou 妙舟, *Meng Zang fojiao shi*.

176. T. *bskang gso*.

177. T. *bsnyen pa*. Brag dgon zhabs drung Dkon mchog bstan pa rab rgyas, *Mdo smad chos byung*, 115.24.

178. T. *gling bsre'i dka' bcu*.

179. It is unclear who this was. The *Mdo smad chos 'byung* simply say, "the Great Scholar Blo bzang rgya mtsho." This may have been Li kya dpon slob blo bzang rgyal mtshan (r. 1675–1680) or Chu bzang II Blo bzang bstan pa'i rgyal mtshan (r. 1680–1688), although this is only my conjecture.

180. T. *gzhi gsum*. I.e., the monastic practices of the fortnightly confession, Summer Retreat, and release from Summer Retreat.

181. T. Te thung dgon chen Thos bsam dar rgyas gling; Ch. Dong da si 東大寺. It is in Liancheng Township 连城镇, Yongdeng County 永登县, Gansu Province, just a few kilometers to the north and east of the Lü Tusi yamen.

182. It is not clear how long Semnyi served as abbot of this monastery. He was certainly still Te thung dgon chen's abbot in 1698 when Lcang skya II passed through there. He is there in 1710, too, when Lcang skya II was again passing through there, although it is unclear whether he was in fact acting as abbot at that time. Lcang skya II Ngag dbang blo bzang chos ldan, "Rnam thar bka' rtsom," 22a.6, 33b.4–5.

183. Brag dgon zhabs drung Dkon mchog bstan pa rab rgyas, *Mdo smad chos 'byung*, 117.4. Emphasis added.

184. His biography in the *Mdo smad chos 'byung* does not specify whether the location of his actions is Te thung dgon chen or his home monastery of Sems nyid.

185. Again, this could instead be referring to Sems nyid Monastery.

186. Brag dgon zhabs drung Dkon mchog bstan pa rab rgyas, *Mdo smad chos 'byung*, 117.14–17.

187. Ibid., 117.19–20.

188. This is an exaggeration. In fact, the number of troops would have been in the thousands. The *Mdo smad chos 'byung* explains that the general Nian Gengyao ordered that only two of the monastery's temples be destroyed. ("Legal custom" (*khrims srol*) demanded that at least two be burned!) So, on the fourth day of the fifth month, two temples were burned. Then, on the fifteenth day, the rest of the monastery was burned to the ground. No explanation is given for this total act of destruction except for the nature of compounded phenomena"; i.e., its impermanence.

189. T. Rgya rdog; Rgya ldog. On Rgya rdog being a branch of Sems nyid, see Brag dgon zhabs drung Dkon mchog bstan pa rab rgyas, *Mdo smad chos 'byung*, 112.11–13, which is citing the *BaiDUrya ser po* of Sde srid Sangs rgyas rgya mtsho.

190. T. Jo mchod smon lam.

191. T. Mgon po *bsnyen sgrub*.

192. Brag dgon zhabs drung Dkon mchog bstan pa rab rgyas, *Mdo smad chos 'byung*, 121.1–6.

193. A commemoration of the death of Tsong kha pa.

194. Sum pa mkhan po Ye shes dpal 'byor, "Dgon sde 'ga' zhig gi bca' yig blang dor snyan sgron," 131/14a.5. Sumba Kanbo also here identifies an overabundance of wealth and laziness as factors.

195. My thanks to Gen Tsetan Chonjore for explaining this proverb to me. Personal communication, 12 July 2017. He further related this proverb to another: *dred mong gis 'phyi ba 'jus pa*, "the bear that grabs the marmot [then reaches for another one and loses/forgets the first one]."

196. T. 'Brom [ston pa].

197. The print is distorted here, although it appears to read: *chos zab mo'i grags pa sngags la 'khul/ las 'khor ba'i gting rdo byas kyis dogs.*

198. Sum pa mkhan po Ye shes dpal 'byor, "Dgon sde 'ga' zhig gi bca' yig blang dor snyan sgron," 131/14a.6–132/14b.2.

199. Ray, *Buddhist Saints in India.*

CHAPTER 4

1. Cabezón, *Buddhism and Language,* 20.

2. Yi, "History of Monastic Textbooks," 23. The term "indoctrination" has become laden with negative connotations due to Cold War–era rhetoric regarding communist parties and states. However, the term originally pertained to religious instruction and had no such negative connotations.

3. See Chapter 1.

4. Examples of Dge lugs constitutions written for and praising the benefits of meditation are nos. 29 and 65.

5. See Cabezón, *Buddhism and Language,* 15; Cabezón, *Scholasticism.*

6. Dreyfus, "Where Do Commentarial Schools Come From?"; Dreyfus, *Sound of Two Hands Clapping,* 111–33.

7. T. Bla brang bkra shis 'khyil.

8. See constitution no. 60. Meanwhile, the rules and procedures of the Tantric College (T. *rgyud grwa*) were to follow the tradition of recitations and chanting found at the Smad rgyud Monastery in Lhasa.

9. Dreyfus points to the use of "*bshad grwa*" (commentary school) to make a similar point: that the early years of such Dge lugs monasteries were not characterized by the sort of rigid scholasticism that later came to characterize them. Dreyfus, "Where Do Commentarial Schools Come From?," 293–96.

10. Newland, "Debate Manuals (*Yig cha*)."

11. Dreyfus, *Sound of Two Hands Clapping,* 106–9; Yi, "History of Monastic Textbooks," 25–26.

12. T. Gung ru chos kyi 'byung gnas.

13. Yi, "History of Monastic Textbooks," 39.

14. Sørensen and Hazod, *Rulers on the Celestial Plain,* 55.

15. T. *gtong chos.* My translation of this word is tentative. The term appears in one other place in the Karma pa's constitutions, but its meaning is somewhat obscure: "Before the noon sounding board has been struck, if the recitations [T. *gtong chos*] have not been completed, then no one of high or low rank is to go anywhere but must remain seated in the debate courtyard." Constitution no. 21, p. 59b.4–5.

16. Emphasis added. Constitution no. 22, p. 62b.5. David DiValerio informs me that "*yig cha*" is also used to refer to collections of the songs and sayings of the Bka' brgyud saint Milarepa. Personal communication, 26 July 2018.

17. T. Kun dga' rgya mtsho; also known as Kun dga' rgyal mtshan. He served as abbot from 1693 through 1701.

18. Sde srid Sangs rgyas rgya mtsho, *Dga' ldan chos 'byung baiDUrya ser po,* 340.

19. Brag dgon zhabs drung Dkon mchog bstan pa rab rgyas, *Mdo smad chos 'byung,* 70–71. It is possible that other monks were responsible for bringing these textbooks to Dgon

lung in the first place. Gung ru chos 'byung himself is said to have traveled extensively in A mdo after fleeing from Gtsang forces sometime in the 1610s. Yi, "History of Monastic Textbooks," 43.

20. Sde srid Sangs rgyas rgya mtsho, *Dga' ldan chos 'byung baiDUrya ser po*, 241–42. The (abbreviated) title of this textbook is *The Lamp of the View* (*Lta ba'i sgron me*). BDRC places Sangs rgyas rgya mtsho's birth in the sixteenth century. "BDRC," P1553.

21. His text is the *Chos mngon rin chen 'dren pa'i shing rta*.

22. Wang IV Blo bzang 'jam pa'i tshul khrims, "Bstan bcos sgo brgya 'byed pa'i zab zing gser gyi sde mig."

23. Maher, "Knowledge and Authority," 216–17. See also the entry for 'Jam dbyangs bzhad pa I at the online biographical encyclopedia "The Treasury of Lives," https://treasuryoflives.org/biographies/view/Jamyang-Zhepai-Dorje/6646.

24. Constitution no. 23, p. 69b.1.

25. Constitution no. 19, pp. 43a.7–43b.5.

26. Ibid., pp. 44b.6–45a.5

27. Constitution no. 22, pp. 63b.7–64a.1, and constitution no. 15, p. 30b.6–7.

28. Ibid., p. 63b.2.

29. Constitution no. 49, pp. 89–90.

30. T. Ra ba stod pa.

31. *The Commentary on the Compendium of Valid Cognition*. Dergé Tenjur no. 4210; Peking Tenjur no. 5709.

32. T. *rtsis gshag*.

33. T. *bgro gleng*. This word is more commonly translated as something like "discussion." However, it also has the narrower meaning of dispute with a partner in a debate courtyard.

34. T. *chos spyod*.

35. Constitution no. 48, p. 85.

36. T. *mtshan nyid kyi grwa sa; chos sde 'di dbu phar gyi gras yin*. Constitution no. 51, pp. 188, 182.

37. For a terrific study of many aspects of this constitution, see Jansen, "How to Tame a Wild Monastic Elephant."

38. Constitution no. 51, p. 185.

39. Jansen, "How to Tame a Wild Monastic Elephant."

40. See Constitution no. 51, p. 185.

41. Constitution no. 51, p. 182.

42. Ibid., pp. 183, passim.

43. Ibid., pp. 182–83. Jansen, "How to Tame a Wild Monastic Elephant," 132–33.

44. Constitution no. 60, pp. 820/2b.6–821/3a.2.

45. On the ritual invocation of Mañjuśrī before debate, see Dreyfus, *Sound of Two Hands Clapping*, 211.

46. Constitution no. 60, p. 821/3a.2–3.

47. T. *bar chos*.

48. Brag dgon zhabs drung Dkon mchog bstan pa rab rgyas, *Mdo smad chos 'byung*, 71.

49. T. *dpyid chos rjes ma*. This is the name given the session by Wang IV's 1885 constitution for Dgon lung.

50. Constitution no. 66, pp. 30b.6–31a.2.

51. T. *chos ra, chos grwa*.

52. T. *mang ja*.

53. Constitution no. 66, p. 22b.2. This corroborates Schram's picture of the Philosophical College as the wealthiest segment of the monastery and of food being a primary motivation for many monks who enroll in that college. Schram, *Monguors of the Kansu-Tibetan Border*, 377.

54. Constitution no. 66, p. 31b.1.

55. Wang IV Blo bzang 'jam pa'i tshul khrims, "Bstan bcos sgo brgya 'byed pa'i zab zing gser gyi sde mig," 3b.4.

56. T. *zla bo*.

57. Constitution no. 66, p. 23a.3.

58. Lempert, *Discipline and Debate*, 55–56.

59. Dreyfus, *Sound of Two Hands Clapping*, 251, 388n50.

60. T. *dbyangs spyangs*.

61. T. *dam bca'*.

62. T. *Rgyan 'jug*. That is, Maitreya's commentary on the Perfection of Wisdom—the *Abhisamayālaṃkāra* (T. *Mngon rtogs rgyan*, The Ornament of Realization)—and Candrakīrti's *Madhyamakāvatāra* (T. *Dbu ma la 'jug pa*, Entrance to the Middle Way), two of the five foundational scriptures of the Dge lugs curriculum. Constitution no. 66, p. 25a.4–5.

63. Constitution no. 66, p. 25b.3–4.

64. T. *dge rgan*.

65. T. *sgrigs lam*.

66. T. *rnam gzhag*.

67. A senior teacher monk at a modern-day Dge lugs scholastic monastery told me that this process can take anywhere from one year to several years. Personal communication, July 2016, Thar shul Monastery, Guinan County, Qinghai Province. Of course, the rate of progress depends also on the individual's abilities. Dreyfus, *Sound of Two Hands Clapping*, 85.

68. Constitution no. 66, pp. 19b.6–20a.1–2.

69. Goldstein, "Revival of Monastic Life in Drepung Monastery," 17–19.

70. Schram concludes that the majority of the monks in Huangzhong 湟中 (eastern Amdo) were enrolled in a college, most of them in a Philosophical College. Schram, *Monguors of the Kansu-Tibetan Border*, 376–77. The Seventh Dalai Lama's constitution for the tantric college of Sku 'bum (constitution no. 61, pp. 279.5, passim) requires recitation lessons (T. *rtsi bzhag*).

71. Constitution no. 66, p. 24b.1–2.

72. T. *'dzin grwa*.

73. T. Bsdus grwa che chung.

74. T. Blo rtags gnyis.

75. T. Don bdun bcu.

76. T. Sems bskyed.

77. T. Chos 'khor.

78. T. Dkyil khang pa.

79. T. *Chos mngon rin chen 'dren pa'i shing rta*.

80. Brag dgon zhabs drung Dkon mchog bstan pa rab rgyas, *Mdo smad chos 'byung*, 70–71.

81. Onoda, "bsDus grwa Literature."

82. Ibid., 187–88; Dreyfus, *Sound of Two Hands Clapping*, 112.

83. T. *gzhung po ti lnga*.

84. These scriptures, which are here studied through the specified Tibetan commentaries, are (1) Nāgārjuna's *Treatise of the Middle Way* (S. *Mūlamadhyamakakārika*) or the Indian commentary on that by Candrakīrti, *Entrance to the Middle Way* (S. *Madhyamakāvartāra*); (2) Vasubandhu's *Treasury of the Abhidharma* (S. *Abhidharmakośa*); (3) Dharmakīrti's *Commentary on Valid Cognition/Knowledge* (*Pramāṇavārttika*), and (4) Guṇaprabha's *Discourse on Vinaya* (S. *Vinaya-sūtra*). Dreyfus, *Sound of Two Hands Clapping*; Lopez, *Prisoners of Shangri-La*, 166–68; Jackson, "Kalachakra in Context," 39–40.

85. See Dreyfus, *Sound of Two Hands Clapping*, ch. 6.

86. Ngawang Dakpa describes in part how this was the case at 'Bras spungs Monastery. Ngawang Dakpa, "The Hours and Days of a Great Monastery," 174–75.

87. Constitution no. 66, p. 24b.4–5.

88. Dreyfus, *Sound of Two Hands Clapping*, 250–51; Lempert, *Discipline and Debate*, 60.

89. These are all Perfection of Wisdom topics. Constitution no. 66, p. 24b.3–4.

90. Constitution no. 66, p. 31b.3–4.

91. Ibid., p. 31b.1–2.

92. T. *zhabs 'dren.*

93. Constitution no. 51, p. 186. The Dalai Lama worries about the presence of foreign monks at 'Bras spungs who do not take their studies seriously and how that might affect the study-abroad connections (*grwa rgyun*) 'Bras spungs has established in Mongolia. My reading of this differs from Berthe Jansen's, who reads "*grwa rgyun*" as "monk-register." Jansen, "How to Tame a Wild Monastic Elephant," 124. 'Od zer rgya mtsho's constitution (Constitution no. 25, p. 292/2b.2–3.) also warns of declining "wealth" that follows in the wake of declining repute. See also Jansen, *The Monastery Rules*, ch. 6.

94. Constitution no. 66, p. 25b.5.

95. Transgressions of the rules of the host monastery, etc., were to be "fervently suppressed and prevented from happening again" (*rjes gnon phyi lam 'khebs pa*). This is a stock phrase that appears in several constitutions in various contexts.

96. T. *dka' rams* or *dka' ram*. This is an abbreviation of *dka' bcu ba*, "Master of the Ten Difficulties [or Texts]" and *rab 'byams pa*, "Universally Learned One."

97. Constitution no. 66, p. 31b.4.

98. Ibid., p. 25b.5–6.

99. Exceptions are made for "those who have been going [to dharma class] for a long time." Constitution no. 66, p. 25b.5.

100. This is Sems nyid dgon dga' ldan dar rgyas gling. The Fifth Dalai Lama's biography of the Third Dalai Lama describes the Third Dalai Lama prophesying the founding of this monastery at its future site. Lamas and monks at Dgon lung consider this to have been a branch monastery of Dgon lung.

101. Brag dgon zhabs drung Dkon mchog bstan pa rab rgyas, *Mdo smad chos 'byung*, 117.20. According to this nineteenth-century source, this is said to have happened sometime after 1707. The entire system of scholasticism at this monastery developed over the course of the seventeenth century under the direction of figures from Dgon lung and others.

102. T. *gling bsre dka' bcu*, or "Master of the Ten Difficulties [i.e., Texts] among Mixed Communities." "Mixed communities" is a reference to the origin of the title *Gling bsre* at Gsang phu Monastery, where members of both the Upper and Lower monastic groups gathered for the formal debate (defense). Dreyfus, *Sound of Two Hands Clapping*, 366n74; Tarab Tulku, *Brief History of Tibetan Degrees*, 17; Zhang Yisun 張怡荪, *Bod rgya tshig mdzod chen mo*, 424–25. At Dgon lung, the "mixing" is all intra-monastic.

103. Sems nyid sprul sku Bstan 'dzin 'phrin las rgya mtsho earned the latter in 1677. Brag dgon zhabs drung Dkon mchog bstan pa rab rgyas, *Mdo smad chos 'byung*, 115.25; See also Thu'u bkwan III Blo bzang chos kyi nyi ma, "Dgon lung gi dkar chag," 739/49a.5; Sagaster, *Subud erike*, 43; Qinghai sheng bianji zu, *Qinghai Tuzu shehui lishi diaocha*, 49; Dreyfus, *Sound of Two Hands Clapping*, 144.

104. T. *thal 'phreng*. This is a style of argumentation that is characteristic of the Dge lugs debate. Hugon, "Arguments by Parallels," 94, 94n2; Onoda, "bsDus grwa Literature," 190; Jackson, *The Entrance Gate for the Wise*, 130.

105. Constitution no. 66, pp. 31b.6–32a.1.

106. Ibid., p. 26a.3.

107. T. *tshogs lang*. Sometimes one finds this spelled "*tshogs gleng*." Liu Shengqi writes that "the result of these Tshogs-langs was not an official assessment for the monks' academic degree. However, it provided the heads and all monks of this monastery with a clear view of a monk's academic performance and based on this decided whether a monk could have a degree or not, though it was a long time before he took formal graduation examinations." Liu Shengqi, "Three Major Monasteries in Lhasa."

108. T. *bla ma dge skos rnams nyis [sic] thad ka thad ka'i rgyug len pa dang / gsar du 'jog pa sogs bcing bskul gyi do dam gang drag byed*.

109. T. *ming btags pa* (lit. title-holder, or one [seeking a] title).

110. T. *rigs lung byed mkhan*. This term is synonymous with "*rigs lam pa*." See Dreyfus, *Sound of Two Hands Clapping*, 211.

111. Constitution no. 66, pp. 25b.6–26a.3.

112. T. *g.yo sgyu'i sbyor ba*.

113. T. *phug tshangs kyi gtam*. My rendering of this is tentative.

114. T. *shags ngan*.

115. T. *don rtogs pa*.

116. T. *lung rigs*.

117. T. *Tshad ma sde bdun*.

118. Constitution no. 66, pp. 24a.4–24b.1.

119. T. *Dpa' re khya kho*. "Dpa' re" is an alternative spelling for "Dpa' ris"; i.e., Pari. I have rendered this phonetically as "Pari" for the sake of consistency.

120. T. *Bstan 'dzin rgya yu ma*. Nietupski writes that he once served as abbot of Dgon lung. I have been unable to corroborate this. Nietupski, *Labrang Monastery*, 129.

121. T. *phyir*. This is my own gloss of the term. For a description of how this taunt is used in actual debate, see Lempert, *Discipline and Debate*, 69–70.

122. T. *phreng kog*.

123. T. *stong zob*.

124. T. *'khor gsum bskor*. See Lempert, *Discipline and Debate*, 69–70, 179n36.

125. T. *thal skad*.

126. T. *chos gos*.

127. The absurdity of this implication of Dpa' re Khya kho's assertions is based on the fact that monks wear robes while laypeople wear pants, but neither wear both. Brag dgon zhabs drung Dkon mchog bstan pa rab rgyas, *Mdo smad chos 'byung*, 382. Emphasis added.

128. T. *ming btags zur pa*.

129. T. *gzhi dgon rang gi grwa pa*.

130. T. *gzhi 'dug gi rigs*. Constitution no. 66, p. 32a.1–3.

131. T. *ka par nas bshad pa*.

132. T. *tshab grwa*. The *Tshigs mdzod chen mo* (Great Chinese-Tibetan Dictionary) defines "*tsha gra*" as "the *tsampa* allotted to monks during the Great Prayer Festival by the Tsampa Office of the former regional government of Tibet." Alternatively, "*tshab grwa*" may be related to the term "*tsha rting*," meaning "mid-morning." I would like to thank Khenpo Ngawang Dorjee for first pointing me in this direction. Constitution no. 66, p. 32a.1–3.

133. T. Phan theb.

134. T. *srang*.

135. T. *dam bca' chen mo*.

136. Constitution no. 66, p. 32a.4.

137. Sum pa mkhan po Ye shes dpal 'byor, "Mkhan po erte ni paN+Di tar grags pa'i spyod tshul brjod pa sgra 'dzin bcud len," 167a.3.

138. Ibid., 114b.7.

139. His full name was Blo bzang 'jam pa'i tshul khrims.

140. Wang IV Blo bzang 'jam pa'i tshul khrims, "Bca' yig blong dor gsal ba'i me long." This and the following draws on Sullivan, "Monastic Customaries."

141. Wang IV Blo bzang 'jam pa'i tshul khrims, "Bstan bcos sgo brgya 'byed pa'i zab zing gser gyi sde mig."

142. Schram claims that the originator of this line was a lama from Kharachin (Liaodong Province). He was then reborn in the vicinity of Dgon lung. That boy is the "First" Wang Khutugtu. Schram, *Monguors of the Kansu-Tibetan Border*, 321.

143. See Borjigin, "Ethnic Conflict in the Frontier."

144. For a translation of this text, see Sullivan, "Monastic Customaries," 95–96.

145. T. *rdo ram pa* (lit. "The Stone Courtyard One").

146. Dreyfus, *Sound of Two Hands Clapping*, 144–45; Tarab Tulku, *Brief History of Tibetan Degrees*, 18–19.

147. See Hopkins and Yi, *The Hidden Teaching*.

148. Sullivan, "Monastic Customaries," 95.

149. T. *thal 'phen*; to point out the absurd consequences of an opponent's assertion or thesis. As such, it is synonymous with the *thal 'phreng*.

150. T. *rtag gsal khyab*.

151. T. *tshogs*.

152. Sullivan, "Monastic Customaries," 95.

153. Ibid., 96.


CHAPTER 5

1. T. mA this zi. Also, Dga' ldan dam chos gling.

2. "Dga' ldan dam chos gling gi 'grig lam dang 'don bsgrigs," 1. One regularly finds these phrases or near synonyms as section titles within *bca' yig*.

3. This is based on an informant at Mati si. The author is said to have studied under "Dpal ldan tshang," who was described as the most important scholar-monk (T. *dge bshes*) at Bla brang bkra shis 'khyil's philosophical college after the 'Jam dbyangs bzhad pa.

4. I have removed certain identifying details to protect the anonymity of the individuals being discussed here. These facts were reported to me by a monk at Mati si.

5. T. Chu bzang dgon. This is Chu bzang Lama's own monastery.

6. For this reason, I disagree with Jansen when she writes, "The preservation of the Vinaya vows was as important—if not more important—than [*sic*] performing the right kinds of rituals." Clearly Vinaya and discipline, as I, too, have argued, are important subjects in monastic constitutions. Nonetheless, Vinaya and discipline are part of a larger, rationalized monastic program, which also includes the proper practice of ritual. Jansen, *The Monastery Rules*, 180.

7. Patte, *Cambridge Dictionary of Christianity*, 735.

8. Ellingson, "The Mandala of Sound," 682–84; Cabezón, *Tibetan Ritual*, 13–15.

9. As such, the reader will notice some continuity between Chapter 3 on tantric colleges and this chapter.

10. My thanks to Matthew Kapstein (personal communication, 7 March 2015) for making this point and for redirecting my attention to the relevant work of Stephan Beyer. See Beyer, *The Cult of Tārā*.

11. Cabezón, *Tibetan Ritual*, 2–3.

12. Davidson, "The Litany of Names of Mañjuśrī."

13. The work of Chris Bell and that of Amy Heller are examples of such careful scholarship. Bell, for instance, has, in effect, created a map of the varying degrees to which the cult of the god Pe har (and the associated liturgy) were connected with Gnas chung Monastery and the liturgical compositions of the Fifth Dalai Lama. Bell, "Nechung," 225–50.

14. Beyer, *The Cult of Tārā*, 20.

15. Constitution no. 4, p. 693/248a.4–5.

16. Constitution no. 8, p. 689/1b.3–5.

17. Ibid., p. 690/2a.5–6.

18. Ibid., pp. 689/1b.4–5, 690/2a.6–691b.2.

19. Constitution no. 9, p. 706/4a.1–3.

20. T. 'Brug pa zhabs drung Ngag dbang rnam rgyal, 1594–1651.

21. On the history of Ngag dbang rnam rgyal's flight to Bhutan, see Ardussi, "Formation of the State of Bhutan," 35–36.

22. T. Sa skya khri chen Ngag dbang kun dga' bsod nams, 1597–1660.

23. Constitution no. 31, p. 40/20b.5–6.

24. Ibid., pp. 40/20b.6–41/21a.1.

25. For instance, the liturgy of the following appears to have been influenced: Sa skya pa Kun dga' blo gros, "Chos grwa chen po thub bstan lha khang chen mo'i bca' yig."

26. Sde srid Sangs rgyas rgya mtsho, *Life of the Fifth Dalai Lama*, 310–11. Emphasis added. I have made some minor emendations to the passage but otherwise left it as translated by Ahmad.

27. This is 'Ba' Dga' ldan phan bde gling.

28. Dalai Lama V Ngag dbang blo bzang rgya mtsho, *Rgyal dbang lnga pa Ngag dbang blo bzang rgya mtsho'i gsung 'bum*, 23 ('a): 91; Brag dgon zhabs drung Dkon mchog bstan pa rab rgyas, *Mdo smad chos 'byung*, 169; Zhiguanba•Gongquehudanbaraoji, *Anduo zhengjiao shi*, 164.

29. T. Gong ra Gzhan phan rdo rje, 1594–1654.

30. T. Sog bzlog pa, 1552–1624.

31. T. Snang rtse ba; also known as Zhig po gling pa, 1524–1583.

32. T. Bsod nams rab brtan, 1595–1657.

33. Khra tshang pa Blo gros mchog gi rdo rje, 1595–1671.

34. Gentry, "Substance and Sense," 470–71; Gentry, *Power Objects in Tibetan Buddhism*.

35. Gentry, "Substance and Sense," 452–53.

36. Another example of the Dalai Lama's direct appointment of an abbot is for Rwa sgreng Monastery. See the note corresponding to constitution no. 33 in the Appendix.

37. Heller, "Protective Deities Srung-Ma Dmar-Nag," 479, 489, 491, passim.

38. For the latter, see Nor brang o rgyan, *Dge lugs pa'i zhal 'don*, 187–93.

39. Constitution no. 34, p. 10.

40. The Fifth Dalai Lama first alludes to the relationship between Lha mo (the Glorious Goddess) and Beg tse (the Armored One) in his biography of the Third Dalai Lama. Later oral tradition builds on this to identify these protectors with the Dalai Lamas and the Dga' ldan pho brang government. Heller, "Étude sur le développement de l'iconographie," 220–25 (ch. 8).

41. Dreyfus, "An Introduction to Drepung's Colleges"; Makransky, "Offering (*mChod pa*) in Tibetan Ritual Literature," 321.

42. Like many prayers and hymns, the title by which this is known is simply the first verse of the prayer. Nor brang o rgyan, *Dge lugs pa'i zhal 'don*, 59–62.

43. Las chen Kun dga' rgyal mtshan, *Bla ma thams cad mkhyen pa'i rnam thar ngo mtshar mdzad pa bcu gnyis.*

44. Nor brang o rgyan, *Dge lugs pa'i zhal 'don*, 153–55.

45. Ibid., 156–58.

46. Ibid., 225–27.

47. T. Blo gros bas pa, 1400–1475.

48. Nor brang o rgyan, *Dge lugs pa'i zhal 'don*, 228–30.

49. Ibid., 231–33.

50. Ibid., 234–36.

51. Ibid., 237–38.

52. This appears in *Chos sde chen po rnams su gsung pa'i chos spyod kyi rim pa dang ser smad thos bsam nor gling grwa tshang gi thun mong ma yin pa'i nye mkho chos spyod*, 222/11b.4–224/112b.1.

53. Nor brang o rgyan, *Dge lugs pa'i zhal 'don*, 657–58.

54. Ibid., 655–56.

55. Tsong kha pa Blo bzang grags pa, *Gsung 'bum*, 2 (kha): 240–48.

56. Mkhas sgrub rje Dge legs dpal bzang, *Gsung 'bum*, 9 (ta): 520–21.

57. Nor brang o rgyan, *Dge lugs pa'i zhal 'don*, 101–2.

58. Ibid., 638–42.

59. This appears in Krung go bod brgyud mtsho rim nang bstan slob gling brgyud nang bstan zhib 'jug khang, *Dge lugs pa'i chos spyod phyogs bsgrigs*, 167–72.

60. On the meaning of "Lcam sring," see Heller, "Étude sur le développement," 25–36 (ch. 2).

61. The example I have relied on most is Nor brang o rgyan, *Dge lugs pa'i zhal 'don*.

62. Constitution no. 40, pp. 43–44. Also listed here is *Rnam rgyal sgrub mchod*, which may refer to Rnam rgyal ma, the Completely Victorious One (Arisen from) the *Uṣṇīṣa*.

63. Constitution no. 40, p. 45.

64. The five specified chapels are Mgon khang (rgyal) mthil, Lhun grub dga' ba'i tshal, Mgon khang po ta la, Wi ko Ti, and Bsil ba tshal.

65. This is the Bsil ba tshal. Panjara Mahākāla and Four-faced Mahākāla (gur zhal) are also worshipped in conjunction with this, we are told.

66. This is the De wi ko Ti, from the Sanskrit Devīkoṭi.

67. This is the Mgon khang po ta la.

68. T. *sku rim*.

69. Constitution no. 40, p. 46.

70. T. *rgyud lugs kyi rjes su 'brags pa'i sngags dgon*. See Constitution no. 42, p. 75.

71. Constitution no. 42, p. 71.

72. This is 'Dul 'dzin Grags pa rgyal mtshan, 1374–1434.

73. This is Mkhas sgrub Nor bzang rgya mtsho.

74. Constitution no. 42, p. 75.

75. T. *Gsang ba'i rnam thar*; by the disciple of Tsong kha pa, Bkra shis dpal ldan (1379–1449). In Nor brang o rgyan, *Dge lugs pa'i zhal 'don*, 198–205.

76. T. *'Dod khams bdag mo'i gtor bsngo*. This appears in Krung go bod brgyud mtsho rim nang bstan slob gling brgyud nang bstan zhib 'jug khang, *Dge lugs pa'i chos spyod phyogs bsgrigs*, 6: 64–137.

77. van Vleet, "Medicine as Impartial Knowledge."

78. Ibid., 264.

79. Dalai Lama VI skal bzang skya mtsho, Dbus 'gyur chos sde chen po dpal ldan 'bras spungs tshogs chen dang dpal ldan bkra shis sgo mang grwa tshang bcas kyi tshogs 'don chos spyod kyi rim pa. The library catalog at the University of Virginia has misattributed the compilation of this breviary to Gung thang Bstan pa'i sgron me. It is not entirely clear which parts of the extant breviary were included by him and which parts might have been added later when the breviary was reprinted. The later colophon suggests that the first half of the breviary, which is made up almost entirely of prayers by or for Tsong kha pa, was compiled by the Seventh Dalai Lama, while the second half of the current edition was added later. Actually, the second half of the print also contains certain liturgical formulas that are found in constitutions from the earlier period, including the litany of praises of the Dalai Lamas (as found in constitution no. 40 for Chos 'khor rgyal) and the dates for commemorating the first four Dalai Lamas (as found in constitution no. 55 for Rta wang).

80. Constitution no. 55, p. 26.

81. T. Drug cu pa'i skyed chog, which I interpret as referring to the Great Sacrificial Cake Offering Ritual to Vajrabhairava discussed in Chapter 3. Constitution no. 55, p. 30.

82. Nor brang o rgyan, *Dge lugs pa'i zhal 'don*, 499–501.

83. Dalai Lama VII Skal bzang skya mtsho, *Dbus 'gyur chos sde chen po dpal ldan 'bras spungs tshogs chen dang dpal ldan bkra shis sgo mang grwa tshang bcas kyi tshogs 'don chos spyod kyi rim pa bskal bzang mgrin rgyan*.

84. Brag dgon zhabs drung Dkon mchog bstan pa rab rgyas, *Mdo smad chos 'byung*, 71.

85. Constitution no. 66, p. 20b.5.

86. Ibid., pp. 20b.6–21b.1.

87. Ibid., p. 34b.3–4.

88. Ellingson, "Tibetan Monastic Constitutions," 212.

89. Constitution no. 66, p. 34a.5. This may, in fact, refer to the practice of the medium going around to villages so that the locals can pay homage to the protector deity.

90. Other rituals in the calendar include *'cham* ritual dancing and the commemoration of the previous 'On Rgyal sras. The latter is described briefly in constitution no. 66, p. 33b.1–2. See also Chapter 3 on Gönlung's tantric college.

91. Lcang skya II Ngag dbang blo bzang chos ldan, "Rnam thar bka' rtsom (Peking Edition)," 12a.3–6.

92. Per Nyi ma 'dzin Ngag dbang legs bshad rgya mtsho, *Bshad sgrub bstan pa'i 'byung gnas chos sde chen po dgon lung byams pa gling gi gdan rabs zur rgyan*, 136; Pu Wencheng, *Gan Qing Zangchuan fojiao siyuan*, 78.

93. Nor brang o rgyan, *Dge lugs pa'i zhal 'don*, 304–8.

94. 'Brug rgyal mkhar, *Mtshan gzungs rgyun khyer phyogs bsgrigs*, 1–2. This was originally composed by Tsong kha pa for his master Red mda' ba (1349–1412). Red mda' ba returned the praise by replacing his own name with that of Tsong kha pa's, and thus the prayer is a praise of the founder of the Dge lugs school and, as Lcang skya III puts it in one constitution, is "the most superior of secret mantras." Lcang skya III Rol pa'i rdo rje, "A lag sha zhes grags pa'i gnas chen gyi phan bde rgya mtsho'i gling gi dge 'dun rnams la khrims su bcas pa'i yi ge bslab gsum rnam par rgyas pa'i nyi 'od."

95. Dreyfus, *Sound of Two Hands Clapping*, 44.

96. According to the *sku rim* liturgy at 'Bras spungs Monastery, at the end of the service special prayers are recited for anyone who is seriously ill. Lodrö, *Geschichte der Kloster-Universität Drepung mit einem Abris der Geistesgeschichte Tibets*, 208.

97. The "Sgrol ma" without introduction verses can be found in Sangs rgyas, *Bstod smon phyogs bsgrigs*, 200–205; Beyer's translation appears in *The Cult of Tārā*, 211–14.

98. Constitution no. 66, p. 31a.6. The precise number is actually ambiguous because at another point in the constitution (p. 24b.6) it says to recite it thirty to fifty times.

99. Wang IV Blo bzang 'jam pa'i tshul khrims, "Bstan bcos sgo brgya 'byed pa'i zab zing gser gyi sde mig," 4b.2.

100. Note that the constitution is said to be *based on* the practices of 'Bras spungs Sgo mang. Apparently, this was not understood by the editors of the *'Bras spungs Sgo mang chos 'byung*, who have labeled it as the monastic constitution *of* 'Bras spungs Sgo mang.

101. Bstan pa bstan 'dzin, *'Bras spungs sgo mang chos 'byung*, 2:686.7.

102. Ibid., 2:688.20.

103. Ibid., 2:692.13.

104. I have not yet had a chance to compare the other sections of the constitution for the Mongol Monastery (Baruun Kheid in Alashaa) to the other components of the 'Bras spungs liturgy as found in Lodrö, *Geschichte der Kloster-Universität Drepung mit einem Abris der Geistesgeschichte Tibets*.

105. Thu'u bkwan Blo bzang chos kyi nyi ma, *Gsung 'bum*, 2 (kha): 675/1–716/21b.6. One constitution was for his personal monastery of Chos bzang ri khrod, located in the valley just east of Dgon lung; another was for monks and laity preparing and empowering *maṇi* pills; the other two were for Mongol monasteries.

106. "*Sbyin bdag wang dpal 'byor yar 'phel gyis zhus pa ltar sde brgyad kyi bka' shog dang tA bla ma sogs kyis bskul ngor bslab mchog gling gi bca' yig ljags rtsom mdzad de gnang/.*" Gung thang III Dkon mchog bstan pa'i sgron me, "Blo bzang chos kyi nyi ma'i gsang gsum rmad du byung ba'i rtogs brjod," 7 (*ja*): 808.

107. Gung thang III Dkon mchog bstan pa'i sgron me, "A ru hor chen dgon pa bkra shis bsam 'grub gling gi bca' yig chos kyi snang ba."

108. Jalsan, "The Reincarnations of Desi Sangye Gyatso," 358n2.

109. See Sullivan, "Monastic Customaries."

110. T. *spyi bskang*. This together with *ltung bshags* is recited every fortnight by Buddhist monastic communities.

111. That is, they are to "make a dedication of merit [by reciting] the Sixty" (*drug cu pa bsngo bar byed*). I am assuming that "*drug cu pa*" corresponds to something like the extracts found in "Drug cu ba'i 'don bsgrigs 'khyer bde nag 'gros su bkod pa las bzhi'i 'phrin las myur 'grub" found in the Krung go bod brgyud mtsho rim nang bstan slob gling brgyud nang bstan zhib 'jug khang, *Dge lugs pa'i chos spyod phyogs bsgrigs*, 6:138–49. The prescription of

"[*bdag*] *'jug tu drug cu pa*," which I understand to mean "self-initiation [as Vajrabhairava] and worship of Yama," appears in the Third Lcang skya's constitution for Baruun Kheid, which I discuss below.

112. Nebesky-Wojkowitz, *Oracles and Demons of Tibet*, 25, 181–98; see also Bell, "Nechung," 518–19.

113. See the index to Nor brang o rgyan, *Dge lugs pa'i zhal 'don*, 7.

114. Thu'u bkwan Blo bzang chos kyi nyi ma, *Gsung 'bum*, 2 (kha): 708/17b.5.

115. Ibid., 706/16b.1–3. Emphasis added.

116. T. *rgyal ba yab sras/ nge kyi ring 'tsho'i bden tshig.*

117. These are the *smon lam* to Samantabhadra; to Undertaking the Way to Awakening (T. *Spyod 'jug*); to Beginning, Middle, and End (T. *Thog mtha' bar*; by Tsong kha pa); to Being Born in the Land of Bliss (T. *Bde ba can du skye ba'i smon lam*); and to Maitreya. These are numbers 111–115 in Nor brang o rgyan, *Dge lugs pa'i zhal 'don*.

118. This refers to the practice of distributing a part of the canon of the Buddha's sutras to each monk for him to read until the entire corpus is recited.

119. Nor brang o rgyan, *Dge lugs pa'i zhal 'don*, 499–501.

120. T. *Cha gsum.*

121. Bell, "Nechung," 32–33, passim.

122. Thu'u bkwan Blo bzang chos kyi nyi ma, *Gsung 'bum*, 2 (kha): 706/16b.3–707/17a.2.

123. Jalsan, "The Reincarnations of Desi Sangye Gyatso." Jalsan (from the Tibetan "Rgyal mtshan"), who died in 2013, was the most recent rebirth of the prime minister. He mentions the Lcang skya constitution on page 358n2 and includes a snapshot of the *dbu med* version of it in Jialasen, *Zaixian huihuang de Guangzong si*. I was able to photograph an *dbu chen* version of it, which had been copied out by Jalsan, in July 2017. I am thankful to Qin Siqin at the Inner Mongolia University for traveling with me and facilitating that trip. The constitution itself is titled "A lag sha zhes grags pa'i gnas chen gyi phan bde rgya mtsho'i gling gi dge 'dun rnams la khrims su bcas pa'i yi ge bslab gsum rnam par rgyas pa'i nyi 'od."

124. Lcang skya III Rol pa'i rdo rje, "A lag sha zhes grags pa'i gnas chen gyi phan bde rgya mtsho'i gling gi dge 'dun rnams la khrims su bcas pa'i yi ge bslab gsum rnam par rgyas pa'i nyi 'od," line 61.

125. T. *Dga' ldan lha brgya ma.* A praise and guru yoga of Tsong kha pa by the Second 'Jam dbyangs bzhad pa. Nor brang o rgyan, *Dge lugs pa'i zhal 'don*, 209–12.

126. T. *Byams pa dam bca' ba'i gzungs.*

127. T. *Gnas mchog dga' ldan.* This is said to be a praise of the Dalai Lama's Potala Palace, although I have not located a corresponding text or ritual manual.

128. T. *'jug tu drug cu pa.* I believe this refers to the ritual act of visualizing oneself as Vajrabhairava and commanding Yama and his retinue to continue protecting the dharma.

129. T. *gung tshig.* This can also mean "lunch."

130. T. *mang ja zur pa med na.*

131. T. *'jug 'dir* DzaM b+ha la'i chu sbyin.

132. T. *Sa la rnam gsum.* Also known as the *Sa lam skabs gsum*, this refers to the *Sa gsum pa* by Mkhas sgrub, the *Lam rim bsdus don* by Tsong kha pa, and the *Skabs gsum pa* by Tsong kha pa. All of these can be found in the Nor brang o rgyan, *Dge lugs pa'i zhal 'don*.

133. T. *sku brtan sku skal yan lag bdun pa'i yan la phul nas.* . . . My translation is tentative. "Arhats" could be a reference to the elders of the monastery.

134. T. *Sangs rgyas chos tshogs ma.* This consists of four verses, the first two being the taking of refuge and the latter two being the aspiration to attain enlightenment for the

benefit of others. One website says that this is attributed to Atiśa. http://www
.gyalwarinpoche.com/node/116, accessed 30 August 2016. This website is no longer available,
and I have not been able to confirm this attribution.

135. Lcang skya III Rol pa'i rdo rje, "A lag sha zhes grags pa'i gnas chen gyi phan bde
rgya mtsho'i gling gi dge 'dun rnams la khrims su bcas pa'i yi ge bslab gsum rnam par rgyas
pa'i nyi 'od," lines 61–71.There is a final section to this regular liturgy, too: "After that, if the
horn is blown for an ancillary assembly [T. *tshogs chung*], then, assemble according to whatever procedures there are for ancillary assemblies, and perform: the complete self visualization and front visualization ritual of Akṣobhya Buddha, extended or abbreviated; the
[regular] liturgy [T. *chos spyod*]; aspiration prayers; and, the Tārā, *Heart Sutra*, and so forth
as circumstances dictate. Assembly disperses. The young monks assemble in the courtyard
and rehearse and practice [their recitations]."

136. Constitution no. 66, p. 25a.2; constitution no. 55, p., 27; and, constitution no. 61,
p. 282.1–2.

137. T. *byams pa mgon po'i snang brnyan skor lam du gdan 'dren pa.*

138. T. Bla ma bsod nams grub.

139. T. *Rdo rje 'phreng ba'i gar gyi bstan bcos.* Rangjung Yeshe suggests the "rdo rje
phreng ba" might be *Gsang 'dus bshad rgyud*, which, in turn, could be *Rgyud kyi rgyal po dpal
gsang ba 'dus pa'i rnam par bshad pa* (S. *Tantrarājaśrīguhyasamājaṭīkā*) found in the Dergé
Tenjur (D1909) and Peking Tenjur (P2772 or Q2772).

140. T. Zla ba dpal rin.

141. T. Bla ma Bsam grub.

142. T. 'Dul 'dzin rin po che

143. T. *Yo ga Ti ka chen yid bzhin nor bu.* This might be his *Rdo rje dbyings kyi dkyil 'khor
gyi cho ga rdo rje thams cad 'byung ba zhes bya ba'i rgya cher bshad pa yid bzhin gyi nor bu*, which
can be found in volume 11 (*da*) of Bu ston Rin chen grub, *Gsung 'bum.*

144. T. *Sngags rim.* Parts of this seminal text have been translated by Jeffrey Hopkins as
*Tantra in Tibet*, vol. 1; Hopkins, *Tantra in Tibet*, vols. 2–3.

145. T. *Slob dpon* a bha ya ka ra.

146. T. *Rdo rje phreng ba.* This is probably Abhyāgaragupta, *Dkyil chog rdo rje phreng ba
dang rdzogs pa'i rnal 'byor gyi 'phreng ba.*

147. Bentor, "Literature on Consecration (*Rab gnas*)," 290.

148. Beyer, *The Cult of Tārā*, 20–21.

149. Some important exceptions include Cuevas, *Tibetan Book of the Dead*; Bell, "Nechung"; Mills, *Identity, Ritual and State in Tibetan Buddhism.* See also the collection of essays
in Cabezón, *Tibetan Ritual.*

150. Lopez, *Prisoners of Shangri-La*, 16; on the use of "popish" as a deprecatory adjec-
tive, see Orsi, *History and Presence*, 33.

151. Waddell, *Tibetan Buddhism*, 145; cited in Lopez, *Prisoners of Shangri-La*, 42; see also
Robert Ekvall's condescending description of the endless "false prayers" resonating throughout Tibet. Bray, "Missionary Images of Tibet," 28.

152. Schram, *Monguors of the Kansu-Tibetan Border*, 399. Emphasis added.

153. This is an estimate. Louis Schram writes, "In 1914 I was told that among the 3,000
lamas of Kumbum, 1,300 were members of the College of Philosophy, 350 of the College of
Ritual, Magic and Astrology, 200 each in the College of Medicine and the College of Sacred
Scripture and Monastic Rules. All these numbers have to be reduced according to the ratio
previously noted for the 3,000 lamas of Kumbum, but the proportion is the same for the

members attending the colleges. Thus, among the 3,000 lamas 2,000 or two-thirds were enjoying a higher educational training in the colleges, and they remained members of the colleges for the whole of their lives. This was generally true for all of the colleges of Huang-chung." Schram, *Monguors of the Kansu-Tibetan Border*, 376–77.

154. Sosis, "Religion and Intragroup Cooperation," 76.

155. Ibid., 78–79; Sosis and Bressler, "Cooperation and Commune Longevity," 215.

156. Zehavi and Zahavi, *The Handicap Principle*.

157. Higher costs did not correlate with greater longevity among secular groups. The reasons for this are unclear, although the authors suggest it may have something to do with the unique features of religious beliefs (unfalsifiable) as opposed to secular beliefs. In short, it would seem costly signals work for religious groups but only because they interact in some still unknown way with other features of religious groups. Sosis and Bressler, "Cooperation and Commune Longevity."

158. McCleary and van der Kuijp also suggest that celibacy may have provided credibility to the Dge lugs monastic system. McCleary and van der Kuijp , "Market Approach," 165.

159. Sosis and Bressler explain that there are limits to the number and magnitude of costs that can be imposed on a religious community beyond which one should see a negative impact on the survivorship of the community. Sosis and Bressler, "Cooperation and Commune Longevity," 234n1, 235n10.

160. Melvyn Goldstein provides a rather lurid description of what he deems the "mass monasticism" of the Geluk school. Goldstein, "Revival of Monastic Life in Drepung Monastery," 17–18; cited in Dreyfus, *Sound of Two Hands Clapping*, 38; Schram, *Monguors of the Kansu-Tibetan Border*, 377–79, 386–90.

161. Religious *kibbutzim* have weathered shifting economies better than their secular counterparts and today are much more financially solvent than their secular counterparts. The authors therefore chose relatively successful secular *kibbutzim* for their study, ones more comparable to the religious *kibbutzim* in the study, even though these secular organizations are not representative of the overall state of secular *kibbutzim*. Sosis and Ruffle, "Religious Ritual and Cooperation."

162. Wiltermuth and Heath, "Synchrony and Cooperation," 4b. A more recent study corroborates and builds on the results of these and other, earlier studies: Jackson et al., "Synchrony and Physiological Arousal."

163. Sum pa mkhan po Ye shes dpal 'byor, "Dgon sde 'ga' zhig gi bca' yig," 129/13a.7. Here is another example taken from the constitution of another of Dgon lung's branch monasteries: "Hats without the *zhwa skro* and *zhwa lag* [i.e., the feather-like part on top and 'tail' that characterize the hat worn by Dge lugs pas during services], worn-out clothes, etc. are not to be worn." Smin grol III Ngag dbang 'phrin las rgya mtsho, "Theg chen thar pa gling gi bca' yig mu tig gi phreng mdzes," line 50.

164. Constitution no. 66, p. 28a.1–2. The language in a decree composed by the regent of Tibet at this time, the Demo Khutugtu, delivered on behalf of a Geluk monastery in Khams is equally disparaging of non-Geluk schools of Buddhism. Schwieger, *The Dalai Lama and the Emperor of China*, 170.

165. Boyer and Liénard, "Why Ritualized Behavior?"

166. Schjoedt et al., "Cognitive Resource Depletion in Religious Interactions."

167. Boyer and Liénard, "Why Ritualized Behavior?," 605b.

168. Interestingly, they find that this effect holds true even as participants gain familiarity with the ritual, although they admit that it is too early to say what the effect of famil-

iarization on cognitive processing during ritual is. Schjoedt et al., "Cognitive Resource Depletion in Religious Interactions," 46.

169. Schjoedt et al., "Cognitive Resource Depletion in Religious Interactions," 46.

170. Indeed, elsewhere, Sørensen and Nielbo write, "We speculate that non-functional actions serve as motivators for the construction of abstract information, giving the non-functional actions purpose and function although not a perceptually tangible one." Sørensen and Nielbo, "Prediction Error," 363.

171. McNeill, *Keeping Together in Time*.

CONCLUSION

1. Tiyavanich, *Forest Recollections*.

2. Ray, *Buddhist Saints in India*.

3. Gellner, *Anthropology of Buddhism and Hinduism*, 172.

4. Dutt, *Buddhist Monks and Monasteries of India*, 324; the distinction is also found in ch. 8, v. 39a–b of Vasubandhu, *L'Abhidharmakośa de Vasubandhu*.

5. DiValerio, *Holy Madmen of Tibet*, 164.

6. Lopez, *Prisoners of Shangri-La*, 3–4.

7. Kaschewsky, "The Image of Tibet in the West," 5, citing Jürgen Aschoff *Tsaparang—Königsstadt in Westtibet: Die vollständigen Berichte des Jesuitenpaters Antônio de Andrade und eine Beschreibung vom heutigen Zustand der Klöster* (Munich: MC-Verlag, 1989), pp. 43 ff.

8. Bishop, *The Myth of Shangri-La*.

9. Bray, "Missionary Images of Tibet," 28 citing Robert Ekvall, *Gateway to Tibet: the Kansu-Tibetan Border* (Harrisburg, PA: Christian Publications, 1938), 188.

10. Lopez, *Prisoners of Shangri-La*, 16–17.

11. Bray, "Missionary Images of Tibet," 27, citing Ekvall, *Gateway to Tibet*, p. 170.

12. He founded the Tantric College of Dgon lung byams pa gling in 1710.

13. Nietupski, *Labrang Monastery*, 19–22.

14. Ibid., 21–22.

15. Bishop, *The Myth of Shangri-La*, 140–41, passim.

16. The twentieth-century Japanese monk Ekai Kawaguchi (1866–1945), who traveled extensively in Tibet and the Himalayas, also judged rather harshly Tibetan Buddhist monsaticism. Kawaguchi, *Three Years in Tibet*, 348.

17. Heather, *The Restoration of Rome*.

18. Ibid., 335–43.

19. Ibid., 408.

20. Ibid., 299–414; a summary statement by Heather appears on p. 408.

21. However, new research on the role of "the Holder-of-the-Teachings Dharma-King" Güüshi Khan and his descendants in the development of law in Tibet and Mongolia promises to complicate too simple a picture of who helped to promote such reforms. Oidtmann, "The Laws of the Kökenuur Oirats."

22. Dreyfus, *Sound of Two Hands Clapping*, 347n42.

23. On the persistence of "patron communities" and the importance of the traditional ties between monasteries and client communities for the revival of Tibetan Buddhism in the post-Mao period, see Caple, *Morality and Monastic Revival in Post-Mao Tibet*, 31–35, 70–71.

24. Heather writes of the importance of the Catholic Church's "ideological force" for achieving its objectives as well as for its longevity. Heather, *The Restoration of Rome*, 409.

## APPENDIX

Note to Appendix title: This includes all extant and reliably datable constitutions that I have come across. Constitutions that I have been unable to assign to a particular date or time period are not included. Jann Ronis has uncovered at least one constitution composed by Situ Paṇchen Chos kyi 'byung gnas (1700–1774) in this period (in 1739). I have not yet had the opportunity to peruse this text. Ronis, "Celibacy, Revelations, and Reincarnated Lamas," 157n288.

1. Rong zom Chos kyi bzang po, "Sngags pa rnams kyi bca' yig"; Rong zom Chos kyi bzang po, "Rang slob dam tshig pa rnams la gsungs pa'i rwa ba brgyad pa'i bca' yig," 2:391–406. My references to Rong zom's text are to the latter unless otherwise noted. My thanks to Steve Weinberger at the University of Virginia for sharing with me his extensive notes of this constitution.

2. 'Jig rten mgon po, *The Collected Works (Bka' 'bum) of Khams gsum chos kyi rgyal po thub dbang rat+na śrī (Skyob pa 'Jig rten gsum mgon)*, 4 (nga): 126–28. I only recently became aware of this text. Attributed to the founder of the 'Bri gung Bka' brgyud school, it appears to describe the impoverished practitioner community of Stag lung thang pa Bkra shis dpal (1142–1209/1210): "Stag lung thang pa has passed away." (p. 126.4). It is clearly written for a community of renunciants, since it instructs them, "Do not engage in painting gods or writing, but focus on spiritual practice [*dge sbyor*]" (p. 127.4). The constitution mostly consists of instructions on how to survive a famine, something the community had apparently experienced over the previous two years: If you have fewer than three *zho* of provisions, then go collect more. If you have more than that, don't; instead, focus on spiritual practice. Moreover, once you have some food and receive your teachings (and resolve whatever questions you have about the dharma), you are urged to move on and not tarry.

3. 'Bri gung Grags pa 'byung gnas, *The Collected Works (Gsung 'bum) of Grags pa 'byung gnas*, 493/247a–499/250a.

4. Tsong kha pa Blo bzang grags pa, *Gsung 'bum*, 2 (kha): 686–98. This was composed in a *bya* year. His other constitution (no. 5) was also composed in a *bya* year, and it was composed at and for the Lhazhöl Hermitage (Lha zhol dben gnas byams pa gling), a place Tsong kha pa spent time in 1394 and again in 1397 or 1398. Thus, 1405, a *bya* year, is a likely year of composition.

5. Tsong kha pa Blo bzang grags pa, *Gsung 'bum*, 2 (kha): 698–713. See the preceding note regarding the year of composition.

6. Blo gros rgyal mtshan, *The Collected Works (Gsung 'bum) of Spyan-snga Blo-gros-rgyal-mtshan*, 4:79–84.

7. Shākya Mchog ldan, *The Complete Works (Gsung 'bum) of Gser-mdog Paṇ-chen Śākya-mchog-ldan*, 17 (tsa): 307–11.

8. Karma pa VIII Mi skyod rdo rje, *Karma pa Mi bskyod rdo rje bzhad pa'i gsung 'bum*, 3:688–93.

9. Ibid., 3:700–715.

10. Ibid., 19:997–1025.

11. A mgon Rin po che, *'Bri gung bka' brgyud chos mdzod chen mo* (The Great Treasury of Dharma of the Drigung Kagyü School), 66 (chu): 411–24. The title page instead gives "Bca' yig 'ching kun grol dri bral shel gyi ri bo."

12. Shes rab 'od zer, *Collected Writings of Shes-rab-'od-zer*, 455–60.

13. Karmapa IX Dbang phyug rdo rje, "Bca' ba chos khrims kyi skor gnang bkag gsal bar ston pa'i snang byed," 14b.7–23a.3.

14. Authorship of this constitution and most of the other constitutions in this compilation (BDRC W8LS16413) is not made explicit. Often, as in this constitution, reference is made to the Eighth Karma pa Mi skyod rdo rje (although it is typically misspelled as Mi spyod rdo rje) (p. 18a.4). These references are always in the third person and refer to the past acts of the Eighth Karma pa. Meanwhile, it is clear that these constitutions are by the lord of the Karma pa estate (*sgar chen*). The logical author is, therefore, the Ninth Karma pa. In addition, the Ninth Karmapa is explicitly mentioned as the author of the constitution of Karma dar rgyas gling (no. 18). Nonetheless, it is possible that some of these are by the Eighth Karma pa or that some of these texts were authored by him and later edited by the Ninth Karma pa.

15. Karmapa IX Dbang phyug rdo rje, "Bca' ba chos khrims kyi skor gnang bkag gsal bar ston pa'i snang byed," 23a.3–28.2.

16. Ibid., 28a.2–31a.7.

17. This is a title ultimately derived from the Chinese, Guanding guoshi 灌頂國師, "Consecration State Preceptor."

18. Karmapa IX Dbang phyug rdo rje, "Bca' ba chos khrims kyi skor gnang bkag gsal bar ston pa'i snang byed," 31a.7–33a.5.

19. Ibid., 1–14b.6.

20. Ibid., 33a.6–36b.6.

21. The Ninth Karmapa is explicitly mentioned as the author on p. 36b.4.

22. Karmapa IX Dbang phyug rdo rje, "Bca' ba chos khrims kyi skor gnang bkag gsal bar ston pa'i snang byed," 36b.6–49a.7.

23. Ibid., 49a.7–55a.3.

24. Ibid., 55a.3–61a.3.

25. Ibid., 61a.3–64a.5.

26. Ibid., 64a.5–73b.4.

27. 'Od zer rgya mtsho, *'Od zer rgya mtsho dpal bzang po'i gsung 'bum*, 683–89.

28. Ibid., 689–92.

29. Ibid., 693–96.

30. Ibid., 697–98.

31. Ibid., 845–76.

32. Paṇchen Lama IV Blo bzang chos kyi rgyal mtshan, *Rje btsun Blo bzang chos kyi rgyal mtshan gyi gsung 'bum*, 4 (nga): 501–16.

33. This text does not actually have a title. The editors have provided the title "Bca' yig chen mo." The text was written by the then head of the 'Brug pa bka' brgyud school at (though not explicitly *for*) his seat of Ra lung thel. Found in Dge 'dun 'dus tshogs of 'Brug gzhung grwa tshang ste ba spung thim chos sde, *Dpal 'brug dge 'dun phyag srol cha shas bstan 'dzin gzhon nu'i dga' tshal*, 2:95–100. My thanks to Manu Lopez for sharing this collection with me.

34. Sa skya khri chen Ngag dbang kun dga' bsod nams, *Dpal Sa skya pa Ngag dbang kun dga' bsod nams kyi gsung 'bum*, 27 (sha): 31–46.

35. The text has no title, although it tells us that it was composed for Khrig se Monastery, in Mang yul [Mar yul?]. It was founded by Dpal ldan shes rab, a disciple of Shes rab bzang po, himself one of the six disciples of Tsong kha pa sent to establish the Dge lugs school in distant lands. The monastery is also known as Khrig rtse and is located in Ladakh. Schuh and Phukhang, *Urkunden und Sendschreiben aus Zentraltibet, Ladakh und Zanskar*, document L.

36. Rdo sbis Tshe ring rdo rje and O rgyan chos 'phel, *Bca' yig phyogs bsgrigs*, 421–33. This was written down in a Wood-Monkey year based on an order issued by the Fifth Dalai Lama. In addition, an edict (T. *yi ge*) was issued in 1648, appointing a new abbot of the monastery, and this edict makes reference to the constitution in question. It is sandwiched between a constitution written for the Dalai Lama's medical school—that is, the Gso rig 'gro phan gling—and a document appointing the abbot of Ri bo bde chen Monastery in Mnga' ris. Dalai Lama V Ngag dbang blo bzang rgya mtsho, "Rwa sgreng dang ri bo bde chen sogs chos sde chung rigs 'gar stsal ba'i bka' yig sogs," 23 ('a): 30–38.

37. Dalai Lama V Ngag dbang blo bzang rgya mtsho, *Rgyal dbang lnga pa Ngag dbang blo bzang rgya mtsho'i gsung 'bum*, 23 ('a): 7–10.

38. The title given by the editors is "Rwa sgreng dang ri bo bde chen sogs chos sde chung rigs 'gar stsal ba'i bka' yig sogs." Dalai Lama V Ngag dbang blo bzang rgya mtsho, 23 ('a): 30–34. One finds on the first page the line, "*gso rig 'gro phan gling gi bca' tshe bri*" ("constitution written for the Medical College Dropen Ling"). As Stacey van Vleet has explained to me (personal communication, 3 June 2019), this is a reference to the Dalai Lama's medical school at 'Bras spungs Monastery, which he established in 1645. This constitution may have been written at the time of its founding. The full name of the famous Lcags po ri medical college founded by Sangs rgyas rgya mtsho in 1696 also includes *'gro phan*: Lcags ri bai DUr+ya *'gro phan* lta nan go mtshar rig byed gling. However, this is actually a reference to the older school established by the Dalai Lama in 1645 and known as the Gso rig 'gro phan gling. The full name of Lcags po ri is found in Sde srid Sangs rgyas rgya mtsho, *Sde srid sman gyi khog 'bubs*, 392. The Dalai Lama mentions his founding of the 'Bras spungs medical school in his autobiography, Dalai Lama V Ngag dbang blo bzang rgya mtsho, "Za hor gyi ban+de Ngag dbang blo bzang rgya mtsho'i 'di sngang 'khrul ba'i rol rtsed rtogs brjod kyi tshul du bkod pa du kU la'i gos bzang," 246/128b; Dalai Lama V Ngagwang Lobzang Gyatsho [Ngag dbang blo bzang rgya mtsho], *The Illusive Play*, 197. My thanks to van Vleet for these references.

39. Dalai Lama V Ngag dbang blo bzang rgya mtsho, *Rgyal dbang lnga pa Ngag dbang blo bzang rgya mtsho'i gsung 'bum*, 23 ('a): 19–23. Composed on the eleventh day of the sixth month.

40. The full title given by the editors is "Rgyal dbang sku phreng lnga pa Ngag dbang blo bzang rgya mtshos smon lam chen mo'i mtshan rtags skor la bstsal ba'i dran tho." However, a more accurate title would be "Me phag smon lam chen mo'i thog nas bzung 'gyur med lag tu len dgos kyi dran tho," as found on p. 3. Rdo sbis Tshe ring rdo rje and O rgyan chos 'phel, *Bca' yig phyogs bsgrigs*, 1–6.

41. Dalai Lama V Ngag dbang blo bzang rgya mtsho, *Rgyal dbang lnga pa Ngag dbang blo bzang rgya mtsho'i gsung 'bum*, 23 ('a): 11–18.

42. Ibid., 23 ('a): 24–29.

43. Ibid., 23 ('a): 39–47.

44. The full title given by the editors is "Rgyal dbang sku phreng lnga pa Ngag dbang blo bzang rgya mtshos sku 'bum byams pa gling la bstsal ba'i bca' yig". Rdo sbis Tshe ring rdo rje and O rgyan chos 'phel, *Bca' yig phyogs bsgrigs*, 7–10.

45. Dalai Lama V Ngag dbang blo bzang rgya mtsho, *Rgyal dbang lnga pa Ngag dbang blo bzang rgya mtsho'i gsung 'bum*, 23 ('a): 69–76.

46. Ibid., 23 ('a): 58–68.

47. The full title given by the editors is "Rgyal dbang sku phreng lnga pa Ngag dbang blo bzang rgya mtshos lha ldan cho 'phrul smon lam chen mo'i tshogs bzhugs dge 'dun spyi la bstsal ba'i bca' yig." Rdo sbis Tshe ring rdo rje and O rgyan chos 'phel, *Bca' yig phyogs bsgrigs*, 14–32.

48. The full title given by the editors is "Rgyal dbang sku phreng lnga pa Ngag dbang blo bzang rgya mtshos chos sde chen po zha lu'u sgrub mchod bco lnga gsar tshugs skabs bstsal ba'i bca' yig shes dkar me long." Rdo sbis Tshe ring rdo rje and O rgyan chos 'phel, *Bca' yig phyogs bsgrigs*, 33–57.

49. The full title given by the editors is "Rgyal dbang sku phreng lnga pa Ngag dbang blo bzang rgya mtshos bstsal ba'i nyang smad bsam don lhun gyis grub pa'i rdzong chen du tshe'i rig byed gso ba rig pa'i grwa tshang drang srong 'dus pa'i gling gi bca' yig." Rdo sbis Tshe ring rdo rje and O rgyan chos 'phel, *Bca' yig phyogs bsgrigs*, 58–70.

50. The full title given by the editors is "Rgyal dbang sku phreng lnga pa Ngag dbang blo bzang rgya mtshos bstsal ba'i pho brang po ta la'i sum skas mgo'i bca' yig." Rdo sbis Tshe ring rdo rje and O rgyan chos 'phel, *Bca' yig phyogs bsgrigs*, 11–13.

51. It is known from other sources that constitutions for other places in Khams were being issued around this time (1679–1680). The date of composition here is an educated guess only.

52. Dalai Lama V Ngag dbang blo bzang rgya mtsho, *Rgyal dbang lnga pa Ngag dbang blo bzang rgya mtsho'i gsung 'bum*, 23 ('a): 77–86.

53. It is known from other sources that constitutions for other places in Khams were being issued around this time (1679–1680). The date of composition here is an educated guess only.

54. Dalai Lama V Ngag dbang blo bzang rgya mtsho, *Rgyal dbang lnga pa Ngag dbang blo bzang rgya mtsho'i gsung 'bum*, 23 ('a): 87–93.

55. This is the title provided by the editors. The colophon of the text includes the following title: "Rdo rje gdan gnyis pa 'bri gung byang chub gling gi 'dus pa rgya mtsho rnams kyi bca' sgrig la skabs su babs pa'i . . . [text missing] kun gsal du bgyis pa'i yi ge." It is found in A mgon Rin po che, *'Bri gung bka' brgyud chos mdzod chen mo* [The Great Treasury of Dharma of the Drigung Kagyü School], 115 (re): 545/273a–556/277b.3.

56. Dalai Lama V Ngag dbang blo bzang rgya mtsho, *Rgyal dbang lnga pa Ngag dbang blo bzang rgya mtsho'i gsung 'bum*, 23 ('a): 157–94. I also consulted the following version, though I found it to contain more spelling and grammatical errors: Krung go bod brgyud mtho rim nang bstan slob gling gi slob gzhi rtsom sgrig tsho chung, *Bca' yig phyogs sgrig*, 169–213.

57. Like constitution no. 50, this is listed under the title "'Bri gdan byang chub gling gi bca' yig nyes brgya kun grol." It is found in A mgon Rin po che, *'Bri gung bka' brgyud chos mdzod chen mo* [The Great Treasury of Dharma of the Drigung Kagyü School], 115 (re): 556/277b.3–565/282a.2.

58. Revised in 1708. Printed in 1717 together with the "*bu*" (child) constitutions (no. 54). In Gter bdag gling pa 'Gyur med rdo rje, *Gsung 'bum* [Collected Works of Tertak Lingpa Gyurmé Dorjé], 16 (*ma*): 61a–95b. See also Cuevas, "Preliminary Remarks on the History of Mindroling"; Townsend, "Materials of Buddhist Culture"; Townsend, "How to Constitute a Field of Merit." Townsend has argued that despite being a constitution for a "Rnying ma" monastery, it also makes several overtures to the Dge lugs school. In particular, the constitution

esteems *both* scholasticism *and* meditation/tantra, *both* celibacy *and* lay practice. This, Townsend suggests, has to do with the dominance of the newly founded Dga' ldan pho brang government of the Dalai Lama as well as the intimate relationships that existed between Gter bdag gling pa, the Fifth Dalai Lama, and Sde srid Sangs rgyas rgya mtsho. My own reading of this constitution corroborates Townsend's findings. In the opening lines of the constitution one immediately gets the impression that this monastery, Smin grol gling, is a place that is supposed to adhere to the ways of *both* scholar-monks *and* tantric adepts (*paN grub*; *bla chen khan rgyud* and *sngags 'chang chen po*). The Vinaya is identified as the basis of both the way of the scriptures (*klog pa thos bsam*) and the way of practice and meditation (*sgrub pa bsam gtan*) (pp. 63a.6–63b.2 / 3a.6–3b.2). Serious study and exegesis of scriptures, including the tantras, is underscored (no. 54, pp. 102a–b / 7a–b), debate takes place (no. 53, p. 86b.6 / 21b.6), and exams are held (pp. 73b / 13b, 81b.6 / 21b.6 and no. 54, pp. 99b.6–10a.1 / 4b.6–5a.1). Expensive offerings, such as instruments and canopies (*bla re*), are to be given directly to the common wealth (*spyi rdzas*) of the monastery, and particular importance is given to the impartiality of monastic officials and especially the disciplinarians (no. 54, p. 109a–b). These and other features of Bter bdag gling pa's constitutions for Smin grol gling parallel features found in Dge lugs constitutions. This constitution (no. 53) even prescribes the annual commemoration of the death (*dgongs rdzogs sgrub mchod*) of the father of the Fifth Dalai Lama (87a.3 / 27a.3). I do not see evidence that Bter bdag gling pa copied directly from the Fifth Dalai lama's constitutions or any other Dge lugs constitution, but the influence of such constitutions and of Dge lugs monastic governance is obvious. However, at the same time, the constitution is less bureaucratic than a Dge lugs constitution insofar as it is more centered on the figure of the lama, Gter bdag gling pa himself, and underscores the importance of tantric commitments (S. *samaya*) (e.g. no. 54, p. 108a.6 / 13a.6). This is a long and complex constitution and deserving of additional study.

59. Compiled in 1707. Printed in 1717 together with the *"ma"* (mother) constitution (no. 53). In Gter bdag gling pa 'Gyur med rdo rje, *Gsung 'bum* [Collected Works of Tertak Lingpa Gyurmé Dorjé], 16 (ma): 96a–113a.

60. Ngag dbang rnam rgyal, *Rta wang dga' ldan rnam rgyal lha rtse'i bca' yig mdor bsdus*. On the importance of this monastery to the new Dga' ldan pho brang government, see Ardussi, "Bhutan Before the British," 328.

61. In Lcang skya II Ngag dbang blo bzang chos ldan, *Gsung 'bum*, vol. 7 (ja). The colophon explains that it was composed at the Bod chos lha khang in Beijing, so it was probably done between 1698 and 1714, although the date could be even earlier and between 1693–1697.

62. The colophon explains that it was composed at Dgon lung Monastery (Dgon klung byams pa gling). Thus, I conjecture it was composed between 1697 and 1714. Also, I suspect that it is based in part on the constitution he composed for Dga' ldan byang chub gling (no. 56) and thus dates to after that constitution.

63. Brag dkar sngags rams pa Blo bzang bstan pa rab rgyas, *Gsung 'bum*, 1:684/4b.6–687/6a.4.

64. Schuh and Phukhang, *Urkunden und Sendschreiben aus Zentraltibet, Ladakh und Zanskar*, 2:61–64. The "mother monastery" is Chos 'khor shar gling in Matho (or Masho, Mang spro). The "children monasteries" referred to are Skyid mang and Gog mig. All of these are associated with the Sa skya school. More information can be found at https://sakyaresearch.org/places, accessed 8 March 2019.

65. The date for the constitution is difficult to calculate with total confidence. The author gives us the date of composition since the time of the Buddha Śākyamuni's birth, en-

lightenment and first teaching, and death. However, it is not clear which system of calculation he is using. He also tells us that it was completed in an Earth-Female-Pig year (p. 2b.4–5). Given that the monastery named in the constitution seems to correspond to the famous Labrang Monastery (Bla brang bkra shis 'khyil) and is found in the *Collected Works* of 'Jam dbyangs bzhad pa I, 1719 seems to be the most logical year. By using Bu ston's dates for the Buddha's life, one also arrives at 1719 or thereabout (1721 based on his birth, 1720 based on his enlightenment and first teaching, and 1719 based on his death).

66. 'Jam dbyangs bzhad pa I Ngag dbang brtson 'grus, *Gsung 'bum* [Collected Works of Jamyang Zhepa I Ngawang Tsöndrü], 817–24. BDRC W21503. The same constitution is also found in the other versions of the author's *Collected Works*.

67. Dalai Lama VII Skal bzang rgya mtsho, *The Collected Works (Gsung 'bum) of the Seventh Dalai Lama*, 3 (ga): 270–87.

68. Rgyal sras 'Jigs med ye shes grags pa, *Gsung 'bum*, 24 ('a): 1–9a.4.

69. Rdo sbis Tshe ring rdo rje and O rgyan chos 'phel, *Bca' yig phyogs bsgrigs*, 71–79.

70. No date is given for this constitution. It was compiled in the author's *Gsung 'bum* alongside his constitutions for Snar thang and Dgon lung Monasteries. In addition, we are told that it was composed in response to the request made by Daichingbaatar (Khang chen nas), who died in 1727.

71. Rgyal sras 'Jigs med ye shes grags pa, *Gsung 'bum*, 24 ('a): 9a.4–17b.6.

72. Cuevas has mistaken the colophon for another of this author's constitutions for the colophon to this text. As a result, he provides the date of composition as the ninth month of 1709. The actual date of composition is the fifth month of a Fire Sheep year, which could only be 1727. Note that this pushes the Brak dkar Sngags rams pa's death date forward in time by at least a year beyond Cuevas's estimate. Cuevas, "Sorcerer of the Iron Castle," 18, 49.

73. Brag dkar sngags rams pa Blo bzang bstan pa rab rgyas, *Gsung 'bum*, 677–84. Cuevas refers the reader to additional constitutions for this hermitage in a modern compilation, although those texts both appear to be unrelated to the constitution in question here and they are twentieth-century compositions (one is dated to 1922; the other does not have a clear date). Cuevas, "Sorcerer of the Iron Castle," 18n49.

74. The colophon does not mention the author's name but an epithet, Su ma ti (Sumati).

75. Rgyal sras 'Jigs med ye shes grags pa, *Gsung 'bum*, 24 ('a): 7b.6–38b.2.

76. In Blo bzang bsam gtan, *Rje Ngag dbang blo bzang bsam gtan gyi gsung 'bum*, 2: 429–35.

77. Rdo sbis Tshe ring rdo rje and O rgyan chos 'phel, *Bca' yig phyogs bsgrigs*, 80–98. The constitution found immediately after this one in this collection, on pp. 99–117, is identical.

78. No date is given in the text. The proposed date is based instead on the author's other constitution (no. 67).

79. In Blo bzang bsam gtan, *Rje Ngag dbang blo bzang bsam gtan gyi gsung 'bum*, 2:395–99.

80. The colophon of the constitution itself does not provide the author's name, but it does provide an epithet, Su ma ti bha dra d+hye na (Sumati Vajra Dhyāna).

# Bibliography

## WESTERN-LANGUAGE SOURCES

Ahmad, Zahiruddhin. *Sino-Tibetan Relations in the Seventeenth Century*. Serie Orientale Roma, XL. Roma: Istituto italiano per il Medio ed Estremo Oriente, 1970.

Apple, James B. *Stairway to Nirvāṇa: A Study of the Twenty* Saṃghas *Based on the Works of Tsong Kha Pa*. Albany: State University of New York Press, 2008.

Ardussi, John A. "Bhutan Before the British: A Historical Study." Ph.D. diss., Australian National University, 1977.

Ardussi, John. "Formation of the State of Bhutan ('Brug gzhung) in the 17th Century and Its Tibetan Antecedents." In *The Relationship Between Religion and State (chos srid zung 'brel) in Traditional Tibet: Proceedings of a Seminar Held in Lumbini, Nepal, March 2000*, edited by Christoph Cüppers, 4:33–48. Monograph Series. Lumbini: Lumbini International Research Institute, 2004.

Aris, Michael. *Hidden Treasures and Secret Lives: A Study of Pemalingpa (1450–1521) and the Sixth Dalai Lama (1683–1706)*. London: Kegan Paul International, 1989.

Ary, Elijah. *Authorized Lives: Biography and the Early Formation of Geluk Identity*. Somerville, Mass.: Wisdom, 2015.

Asad, Talal. *Genealogies of Religion: Discipline and Reasons of Power in Christianity and Islam*. Baltimore: Johns Hopkins University Press, 1993.

Bell, Christopher. "Nechung: The Ritual History and Institutionalization of a Tibetan Buddhist Protector Deity." Ph.D. diss., University of Virginia, 2013.

Bell, Christopher. "The Nechung Record." *Revue d'Études Tibétaines* 36 (October 2016): 143–249.

Bentor, Yael. "Literature on Consecration (*Rab gnas*)." In *Tibetan Literature: Studies in Genre*, edited by José Ignacio Cabezón and Roger R. Jackson, 290–311. Ithaca, N.Y.: Snow Lion Publications, 1996.

Berry, Beth. "Public Life in Authoritarian Japan." *Daedalus* 127, no. 3 (Summer 1998): 133–65.

Berry, Beth. "Public Peace and Private Attachment: The Goals and Conduct of Power in Early Modern Japan." *Journal of Japanese Studies* 12, no. 2 (Summer 1986): 237–71.

Berzin, Alexander. "A Brief History of Gyumay and Gyuto Lower and Upper Tantric Colleges." Berzin Archives, 2003. www.berzinarchives.com/web/en/index.html.

Beyer, Stephan. *The Cult of Tārā: Magic and Ritual in Tibet*. Berkeley: University of California Press, 1973.

Bishop, Peter. *The Myth of Shangri-La: Tibet, Travel Writing and the Western Creation of Sacred Landscape*. Berkeley: University of California Press, 1989.

Blo bzang 'phrin las, Dung dkar. *The Merging of Religious and Secular Rule in Tibet.* Translated by Chen Guangsheng. Beijing: Foreign Languages Press, 1991.

Borjigin, Burensain. "The Complex Structure of Ethnic Conflict in the Frontier: Through the Debates Around the 'Jindandao Incident' in 1891." *Inner Asia* 6, no. 1 (1 January 2004): 41–60.

Boyer, Pascal, and Pierre Liénard. "Why Ritualized Behavior? Precaution Systems and Action Parsing in Developmental, Pathological and Cultural Rituals." *Behavioral and Brain Sciences* 29, no. 6 (2006): 595–613.

Bray, John. "Nineteenth- and Early Twentieth-Century Missionary Images of Tibet." In *Imagining Tibet: Perceptions, Projections, & Fantasies,* edited by Thierry Dodin and Heinz Räther, 21–45. Boston: Wisdom Publications, 2001.

Bstan-'dzin-rgya-mtsho, Daniel Goleman, Robert A. F. Thurman, and Howard Gardner. *MindScience: An East-West Dialogue.* Boston: Wisdom Publications, 1991.

Buddhist Digital Resource Center (BDRC, formerly Tibetan Buddhist Resource Center), 1999. www.tbrc.org.

Burbank, Jane, and Frederick Cooper. *Empires in World History: Power and the Politics of Difference.* Princeton, N.J.: Princeton University Press, 2010.

Cabezón, José Ignacio. *Buddhism and Language: A Study of Indo-Tibetan Scholasticism.* Albany: State University of New York Press, 1994.

Cabezón, José Ignacio. "An Introduction to Sera's Colleges." The Tibetan and Himalayan Library, 2006. www.thlib.org/places/monasteries/sera/essays/#!essay=/cabezon/sera/colleges/intro/s/b24.

Cabezón, José Ignacio, ed. *Scholasticism: Cross-Cultural and Comparative Perspectives.* Albany: State University of New York Press, 1998.

Cabezón, José Ignacio. *Tibetan Ritual.* New York: Oxford University Press, 2010.

Caple, Jane E. *Morality and Monastic Revival in Post-Mao Tibet.* Contemporary Buddhism. Honolulu: University of Hawai'i Press, 2019.

Carrasco Pizana, Pedro. *Land and Polity in Tibet.* Seattle: University of Washington Press, 1959.

Cassinelli, C. W., and Robert B. Ekvall. *A Tibetan Principality: The Political System of Sa SKya.* Ithaca, N.Y.: Cornell University Press, 1969.

Caumanns, Volker. "Paṇ chen Shākya mchog ldan's Monastic Seat Thub bstan gser mdog can (Part 1): The History of Its Foundation." In *Nepalica-Tibetica: Festgabe for Christoph Cüppers,* edited by Franz-Karl Ehrhard and Petra Maurer, 65–88. Andiast: IITBS, International Institute for Tibetan and Buddhist Studies, 2013.

Chaney, Wesley Byron. "Land, Trade, and the Law on the Sino-Tibetan Border, 1723–1911." Ph.D. diss., Stanford University, 2016.

Charleux, Isabelle. *Temples et monastères de Mongolie-Intérieure.* Archéologie et histoire de l'art 23. Paris: Éditions du Comité des travaux historiques et scientifiques: Institut national d'histoire de l'art, 2006.

Chayet, Anne. "The Potala, Symbol of the Power of the Dalai Lamas." In *Lhasa in the Seventeenth Century: The Capital of the Dalai Lamas,* edited by Françoise Pommaret, translated by Howard Solverson, 39–52. Boston: Brill, 2003.

*Chinese Legal Documents Series: International Society for Chinese Law and History* (blog); "A Document from the Xunhua Archives," by Max Oidtmann, http://chineselawandhistory.com/blog/2014/10/23/chinese-legal-documents-series-001/, posted November 2014.

Chou, Wen-shing. "Reimagining the Buddhist Universe: Pilgrimage and Cosmography in the Court of the Thirteenth Dalai Lama (1876–1933)." *Journal of Asian Studies* 73, no. 2 (May 2014): 419–45.

Cowell, E. B., ed. *The Jātaka: Or, Stories of the Buddha's Former Births*. Translated by Robert Chalmers. Cambridge: University Press [of Cambridge], 1895.

Cuevas, Bryan J. *The Hidden History of the Tibetan Book of the Dead*. New York: Oxford University Press, 2003.

Cuevas, Bryan J. "Preliminary Remarks on the History of Mindroling: The Founding and Organization of a Tibetan Monastery in the Seventeenth Century." n.p., n.d.

Cuevas, Bryan J. "Sorcerer of the Iron Castle: The Life of Blo bzang bstan pa rab rgyas, the First Brag dkar sngags rams pa of A mdo (c. 1647–1726)." *Revue d'Études Tibétaines* 39 (April 2017): 5–59.

Dalai Lama V Ngagwang Lobzang Gyatsho [Ngag dbang blo bzang rgya mtsho]. *The Illusive Play: The Autobiography of the Fifth Dalai Lama*. Translated by Samten G. Karmay. Chicago: Serindia Publications, 2014.

Das, Sarat Chandra. "The Monasteries of Tibet." *Journal of the Asiatic Society of Bengal*, New Series, 1 (1905): 106–16.

Das, Sarat Chandra. *Narrative of a Journey Round Lake Yamdo (Palti), and in Lhokha, Yarlung, and Sakya, in 1882*. Calcutta, 1887.

Davidson, Ronald M. "The Litany of Names of Mañjuśrī: Text and Translation of the Mañjuśrīnāmasaṃgīti." In *Tantric and Taoist Studies in Honour of R.A. Stein*, edited by Michel Strickmann, 1:1–69. Mélanges Chinois et Bouddhiques 20. Bruxelles: Institut belge des hautes études chinoises, 1981.

Davidson, Ronald M. *Tibetan Renaissance: Tantric Buddhism in the Rebirth of Tibetan Culture*. New York: Columbia University Press, 2005.

DiValerio, David M. *The Holy Madmen of Tibet*. New York: Oxford University Press, 2015.

Dorje, Gyurme. *Footprint Tibet Handbook*. 4th ed. Bath: Footprint Handbooks, 2009.

Doyle, Michael W. *Empires*. Ithaca, N.Y.: Cornell University Press, 1986.

Dreyfus, Georges. "An Introduction to Drepung's Colleges." The Drepung Monastery Project, 2006. www.thlib.org/places/monasteries/drepung/essays/#!essay=/dreyfus/drepung/colleges/s/b1.

Dreyfus, Georges. "Proto-Nationalism in Tibet." In *Tibetan Studies*, edited by Per Kvaerne, 1:205–18. Oslo: Institute for Comparative Research, 1994.

Dreyfus, Georges. *The Sound of Two Hands Clapping: The Education of a Tibetan Buddhist Monk*. Berkeley: University of California Press, 2003.

Dreyfus, Georges. "Tibetan Religious Nationalism." In *Tibet, Self, and the Tibetan Diaspora: Voices of Differences: Proceedings of the Ninth Seminar of the International Association for Tibetan Studies*, 37–56. Leiden: Brill, 2002.

Dreyfus, Georges. "Where Do Commentarial Schools Come From? Reflections on the History of Tibetan Scholasticism." *Journal of the International Association of Buddhist Studies* 28, no. 2 (2005): 273–97.

Dutt, Sukumar. *Buddhist Monks and Monasteries of India: Their History and Their Contribution to Indian Culture*. Delhi: Motilal Banarsidass Publishers, 1962.

Ehrhard, Franz-Karl. "A 'Hidden Land' at the Border of 'Ol-kha and Dvags-po." Edited by Roberto Vitali. *The Tibet Journal: The Earth Ox Papers; Proceedings of the International Seminar on Tibetan and Himalayan Studies, Dharamsala, 2009* 34–35, no. 3–4 and 1–2 (Autumn 2009 through Summer 2010): 493–522.

Ellingson, Ter. "Don rta dbyangs gsum: Tibetan Chant and Melodic Categories." *Asian Music* 10, no. 2 (1 January 1979): 112–56.

Ellingson, Ter. "The Mandala of Sound: Concepts and Sound Structures in Tibetan Ritual Music." Ph.D. diss., University of Wisconsin-Madison, 1979.

Ellingson, Ter. "Tibetan Monastic Constitutions: The Bca' yig." In *Reflections on Tibetan Culture: Essays in Memory of Turrell V. Wylie*, edited by Lawrence Epstein and Richard F. Sherburne, 12:205–29. Studies in Asian Thought and Religion. Lewiston, N.Y.: Edwin Mellen Press, 1990.

Elverskog, Johan. *The Jewel Translucent Sūtra: Altan Khan and the Mongols in the Sixteenth Century*. Leiden: Brill, 2003.

Elverskog, Johan. "Tibetocentrism, Religious Conversion and the Study of Mongolian Buddhism." In *The Mongolia-Tibet Interface: Opening New Research Terrains in Inner Asia; Proceedings of the Tenth Seminar of the International Association for Tibetan Studies, Oxford, 2003*, edited by Uradyn E. Bulag and Hildegard Diemberger, 10/9:59–81. Boston: Brill, 2007.

Everding, Karl-Heinz. "gSang phu Ne'u thog, Tibet's Earliest Monastic School (1073): Reflections on the Rise of Its Grva tshang bcu gsum and Bla khag bcu." *Zentralasiatische Studien (Festschrift Für Prof. Dr. Veronika Veit)* 38 (2009): 137–54.

Foulk, Theodore Griffith. "The 'Ch'an School' and Its Place in the Buddhist Monastic Tradition (Zen, Japan, China)." Ph.D. diss., University of Michigan, 1987.

Gellner, David N. *The Anthropology of Buddhism and Hinduism: Weberian Themes*. New Delhi: Oxford University Press, 2001.

Gentry, James Duncan. *Power Objects in Tibetan Buddhism: The Life, Writings, and Legacy of Sokdokpa Lodrö Gyeltsen*. Boston: Brill, 2017.

Gentry, James Duncan. "Substance and Sense: Objects of Power in the Life, Writings, and Legacy of the Tibetan Ritual Master Sog Bzlog Pa Blo Gros Rgyal Mtshan." Ph.D. diss., Harvard University, 2014.

Germano, David. "Food, Clothes, Dreams, and Karmic Propensities." In *Religions of Tibet in Practice*, edited by Donald S. Lopez, 293–312. Princeton, N.J.: Princeton University Press, 1997.

Goldstein, Melvyn C. "Bouddhisme tibétain et monachisme de masse" [Tibetan Buddhism and mass monasticism]. In *Des moines et des moniales dans le monde: La vie monastique dans le miroir de la parenté*, edited by Adeline Herrou and Gisèle Krauskopff, 409–24. Paris: L'Harmattan, 2009.

Goldstein, Melvyn C. *A History of Modern Tibet, 1913–1951: The Demise of the Lamaist State*. Berkeley: University of California Press, 1989.

Goldstein, Melvyn C., T. N. Shelling, and J. T. Surkhang, eds. *The New Tibetan-English Dictionary of Modern Tibetan*. Berkeley: University of California Press, 2001.

Goldstein, Melvyn C. "The Revival of Monastic Life in Drepung Monastery." In *Buddhism in Contemporary Tibet: Religious Revival and Cultural Identity*, edited by Matthew T. Kapstein and Melvyn C. Goldstein, 15–52. Berkeley: University of California Press, 1998.

Goldstein, Melvyn C. "Tibetan Buddhism and Mass Monasticism" [English translation of "Bouddhisme tibétain et monachisme de masse"]. The Center for Research on Tibet, n.d. www.case.edu/affil/tibet/currentStaff/goldstein.htm.

Gorski, Philip S. *The Disciplinary Revolution: Calvinism and the Rise of the State in Early Modern Europe*. Chicago: University of Chicago Press, 2003.

Gorski, Philip S. "The Protestant Ethic and the Bureaucratic Revolution: Ascetic Protestantism and Administrative Rationalization in Early Modern Europe." In *Max Weber's Economy and Society: A Critical Companion*, edited by Charles Camic, David M. Trubek, and Philip S. Gorski, 267–96. Stanford, Calif.: Stanford University Press, 2005.

Gorski, Philip S. "The Return of the Repressed: Religion and the Political Unconscious of Historical Sociology." In *Remaking Modernity: Politics, History, and Sociology*, edited by Julia Adams, Elisabeth S. Clemens, and Ann Shola Orloff, 161–89. Durham, N.C.: Duke University Press, 2005.

Graeber, David. *The Utopia of Rules on Technology, Stupidity, and the Secret Joys of Bureaucracy.* Brooklyn, N.Y.: Melville House, 2016.

Griffiths, Rachael. "A Polymath from Amdo: The Many Hats of Sumpa Khenpo Yeshe Paljor (1704–1788)." Ph.D. diss., University of Oxford, anticipated 2020.

Guy, R. Kent. "Who Were the Manchus? A Review Essay." *Journal of Asian Studies* 61, no. 1 (2002): 151–64.

Hartley, Lauran. "Self as a Faithful Public Servant: The Autobiography of Mdo mkhar ba Tshe ring dbang rgyal (1697–1763)." In *Mapping the Modern in Tibet*, edited by Gray Tuttle, 45–72. Andiast, Switzerland: IITBS, International Institute for Tibetan and Buddhist Studies GmbH, 2011.

Heather, Peter. *The Restoration of Rome: Barbarian Popes and Imperial Pretenders.* New York: Oxford University Press, 2013.

Heissig, Walther. *Die Pekinger lamaistischen Blockdrucke in mongolischer Sprache Materialien zur mongolischen Literaturgeschichte.* Wiesbaden: O. Harrassowitz, 1954.

Heller, Amy. "Étude sur le développement de l'iconographie et du culte de Beg-tse, divinité protectrice tibétaine." Ph.D. diss., l'École Pratique des Hautes Études, 1992.

Heller, Amy. "The Great Protector Deities of the Dalai Lamas." In *Lhasa in the Seventeenth Century: The Capital of the Dalai Lamas*, edited by Françoise Pommaret, translated by Howard Solverson, 81–98. Boston: Brill, 2003.

Heller, Amy. "Historic and Iconographic Aspects of the Protective Deities Srung-Ma Dmar-Nag." In *Tibetan Studies: Proceedings of the 5th Seminar of the International Association for Tibetan Studies, Narita 1989*, edited by Ihara Shōren and Yamaguchi Zuihō, 2:497–92. Tokyo: Naritasan Sinshoji, 1992.

Hendrickx, Jeroom. "Louis J. M. Schram, CICM: Missionary and Ethnologist." In *The Monguors of the Kansu-Tibetan Border*, edited by Charles Kevin Stuart, 51–59. Xining: Plateau Publications, 2006.

Hopkins, Jeffrey, ed. *Tantra in Tibet: The Great Exposition of Secret Mantra.* Vol. 1. London: Allen and Unwin, 1977.

Hopkins, Jeffrey, ed. *Tantra in Tibet: The Great Exposition of Secret Mantra.* Vols. 2–3. London: Allen and Unwin, 1981.

Hopkins, Jeffrey, and Jongbok Yi. *The Hidden Teaching of the Perfection of Wisdom Sutras: Jamyang-shay-pa's Seventy Topics and Kon-chog-jig-may-wang-po's Supplement.* Dyke, Va.: UMA Institute for Tibetan Studies, 2013.

Horner, I. B. *The Book of the Discipline: (Vinaya-Piṭaka).* Translated by I. B. Horner. 4 vols. London: Pali Text Society, 1963 (1951).

Huber, Toni. *The Cult of Pure Crystal Mountain: Popular Pilgrimage and Visionary Landscape in Southeast Tibet.* New York: Oxford University Press, 1999.

Hugon, Pascale. "Arguments by Parallels in the Epistemological Works of Phya pa Chos kyi seng ge." *Argumentation* 22, no. 1 (6 February 2008): 93–114.

Illich, Marina. "Imperial Stooge or Emissary to the Dge Lugs Throne? Rethinking the Bi-ographies of Changkya Rolpé Dorjé." In *Power, Politics, and the Reinvention of Tradition: Tibet in the Seventeenth and Eighteenth Centuries; Proceedings of the Tenth Seminar of the International Association for Tibetan Studies, Oxford, 2003*, edited by Bryan J. Cuevas and Kurtis R. Schaeffer, 17–32. Boston: Brill, 2006.

Ishihama Yumiko 石濱裕美子. "On the Dissemination of the Belief in the Dalai Lama as a Manifestation of the Bodhisattva Avalokiteśvara." *Acta Asiatica* 64 (1993): 38–56.

Jackson, David Paul. *The Entrance Gate for the Wise (Section III): Sa-Skya Paṇḍita on Indian and Tibetan Traditions of Pramāṇa and Philosophical Debate.* Vienna: Arbeitskreis für Tibetische und Buddhistische Studien, Universität Wien, 1987.

Jackson, Joshua Conrad, Jonathan Jong, David Bilkey, Harvey Whitehouse, Stefanie Zoll-mann, Craig McNaughton, and Jamin Halberstadt. "Synchrony and Physiological Arousal Increase Cohesion and Cooperation in Large Naturalistic Groups." *Scientific Reports* 8, no. 1 (9 January 2018): 1–8.

Jackson, Roger R. "The dGe ldan-bKa' brgyud Tradition of Mahāmudrā: How Much dGe ldan? How Much bKa' brgyud?" In *Changing Minds: Contributions to the Study of Buddhism and Tibet in Honor of Jeffrey Hopkins*, edited by Guy Newland, 155–91. Ithaca, N.Y.: Snow Lion Publications, 2001.

Jackson, Roger R. "Kalachakra in Context." In *The Wheel of Time: The Kalachakra in Context*, edited by John Newman, Geshé Lhundub Sopa, and Roger R. Jackson. Ithaca, N.Y.: Snow Lion Publications, 1991.

Jalsan. "The Reincarnations of Desi Sangye Gyatso in Alasha and the Secret History of the Sixth Dalai Lama." *Inner Asia* 4, no. 2 (2002): 347–59.

Jansen, Berthe. "How to Tame a Wild Monastic Elephant: Drepung Monastery According to the Great Fifth." In *Tibetans Who Escaped the Historian's Net: Studies in the Social History of Tibetan Societies*, edited by Charles Ramble, Peter Schwieger, and Alice Travers, 111–40. Kathmandu: Vajra Books, 2013.

Jansen, Berthe. "The Monastery Rules: Buddhist Monastic Organization in Pre-Modern Tibet." Ph.D. diss., Leiden University, 2014.

Jansen, Berthe. *The Monastery Rules: Buddhist Monastic Organization in Pre-Modern Tibet.* Oakland: University of California Press, 2018.

Kapstein, Matthew T. "Buddhism, Schools of: Tibetan and Mongolian Buddhism." In *Encyclopedia of Religion*, edited by Lindsay Jones, 2:1222–29. Detroit: Macmillan Reference USA, 2005.

Kapstein, Matthew T. "A Pilgrimage of Rebirth Reborn: The 1992 Celebration of the Drigung Powa Chenmo." In *Buddhism in Contemporary Tibet: Religious Revival and Cultural Identity*, edited by Melvyn C. Goldstein and Matthew T. Kapstein, 95–119. Berkeley: University of California Press, 1998.

Kapstein, Matthew. *The Tibetan Assimilation of Buddhism: Conversion, Contestation, and Memory.* New York: Oxford University Press, 2000.

Kapstein, Matthew T. *The Tibetans.* Malden, MA: Blackwell Publishing, 2006.

Karsten, Joachim Günter. "A Study on the Sku-'bum/T'a-Erh Ssu Monastery in Ching-Hai." Thesis, University of Auckland, 1996.

Kaschewsky, Rudolf. "The Image of Tibet in the West Before the Nineteenth Century." In *Imagining Tibet: Perceptions, Projections, & Fantasies*, edited by Thierry Dodin and Heinz Räther, 3–20. Boston: Wisdom Publications, 2001.

Kawaguchi, Ekai. *Three Years in Tibet.* Thailand: Orchid Press, 2005.

Kieffer-Pülz, Petra. "Rules for the Sīmā Regulation in the Vinaya and Its Commentaries and Their Application in Thailand." *Journal of the International Association of Buddhist Studies* 20, no. 2 (31 December 1997): 141–53.

Kim, Hanung. "A mdo, Collected Works (gSung 'bum), and Prosopography." *Revue d'Études Tibétaines* 37 (December 2016): 162–77.

Kim, Hanung. "Renaissance Man from Amdo: The Life and Scholarship of the Eighteenth-Century Amdo Scholar Sum Pa Mkhan Po Ye Shes Dpal 'byor (1704–1788)." Ph.D. diss., Harvard University, 2018.

Kraft, Kenneth. *Inner Peace, World Peace: Essays on Buddhism and Nonviolence.* Albany: State University of New York Press, 1992.

Lattimore, Owen. "Introduction." In *The Monguors of the Kansu-Tibetan Border*, edited by Charles Kevin Stuart, 86–108. Xining: Plateau Publications, 2006.

Lempert, Michael. *Discipline and Debate: The Language of Violence in a Tibetan Buddhist Monastery.* Berkeley: University of California Press, 2012.

Limusishiden (Li Dechun 李得春) and Jugui (Lu Wanfang 鲁万芳). "Passions and Colored Sleeves: Mongghul Lives in Eastern Tibet." Edited by C. K. Stuart, G. Roche, and R. Johnson. *Asian Highlands Perspectives* 7 (2010).

Liu Shengqi. "The Education System of Three Major Monasteries in Lhasa." Translated by Qin Lili. *China Tibetology* 8. Accessed 5 September 2012. http://zt.tibet.cn/english/zt /TibetologyMagazine/200312007421135337.htm.

Lodrö, Geshe G. *Geschichte der Kloster-Universität Drepung mit einem Abris der Geistesgeschichte Tibets: 1. Teil: Tibetischer Text.* Wiesbaden: Franz Steiner Verlag, 1974.

Lopez, Donald S. *Prisoners of Shangri-La: Tibetan Buddhism and the West.* Chicago: University of Chicago Press, 1998.

Maher, Derek Frank. "Knowledge and Authority in Tibetan Middle Way Schools of Buddhism: A Study of the Gelukba (dge lugs pa) Epistemology of Jamyang Shayba ('jam dbyangs bzhad pa) in Its Historical Context." Ph.D. diss., University of Virginia, 2003.

Makransky, John. "Offering (*mChod pa*) in Tibetan Ritual Literature." In *Tibetan Literature: Studies in Genre*, edited by José Ignacio Cabezón and Roger R. Jackson, 312–30. Ithaca, N.Y.: Snow Lion Publications, 1996.

Martin, Dan. *Tibetan Histories: A Bibliography of Tibetan-Language Historical Works.* London: Serindia Publications, 1997.

Martin, Dan. "Tibetan Histories: Addenda & Corrigenda," Accessed January 15, 2011. https:// sites.google.com/site/tibetological/tibetan-histories-addenda-et-corrigenda.

McCleary, Rachel M., and Leonard W. J. van der Kuijp. "The Market Approach to the Rise of the Geluk School, 1419–1642." *Journal of Asian Studies* 69, no. 1 (2010): 149–80.

McNeill, William Hardy. *Keeping Together in Time: Dance and Drill in Human History.* Cambridge, Mass.: Harvard University Press, 1995.

Miller, Robert J. "Buddhist Monastic Economy: The Jisa Mechanism." *Comparative Studies in Society and History* 3, no. 4 (July 1961): 427–38.

Miller, Robert James. *Monasteries and Culture Change in Inner Mongolia.* Wiesbaden: O. Harrassowitz, 1959.

Mills, Martin A. *Identity, Ritual and State in Tibetan Buddhism: The Foundations of Authority in Gelukpa Monasticism.* London RoutledgeCurzon, 2003.

Murphy, George. "Buddhist Monastic Economy: The Jisa Mechanism: Comment." *Comparative Studies in Society and History* 3, no. 4 (July 1961): 439–42.

Namri Dagyab. "Vergleich von Verwaltungsstrukturen und wirtschaftlichen Entscheidung-sprozessen tibetisch- buddhistischer Klöster in der Autonomen Region Tibet, China und Indien." Ph.D. diss., Philosophische Fakultät der Rheinischen Friedrich-Wilhelms-Universität, Bonn, 2009.

Nebesky-Wojkowitz, Réne. *Oracles and Demons of Tibet: The Cult and Iconography of the Tibetan Protective Deities*. Kathmandu: Tiwari's Pilgrims Book House, 1993.

Newland, Guy. "Debate Manuals (*Yig cha*) in dGe lugs Monastic Colleges." In *Tibetan Literature: Studies in Genre*, edited by José Ignacio Cabezón and Roger R. Jackson, 202–16. Ithaca, N.Y.: Snow Lion Publications, 1996.

Ngawang Dakpa. "The Hours and Days of a Great Monastery: Drepung." In *Lhasa in the Seventeenth Century: The Capital of the Dalai Lamas*, edited by Françoise Pommaret, translated by Howard Solverson, 167–78. Boston: Brill, 2003.

Nietupski, Paul. *Labrang Monastery: A Tibetan Buddhist Community on the Inner Asian Borderlands, 1709–1958*. Lanham, Md.: Lexington Books, 2011.

Nietupski, Paul. "The 'Reverend Chinese' (Gyanakapa Tsang)." In *Buddhism Between Tibet and China*, edited by Matthew Kapstein, 181–214. Somerville, Mass.: Wisdom Publications, 2009.

Nonomura, Kaoru. *Eat Sleep Sit: My Year at Japan's Most Rigorous Zen Temple*. Translated by Juliet Winters Carpenter. New York: Kodansha USA, 2015.

Nornang, Nawang L. "Monastic Organization and Economy at Dwags-Po Bshad-Grub-Gling." In *Reflections on Tibetan Culture: Essays in Memory of Turrell V. Wylie*, edited by Lawrence Epstein and Richard F. Sherburne, 12:249–68. Studies in Asian Thought and Religion. Lewiston, N.Y.: Edwin Mellen Press, 1990.

Nourse, Ben. "Revolutions of the Dharma Wheel: Uses of Tibetan Printing in the Eighteenth Century." In *Tibetan Printing: Comparisons, Continuities and Change*, edited by Hildegard Diemberger, Franz-Karl Ehrhard, and Peter Kornicki, 424–50. Brill's Tibetan Studies Library, vol. 39. Boston: Brill, 2016.

Oidtmann, Max Gordon. "Between Patron and Priest: Amdo Tibet Under Qing Rule, 1792–1911." Ph.D. diss., Harvard University, 2014.

Oidtmann, Max. "A 'Dog-Eat-Dog' World: Qing Jurispractices and the Legal Inscription of Piety in Amdo." *Extrême-Orient, Extrême-Occident* 40 (2016): 151–82.

Oidtmann, Max. *Forging the Golden Urn: The Qing Empire and the Politics of Reincarnation in Tibet*. New York: Columbia University Press, 2018.

Oidtmann, Max. "The Laws of the Kökenuur Oirats and Their Ramifications for the Legal Culture of Amdo." Presented at the Fifteenth Seminar of the International Association for Tibetan Studies, Paris, July 2019.

Oidtmann, Max. "Overlapping Empires: Religion, Politics, and Ethnicity in Nineteenth-Century Qinghai." *Late Imperial China* 37, no. 2 (2016): 41–91.

Onoda, Shunzo. "bsDus grwa Literature." In *Tibetan Literature: Studies in Genre*, edited by José Ignacio Cabezón and Roger R. Jackson, 187–201. Ithaca, N.Y.: Snow Lion Publications, 1996.

Orsi, Robert A. *History and Presence*. Cambridge, Mass.: Belknap Press of Harvard University Press, 2016.

Osterhammel, Jürgen. *Colonialism: A Theoretical Overview*. Translated by Shelley L. Frisch. 2nd ed. Princeton, N.J.: Markus Wiener Publishers, 2005.

Patte, Daniel, ed. *The Cambridge Dictionary of Christianity*. New York: Cambridge University Press, 2010.

Petech, Luciano. *China and Tibet in the Early 18th Century*. Leiden: Brill, 1972.

Pommaret, Françoise, ed. *Lhasa in the Seventeenth Century: The Capital of the Dalai Lamas*. Translated by Howard Solverson. Boston: Brill, 2003.

Powers, John. *Introduction to Tibetan Buddhism*. Ithaca, N.Y.: Snow Lion Publications, 1995.

Prebish, Charles S. *Buddhist Monastic Discipline: The Sanskrit Prātimokṣa Sūtras of the Mahāsāṃghikas and Mūlasarvāstivādins*. University Park, Pa.: Pennsylvania State University Press, 1975.

Ray, Reginald A. *Buddhist Saints in India: A Study in Buddhist Values and Orientations*. New York: Oxford University Press, 1994.

Roche, Gerald. "The Vitality of Tibet's Minority Languages in the Twenty-First Century." *Multiethnica* 35 (2014): 24–31.

Rockhill, William Woodville. "Tibet: Geographical, Ethnographical, and Historical Sketch, Derived from Chinese Sources." *Journal of the Royal Asiatic Society* 23, no. 1–2 (1891): 1–133, 185–291.

Ronis, Jann. "Celibacy, Revelations, and Reincarnated Lamas: Contestation and Synthesis in the Growth of Monasticism at Katok Monastery from the 17th Through 19th Centuries." Ph.D. diss., University of Virginia, 2009.

Sack, Robert. *Human Territoriality: Its Theory and History*. Cambridge Studies in Historical Geography. New York: Cambridge University Press, 1986.

Sagaster, Klaus. *Subud erike: "Ein Rosenkranz aus Perlen," Die Biographie des 1. Pekinger lČaṅ skya Khutukhtu Ṅag dbaṅ blo bzaṅ čʼos ldan, verfasst von Ṅag dbaṅ čʼos ldan alias Šes rab dar rgyas* [Subud erike: "A Rosary of Pearls," [Being] the biography of the First Beijinger Lcang skya Khutukhtu Ngag dbang blo bzang chos ldan, written by Ngag dbang chos ldan, alias Shes rab dar rgyas]. Wiesbaden: O. Harrassowitz, 1967.

Samuel, Geoffrey. *Civilized Shamans: Buddhism in Tibetan Societies*. Washington, D.C.: Smithsonian Institution Press, 1993.

Śāntideva. *The Bodhicaryāvatāra*. Translated by Kate Crosby and Andrew Skilton. Oxford: Oxford University Press, 1995.

Schaeffer, Kurtis R. "The Beginnings of the Gandenpa School." In *Sources of Tibetan Tradition*, edited by Kurtis R. Schaeffer, Matthew T. Kapstein, and Gray Tuttle, 507–8. New York: Columbia University Press, 2013.

Schaeffer, Kurtis R. "Fifth Dalai Lama Ngawang Lopsang Gyatso." In *The Dalai Lamas: A Visual History*, edited by Martin Brauen, 64–91. Chicago: Serindia Publications, 2005.

Schaeffer, Kurtis R. "Indian Intellectuals at the Court of the Fifth Dalai Lama, 1654–1682." presented at the Tibet and Her Neighbors Symposium, Harvard University, 23 April 2004.

Schaeffer, Kurtis R. "Ritual, Festival and Authority Under the Fifth Dalai Lama." In *Power, Politics, and the Reinvention of Tradition: Tibet in the Seventeenth and Eighteenth Centuries; Proceedings of the Tenth Seminar of the International Association for Tibetan Studies, Oxford, 2003*, edited by Bryan J. Cuevas and Kurtis R. Schaeffer, 187–202. Boston: Brill, 2006.

Schaeffer, Kurtis R., Matthew T. Kapstein, and Gray Tuttle, eds. *Sources of Tibetan Tradition*. New York: Columbia University Press, 2013.

Schjoedt, Uffe, Jesper Sørensen, Kristoffer Laigaard Nielbo, Dimitris Xygalatas, Panagiotis Mitkidis, and Joseph Bulbulia. "Cognitive Resource Depletion in Religious Interactions." *Religion, Brain & Behavior* 3, no. 1 (2013): 39–86.

Schopen, Gregory. *Bones, Stones, and Buddhist Monks: Collected Papers on the Archaeology, Epigraphy, and Texts of Monastic Buddhism in India.* Honolulu: University of Hawai'i Press, 1997.

Schopen, Gregory. *Buddhist Monks and Business Matters: Still More Papers on Monastic Buddhism in India.* Honolulu: University of Hawai'i Press, 2004.

Schopen, Gregory. *Buddhist Nuns, Monks, and Other Worldly Matters: Recent Papers on Monastic Buddhism in India.* Honolulu: University of Hawai'i Press, 2014.

Schopen, Gregory. "Deaths, Funerals, and the Division of Property." In *Buddhism in Practice,* edited by Donald S. Lopez, 473–502. Princeton, N.J.: Princeton University Press, 1995.

Schopen, Gregory. *Figments and Fragments of Mahayana Buddhism in India: More Collected Papers.* Honolulu: University of Hawai'i Press, 2005.

Schram, Louis M. J. *The Monguors of the Kansu-Tibetan Border.* Edited by Charles Kevin Stuart. Xining: Plateau Publications, 2006.

Schuh, Dieter, and J. K. Phukhang. *Urkunden und Sendschreiben aus Zentraltibet, Ladakh und Zanskar.* 2 vols. Monumenta Tibetica Historica 4. S[ank]t Augustin: VGH, Wissenschaftsverlag, 1979.

Schwieger, Peter. *The Dalai Lama and the Emperor of China: A Political History of the Tibetan Institution of Reincarnation.* New York: Columbia University Press, 2015.

Schwieger, Peter. "A Nearly-Forgotten Dge lugs pa Incarnation Line as Manorial Lord in Bkra shis ljongs, Central Tibet." In *Tibetans Who Escaped the Historian's Net: Studies in the Social History of Tibetan Societies,* edited by Charles Ramble, Peter Schwieger, and Alice Travers, 89–109. Kathmandu: Vajra Books, 2013.

Scott, James C. *The Art of Not Being Governed: An Anarchist History of Upland Southeast Asia.* New Haven, Conn.: Yale University Press, 2009.

Sde srid Sangs rgyas rgya mtsho. *Life of the Fifth Dalai Lama.* Edited and translated by Zahiruddhin Ahmad. Śata-Piṭaka 392. New Delhi: International Academy of Indian Culture and Aditya Prakashan, 1999.

Shakabpa, Tsepon Wangchuk Deden. *One Hundred Thousand Moons: An Advanced Political History of Tibet* (bod kyi srid don rgyal rabs). Translated by Derek F. Maher. 2 vols. Tibetan Studies Library 23. Leiden: Brill, 2010.

Slater, Keith W. *A Grammar of Mangghuer: A Mongolic Language of China's Qinghai-Gansu Sprachbund.* New York: RoutledgeCurzon, 2003.

Smith, E. Gene. *Among Tibetan Texts: History and Literature of the Himalayan Plateau.* Boston: Wisdom Publications, 2001.

Sørensen, Jesper, and Kristoffer L. Nielbo. "Prediction Error During Functional and Non-Functional Action Sequences: A Computational Exploration of Ritual and Ritualized Event Processing." *Journal of Cognition & Culture* 13, no. 3/4 (September 2013): 347–65.

Sorensen, Michelle Janet. "Making the Old New Again and Again: Legitimation and Innovation in the Tibetan Buddhist Chod Tradition." Ph.D. diss., Columbia University, 2013.

Sørensen, Per K. "The Dalai Lama Institution: Its Origin and Genealogical Succession." *Orientations,* September 2005: 53–60.

Sørensen, Per K. "The Sacred Junipers of Reting: The Arboreal Origins Behind the Dalai Lama Lineage." *Orientations,* September 2008: 74–87.

Sørensen, Per K., and Guntram Hazod. *Rulers on the Celestial Plain: Ecclesiastic and Secular Hegemony in Medieval Tibet: A Study of Tshal Gung-Thang.* Vienna: Verlag der Österreichischen Akademie der Wissenschaften, 2007.

Sosis, Richard. "Religion and Intragroup Cooperation: Preliminary Results of a Comparative Analysis of Utopian Communities." *Cross-Cultural Research* 34 (2000): 70–87.

Sosis, Richard, and Eric R. Bressler. "Cooperation and Commune Longevity: A Test of the Costly Signaling Theory of Religion." *Cross-Cultural Research* 37, no. 2 (1 May 2003): 211–39.

Sosis, Richard, and Bradley Ruffle. "Religious Ritual and Cooperation: Testing for a Relationship on Israeli Religious and Secular Kibbutzim." *Current Anthropology* 44 (2003): 713–22.

Spiro, Melford E. *Buddhism and Society: A Great Tradition and Its Burmese Vicissitudes.* 2nd ed. Berkeley: University of California Press, 1982.

Stein, R. A. *La civilisation tibétaine.* Paris: Dunod, 1962.

Stein, R. A. *Tibetan Civilization.* Translated by J. E. Stapleton Driver. Stanford, Calif.: Stanford University Press, 1972.

Sullivan, Brenton. "Administering Tibet: Don't Forget the Monasteries!" presented at the Fourteenth Seminar of the International Association for Tibetan Studies, Bergen, Norway, June 2016.

Sullivan, Brenton. "The Body of Skyid shod sprul sku: The Mid-Seventeenth Century Ties Between Central Tibet, the Oirat Mongols, and Dgon lung Monastery in Amdo." *Revue d'Études Tibétaines* 52 (2019): 294–327.

Sullivan, Brenton. "Convincing the Mongols to Join Mañjuśrī's Realm: The Diplomacy of the Second Changkya Ngawang Lozang Chöden (1642–1714)." In *Sino-Tibetan Buddhism: Essays in Memory of Monica Esposito,* edited by Ester Bianchi and Weirong Shen, forthcoming.

Sullivan, Brenton. "The First Generation of Dge lugs Evangelists in Amdo: The Case of 'Dan ma Tshul khrims rgya mtsho (1578–1663/65)." *Études mongoles et sibériennes, centrasiatiques et tibétaines,* forthcoming.

Sullivan, Brenton. "The Manner in Which I Went to Worship Mañjuśrī's Realm, The Five-Peaked Mountain (Wutai), by Sumba Kanbo (1704–1788)." *Inner Asia* 20, no. 1 (16 April 2018): 64–106.

Sullivan, Brenton. "Monastic Customaries and the Promotion of Dge lugs Scholasticism in A mdo and Beyond." *Asian Highlands Perspectives* 36 (2015): 84–105.

Sullivan, Brenton. "The Qing Regulation of the Sangha in Amdo." *Journal of the Royal Asiatic Society,* forthcoming.

Sur, Dominic. "Constituting Canon and Community in Eleventh Century Tibet: The Extant Writings of Rongzom and His *Constitution of Mantrins (sngags pa'i bca' yig)." Religions* 8, no. 3 (15 March 2017): 40.

Swidler, Ann. "Foreword." In *The Sociology of Religion,* by Max Weber, ix–xviii. Boston: Beacon Press, 1993.

Tambiah, Stanley Jeyaraja. *World Conqueror and World Renouncer: A Study of Buddhism and Polity in Thailand Against a Historical Background.* Cambridge Studies in Social Anthropology 15. New York: Cambridge University Press, 1976.

Tarab Tulku. *A Brief History of Tibetan Degrees in Buddhist Philosophy.* Copenhagen: Nordic Institute of Asian Studies, 2000.

Thuken Losang chökyi nyima [Thu'u bkwan Blo bzang chos kyi nyi ma]. *The Crystal Mirror of Philosophical Systems: A Tibetan Study of Asian Religious Thought.* Edited by

Roger R. Jackson. Translated by Geshé Lhundub Sopa. Library of Tibetan Classics 25. Boston: Wisdom Publications, 2009.

Thurman, Robert A. F. *The Life and Teachings of Tsong Khapa.* Rev. ed. Dharamsala: Library of Tibetan Works and Archives, 2006.

Tiyavanich, Kamala. *Forest Recollections: Wandering Monks in Twentieth-Century Thailand.* Honolulu: University of Hawai'i Press, 1997.

Townsend, Dominique. "How to Constitute a Field of Merit: Structure and Flexibility in a Tibetan Buddhist Monastery's Curriculum." *Religions* 8, no. 9 (7 September 2017).

Townsend, Dominique. "Materials of Buddhist Culture: Aesthetics and Cosmopolitanism at Mindrolling Monastery." Ph.D. diss., Columbia University, 2012.

"Treasury of Lives, The" 2007. https://treasuryoflives.org/.

Tsongkhapa. *Tantric Ethics: An Explanation of the Precepts for Buddhist Vajrayna Practice.* Translated by Gareth Sparham. Boston: Wisdom Publications, 2005.

Tsyrempilov, Nikolay. "Dge lugs pa Divided: Some Aspects of the Political Role of Tibetan Buddhism in the Expansion of the Qing Dynasty." In *Power, Politics, and the Reinvention of Tradition: Tibet in the Seventeenth and Eighteenth Centuries; Proceedings of the Tenth Seminar of the International Association for Tibetan Studies, Oxford, 2003,* edited by Bryan J. Cuevas and Kurtis R. Schaeffer, 47–64. Boston: Brill, 2006.

Tucci, Giuseppe. *Tibetan Painted Scrolls.* 2nd ed. 2 vols. Bangkok: SDI Publications, 1999.

Tuttle, Gray. "Building Up the Dge lugs pa Base in A mdo: The Roles of Lhasa, Beijing and Local Agency." *Zangxue xuekan* [Journal of Tibetology] 7 (2012): 126–40.

Tuttle, Gray. "Local History in A mdo: The Tsong kha Range (ri rgyud)." *Asian Highlands Perspectives* 6 (2010): 23–97.

Tuttle, Gray. "Pattern Recognition: Tracking the Speed of the Incarnation Institution Through Time and Across Tibetan Territory." *Revue d'Études Tibétaines,* no. 38 (February 2017): 29–64.

Tuttle, Gray. "The Role of Mongol Elite and Educational Degrees in the Advent of Reincarnation Lineages in Seventeenth Century Amdo." In *The Tenth Karmapa and Tibet's Turbulent Seventeenth Century,* edited by Karl Debreczeny and Gray Tuttle, UK ed., 235–62. Chicago: Serindia Publications, 2016.

U, Eddy. *Disorganizing China: Counter-Bureaucracy and the Decline of Socialism.* Stanford, Calif.: Stanford University Press, 2007.

van Vleet, Stacey. "Medicine as Impartial Knowledge: The Fifth Dalai Lama, the Tsarong School, and Debates of Tibetan Medical Orthodoxy." In *The Tenth Karmapa and Tibet's Turbulent Seventeenth Century,* edited by Karl Debreczeny and Gray Tuttle, UK ed. Chicago: Serindia Publications, 2016.

Vasubandhu. *L'Abhidharmakośa de Vasubandhu.* Translated by Louis de La Vallée Poussin. 2nd ed. 6 vols. Bruxelles: Institut belge des hautes études chinoises, 1971.

Vetturini, Gianpaolo. "The bKa' gdams pa School of Tibetan Buddhism." Ph.D. diss., SOAS University of London, 2007.

Vidyabhusana, Satis Chandra, ed. "So-Sor-Thar-Pa; or, a Code of Buddhist Monastic Laws: Being the Tibetan Version of the Prātimokṣa of the Mūla-Sarvāstivāda School." Translated by Satis Chandra Vidyabhusana. *Journal of the Asiatic Society of Bengal.* New Series, 9, no. 3–4 (1915): 29–139.

Vostrikov, A. I. *Tibetan Historical Literature.* Translated by Harish Chandra Gupta. Richmond, Surrey: Curzon Press, 1994.

Waddell, L. Austine. *Tibetan Buddhism: With Its Mystic Cults, Symbolism and Mythology, and in Its Relation to Indian Buddhism*. New York: Dover Publications, 1972.

Wakeman, Jr., Frederic. "Boundaries of the Public Sphere in Ming and Qing China." *Daedalus* 127, no. 3 (Summer 1998): 167–89.

Weber, Max. *Economy and Society: An Outline of Interpretive Sociology*. Edited by Guenther Roth and Claus Wittich. Vol. 1. 2 vols. Berkeley: University of California Press, 2013.

Weber, Max. *The Protestant Ethic and the Spirit of Capitalism*. Translated by Talcott Parsons. New York: Routledge, 1992.

Weber, Max. *The Religion of China: Confucianism and Taoism*. New York: Macmillan, 1964.

Weber, Max. "The Social Psychology of the World Religions." In *From Max Weber: Essays in Sociology*, edited by H. H. Gerth and C. Wright Mills, 267–301. New York: Oxford University Press, 1946.

Weber, Max. *The Sociology of Religion*. Translated by Ephraim Fischoff. Boston: Beacon Press, 1993.

Welch, Holmes. *The Practice of Chinese Buddhism, 1900–1950*. Harvard East Asian Studies 26. Cambridge, Mass.: Harvard University Press, 1967.

Whyte, William H. *The Organization Man*. Philadelphia: University of Pennsylvania Press, 2002 (1956).

Willis, Janice D. *Enlightened Beings: Life Stories from the Ganden Oral Tradition*. Boston: Wisdom Publications, 1995.

Wiltermuth, Scott S., and Chip Heath. "Synchrony and Cooperation." *Psychological Science* 20, no. 1 (1 January 2009): 1–5.

Wylie, Turrell V. "Monastic Patronage in 15th-Century Tibet." *Acta Orientalia Academiae Scientiarum Hungaricae* 34, no. 1–3 (1980): 319–28.

Ye shes dpal 'byor, Sum pa mkhan po. *Chronology of Tibet According to the Re'u mig of Sum pa mkhan po*. Edited and translated by Bireshwar Prasad Singh. Patna, India: Bihar Research Society, 1991.

Yi, Jongbok. "The History of Monastic Textbooks in Gomang Monastic College (I): 15th Century to 17th Century." *ChiMoKoJa: Histories of China, Mongolia, Korea and Japan* 2 (2016): 23–46.

Yijing 義淨. *Buddhist Monastic Traditions of Southern Asia: A Record of the Inner Law Sent Home from the South Seas*. Edited and translated by Li Rongxi. BDK English Tripitaka 93–I. Berkeley, Calif.: Numata Center for Buddhist Translation and Research, 2000.

Zahavi, Amotz, and Avishag Zahavi. *The Handicap Principle: A Missing Piece of Darwin's Puzzle*. New York: Oxford University Press, 1997.

ASIAN-LANGUAGE SOURCES

A mgon Rin po che, ed. *'Bri gung bka' brgyud chos mdzod chen mo* [The great treasury of Dharma of the Drigung Kagyü school]. 151 vols. [Lhasa]: s.n., 2004. Compendium W00JW501203.

Abhyāgaragupta. *Dkyil chog rdo rje phreng ba dang rdzogs pa'i rnal 'byor gyi 'phreng ba*. Darjeeling: Kargyud Sungrab Nyamso Khang, 1983. BDRC W23203.

BAN Shinichiro. "Darai rama seiken seiritsu zen'ya ni okeru geruku-ha no amudo fukyō: Geruku-ha sōryo depa choje no katsudō o chūshin ni mita" [Propagation of Buddhism

in Amdo by the dGe lugs pa sect just before the establishment of the Dalai-Lama administration: With special reference to the activities of sDe pa chos rje]. *Nihon chibetto
gakkai kaihō* [Report of the Japanese Association for Tibetan Studies] 62 (March 2017):
1–11.

Blo bzang bsam gtan. *Rje Ngag dbang blo bzang bsam gtan gyi gsung 'bum* [Collected works of
Ngawang Lozang Samten]. 4 vols. Lan kru'u [Lanzhou]: Kan su'u mi rigs dpe skrun
khang, 2005.

Blo gros rgyal mtshan. *The Collected Works (Gsung 'bum) of Spyan-snga Blo-gros-rgyal-mtshan
of Rgya-ma rin-chen sgang: Reproduced from a set of prints from the 'Bras-spungs Dga'-ldan
Pho-brang blocks under the supervision of Ngawang Gelek Demo.* 5 vols. New Delhi: Ngawang Gelek Demo, 1983. BDRC W447.

Brag dgon zhabs drung Dkon mchog bstan pa rab rgyas. *Mdo smad chos 'byung [Deb ther rgya
mtsho = Ocean Annals].* Lanzhou: Kan su'u mi dmangs dpe skrun khang, 1982.

Brag dkar sngags rams pa Blo bzang bstan pa rab rgyas. *Gsung 'bum* [Collected works of Dra-
kar Ngarampa Lozang Tenpa Rabgyé]. 2 vols. Rong bo, Qinghai Province: Rong po
dgon chen gyi par khang, n.d. BDRC W28897.

'Bri gung Grags pa 'byung gnas. *The Collected Works (Gsung 'bum) of Grags pa 'byung gnas: A
Chief Disciple of the Skyob-pa-'Jig-rten-gsum-mgon, 1175–1255.* Edited by H. H. Drikung
Kyabgon Chetsang (Konchog Tenzin Kunzang Thinley Lhundub). Delhi: Drikung Ka-
gyu Publications, 2002. BDRC W23785.

'Brom Shes rab me lce. An Early Text on the History of Rwa sgreng Monastery: The *Rgyal
ba'i dben gnas rwa sgreng gi bshad pa nyi ma'i 'od zer* of 'Brom shes rab me lce. Edited by
Maho Iuchi. Vol. 82. Harvard Oriental Series. Cambridge, Mass.: Harvard University
Press, 2016.

'Brug rgyal mkhar, ed. *Mtshan gzungs rgyun khyer phyogs bsgrigs.* Lan kru'u [Lanzhou]: Kan
su'u mi rigs dpe skrun khang, 1996.

'Brug thar and Sangs rgyas tshe ring. *Mdo smad rma khug tsha 'gram rong 'brog yul gru'i sngon
byung mes po'i ngag gi lo rgyus deb ther chen mo* [The great annals of the oral history of
the ancestors of the farming and nomadic places along the bend of the Yellow River in
Domé] Beijing: Mi rig dpe skrun khang, 2005.

Bsod nam ye shes dbang po. "Bsang rnam dag ma." In *Bsang mchod phyogs bsgrigs*, 139–49.
Beijing: Mi rigs dpe skrun khang, 2003.

Bstan pa bstan 'dzin, ed. *Chos sde chen po dpal ldan 'bras spungs sgo mang grwa tshang gi chos
'byung dung g.yas su 'khyil ba'i sgra dbyangs* [History of the dharma at Gomang College
of Drepung Monastery, the Rightward-Turning Sound]. Vol. 1. 2 vols. Karnataka, India: Dpal ldan 'bras spungs bkra shis sgo mang dpe mdzod khang, 2003.

Bu ston Rin chen grub. *Gsung 'bum* [Collected works of Butön Rinchen Drup]. Beijing: Krung
go'i bod rig pa dpe skrun khang, 2008. BDRC W1PD45496.

*Chos sde chen po rnams su gsung pa'i chos spyod kyi rim pa dang ser smad thos bsam nor gling grwa
tshang gi thun mong ma yin pa'i nye mkho chos spyod* [The liturgy recited at the great monasteries and the uncommon, daily liturgy of the Mé College at Sera [Monastery]].
Delhi: Lama Gurudeva, 1982. BDRC W1KG10780.

Dalai Lama V Ngag dbang blo bzang rgya mtsho. *Rgyal dbang lnga pa Ngag dbang blo bzang
rgya mtsho'i gsung 'bum* [Collected works of the Fifth Dalai Lama]. 28 vols. Beijing:
Krung go'i bod rig pa dpe skrun khang, 2009. BDRC W1PD107937.

Dalai Lama V Ngag dbang blo bzang rgya mtsho. "Rwa sgreng dang ri bo bde chen sogs chos
sde chung rigs 'gar stsal ba'i bka' yig sogs" [Edicts [bka' yig] bestowed for Rwa sgreng

and some small monasteries such as Ri bo bde chen]. In *Rgyal dbang lnga pa Ngag dbang blo bzang rgya mtsho'i gsung 'bum* [Collected works of the Fifth Dalai Lama], 23 ('a): 30–38. Beijing: Krung go'i bod rig pa dpe skrun khang, 2009. BDRC W1PD107937.

Dalai Lama V Ngag dbang blo bzang rgya mtsho. "Za hor gyi ban+de Ngag dbang blo bzang rgya mtsho'i 'di sngang 'khrul ba'i rol rtsed rtogs brjod kyi tshul du bkod pa du kU la'i gos bzang." In *Gsung 'bum* (Collected works), Vol. 5. Lhasa: Zhol par khang, 1991. BDRC W294.

Dalai Lama VII Skal bzang rgya mtsho. *The Collected Works (Gsung 'bum) of the Seventh Dalai Lama Blo-bzang-bskal-bzang-rgya-mtsho: Reproduced from a Set of Prints from the 1945 'Bras-spungs Blocks from the Library of Ven. Dhardo Rimpoche by Lama Dodrup Sangye*. 13 vols. Gangtok: Dodrup Sangye, 1976. BDRC W2623.

Dalai Lama VII Skal bzang skya mtsho. *Dbus 'gyur chos sde chen po dpal ldan 'bras spungs tshogs chen dang dpal ldan bkra shis sgo mang grwa tshang bcas kyi tshogs 'don chos spyod kyi rim pa bskal bzang mgrin rgyan* [The sequence of the assembly recitations and ritual breviary of the General Assembly of the Great and Glorious Drepung Monastery and its College of Gomang in Ü: The ornament of the voice of the good eon]. New Delhi: Chos 'phel legs ldan, 1974. BDRC W00EGS1016242.

Dalai Lama VII Skal bzang rgya mtsho. "Khri chen sprul pa'i sku Blo bzang stan pa'i nyi ma dpal bzang po'i rnam par thar pa dpyod ldan yid dbang 'gugs pa'i pho nya" [The biography of the incarnation of the Great [Golden] Throne-holder, the Glorious Lozang Tenpé Nyima: The Sagacious Messenger that allures the mind]. In *Gsung 'bum of the Seventh Dalai Lama Skal bzang rgya mtsho: Reproduced from a Set of Prints from the 1945 'Bras spungs Blocks from the Library of the Ven. Dhardo Rimpoche by Lama Dodrup Sangye*, 10:328–430. Gangtok: Dodrup Sangye and Deorali Chorten, 1977. BDRC W2623.

Dbal mang paN+Di ta Dkon mchog rgyal mtshan. "'Jam dbyangs bla ma rje btsun bstan pa'i sgron me'i rnam par thar pa brjod pa'i gtam dad pa'i pad+mo bzhad pa'i nyin byed." In *Gsung 'bum* [Collected works of Gung thang III Dkon mchog bstan pa'i sgron me], 8:525–912. Lhasa: Zhol par khang gsar pa, 2000. BDRC W22112.

"Dga' ldan dam chos gling gi 'grig lam dang 'don bsgrigs [The Path of Discipline and procedures for arranging the liturgy of Mati Monastery]." Manuscript at Mati si 马蹄寺, Gansu, 1999.

Dge 'dun 'dus tshogs of 'Brug gzhung grwa tshang ste ba spung thim chos sde, ed. *Dpal 'brug dge 'dun phyag srol cha shas bstan 'dzin gzhon nu'i dga' tshal*. Vol. 2. Thimphu, Bhutan: Dratshang Lhentshog [Grwa tshang lhan tshogs], 2011.

Dkon mchog bstan pa rab rgyas. *Yul mdo smad kyi ljongs su thub bstan rin po che ji ltar dar ba'i tshul gsal bar brjod pa: Deb ther rgya mtsho* [The ocean annals of Amdo]. Edited by Lokesh Chandra. 3 vols. Śata-piṭaka 226. New Delhi: Mrs. Sharada Rani, Hauzkhas Enclave, 1977.

Dung dkar Blo bzang 'phrin las. *Bod kyi chos srid zung 'brel skor bshad pa* [The merging of religious and secular rule in Tibet]. Dharamsala: Bod kyi dpe mdzod khang, 1982.

Duo Zang, and Pu Wencheng, eds. *Youning si zhi: san zhong* 佑宁寺志：三种 [Three gazetteers of Gönlung Monastery]. Qinghai shaoshu minzu guji congshu. Xining: Qinghai renmin chubanshe, 1990.

Gter bdag gling pa 'Gyur med rdo rje. *Gsung 'bum* [Collected works of Tertak Lingpa Gyurmé Dorjé]. 16 vols. D. G. Khochhen Tulku: Dehra Dun, 1998. BDRC W22096.

Gung thang III Dkon mchog bstan pa'i sgron me. "A ru hor chen dgon pa bkra shis bsam 'grub gling gi bca' yig chos kyi snang ba." In *Gsung 'bum* [Collected works of Gungtang

III Könchok Tenpé Drönmé], 10:429–36. Beijing: Mi rigs dpe skrun khang, 2003. BDRC W2DB4591.

Gung thang III Dkon mchog bstan pa'i sgron me. "Blo bzang chos kyi nyi ma'i gsang gsum rmad du byung ba'i rtogs brjod pad+ma dkar po [The marvelous tale of realization of the three secrets of Thu'u bkwan III Blo bzang chos kyi nyi ma: The White Lotus]." In *Gung thang bstan pa'i sgron me'i gsung 'bum* [Collected works of Gungtang Könchok Tenpé Drönmé (1762–1823)], Vols. 6–7. Beijing: Mi rigs dpe skrun khang, 2003. BDRC W2DB4591.

Han Rulin 韓儒林. "Qinghai Youning si ji qi ming seng 青海佑寧寺及其名僧" [Qinghai's Youning Monastery and its famous monks]. *Bianzheng gonglun* 邊政公論 [Frontier affairs] 3, nos. 1, 4, and 5 (May 1944): 45–48, 10–16, and 12–17 respectively.

'Jam dbyangs bzhad pa I Ngag dbang brtson 'grus. *Gsung 'bum* [Collected works of Jamyang Zhepa I Ngawang Tsöndrü]. 15 vols. New Delhi: Ngawang Gelek Demo, 1972. BDRC W1KG9409.

Jialasen 贾拉森 (Jalsan), ed. *Zaixian huihuang de Guangzong si: Qingzhu Alashan Guangzong si jian si 250 zhou nian ji Liu shi Dalai lama zhuang cheng shu 250 zhou nian (1757–2005)* 再现辉煌的广宗寺：庆祝阿拉善广宗寺建寺250 周年暨《六世达赖喇嘛传》成书250 周年 (*1757 –2005*) [The revived and glorious Guangzong Monastery: Celebrating the 250th anniversary of the founding of Alashan's Guangzong Monastery and the 250th anniversary of the composition of the biography of the Sixth Dalai Lama (1757–2005)]. Alashan Guangzong si: Alashan Guangzong si, 2005.

Jibzundamba I Lubsang-Danbi-Jaltsan (Rje btsun dam pa Blo bzang bstan pa'i rgyal mtshan), Jibzundamba II Lubsang-Danbi-Döngmi (Blo bzang bstan pa'i sgron me), Jibzundamba III Ishi-Danbi-Nima (Ye shes bstan pa'i nyi ma), Jibzundamba IV Lubsang-Tubdan-Wangchug (Blo bzang thub bstan dbang phyug), Jibzundamba V Lubsang-Tsültem-Jigmed (Blo bzang tshul khrims 'jigs med), Jibzundamba VI Lubsang-Danbi-Jaltsan (Blo bzang bstan pa'i rgyal mtshan), Jibzundamba VII Agwang-Choijin-Wangchug-Perenlai-Jamtsu (Ngag dbang chos kyi dbang phyug 'phrin las rgya mtsho), and Jibzundamba VIII Agwang-Lubsang-Choijin-Nima-Danzin-Wangchug (Ngag dbang blo bzang chos kyi nyi ma bstan 'dzin dbang phyug). *Khal kha rje btsun dam pa sku phreng rim byon gyi gsung 'bum* [Collected works of the succession of incarnations of the Khalkha Jibzundamba]. 4 vols. Ulaanbaatar: R. Byambaa, 2004. BDRC W2DB25419.

'Jig rten mgon po. *The Collected Works (Bka' 'bum) of Khams gsum chos kyi rgyal po thub dbang rat+na śrī (Skyob pa 'Jig rten gsum mgon)*. Edited by H. H. Drikung Kyabgon Chetsang (Konchog Tenzin Kunzang Thinley Lhundub). 12 vols. Delhi: Drikung Kagyu Ratna Shri Sungrab Nyamso Khang, 2001. BDRC W23743.

Karma pa VIII Mi skyod rdo rje. *Rgyal ba thams cad kyi ye shes kyi sku rnam pa thams cad pa'i thugs can Karma pa Mi bskyod rdo rje bzhad pa'i gsung 'bum*. Edited by Karma Bde legs. 26 vols. [Lhasa]: s.n., 2004. BDRC W8039.

Karmapa IX Dbang phyug rdo rje. "Bca' ba chos khrims kyi skor gnang bkag gsal bar ston pa'i snang byed" [Concerning the institution of religious law: That which clarifies what is permitted and what is prohibited]. s.l., n.d. BDRC W8LS16413.

Krung go bod brgyud mtho rim nang bstan slob gling gi slob gzhi rtsom sgrig tsho chung, ed. *Bca' yig phyogs sgrig. Gangs can rig brgya'i sgo 'byed lde mig ces bya ba bzhugs so* 11. Beijing: Mi rigs dpe skrun khang, 1989.

Krung go bod brgyud mtsho rim nang bstan slob gling brgyud nang bstan zhib 'jug khang, ed. *Dge lugs pa'i chos spyod phyogs bsgrigs* [Collected ritual hymns of the Geluk]. 6 vols. Zi ling: Mtsho sngon mi rigs dpe skrun khang, 1995.

Las chen Kun dga' rgyal mtshan. *Bka' gdams kyi rnam par thar pa bka' gdams chos 'byung gsal ba'i sgron me*. [Lhasa]: s.n., 1494. BDRC W23748.

Las chen Kun dga' rgyal mtshan. *Bla ma thams cad mkhyen pa'i rnam thar ngo mtshar mdzad pa bcu gnyis* [The complete liberation of the Omniscient Lama, the First Dalai lama: His Twelve Miraculous Deeds]. Lhasa: Dga' ldan pho brang, 1497. BDRC W2CZ7861.

Lcang skya II Ngag dbang blo bzang chos ldan (1642–1714). *Gsung 'bum* [Collected works, Peking ed.]. 7 vols. Beijing: s.n., 19th century. BDRC W1KG1321.

Lcang skya II Ngag dbang blo bzang chos ldan. "Rje btsun bla ma ngag dbang blo bzang chos ldan dpal bzang po'i rnam par thar pa dad pa'i rol mtsho" [Autobiography of the Glorious Ngakwang Lozang Chöden, Zhol Edition], Vol. 5 (*ca*), 1713. BDRC W30098.

Lcang skya II Ngag dbang blo bzang chos ldan. "Rnam thar bka' rtsom [Autobiography of the Glorious Ngakwang Lozang Chöden, Peking ed.]." In *Gsung 'bum* [Collected Works], Vol. 2. Peking, 1713. BDRC W1KG1321.

Lcang skya III Rol pa'i rdo rje. "A lag sha zhes grags pa'i gnas chen gyi phan bde rgya mtsho'i gling gi dge 'dun rnams la khrims su bcas pa'i yi ge bslab gsum rnam par rgyas pa'i nyi 'od" [The document that institutes discipline for the Sangha of Pendé Gyatso Ling, the renowned sacred site of Alashaa: The sun that fully develops the three trainings]. Text is printed on a cloth scroll and held at Baruun Heid, otherwise known as Phan bde rgya mtsho'i gling in Alashaa, Inner Mongolia. This is a recent (20th or 21st century) copy of a handwritten scroll, some images of which can be found in Jialasen, *Zaixian huihuang de Guangzong si*.

Miaozhou 妙舟 Shi 釋. *Meng Zang fojiao shi* 蒙藏佛教史 [History of Tibetan and Mongolian Buddhism]. Yangzhou shi 揚州市: Jiangsu Guangling gu ji ke yin she 江蘇廣陵古籍刻印社, 1993.

Mkhas sgrub rje Dge legs dpal bzang. *Gsung 'bum* [Collected works of Khedrup Jé Gelek Pelzang]. 12 vols. New Delhi: Lama Gurudeva, 1980. BDRC W384.

Ngag dbang rnam rgyal, 'Phyong rgyas pa. *Rta wang dga' ldan rnam rgyal lha rtse'i bca' yig mdor bsdus*. Mundgod, Karnataka: Blo gling gtsug lag gter mdzod 'phrul spar khang, 1979.

Nor brang o rgyan, ed. *Dge lugs pa'i zhal 'don phyogs sgrig dgos pa kun tshang* [Collected liturgy of the Gelukpas]. [Lhasa]: Bod ljongs mi dmangs dpe skrun khang, 1997.

'Od zer rgya mtsho. *'Od zer rgya mtsho dpal bzang po'i gsung 'bum* [Complete Works of Özer Gyatso]. s.l.: s.n., s.d. BDRC W1KG4219.

Panchen Bsod nams grags pa. *Bka' gdams gsar rnying gi chos 'byung* [The history of the Old and New Kadam, i.e. Geluk]. Lhasa: Bod ljongs bod yig dpe rnying dpe skrun khang, 2001 [1529].

Panchen Lama IV Blo bzang chos kyi rgyal mtshan. *Rje btsun Blo bzang chos kyi rgyal mtshan gyi gsung 'bum* [Collected works of the Fourth Panchen Lama Lozang Chökyi Gyeltsen]. s.l.: s.n., s.d. [1990s]. BDRC W9848.

Per Nyi ma 'dzin Ngag dbang legs bshad rgya mtsho. *Bshad sgrub bstan pa'i 'byung gnas chos sde chen po dgon lung byams pa gling gi gdan rabs zur rgyan g.yas 'khyil dung gi sgra dbyangs* [The place where originated expounding on and practicing the Dharma: An addition to the [record of] the succession of abbots of the Great Religious Establishment Gönlung Jampa Ling, the sound of the clockwise-turning conch shell]. Printed book without official publication information. A Chinese translation of it also exists. The author is from Huzhu County, Qinghai Province.

Pu Wencheng 蒲文成. *Gan Qing Zangchuan fojiao siyuan* 甘青藏传佛教寺院. Xining 西寧: Qinghai renmin chubanshe 青海人民出版社, 1990.

Qinghai sheng bianji zu, ed. *Qinghai Tuzu shehui lishi diaocha* 青海土族社会历史调查 [An investigation of the social history of the Tu ethnicity of Qinghai]. Xining: Qinghai renmin chubanshe, 1985.

Rdo sbis Tshe ring rdo rje and O rgyan chos 'phel, eds. *Bca' yig phyogs bsgrigs* [Compendium of constitutions]. 2nd ed. Bod sa gnas kyi lo rgyus. Lhasa: Bod rang skyong ljongs yig tshangs khang, 2011.

Rgyal mtshan seng+ge. "Zha ser cod paN 'dzin pa'i 'dus sde chen po dge ldan bshad sgrub gling gi bca' yig blang dor gsal ba'i me long." In *Gsung 'bum* [Collected works of Lozang Gyeltsen Sengé, the rebirth of Rgyal mtshan seng+ge), edited by Blo bzang rgyal mtshan seng+ge, Vol. 2 *(kha)*. Gtsos Dge ldan chos gling gi par khang, n.d. BDRC WıKG1656.

Rgyal sras Blo bzang bstan 'dzin. "Sbas yul dkar po'i ljongs kyi gnas bstod ka la ping ka'i sgra dbyangs" [Praises of the Place of the Hidden White Land: The song of the cuckoo]. In Thu'u bkwan III Blo bzang chos kyi nyi ma, *Bshad sgrub bstan pa'i byung gnas chos sde chen po dgon lung byams pa gling gi dkar chag dpyod ldan yid dbang 'gugs pa'i pho nya*, 157–73. Zi ling: Mtsho sngon mi rigs dpe skrun khang, 1988.

Rgyal sras 'Jigs med ye shes grags pa. *Gsung 'bum* [Collected works of Gyelsé Jikmé Yeshé Drakpa]. N.p., n.d. A copy is held at the Library of the Research Institute for Ethnology and Anthropology, Chinese Academy of Social Sciences, Minzu University, Beijing. A scan of the same is held at the China Tibetology Research Center in Beijing.

Ser gtsug nang bstan dpe rnying 'tshol bsdu phyogs sgrig khang, ed. *Rgyud smad chos thog khag gi lo rgyus*. Gangs can khyad nor dpe tshogs 81. Lhasa: Ser gtsug nang bstan dpe rnying 'tshol bsdu phyogs sgrig khang, 2009.

Rong po grub chen I Skal ldan rgya mtsho. "Rje skal ldan rgya mtsho'i gsung las mdo smad a mdo'i phyogs su bstan pa dar tshul gi lo rgyus mdor bsdus" ["A mdo'i chos 'byung;" A concise history of the manner in which the teachings arose in the land of Domé]. In *Mdo smad sgrub brgyud bstan pa'i shing rta ba chen po phyag na pad+mo yab rje bla ma Skal ldan rgya mtho'i gsung 'bum* [Collected works of Kelden Gyatso], 1:341–55. Gangs can skal bzang dpe tshogs 1. [Lanzhou]: Kan su'u mi rigs dpe skrun khang, 1999.

Rong po grub chen I Skal ldan rgya mtsho. "Sde ba chos rje Bstan 'dzin blo bzang rgya mtsho'i rnam thar dad pa'i sgo 'byed" [Biography of Dewa Chöjé Tendzin Lozang Gyatso, 1593–1638]. In *Mdo smad sgrub brgyud bstan pa'i shing rta ba chen po phyag na pad+mo yab rje bla ma Skal ldan rgya mtho'i gsung 'bum* [Collected works of Kelden Gyatso], 1:180–255. Gangs can skal bzang dpe tshogs 1. [Lanzhou]: Kan su'u mi rigs dpe skrun khang, 1999.

Rong zom Chos kyi bzang po. "Rang slob dam tshig pa rnams la gsungs pa'i rwa ba brgyad pa'i bca' yig." In *Rong zom chos bzang gi gsung 'bum* [Collected works of Rong zom chos kyi bzang po], 2:391–406. Chengdu: Si khron mi rigs dpe skrun khang, 1999. BDRC W21617.

Rong zom Chos kyi bzang po. "Sngags pa rnams kyi bca' yig," n.d. W29622. Buddhist Digital Resource Center. BDRC W29622.

Sa skya khri chen Ngag dbang kun dga' bsod nams. *Dpal Sa skya pa chen po Sngags 'chang bla ma Thams cad mkhyen pa Ngag dbang kun dga' bsod nams kyi gsung 'bum* [Collected works of Sakyapa Ngawang Künga Sönam). 29 vols. [Kathmandu]: Sa skya rgyal yongs gsung rab slob gnyer khang, 2000. BDRC W29307.

Sa skya pa Kun dga' blo gros. "Chos grwa chen po thub bstan lha khang chen mo'i bca' yig ngo mtshar nying khu nyes sel legs spel gyi sman 'chi ba med pa'i bdud rtsi." In *Gsung* 'bum [Collected works], 4 (nga): 233–313. [Kathmandu]: Sa skya rgyal yongs gsung rab slob gnyer khang, 2008. BDRC W1KG1880.

Sangs rgyas, ed. *Bstod smon phyogs bsgrigs* [Collection of praises and prayers]. Zi ling: Mtsho sngon mi rigs dpe skrun khang, 1993.

Sde srid Sangs rgyas rgya mtsho. *Dga' ldan chos 'byung baiDUrya ser po* [Yellow Beryl history of the Ganden School]. Edited by Rdo rje rgyal po. [Beijing]: Krung go'i bod kyi shes rig dpe skrun khang, 1998.

Sde srid Sangs rgyas rgya mtsho. *Drin can rtsa ba'i bla ma Ngag dbang blo bzang rgya mtsho'i thun mong phyi'i rnam thar du kU la'i gos bzang* [A continuation of the ordinary, ourter life of my Gracious Root Lama, Ngag dbang blo bzang rgya mtsho: The fine silken dress]. 3 vols. Lhasa: Dga' ldan pho brang, 1679–1705. BDRC W8239.

Sde srid Sangs rgyas rgya mtsho. *Sde srid sman gyi khog 'bubs* [The minister's layout of medicine]. Bod kyi gso ba rig pa'i gna' dpe phyogs bsgrigs dpe tshogs 8. Mi rigs dpe skrun khang, 2004.

Shākya Mchog ldan. *The Complete Works (Gsung 'bum) of Gser-mdog Paṇ-chen Śākya-mchog-ldan: Reproduced from the Unique Manuscript Prepared in the 18th Century at the Order of Rje Sakya-rin-chen, the 9th Rje Mkhan-po [of] Bhutan Preserved at the Monastery of Pha-jo sdings 'og-min-gnyis-pa.* 24 vols. New Delhi: Nagwang Topgyel, 1995. BDRC W23200.

Shes rab dar rgyas. *Rje ngag dbang blo bzang chos ldan dpal bzang po'i rnam par thar pa mu tig 'phreng ba* [Biography of the Glorious Lord Ngakwang Lozang Chöden: A rosary of pearls]. Beijing: n.p., 1729. Print is held at the Cultural Palace of Nationalities (Minzu wenhua gong) in Beijing.

Shes rab 'od zer. *Collected Writings of 'Phreng-po Gter-chen Shes-rab-'od-zer: Reproduced from a Manuscript Collection Belonging to Lopon Sonam Sangpo for the Benefit of the Jamyang Chhentse Rimpoche.* Gangtok: Gonpo Tseten, 1977. BDRC W23423.

Smin grol III Ngag dbang 'phrin las rgya mtsho. "Theg chen thar pa gling gi bca' yig mu tig gi phreng mdzes" [The constitution of [Kenchen] Thekchen Tharpa Ling: the beautiful pearl necklace]. [Qinghai Province: Serkhok Monastery], 1758. Manuscript held at Kan chen Monastery in Huzhu County, Qinghai Province.

Sum pa mkhan po Ye shes dpal 'byor. "Dgon sde 'ga' zhig gi bca' yig blang dor snyan sgron" [Constitution for a few monasteries: an inquiry regarding what is to be accepted and what is to be rejected]. In *Gsung 'bum* [Collected works], 8:105–39. Śata-piṭaka. New Delhi: International Academy of Indian Culture, 1975. BDRC W29227.

Sum pa mkhan po Ye shes dpal 'byor. "Mkhan po erte ni paN+Di tar grags pa'i spyod tshul brjod pa sgra 'dzin bcud len" [Autobiography of Sumba Kanbo Yeshe Baljor]. In *Gsung 'bum* [Collected works], 8:371–957. Śata-piṭaka 221. New Delhi: International Academy of Indian Culture, 1975. BDRC W29227.

Sum pa mkhan po Ye shes dpal 'byor. *PaN+Di ta Sum pa Ye shes dpal 'byor mchog gi spyod tshul brjod pa sgra 'dzin bcud len* [Autobiography of Sumba Kanbo Yeshe Baljor]. Mtsho sngon bod yig gna' gzhung 3. Beijing: Krung go'i bod kyi shes rig dpe skrun khang, 2001.

Sum pa mkhan po Ye shes dpal 'byor. "Sgrub sde 'ga' zhig gi bca' yig" [Constitution for a few practice sites]. In *Gsung 'bum (Collected Works)*, 8:141–70. Śata-piṭaka. New Delhi: International Academy of Indian Culture, 1975.

Thub bstan phun tshogs. "Karma pa'i chos tshogs sgar chen 'dzam gling rgyan zhes pa'i skor mdor bsdus tsam brjod pa." *Krung go'i bod kyi shes rig* 21, no. 1 (1993): 52–65.

Thu'u bkwan Blo bzang chos kyi nyi ma. *Gsung 'bum* [Collected works of Tuken III Lozang Chökyi Nyima]. 10 vols. [Lhasa: Zhol par khang gsar pa, 2000]. BDRC W21507.

Thu'u bkwan III Blo bzang chos kyi nyi ma. *Bshad sgrub bstan pa'i byung gnas chos sde chen po dgon lung byams pa gling gi dkar chag dpyod ldan yid dbang 'gugs pa'i pho nya* [The monastic chronicle of Gönlung Monastery]. Xining: Mtsho sngon mi rigs dpe skrun khang, 1988.

Thu'u bkwan III Blo bzang chos kyi nyi ma. "Bshad sgrub bstan pa'i byung gnas chos sde chen po dgon lung byams pa gling gi dkar chag dpyod ldan yid dbang 'gugs pa'i pho nya" [The monastic chronicle of Gönlung Monastery; the "Dgon lung gi dkar chag"]. In *Gsung 'bum* [Collected works], 2:647–788. Lhasa: Zhol par khang gsar pa, 2000 [1775]. BDRC W21507.

Thu'u bkwan III Blo bzang chos kyi nyi ma. "Dben gnas bde chen chos gling gi bsam gtan pa rnams kyi bca' khrims bstan pa'i pad tshal rgyas pa'i nyin byed sogs bca' yig gi rim pa phyogs gcig tu bkod pa bzhugs so" [The constitution that clearly elucidates the processes of ethical decision making for the monks residing at the great place of accomplishment, Dechen Chöling, and other places. Also known as the Sun that Makes Grow the Lotus Garden of the Teachings]." In *Gsung 'bum* (Collected works), 2 (*kha*): 676–716. Lhasa: Zhol par khang gsar pa, 2000 [1781]. BDRC W21507.

Thu'u bkwan III Blo bzang chos kyi nyi ma (1737–1802). "Dpal ldan lha mo la tshes gtor 'bul tshul gyi lag len khrigs chags su bkod pa 'gag med rdo rje'i sgra dbyangs" [The presentation of the Series of Practices for Offering the Day *Torma* to the Glorious Lhamo]. In *Gsung 'bum* [Collected works], 5: part 21. New Delhi: Ngawang Gelek Demo, 1969. BDRC W21506.

Thu'u bkwan III Blo bzang chos kyi nyi ma. "Rta mgrin gsang sgrub kyi chos skor las/ rgyal gsol gyi cho ga phrin las lhun grub." In *Gsung 'bum* [Collected works], 7:791–803. Lhasa: Zhol par khang gsar pa, 2000 [1783]. BDRC W21507.

"Tianzhu Songshan Dalong si jieshao 天祝松山达隆寺简介," 2009. http://blog.sina.com.cn /s/blog_4d04c10a0100c6ez.html.

Tshan chung, ed. *Dag yig gsar bsgrigs* [The new compilation of orthography]. Xining: Mtsho sngon mi rigs dpe skrun khang, 2004.

Tsong kha pa Blo bzang grags pa. *The Collected Works (Gsung 'bum) of the Incomparable Lord Tsong-kha-pa Blo-bzang-grags-pa: Reproduced from Prints from the 1897 Lha-sa Old Zhol (Dga'-ldan-phun-tshogs-gling) Blocks.* 18 vols. New Delhi: Lama Gurudeva, 1978–1979. BDRC W635.

Wang IV Blo bzang 'jam pa'i tshul khrims. "Bca' yig blong dor gsal ba'i me long" [The constitution of the mirror that illuminates [what should be] accepted and rejected]. Constitution for Eren Monastery, Inner Mongolia. Composed in 1898. Manuscript held at Dgon lung Monastery, Qinghai Province.

Wang IV Blo bzang 'jam pa'i tshul khrims. "Bstan bcos sgo brgya 'byed pa'i zab zing gser gyi sde mig" [Profound and secret golden key of a hundred doors to [Buddhist] treatises]. Constitution for Dgon lung Monastery. Composed in 1885. Manuscript held at Dgon lung Monastery, Qinghai Province.

Wang V Ngag dbang mkhyen rab rgya mtsho. "Chos sde chen po dgon lung byams pa gling gi gdan rabs rten dang brten par bcas pa'i dkar chag ched du brjod pa gdangs snyan chos kyi gaNDi" [The chronicle of the abbatial succession of the Great Monastery, Gönlung Jampa Ling, its abodes and its residents: The pleasant melody of the sounding board of the Dharma)." Composed in 1932. Manuscript held at Dgon lung Monastery. This has been translated into Chinese in Duo Zang and Pu Wencheng, *Youning si: san zhi*.

Wei Yuan 魏源. *Sheng wu ji* 聖武記. Beijing: Zhonghua shuju, 1984.

Ye shes rgyal mtshan. "Rgyal ba Bsod nams rgya mtsho'i rnam thar." In *Lam rim bla ma brgyud pa'i rnam thar* [Biographies of the succession of lamas of the stages of the Path]. 'Bar khams: Rnga khul bod yig rtsom sgyur cus, n.d. [1787]. BDRC W2DB4613.

Yon tan rgya mtsho. "Skyid shod sde pa'i skor [On the Kyishö governors]." *Journal of the International Association of Tibetan Studies*, no. 2 (August 2006): 1–48.

Zhang Yisun 张怡荪, ed. *Bod rgya tshig mdzod chen mo* [The Great Chinese-Tibetan dictionary]. Beijing: Minzu chubanshe, 2008.

Zhiguanba•Gongquehudanbaraoji 智观巴• 贡却乎丹巴绕吉 [Brag dgon zhabs drung Dkon mchog bstan pa rab rgyas]. *Anduo zhengjiao shi* 安多政教史 [Political and religious history of Amdo; Mdo smad chos 'byung]. Translated by Wu Jun, Mao Jizu, and Ma Shilin. Gansu sheng shaoshu minzu guji congshu. Lanzhou: Gansu minzu chubanshe, 1989.

# Index

# Acknowledgments

I began thinking in earnest about the history of the Geluk school of Tibetan Buddhism and the genre of monastic constitutions as a graduate student in Kurtis Schaeffer's seminar on the Dalai Lamas. That was in the spring of 2009. In the decade since, countless people have contributed to the intellectual development of this project. I endeavor to acknowledge these contributions in the notes throughout this book. Here I wish to thank those individuals and institutions that have commented on drafts of the manuscript or otherwise directly supported the research for this book.

Kurtis Schaeffer, David Germano, Paul Groner, John Shepherd, and Gray Tuttle read some of the earliest formulations of the ideas presented in this book; their feedback motivated me to expand on those nascent ideas and dig deeper into the available primary sources. Khenpo Ngawang Dorjee and Mönlam Gyatso were extremely charitable with their time; they helped me read and understand many of the monastic constitutions and other primary sources presented here. Gerald Roche and Wes Chaney pointed me toward the solutions to the historical and cultural puzzles I encountered throughout this project. Christopher Atwood helped me connect the religious and patronage networks that existed between Inner Mongolia and Amdo. Paul Nietupski responded to my presentations of various parts of this book, drawing upon his own deep knowledge of the history of monasteries and the history of Amdo. Eddy U elucidated Weber's study of bureaucracy and its relevance to my argument. I would also like to thank the two anonymous reviewers of this manuscript for their close reading and critical feedback.

Here at Colgate University Heather Roller guided me through the final stages of writing and publishing, and David Robinson built a wonderful space for the exchange of ideas and research relating to Inner Asian history.

I am lucky to have as friends and colleagues Tobias Smith, Max Oidmtann, Wu Lan, Benno Weiner, and David Divalerio. On untold occasions they have read various parts of this book and provided immediate, indispensable feedback.

I also wish to thank the Buddhist Digital Resource Center (previously Tibetan Buddhist Resource Center) in Cambridge, Massachusetts, without which no scholarship on the history of Tibet worthy of the name could proceed.

Various funding agencies have made possible my research excursions to Asia as well as the writing of this book. The earliest research for this book was supported by a Fulbright-Hays DDRA (2010–11), the Sheng-Yen Education Foundation (summer 2008), and grants and fellowships from the University of Virginia for travel, language study, and research. More recently, the Fulbright Scholar Program, the Chiang Ching-kuo Foundation, and the Picker Research Fellowship at Colgate University provided me with time and resources to write this book while simultaneously commencing research for a new project.

Numerous scholars in China assisted me and made possible my research; I would like to single out two in particular here. Huang Xianian, formerly of the Institute of World Religions at the Chinese Academy of Social Sciences, helped me to build many of the professional connections in China that were instrumental to my research. Pu Wencheng of the Qinghai Academy of Social Sciences is perhaps more familiar than anyone with the religious landscape of Amdo, and his knowledge and guidance was essential to my research and writing.

Finally, by far the most important people for the production of this book are those Tibetans, Monguors, Mongols, and others of the Tibetan Plateau whose time, hospitality, and intellect supported my stays and research there. I do not name them so as to spare them further scrutiny by authorities for having "associated" with a foreigner, but I wish to signal my immense gratitude and debt to them.